These safety symbols are used in laboratory and field investigations in this book to indicate possible hazards. Learn the meaning of each symbol and refer to this page often. *Remember to wash your hands thoroughly after completing lab procedures.*

PROTECTIVE EQUIPMENT   Do not begin any lab without the proper protection equipment.

GOGGLES	Proper eye protection must be worn when performing or observing science activities that involve items or conditions as listed below.	
APRON	Wear an approved apron when using substances that could stain, wet, or destroy cloth.	
SOAP	Wash hands with soap and water before removing goggles and after all lab activities.	
GLOVES	Wear gloves when working with biological materials, chemicals, animals, or materials that can stain or irritate hands.	

LABORATORY HAZARDS

Symbols	Potential Hazards	Precaution	Response
DISPOSAL	contamination of classroom or environment due to improper disposal of materials such as chemicals and live specimens	• DO NOT dispose of hazardous materials in the sink or trash can. • Dispose of wastes as directed by your teacher.	• If hazardous materials are disposed of improperly, notify your teacher immediately.
EXTREME TEMPERATURE	skin burns due to extremely hot or cold materials such as hot glass, liquids, or metals; liquid nitrogen; dry ice	• Use proper protective equipment, such as hot mitts and/or tongs, when handling objects with extreme temperatures.	• If injury occurs, notify your teacher immediately.
SHARP OBJECTS	punctures or cuts from sharp objects such as razor blades, pins, scalpels, and broken glass	• Handle glassware carefully to avoid breakage. • Walk with sharp objects pointed downward, away from you and others.	• If broken glass or injury occurs, notify your teacher immediately.
ELECTRICAL	electric shock or skin burn due to improper grounding, short circuits, liquid spills, or exposed wires	• Check condition of wires and apparatus for fraying or uninsulated wires, and broken or cracked equipment. • Use only GFCI-protected outlets.	• DO NOT attempt to fix electrical problems. Notify your teacher immediately.
CHEMICAL	skin irritation or burns, breathing difficulty, and/or poisoning due to touching, swallowing, or inhalation of chemicals such as acids, bases, bleach, metal compounds, iodine, poinsettias, pollen, ammonia, acetone, nail polish remover, heated chemicals, mothballs, and any other chemicals labeled or known to be dangerous	• Wear proper protective equipment such as goggles, apron, and gloves when using chemicals. • Ensure proper room ventilation or use a fume hood when using materials that produce fumes. • NEVER smell fumes directly. • NEVER taste or eat any material in the laboratory.	• If contact occurs, immediately flush affected area with water and notify your teacher. • If a spill occurs, leave the area immediately and notify your teacher.
FLAMMABLE	unexpected fire due to liquids or gases that ignite easily such as rubbing alcohol	• Avoid open flames, sparks, or heat when flammable liquids are present.	• If a fire occurs, leave the area immediately and notify your teacher.
OPEN FLAME	burns or fire due to open flame from matches, Bunsen burners, or burning materials	• Tie back loose hair and clothing. • Keep flame away from all materials. • Follow teacher instructions when lighting and extinguishing flames. • Use proper protection, such as hot mitts or tongs, when handling hot objects.	• If a fire occurs, leave the area immediately and notify your teacher.
ANIMAL SAFETY	injury to or from laboratory animals	• Wear proper protective equipment such as gloves, apron, and goggles when working with animals. • Wash hands after handling animals.	• If injury occurs, notify your teacher immediately.
BIOLOGICAL	infection or adverse reaction due to contact with organisms such as bacteria, fungi, and biological materials such as blood, animal or plant materials	• Wear proper protective equipment such as gloves, goggles, and apron when working with biological materials. • Avoid skin contact with an organism or any part of the organism. • Wash hands after handling organisms.	• If contact occurs, wash the affected area and notify your teacher immediately.
FUME	breathing difficulties from inhalation of fumes from substances such as ammonia, acetone, nail polish remover, heated chemicals, and mothballs	• Wear goggles, apron, and gloves. • Ensure proper room ventilation or use a fume hood when using substances that produce fumes. • NEVER smell fumes directly.	• If a spill occurs, leave area and notify your teacher immediately.
IRRITANT	irritation of skin, mucous membranes, or respiratory tract due to materials such as acids, bases, bleach, pollen, mothballs, steel wool, and potassium permanganate	• Wear goggles, apron, and gloves. • Wear a dust mask to protect against fine particles.	• If skin contact occurs, immediately flush the affected area with water and notify your teacher.
RADIOACTIVE	excessive exposure from alpha, beta, and gamma particles	• Remove gloves and wash hands with soap and water before removing remainder of protective equipment.	• If cracks or holes are found in the container, notify your teacher immediately.

Authors and Contributors

Alton Biggs 🔺
Biggs Educational Consulting
Commerce, TX

Ralph M. Feather, Jr., Ph.D.
Associate Professor
  Chair, Dept. of Educational
  Studies and Secondary Education
Bloomsburg University
Bloomsburg, PA

Douglas Fisher, Ph.D.
Professor of Teacher Education
San Diego State University
San Diego, CA

S. Page Keeley, M.Ed.
Maine Mathematics and
  Science Alliance
Augusta, ME

Margaret Kilgo 🔺
Educational Consultant
Kilgo Consulting, Inc.
Austin, TX

Michael Manga, Ph.D.
University of California, Berkeley
Berkeley, CA

Edward Ortleb
Science/Safety Consultant
St. Louis, MO

Dinah Zike, M.Ed. 🔺
Author, Consultant,
  Inventor of FOLDABLES
Dinah Zike Academy;
  Dinah Might Adventures, LP
San Antonio, TX

**AMERICAN MUSEUM
ᵒꜰ NATURAL HISTORY**
New York, NY

Texas Advisory Board

Texas Reviewers and Consultants

Lead Consultants:

Lisa K. Felske
Science Specialist
Harris County Department of
  Education
Houston, Texas

Ann C. Mulvihill
Pre-K–12 Science Coordinator
Irving ISD
Irving, Texas

Tracy Ake
7th Grade Science Teacher
Fortbend ISD

Felecia Joiner
Stony Point Ninth Grade Center
Round Rock, TX

Carlos E. Salinas
7th Grade Science Teacher
East Central ISD

Meg Choate
**6th Grade Science
  Teacher**
Northside ISD

Joseph L. Kowalski, MS
Lamar Academy
McAllen, TX

Toni D. Sauncy
Associate Professor of Physics
Dept. of Physics
Angelo State University
St Angelo, TX

Tripp Givens
7th Grade Science Teacher
Mesquite ISD

Ginger Meeks
8th Grade Science Teacher
Austin, TX

Alison Welch
Wm. D. Slider Middle School
El Paso, TX

**Jose Miguel Hurtado
  Jr., Ph.D.**
Associate Professor
Dept. of Geological Sciences
University of Texas at El Paso
El Paso, TX

Paula Noe, M.Ed.
Science Specialist
Austin ISD
Austin, TX

Contributing Writers

Michelle Anderson, MS
Lecturer
The Ohio State University
Columbus, OH

Juli Berwald, Ph.D.
Science Writer
Austin, TX

John E. Bolzan, Ph.D.
Science Writer
Columbus, OH

Rachel Clark, MS
Science Writer
Moscow, ID

Patricia Craig, MS
Science Writer
Moscow, ID

Randall Frost, Ph.D.
Science Writer
Pleasanton, CA

Lisa S. Gardiner, Ph.D.
Science Writer
Denver, CO

Jennifer Gonya, Ph.D.
The Ohio State University
Columbus, OH

Mary Ann Grobbel, MD
Science Writer
Grand Rapids, MI

**Whitney Crispen Hagins,
MA, MAT**
Biology Teacher
Lexington High School
Lexington, MA

Carole Holmberg, BS
Planetarium Director
Calusa Nature Center and
  Planetarium, Inc.
Fort Myers, FL

Tina C. Hopper
Science Writer
Rockwall, TX

Jonathan D. W. Kahl, Ph.D.
Professor of Atmospheric
  Science
University of Wisconsin–
  Milwaukee
Milwaukee, WI

Nanette Kalis
Science Writer
Athens, OH

Cindy Klevickis, Ph.D.
Professor of Integrated
  Science and Technology
James Madison University
Harrisonburg, VA

Kimberly Fekany Lee, Ph.D.
Science Writer
La Grange, IL

Devi Ried Mathieu
Science Writer
Sebastopol, CA

William D. Rogers, DA
Professor of Biology
Ball State University
Muncie, IN

Donna L. Ross, Ph.D.
Associate Professor
San Diego State University
San Diego, CA

Marion B. Sewer, Ph.D.
Assistant Professor
  School of Biology
Georgia Institute of
  Technology
Atlanta, GA

Julia Meyer Sheets, Ph.D.
Lecturer
School of Earth Sciences
The Ohio State University
Columbus, OH

Michael J. Singer, Ph.D.
Professor of Soil Science
Department of Land, Air and
  Water Resources
University of California
Davis, CA

Karen S. Sottosanti, MA
Science Writer
Pickerington, OH

Paul K. Strode, Ph.D.
I.B. Biology Teacher
Fairview High School
Boulder, CO

Jan M. Vermilye, Ph.D.
Research Geologist
Seismo-Tectonic Reservoir
Monitoring (STRM)
Boulder, CO

Judith A. Yero, MA
Direct
Teac   Mind Resources
Ham   , MT

Margaret Zorn, MS
Scien   Writer
Yorkt   in, VA

Your assignment's due tomorrow...
**but your book is
in your locker!**

NOW WHAT?

Even in crunch time, with ConnectED, we've got you covered!

With ConnectED, you have instant access to all of your study materials—anytime, anywhere. From homework materials to study guides—it's all in one place and just a click away. ConnectED even allows you to collaborate with your classmates and use mobile apps to make studying easy.

Resources built for you—available 24/7:

- Your eBook available wherever you are

- Personal Tutors and Self-Check Quizzes to help your learning

- An Online Calendar with all of your due dates

- eFlashcard App to make studying easy

- A message center to stay in touch

Reimagine Learning

Go Online!
connectED.mcgraw-hill.com

Vocab
Learn about new vocabulary words.

Watch
Watch animations and videos.

Tutor
See and hear a teacher explain science concepts

Tools
Find tools to help you study.

Check
Check your progress.

Lab
Get all of your labs and lab worksheets.

Resources
Access practice worksheets.

CHAPTER 1
Scientific Investigations

Center for Nano and Molecular Science at the University of Texas in Austin, Texas

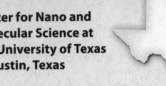

LAB Manager

Go to your Lab Manual or visit connectED.mcgraw-hill.com to perform the labs for this lesson.

Lesson 1.2
  Skill Practice: *How can you build your own scientific instrument?*
  TEKS 7.1(A); 7.2(A), (E); 7.4(A), (B)

  LAB: *How can you design a bioreactor?* **TEKS** 7.1(A); 7.2(A), (C), (D), (E); 7.3(A); 7.4(A), (B)

Virtual Lab: How is a controlled experiment performed?

Go Online! connectED.mcgraw-hill.com

Watch   Resources   Vocab   Tutor   IWB   Check   Lab

CHAPTER 2

Interactions of Matter and Energy

**Botanical Gardens in
San Antonio, Texas**

TEKS 7.5(A); 7.13(B); Also covers
7.1(A); 7.2(A), (C), (E); 7.4(A), (B)

TEKS 7.5(B); Also covers 7.1(A);
7.2(A), (C), (E); 7.3(B); 7.4(A), (B)

TEKS 7.5(A), (C); Also covers
7.1(A); 7.2(A), (C), (E); 7.4(A), (B)

✔ LAB Manager

Go to your Lab Manual or visit
connectED.mcgraw-hill.com to
perform the labs for this lesson.

Lesson 2.1
  MiniLAB: *Can you observe plant
  processes?*
  TEKS 7.1(A); 7.2(A), (C), (E); 7.4(A),
  (B); 7.5(A)

Lesson 2.2
  MiniLAB: *Is your soil rich in
  nitrogen?*
  TEKS 7.1(A); 7.2(A), (C), (E); 7.4(A),
  (B); 7.5(B)

Lesson 2.3
  MiniLAB: *How can you classify
  organisms?*
  TEKS 7.2(A), (E)

  LAB: *Photosynthesis and Light*
  TEKS 7.1(A); 7.2(A), (C), (E); 7.4(A),
  (B); 7.5(A)

BrainPOP®: Photosynthesis and Respiration

Go Online! connectED.mcgraw-hill.com

Watch Resources Vocab Tutor IWB Check Lab
▶   📄   ᵃᵇᶜ   💬   📈   ✔   🔺

CHAPTER 3
Carbon Chemistry

Sloth at the Dallas Aquarium in Dallas, Texas

🖌 **LAB** Manager
Go to your Lab Manual or visit connectED.mcgraw-hill.com to perform the labs for this lesson.

Lesson 3.1
MiniLAB: *How do carbon atoms bond with carbon and hydrogen atoms?* **TEKS** 7.1(A); 7.2(A), (C), (E); 7.3(B); 7.4(B); 7.6(A)

Lesson 3.2
MiniLAB: *How can you make a polymer?* **TEKS** 7.1(A), (B); 7.2(A), (C), (E); 7.4(A), (B); 7.6(A)

Skill Practice: *How do you test for vitamin C?* **TEKS** 7.1(A), (B); 7.2(A), (C), (E); 7.4(A), (B); 7.6(A)

Lesson 3.3
LAB: *Testing for Carbon Compounds* **TEKS** 7.1(A), (B); 7.2(A), (C), (E); 7.3(A); 7.4(A), (B); 7.6(A)

Animation: Polymers

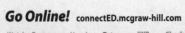
Go Online! connectED.mcgraw-hill.com

Watch   Resources   Vocab   Tutor   IWB   Check   Lab

Strand 3: Force, Motion, and Energy

CHAPTER 4
Forces, Energy, and Work

Solar-powered car at the University of Texas in Austin, Texas

◀ LAB Manager

Go to your Lab Manual or visit connectED.mcgraw-hill.com to perform the labs for this lesson.

Lesson 4.1
MiniLAB: *How does friction affect an object's motion?*
TEKS 7.1(A); 7.2(A), (C), (D), (E); 7.3(A); 7.4(A), (B); 7.7(C)

Lesson 4.2
MiniLAB: *What affects an object's potential energy?*
TEKS 7.1(A); 7.2(A), (C), (E); 7.3(A); 7.4(A), (B)

Lesson 4.3
MiniLAB: *How do energy transformations work for you?*
TEKS 7.4(A)

Skill Practice: *How can you transfer energy to make a vehicle move?* *TEKS* 7.1(A); 7.2(A), (E); 7.4(A), (B); 7.7(A)

Lesson 4.4
MiniLAB: *Does a wheel and axle make work easier?*
TEKS 7.1(A); 7.2(A), (C), (E); 7.4(A), (B); 7.7(A)

LAB: *Build a Powered Vehicle*
TEKS 7.1(A); 7.2(B), (E); 7.4(A), (B); 7.7(A)

Science Video: Get Moving

Go Online! connectED.mcgraw-hill.com

Watch   Resources   Vocab   Tutor   IWB   Check   Lab

Copyright © McGraw-Hill Education

Tornado outside Amarillo, Texas

CHAPTER 5
Weather and Its Impacts

⚑ LAB Manager

Go to your Lab Manual or visit connectED.mcgraw-hill.com to perform the labs for this lesson.

Lesson 5.1
MiniLAB: *What does it take to make a cloud?*
TEKS 7.1(A); 7.2(A), (C), (E); 7.4(A), (B)

Lesson 5.2
MiniLAB: *Can you measure what you cannot see?*
TEKS 7.1(A); 7.2(A), (C), (E); 7.3 (A); 7.4(A), (B)

Skill Practice: *How can you collect weather data and predict the weather?* **TEKS** 7.1(A); 7.2(A), (C), (E); 7.3(A); 7.4(A), (B)

Lesson 5.3
MiniLAB: *What is the "recipe" for a tornado?*
TEKS 7.2(E); 7.8(A)

Lesson 5.4
MiniLAB: *How can watersheds be cleaned up?*
TEKS 7.1(A); 7.2(A), (C), (E); 7.3(B); 7.4(A), (B); 7.8(C)

LAB: *Hurricanes and Their Effects*
TEKS 7.1(B); 7.2(A), (C), (E); 7.4(A); 7.8(A)

BrainPOP®: Clouds

Go Online! connectED.mcgraw-hill.com

Watch   Resources   Vocab   Tutor   IWB   Check   Lab

Wetlands in Galveston, Texas

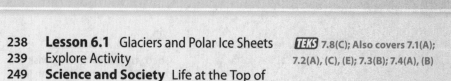

CHAPTER 6

Impacts on Water Systems

TEKS 7.8(C); Also covers 7.1(A);
7.2(A), (C), (E); 7.3(B); 7.4(A), (B)

TEKS 7.8(C); Also covers 7.1(A);
7.2(A), (C), (E); 7.3(B); 7.4(A), (B)

TEKS 7.8(C); Also covers 7.1(A);
7.2(A), (C), (E); 7.3(B); 7.4(A), (B)

LAB Manager

Go to your Lab Manual or visit
connectED.mcgraw-hill.com to
perform the labs for this lesson.

Lesson 6.1
  MiniLAB: *Does the ground's color
  affect temperature?*
  TEKS 7.1(A); 7.2(A), (C), (E); 7.3(B);
  7.4(A); 7.8(C)

Lesson 6.2
  MiniLAB: *How does a
  thermocline affect pollution in a
  lake?* **TEKS** 7.1(A); 7.2(A), (C), (E);
  7.3(B); 7.4(A), (B); 7.8(C)

  Skill Practice: *How does water
  flow into and out of streams?*
  TEKS 7.1(A); 7.2(A), (E); 7.3(B);
  7.4(A), (B); 7.8(C)

Lesson 6.3
  MiniLAB: *Can you model
  freshwater environments?*
  TEKS 7.1(A); 7.2(A), (C), (E); 7.3(B);
  7.4(A), (B); 7.8(C)

  LAB: *What can be done about
  pollution?* **TEKS** 7.1(A); 7.2(A), (C),
  (E); 7.3(B); 7.4(A), (B); 7.8(C)

Animation: Glacier Formation

Accumulation
area

CHAPTER 7
Exploring the Solar System

Saturn V rocket at
Johnson Space
Center in
Houston, Texas

◀ LAB Manager
Go to your Lab Manual or visit
connectED.mcgraw-hill.com to
perform the labs for this lesson.

Lesson 7.1
MiniLAB: *What is one factor that*
makes Earth "just right" for life?
TEKS 7.1(A); 7.2(A), (C), (E); 7.3(B);
7.4(A), (B); 7.9(A)

Skill Practice: *What solar system*
objects beyond Earth might have
conditions that support life?
TEKS 7.1(A); 7.2(A), (C), (E); 7.9(A)

Lesson 7.2
MiniLAB: *How hard is it to hit a*
target?
TEKS 7.1(A); 7.2(A), (C), (E); 7.3(B);
7.4(A)

Personal Tutor: Gravity

Go Online! connectED.mcgraw-hill.com

Watch   Resources   Vocab   Tutor   IWB   Check   Lab

CHAPTER 8

Relationships Between Organisms and Environments

South Padre Island
Bird Center in South
Padre Island, Texas

TEKS 7.10(A), (B); Also covers
7.1(A); 7.2(A), (C), (E); 7.3(B);
7.4(A), (B)

TEKS 7.10(A), (B); Also covers
7.1(A); 7.2(A), (C), (E); 7.3(A), (B),
(D); 7.4(A), (B)

TEKS 7.10(C); Also covers
7.2(A), (E)

LAB Manager

Go to your Lab Manual or visit
connectED.mcgraw-hill.com to
perform the labs for this lesson.

Lesson 8.1
 MiniLAB: *How hot is sand?*
 TEKS 7.1(A); 7.2(A), (C), (E); 7.3(B);
 7.4(A), (B); 7.10(A)

 Skill Practice: *Which biome is it?*
 TEKS 7.2(C), (E); 7.4(A); 7.10(A)

Lesson 8.2
 MiniLAB: *How do ocean
 ecosystems differ?*
 TEKS 7.1(A); 7.2(A), (C), (E); 7.3(B);
 7.4(A), (B); 7.10(A), (B)

 LAB: *A Biome for Radishes*
 TEKS 7.1(A); 7.2(A), (C), (E); 7.3(A),
 (B); 7.4(A), (B); 7.10(A)

BrainPOP®: Ecosystems

Go Online! connectED.mcgraw-hill.com

Watch   Resources   Vocab   Tutor   IWB   Check   Lab

ECOSYSTEMS MOVIE

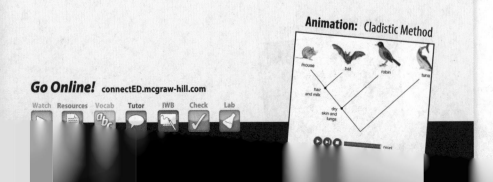

Prairie dogs in the
Panhandle
Plains region
of Texas

CHAPTER 9

Inheritance and Adaptations

LAB Manager

Go to your Lab Manual or visit
connectED.mcgraw-hill.com to
perform the labs for this lesson.

Lesson 9.1
MiniLAB: *How would you name
an unknown organism?*
TEKS 7.2(A), (E); 7.3(A)

Skill Practice: *How can you
identify a beetle?*
TEKS 7.2(A), (C), (E); 7.11(A)

LAB: *Constructing a
Dichotomous Key*
TEKS 7.1(A); 7.2(A), (C), (E); 7.4(A);
7.11(A)

Lesson 9.2
MiniLAB: *Can you change a
caribou to fit your environment?*
TEKS 7.2(A), (C), (E); 7.4(A); 7.11(B);
7.12(A)

LAB: *Adaptations in Bird Beaks*
TEKS 7.1(A); 7.2(A), (C), (E); 7.3(B);
7.4(A), (B); 7.11(B), (C)

Animation: Cladistic Method

Go Online! connectED.mcgraw-hill.com

Watch   Resources   Vocab   Tutor   IWB   Check   Lab

CHAPTER 10

Structure and Function of Organisms

390 **The BIG Idea**

391 **Page Keeley SCIENCE PROBES**

Giraffe at the Dallas
Zoo in Dallas, Texas

LAB Manager
Go to your Lab Manual or visit
connectED.mcgraw-hill.com to
perform the labs for this lesson.

Lesson 10.1
MiniLAB: *How can you observe DNA?*
TEKS 7.1(A); 7.2(A), (C), (D), (E); 7.4(A), (B); 7.12(F)

Lesson 10.2
MiniLAB: *What can you see in a cell?*
TEKS 7.1(A); 7.2(A), (C), (E); 7.4(A), (B); 7.12(D)

Skill Practice: *How are plant cells and animal cells similar and how are they different?*
TEKS 7.1(A), (B); 7.2(A), (C), (E); 7.4(A), (B); 7.12(D)

Lesson 10.3
MiniLAB: *How do cells work together to make an organism?*
TEKS 7.1(A); 7.2(E); 7.3(B); 7.4(A), (B); 7.12(C)

LAB: *Cell Differentiation*
TEKS 7.1(A), (B); 7.2(A), (C), (E); 7.4(A), (B); 7.12(C)

BrainPOP®: *Cell Specialization*

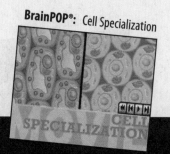

Go Online! connectED.mcgraw-hill.com

Watch   Resources   Vocab   Tutor   IWB   Check   Lab

CHAPTER 11

Human Body Systems

Ice skating at Space City Ice Station in Friendswood, Texas

◀ LAB Manager

Go to your Lab Manual or visit connectED.mcgraw-hill.com to perform the labs for this lesson.

Lesson 11.1
MiniLAB: *How can you model digestion?*
TEKS 7.1(A); 7.2(A), (C), (E); 7.3(B); 7.4(A), (B); 7.6(B)

Skill Practice: *How can you model the function of blood cells?*
TEKS 7.1(A); 7.2(A); 7.3(B); 7.4(A), (B); 7.12(B)

Lesson 11.2
MiniLAB: *Does your sight help you keep your balance?*
TEKS 7.1(A); 7.2(A), (C), (E); 7.4(A); 7.12(B)

Lesson 11.3
LAB: *Model the Body Systems*
TEKS 7.1(A); 7.2(A), (E); 7.3(B), (C); 7.4(A); 7.12(B)

Animation: Neuron

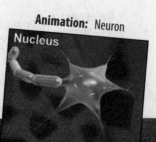

Nucleus

Go Online! connectED.mcgraw-hill.com

Watch   Resources   Vocab   Tutor   IWB   Check   Lab

CHAPTER 12
Plant and Animal Responses

A day at the pond in Houston, Texas

 LAB Manager

Go to your Lab Manual or visit connectED.mcgraw-hill.com to perform the labs for this lesson.

Lesson 12.1
MiniLAB: *When will plants flower?*
TEKS 7.2(A), (C), (E); 7.13(A)

Skill Practice: *What happens to seeds if you change the intensity of light?*
TEKS 7.1(A), (B); 7.2(A), (C), (E); 7.3(A); 7.4(A), (B); 7.13(A)

LAB: *Design a Stimulating Environment for Plants*
TEKS 7.1(A), (B); 7.2(B), (C), (E); 7.3(A); 7.4(A), (B); 7.13(A)

Lesson 12.2
MiniLAB: *How do young birds recognize predators?*
TEKS 7.2(A), (C), (E); 7.4(A); 7.13(A)

Skill Practice: *Can the color or surface of an area determine how a mealworm will move?*
TEKS 7.1(A), (B); 7.2(A), (C), (D), (E); 7.4(A), (B); 7.13(A)

LAB: *What changes an earthworm's behavior?*
TEKS 7.1(A), (B); 7.2(B), (C), (E); 7.4(A), (B); 7.13(A)

BrainPOP®: Plant Growth

Go Online! connectED.mcgraw-hill.com

Watch   Resources   Vocab   Tutor   IWB   Check   Lab

Texas longhorn in
Van Alstyne,
Texas

CHAPTER 13

Inheritance and Reproduction

TEKS 7.14(A), (C); Also covers
7.1(A); 7.2(A), (C); 7.3(B);
7.4(A), (B)

TEKS 7.14(C); Also covers 7.1(A);
7.2(A), (E); 7.3(B)

TEKS 7.14(B), (C); Also covers
7.1(A); 7.2(A), (C), (E); 7.3(B);
7.4(A)

TEKS 7.14(B); Also covers 7.1(A);
7.2(A), (C), (E); 7.3(A), (B);
7.4(A), (B)

◀ **LAB** Manager

Go to your Lab Manual or visit
connectED.mcgraw-hill.com to
perform the labs for this lesson.

Lesson 13.1
MiniLAB: *Can you mutate a
word?*
TEKS 7.4(A); 7.14(C)

Lesson 13.2
MiniLAB: *How does mitosis
work?*
TEKS 7.1(A); 7.2(E); 7.3(B); 7.14(C)

Lesson 13.3
MiniLAB: *How does one cell
produce four cells?*
TEKS 7.1(A); 7.2(A); 7.3(B); 7.4(A);
7.14(B)

Lesson 13.4
MiniLAB: *What parts of plants
can grow?*
TEKS 7.2(A), (C), (E); 7.4(A); 7.14(B)

LAB: *Mitosis and Meiosis*
TEKS 7.1(A); 7.2(A), (E); 7.3(A), (B);
7.4(A); 7.14(B)

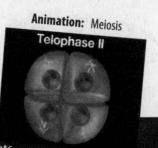

Animation: Meiosis
Telophase II

Go Online! connectED.mcgraw-hill.com

Watch Resources Vocab Tutor IWB Check Lab

TEKS Strand 1
Scientific Investigation and Reasoning

TEKS in this strand

✓ **7.1** The student, for at least 40% of instructional time, conducts laboratory and field investigations following safety procedures and environmentally appropriate and ethical practices.

✓ **7.2** The student uses scientific inquiry methods during laboratory and field investigations.

✓ **7.3** The student uses critical thinking, scientific reasoning, and problem solving to make informed decisions and knows the contributions of relevant scientists.

✓ **7.4** The student knows how to use a variety of tools and safety equipment to conduct science inquiry.

Texas Fun Fact

Did You Know? In 1995, scientists at Rice University in Houston, Texas, discovered a new form of carbon. Buckminsterfullerene—also known as a buckyball— is shaped like a soccer ball. Buckyballs naturally occur in soil. They also have been found in space. They can be used as a drug delivery system or in fiber optics.

1

Scientific Investigations

💡 The **BIG** Idea

The process of scientific inquiry and performing scientific investigations can provide answers about your world.

1.1 Understanding Science

Scientific inquiry is a process that uses a set of skills to answer questions or to test ideas about the natural world.

TEKS 7.1(A); 7.2(A), (B), (C), (D), (E); 7.3(A), (B), (C); 7.4(A), (B)

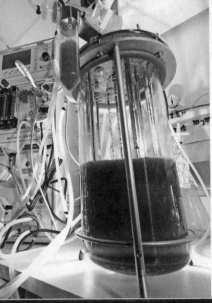

1.2 Case Study: Biodiesel from Microalgae

Scientific inquiry is used in real-life investigations.

TEKS 7.1(A); 7.2(A), (B), (C), (D), (E); 7.3(A), (D); 7.4(A), (B)

4

Go Online!
connectED.mcgraw-hill.com

Watch
Resources
Vocab
Tutor
IWB
Check
Lab

Scientific Explanations

An explanation helps provide answers to a question a scientist might be wondering about. Which of the following do you think involves providing a scientific explanation? Select the best response.

☐ **A.** hypothesis

☐ **B.** scientific theory

☐ **C.** scientific law

☐ **D.** hypothesis and scientific theory

☐ **E.** scientific theory and scientific law

☐ **F.** hypothesis, scientific theory, and scientific law

☐ **G.** None of the above. An explanation is something else.

Explain your thinking. Describe how explanations are used in science.

1.1 Understanding Science

Vacuuming Corals? No, these two divers are collecting data about corals in waters near Sulawesi, Indonesia. They are marine biologists—scientists who study living things in oceans and other saltwater environments. What information about corals do you think these scientists are collecting? What questions might they hope to answer? How do you think science can provide answers to their questions and your questions?

 Write your responses in your interactive notebook.

Explore Activity

TEKS 7.1(A); 7.2(A), (C), (E); 7.4(A)

How does scientific research begin?

Scientists observe what goes on around them. They ask questions about their observations and try to find answers to their questions. By observing and trying to answer some questions in the following activity, you will start to think like a scientist.

Procedure

1. Read and complete a lab safety form.

2. Cut a strip of **coffee filter paper** 3 cm × 12 cm.

3. Use a **black felt-tip pen** to draw a line across the paper 2 cm from the end. Describe the line in your Lab Manual or interactive notebook.

4. Put 1 cm of water in a **beaker**. Place the filter paper strip in the beaker so the end is in the water and the black line is above the water.

5. Predict what will happen to the black line.

6. Observe the black line after 5 min. Record your observations.

Think About This

1. What did you observe as the paper absorbed the water? Did the black line change? If so, how?

_____

_____

_____

_____

2. Did your observations support your prediction? Explain.

_____

_____

_____

_____

TEKS in this Lesson

7.2(B) Design and implement experimental investigations by making observations, asking well-defined questions, formulating testable hypotheses, and using appropriate equipment and technology

7.3(A) In all fields of science, analyze, evaluate, and critique scientific explanation by using empirical evidence, logical reasoning, and experimental and observational testing, including examining all sides of scientific evidence of those scientific explanations, so as to encourage critical thinking by the student

7.4(B) Use preventative safety equipment, including chemical splash goggles, aprons, and gloves, and be prepared to use emergency safety equipment, including an eye/face wash, a fire blanket, and a fire extinguisher.

Also covers Process Standards: 7.1(A); 7.2(A), (C), (D), (E); 7.3(B), (C); 7.4(A)

? Essential Questions

- What is scientific inquiry?
- How can scientific evidence be evaluated?
- Why is safety important in science?

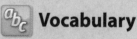 Vocabulary

science
observation
inference
hypothesis
prediction
technology
scientific theory
scientific law
critical thinking

What is science?

The last time that you watched squirrels play in a park or in your yard, did you realize that you were practicing science? Every time you observe the natural world, you are practicing science. **Science** *is the investigation and exploration of natural events and of the new information that results from those investigations.*

When you observe the natural world, you might form questions about what you see. While you are exploring those questions, you probably use reasoning, creativity, and skepticism to help you find answers to your questions. People use these behaviors in their daily lives to solve problems, such as how to keep a squirrel from eating bird seed, as shown in **Figure 1**. Similarly, scientists use these behaviors in their work.

Scientists use a reliable set of skills and methods in different ways to find answers to questions. After reading this lesson, you will have a better understanding of how science works, the limitations of science, and scientific ways of thinking. In addition, you will recognize that when you practice science at home or in the classroom, you use scientific methods to answer questions just as scientists do.

Identify

1. What are three behaviors that scientists might use in exploring questions and in solving problems?

Infer

2. Highlight the meaning of the term *scientific methods*.

Figure 1 Someone used reasoning and creativity to design each of these squirrel-proof bird feeders. However, some solutions don't work. Scientists use similar methods to try to solve problems.

Branches of Science

No one person can study all the natural world. Therefore, people tend to focus their efforts on one of the three fields or branches of science—life science, Earth science, or physical science, as described below. Then people or scientists can seek answers to specific problems within one field of science.

Word Origin

biology from Greek *bios*, means "life"; and *logia*, means "study of"

Life Science

Biology, or life science, is the study of all living things. This forest ecologist, a life scientist who studies interactions in forest ecosystems, is studying lichens growing on Douglas firs. Biologists ask questions such as

- How do plants produce their own food?

- Why do some animals give birth to live young and others lay eggs?

- How are reptiles and birds related?

Earth Science

The study of Earth, including its landforms, rocks, soil, and forces that shape Earth's surface, is Earth science. These Earth scientists are collecting soil samples in Africa. Earth scientists ask questions such as

- How do rocks form?

- What causes earthquakes?

- What substances are in soil?

Physical Science

The study of chemistry and physics is physical science. Physical scientists study the interactions of matter and energy. This chemist is preparing antibiotic solutions. Physical scientists ask questions such as

- How do substances react and form new substances?

- Why does a liquid change to a solid?

- How are force and motion related?

Scientific Inquiry **TEKS** 7.2(A), (B), (E)

As scientists study the natural world, they ask questions about what they observe. To find the answers to these questions, they usually use certain skills, or methods. The chart in **Figure 2** shows a sequence of the skills that a scientist might use in an investigation. However, it is important to know that, sometimes, not all of these skills are performed in an investigation or performed in this order. Scientists practice scientific inquiry—a process that uses a variety of skills and tools to answer questions or to test ideas about the natural world.

Ask Questions

Like a scientist, you use scientific inquiry in your life, too. Suppose you decide to plant a vegetable garden. As you plant the vegetable seeds, you water some seeds more than others. Then, you weed part of the garden and mix fertilizer into some of the soil. After a few weeks, you observe that some vegetable plants are growing better than others. *An* **observation** *is using one or more of your senses to gather information and take note of what occurs.*

Observations often are the beginning of the process of inquiry and can lead to questions such as "Why are some plants growing better than others?" As you are making observations and asking questions, you recall from science class that plants need plenty of water and sunlight to grow. Therefore you infer that perhaps some vegetables are receiving more water or sunlight than others and, therefore, are growing better. *An* **inference** *is a logical explanation of an observation that is drawn from prior knowledge or experience.*

Hypothesize

After making observations and inferences, you are ready to develop a hypothesis and investigate why some vegetables are growing better than others. *A possible explanation about an observation that can be tested by scientific investigations is a* **hypothesis.** Your hypothesis might be: Some plants are growing taller and more quickly than others because they are receiving more water and sunlight. Or, your hypothesis might be: The plants that are growing quickly have received fertilizer and fertilizer helps plants grow.

Steps of Scientific Inquiry

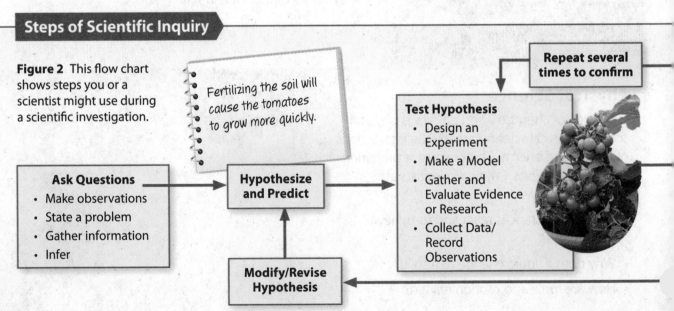

Figure 2 This flow chart shows steps you or a scientist might use during a scientific investigation.

Fertilizing the soil will cause the tomatoes to grow more quickly.

Ask Questions
- Make observations
- State a problem
- Gather information
- Infer

Hypothesize and Predict

Modify/Revise Hypothesis

Test Hypothesis
- Design an Experiment
- Make a Model
- Gather and Evaluate Evidence or Research
- Collect Data/ Record Observations

Repeat several times to confirm

Predict

After you state a hypothesis, you might make a prediction to help you test your hypothesis. A **prediction** is a statement of what will happen next in a sequence of events. For instance, based on your hypotheses, you might predict that if some plants receive more fertilizer, then they will grow taller.

Test Your Hypothesis

When you test a hypothesis, you often are testing your predictions. You might design an experiment to test your hypothesis on the fertilizer. You set up an experiment in which you plant seeds and add fertilizer to only some of them. Your prediction is that the plants that get the fertilizer will grow taller. If your prediction is confirmed, it supports your hypothesis. If your prediction is not confirmed, your hypothesis might need revision.

Analyze Results

During the experiment, you should collect data about the plants' rates of growth and how much fertilizer each plant receives. Initially, it might be difficult to recognize patterns and relationships in data. Your next step might be to organize and analyze your data.

You can create graphs, classify information, or make models and calculations. Organized data are easier to study. Other methods of testing a hypothesis and analyzing results are shown in **Figure 2**.

Draw Conclusions

Now you must decide whether your data do or do not support your hypothesis and then draw conclusions. A conclusion is a summary of the information gained from testing a hypothesis. You might make more inferences when drawing conclusions. If your hypothesis is supported, you can repeat your experiment several times to confirm your results. If your hypothesis is not supported, you can modify it and repeat the scientific inquiry process.

Communicate Results

An important step in scientific inquiry is communicating results to others. Professional scientists write scientific articles, speak at conferences, or exchange information on the Internet. This part of scientific inquiry is important because scientists use new information in their research or perform other scientists' investigations to verify results.

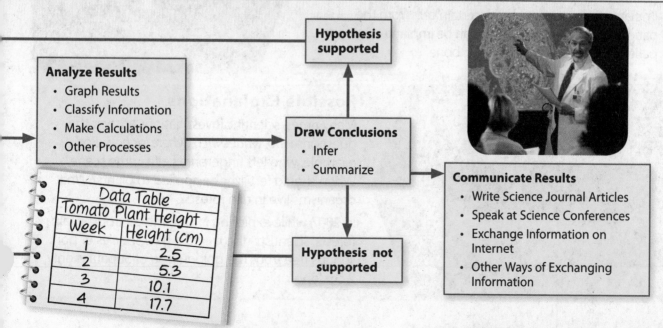

Analyze Results
- Graph Results
- Classify Information
- Make Calculations
- Other Processes

Data Table	
Tomato Plant Height	
Week	Height (cm)
1	2.5
2	5.3
3	10.1
4	17.7

Hypothesis supported

Draw Conclusions
- Infer
- Summarize

Hypothesis not supported

Communicate Results
- Write Science Journal Articles
- Speak at Science Conferences
- Exchange Information on Internet
- Other Ways of Exchanging Information

Results of Science

Both you and scientists perform scientific inquiry to find answers to questions. There are many outcomes of scientific inquiry, as shown below.

> **Determine**
>
> 3. <u>Underline</u> the three results of scientific inquiry identified below.

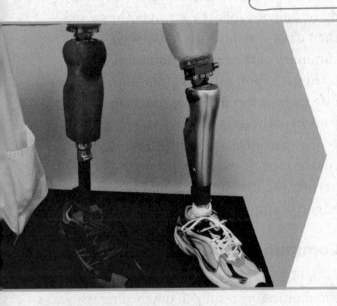

Technology

The practical use of scientific knowledge, especially for industrial or commercial use is **technology.** Televisions, mp3 players, and computers are examples of technology. The C-Leg, shown to the left, is one of the latest designs of computer-aided limbs. The prosthetic leg has sensors that anticipate the user's next move, which prevents him or her from stumbling or tripping. In addition, this new technology has several modes that can enable the user to walk, stand for long periods of time, and even ride a bike.

New Materials

Another possible outcome of an investigation is a new material. For example, scientists have developed a bone bioceramic. A bioceramic is a natural calcium-phosphate mineral complex that is part of bones and teeth. This synthetic bone mimics natural bone's structure. Its porous structure allows a type of cell to grow and develop into new bone tissue. The bioceramic can be shaped into implants that are treated with certain cells from the patient's bone marrow. It then can be implanted into the patient's body to replace missing bone.

Possible Explanations

Many times, scientific investigations answer the questions *who, what, when, where,* or *how.* For example, who left fingerprints at a crime scene? When should fertilizer be applied to plants? What organisms live in rain forests?

In 2007, while exploring in Colombia's tropical rain forests, scientists discovered a new species of poisonous tree frog. The golden frog of Supatá is only 2 cm long.

Scientific Theory and Scientific Laws

Scientists often repeat scientific investigations to verify that the results for a hypothesis or a group of hypotheses are correct. This can lead to a scientific theory.

Scientific Theories The everyday meaning of the word *theory* is an untested idea or an opinion. However, *a* **scientific theory** *is an explanation of observations or events based on knowledge gained from many observations and investigations.* For example, when scientists began looking at organisms through the first microscopes, they noticed that all the organisms were made of tinier units, or cells, such as the ones in **Figure 3**. As more scientists observed cells in other organisms, their observations became known as the cell theory. This theory explains that all living things are made of cells. A scientific theory is assumed to be the best explanation of observations unless it is disproved. The cell theory will continue to explain the makeup of all organisms until an organism is discovered that is not made of cells.

Scientific Laws Scientific laws are different from societal laws, which are agreements on a set of behaviors. *A* **scientific law** *describes a pattern or an event in nature that is always true.* A scientific theory might explain how and why an event occurs. But a scientific law states only that an event in nature will occur under specific conditions. For example, the law of conservation of mass states that the mass of materials will be the same before and after a chemical reaction. This scientific law does not explain why this occurs—only that it will occur. **Table 1** compares a scientific theory and a scientific law.

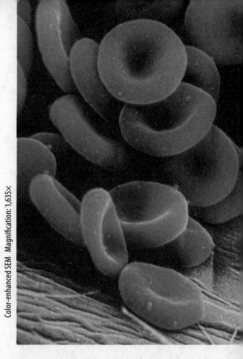

Color-enhanced SEM Magnification: 1,635×

Figure 3 When you view blood using a microscope, you will see that it contains red blood cells.

Table 1	Comparing Scientific Theory and Scientific Law	
Scientific Theory	**Scientific Law**
A scientific theory is based on repeated observations and scientific investigations.	Scientific laws are observations of similar events that have been observed repeatedly.
If new information does not support a scientific theory, the theory will be modified or rejected.	If many new observations do not follow the law, the law is rejected.
A scientific theory attempts to explain why something happens.	A scientific law states that something will happen.
A scientific theory usually is more complex than a scientific law and might contain many well-supported hypotheses.	A scientific law usually is based on one well-supported hypothesis that states that something will happen.

Table 1 There are several key differences between a scientific theory and a scientific law.

Interpret

4. Based on the information in the table, which is more complex—a scientific theory or a scientific law?

_____

_____

Skepticism in Media

When you see scientific issues in the media, such as newspapers, radio, television, and magazines, it is important to be skeptical. When you are skeptical, you question information that you read or hear or events you observe. Is the information truthful? Is it accurate? It also is important that you question statements made by people outside their area of expertise and claims that are based on vague statements.

Evaluating Scientific Evidence

An important skill in scientific inquiry is critical thinking. **Critical thinking** *is comparing what you already know with the information you are given in order to decide whether you agree with it.* Identifying and minimizing bias also is important when conducting scientific inquiry. To minimize bias in an investigation, sampling, repetition, and blind studies can be helpful, as shown in **Figure 4.**

Figure 4 Scientists use different methods to help prevent bias.

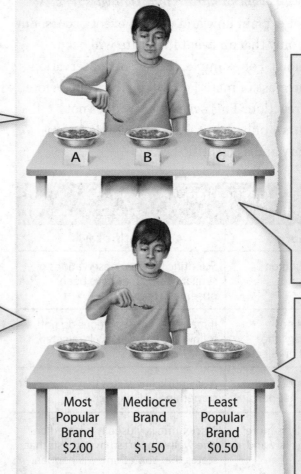

1 Sampling
A method of data collection that involves studying small amounts of something in order to learn about the larger whole is sampling. A sample should be a random representation of the whole.

2 Bias
It is important to reduce bias during scientific investigations. Bias is intentional or unintentional prejudice toward a specific outcome. Sources of bias in an investigation can include equipment choices, hypothesis formation, and prior knowledge.
Suppose you were a part of a taste test for a new cereal. If you knew the price of each cereal, you might think that the most expensive one tastes the best. This is a bias.

3 Blind Study
A procedure that can reduce bias is a blind study. The investigator, subject, or both do not know which item they are testing. Personal bias cannot affect an investigation if participants do not know what they are testing.

4 Repetition
If you get different results when you repeat an investigation, then the original investigation probably was flawed. Repetition of experiments helps reduce bias.

Science cannot answer all questions.

You might think that any question can be answered through a scientific investigation. But there are some questions that science cannot answer, such as the one posed in **Figure 5**. Questions about personal opinions, values, beliefs, and feelings cannot be answered scientifically. However, some people use scientific evidence to try to strengthen their claims about these topics.

Safety in Science TEKS 7.1(A); 7.4(B)

Scientists follow safety procedures when they conduct investigations. You too should follow safety procedures when you do any experiments. You should wear appropriate safety equipment and listen to your teacher's instructions. You should also have proper safety equipment easily accessible in the lab in case an accident would occur. For example, fire extinguishers and fire blankets are necessary safety equipment when using open flames or flammable materials. Also, you should learn to recognize potential hazards and to know the meaning of safety symbols.

Ethics are especially important when using living things during investigations. Animals should be treated properly. Scientists also should tell research participants about the potential risks and benefits of the research. Anyone can refuse to participate in scientific research.

Figure 5 Science cannot answer questions based on opinions or feelings, such as which paint color is the prettiest.

Academic Vocabulary

ethics *(noun)* rules of conduct or moral principles

FOLDABLES®

Cut out the Lesson 1.1 Foldable in the back of the book. Use it to organize your notes on scientific investigations.

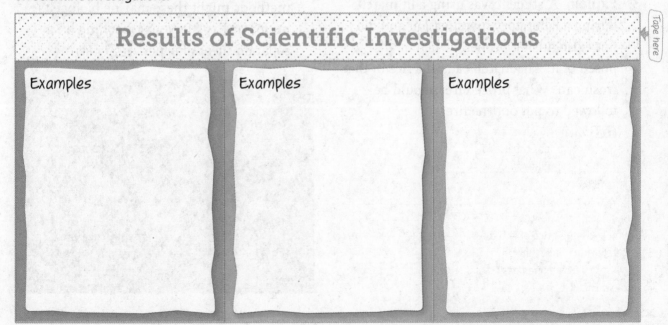

Results of Scientific Investigations

Examples

Examples

Examples

Tape here

Use Vocabulary

1. **Explain** the relationship between observations and hypotheses. **TEKS** 7.2(B)

Apply the Essential Questions

2. **Describe** how to test a hypothesis using scientific inquiry. **TEKS** 7.2(B)

3. **Explain** A student was using a lit match during a laboratory investigation and did not extinguish it properly when he disposed of it. The match caused a fire in the trash can. What procedures should be followed to put out the fire? **TEKS** 7.4(B)

4. **List** three ways that scientists can reduce bias. **TEKS** 7.3(A)

 H.O.T. Questions (Higher Order Thinking)

5. **Evaluate** In a magazine, you read that two scientific investigations attempted to answer the same question. However, the two teams of scientists came to opposite conclusions. How do you decide which investigation was valid? **TEKS** 7.2(E)

Writing in Science

6. **Analyze** What next step of scientific methods might these marine biologists perform? Explain your reasoning on a separate sheet of paper. **TEKS** 7.2(B)

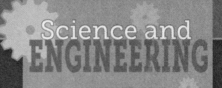

The Design Process

Create a Solution to a Problem

Scientists investigate and explore natural events and then interpret data and information learned from those investigations. How do engineers differ from scientists? Engineers create and maintain the designed world, or everything that does not occur in nature. Roadways, submarines, toys, microscopes, medical equipment, amusement park rides, and video games are the result of engineering. While science involves the practice of scientific inquiry, engineering involves the Design Process—a set of methods to create a solution to a problem or need.

Alvin, a deep sea submersible, has been in operation since 1964. It makes about 200 dives into the ocean each year and has aided in the discovery of human artifacts, deep sea creatures, and sea floor processes. Microscopes enable scientists to closely examine materials that are not easily visible to the unaided eye. Whether studies take place underwater, in a lab, or out in the rainforest, engineers have developed tools that allow scientists to better explore the biological, physical, and chemical world.

The Design Process

1. Identify a Problem or Need
- Determine a problem or need
- Document all questions, research, and procedures throughout the process.

2. Research and Develop Solutions
- Research any existing solutions that address the problem or need.
- Suggest some limitations to developing a solution
- Brainstorm possible solutions

3. Construct a Prototype
- Create several plans to solve the problem or need
- Determine materials, costs, resources, and time to develop the solution(s)

4. Test and Evaluate Solutions
- Use models to test the solutions
- Use graphs, charts, and tables to evaluate results
- Evaluate the process and identify strengths and weaknesses of the solution(s)

5. Communicate Results and Redesign
- Communicate the entire design process and results to others
- Modify and redesign solutions
- Construct actual solutions

Design a Magnifying Tool While on a rain forest field study with a group of fellow scientists, you discover a plant you do not recognize. Because the rain forest contains some species of plants that are poisonous, you know not to touch the plant as you examine its physical structures. Unfortunately, you lost your scientific backpack earlier when you crossed the Deepenphast River. You could become famous with this new discovery! How can you examine the specimen more closely? Record your responses in your interactive notebook.

Identify the Problem

You are anxious to examine and identify the plant species. You do not have your microscope or other tools to magnify the plant's structures. When you were young, you read how microscopes and lenses were first developed. You remember that water and glass were used to view small details of objects. How can you engineer a tool to enlarge your view using only the limited supplies in your day pack—a bottle of water, a plastic bag of paper clips, a test tube and stopper, a glass slide, a dropper, forceps, and disposable gloves?

Research Existing Solutions

Begin answering your questions by researching existing magnifying devices. How could you design and construct such a tool? Make note of possible limitations to your solutions, such as materials, location, or other restraints.

Brainstorm Possible Solutions

Write down ideas for engineering a device to magnify tiny objects. Note how curved surfaces change the size and shape of an object, how distance from an object changes the view, and how both the amount of light and the angle of light affect the image. Record any limitations to your construction.

Construct a Prototype

Discuss how the limited supplies in your day pack could be used to design and construct a magnifying tool. Draw several plans in your interactive notebook or on a separate sheet of paper. Use your materials to construct several models of a magnifier.

Test and Evaluate Solutions

Test your model many times to compare the ability to increase the size and clarity of the image. Use graphs, charts, and tables to evaluate the process and identify strengths and weaknesses in your solutions.

Communicate Your Results and Redesign Your Magnifying Tool

Share your design process and solution with peers using your visual displays and models. Discuss and critique your working solutions with other students. Do further research and testing, if necessary. Redesign and modify your solution to meet the design objectives. Then construct a final model of your magnifying tool.

1.2 Case Study: Biodiesel from Microalgae

Pea Soup? The green liquid in this container might look like soup, but you probably wouldn't want to eat it. The green liquid is actually algae growing in a closed system called a fermentation bioreactor. The temperature and pressure in the bioreactor are controlled to enhance the growth of the algae. Why do you think scientists might grow algae like this?

Write your response in your interactive notebook.

🧪 LAB Manager

Go to your Lab Manual or visit connectED.mcgraw-hill.com to perform the labs for this lesson.

Skill Practice: *How can you build your own scientific instrument?*
TEKS 7.1(A); 7.2(A), (E); 7.4(A), (B)

LAB: *How can you design a bioreactor?*

TEKS 7.1(A); 7.2(A), (C), (D), (E); 7.3(A); 7.4(A), (B)

Explore Activity

How are scientific discoveries made?

Many antibiotics are produced by molds and fungi. A scientist, while trying to grow bacteria in a petri dish, discovered a mold also growing on the plate. The area around this mold was free of bacteria. This event led to the discovery of penicillin, a common antibiotic. Streptomycin, another common antibiotic, was initially discovered in soil fungi. Soil containing this fungi was spread on agar in a petri dish that had bacteria previously growing on it. Again, this fungal growth prevented the bacteria from growing in the dish. Suppose a new fungus has been discovered. How could you test the fungus for antibiotic action?

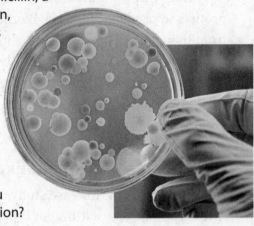

Think About This

1. Write a hypothesis about the new fungus and its possible antibiotic properties.

   _____

   _____

   _____

   _____

2. How would you design an experiment to test your hypothesis? Describe the basic steps of the experiment.

   _____

   _____

   _____

   _____

   _____

   _____

TEKS in this Lesson

7.3(A) In all fields of science, analyze, evaluate, and critique scientific explanation by using empirical evidence, logical reasoning, and experimental and observational testing, including examining all sides of scientific evidence of those scientific explanations, so as to encourage critical thinking by the student

7.3(D) Relate the impact of research on scientific thought and society, including the history of science and contributions of scientists as related to the content.

Also covers Process Standards 7.1(A); 7.2(A), (B), (C), (D), (E); 7.4(A), (B)

? Essential Questions

- How is scientific inquiry used in a real-life scientific investigation?
- How does research impact scientific thought?

abc Vocabulary

variable
dependent variable
independent variable
constants

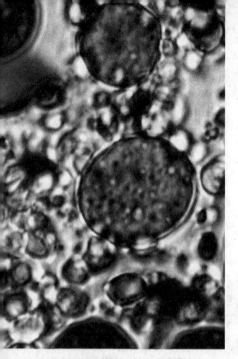

Figure 1 Microalgae are plantlike organisms that can make oils.

Case Study: Biodiesel from Microalgae

TEKS 7.3(A), (D)

For the last few centuries, fossil fuels have been the main sources of energy for industry and transportation. But, scientists have shown that burning fossil fuels negatively affects the environment. Also, some people are concerned about eventually using up the world's reserves of fossil fuels.

During the past few decades, scientists have explored using protists to produce biodiesel. Biodiesel is a fuel made primarily from living organisms. Protists, shown in **Figure 1,** are a group of microscopic organisms that usually live in water or moist environments. Some of these protists are plantlike because they make their own food using a process called photosynthesis. Microalgae are plantlike protists.

Designing a Controlled Experiment

The scientists in this case study used scientific inquiry to investigate the use of different types of protists to make biodiesel. They designed controlled experiments to test their hypotheses. This lesson contains examples of how scientists in the study practiced inquiry. The sample notebook pages throughout the lesson contain information that a scientist might have written in a science journal.

A controlled experiment is a scientific investigation that tests how one variable affects another. *A* **variable** *is any factor in an experiment that can have more than one value.* In controlled experiments, there are two types of variables. *The* **dependent variable** *is the factor measured or observed during an experiment. The* **independent variable** *is the factor that you want to test.* It is changed by the investigator to observe how it affects a dependent variable. **Constants** *are the factors in an experiment that remain the same.*

A controlled experiment has two groups—an experimental group and a control group. The experimental group is used to study how a change in the independent variable changes the dependent variable. The control group contains the same factors as the experimental group, but the independent variable is not changed. Without a control, it is difficult to know whether your experimental observations result from the variable you are testing or from another factor.

Contrast

1. Think back to the experiment you designed in the Explore Activity at the beginning of this lesson. In that experiment, what is the dependent variable? The independent variable? How do the dependent and independent variables differ? Write your responses in your interactive notebook.

Biodiesel

The idea of engines running on fuel made from plant or plantlike sources is not entirely new. Rudolph Diesel, shown in **Figure 2,** invented the diesel engine. He used peanut oil to demonstrate how his engine worked. However, when petroleum was introduced as a diesel fuel source, it was preferred over peanut oil because it was cheaper.

Oil-rich food crops, such as soybeans, can be used as a source of biodiesel. However, some people are concerned that crops grown for fuel sources will replace crops grown for food. If farmers grow more crops for fuel, then the amount of food available worldwide will be reduced. Because of food shortages in many parts of the world, replacing food crops with fuel crops is not a good solution.

Figure 2 Rudolph Diesel invented the first diesel engine in the early 1900s.

Identify

2. Underline the three sources of diesel fuel mentioned above.

Aquatic Species Program

In the late 1970s the U.S. Department of Energy began funding its Aquatic Species Program (ASP) to investigate ways to remove air pollutants. Coal-fueled power plants produce carbon dioxide (CO_2), a pollutant, as a by-product. In the beginning, the study examined all aquatic organisms that use CO_2 during photosynthesis—their food-making process. These included large plants, commonly known as seaweeds, plants that grow partially underwater, and microalgae. It was hoped these organisms might remove excess CO_2 from the atmosphere. During the studies, however, the project leaders noticed that some microalgae produced large amounts of oil. The program's focus soon shifted to using microalgae to produce oils that could be processed into biodiesel.

Scientific investigations often begin when someone observes an event in nature and wonders why or how it occurs.

A hypothesis is a tentative explanation that can be tested by scientific investigations. A prediction is a statement of what someone expects to happen next in a sequence of events.

Observation A:
While testing microalgae to discover if they would absorb carbon pollutants, ASP project leaders noticed that some species of microalgae had high oil content.

Hypothesis A:
Some microalgae species can be used as a source of biodiesel fuel because the microalgae produce a large amount of oil.

Prediction A:
If the correct species is found and the growing conditions are isolated, then large oil amounts will be collected.

Design an Experiment and Collect Data: The ASP scientists developed a rapid screening test to discover which microalgae species produced the most oil.

Independent Variable: amount of nitrogen available

Dependent Variable: amount of oil produced

Constants: the growing conditions of algae (temperature, water quality, exposure to the Sun, etc.)

During an investigation, observations, hypotheses, and predictions are often revised when new information is discovered.

Observation B: Based on previous microalgae studies, starving microalgae of nutrients could result in more oil production.

Hypothesis B: Microalgae grown with inadequate amounts of nitrogen alter their growth processes and produce more oil.

Prediction B: If microalgae receive inadequate amounts of nitrogen then they will produce more oil.

Figure 3 Green microalgae and diatoms showed the most promise during testing for biodiesel production.

Which Microalgae?

Microalgae are microscopic organisms that live in marine (salty) or freshwater environments. Like many plants and other plantlike organisms, they use photosynthesis and make sugar. The process requires light energy. Microalgae make more sugar than they can use as food. They convert excess sugar to oil. Scientists focused on these microalgae because their oil then could be processed into biodiesel.

The scientists began their research by collecting and identifying promising microalgae species. The search focused on microalgae in shallow, inland, saltwater ponds. Scientists predicted that these microalgae were more resistant to changes in temperature and salt content in the water.

By 1985 a test was in place for identifying microalgae with high oil content. Two years later 3,000 microalgae species had been collected. Scientists checked these samples for tolerance to acidity, salt levels, and temperature and selected 300 species. Of these, green microalgae and diatoms, as shown in **Figure 3,** showed the most promise. However, it was obvious that no one species was going to be perfect for all climates and water types.

Oil Production in Microalgae

Scientists also began researching how microalgae produce oil. Some studies suggested that starving microalgae of nutrients, such as nitrogen, could increase the amount of oil they produced. However, starving microalgae also caused them to be smaller, resulting in no overall increase in oil production.

Outdoor Testing v. Bioreactors

By the 1980s the ASP scientists were growing microalgae in outdoor ponds in New Mexico. However, outdoor conditions were very different from those in the laboratory. Cooler temperatures in the outdoor ponds resulted in smaller microalgae. Native algae species also invaded the ponds, forcing out the high-oil-producing laboratory microalgae species.

The scientists continued to focus on growing microalgae in open ponds, such as the one shown in **Figure 4.** Many scientists still think these open ponds are better for producing large quantities of biodiesel from microalgae. But, some researchers are now growing microalgae in closed glass containers called bioreactors, also shown in **Figure 4.** Inside these bioreactors, organisms live and grow under controlled conditions. This method avoids many of the problems associated with open ponds. However, bioreactors are more expensive than open ponds.

A biofuel company in the western United States has been experimenting with a low-cost bioreactor. A scientist at the company explained that they examined the ASP program and hypothesized that they could use long plastic bags, shown in **Figure 4,** instead of closed glass containers.

Open ponds are less expensive than bioreactors for growing microalgae.

Figure 4 These three methods of growing microalgae are examples of three different hypotheses that are being tested in controlled experiments.

Microalgae grown in plastic bags are very expensive to harvest.

Microalgae grow under controlled conditions in glass bioreactors.

Observation C.
Microalgae use light energy, water, and carbon dioxide to make sugar, which is converted to oil.

Hypothesis C.
Microalgae will produce more oil if light is distributed evenly throughout because they need light energy to grow and produce more oil.

Prediction C.
If light is distributed more evenly then more microalgae will grow, and more oil will be produced.

Why So Many Hypotheses?

According to Dr. Richard Sayre, a biofuel researcher, all the ASP research was based on forming hypotheses. Dr. Sayre says, "It was hypothesis-driven. You just don't go in and say 'Well, I have a feeling this is the right way to do it.' You propose a hypothesis. Then you test it."

Dr. Sayre added, "Biologists have been trained over and over again to develop research strategies based on hypotheses. It's sort of ingrained into our culture. You don't get research support by saying, 'I'm going to put together a system, and it's going to be wonderful.' You have to come up with a question. You propose some strategies for answering the question. What are your objectives? What outcomes do you expect for each objective?"

Infer

3. Why is it important for a scientific researcher to develop a good hypothesis?

_____

_____

_____

Increasing Oil Yield

Scientists from a biofuel company in Washington State thought of another way to increase oil production. Researchers knew microalgae use light energy, water, and carbon dioxide and make sugar. The microalgae eventually convert sugar into oil. The scientists wondered if they could increase microalgae oil production by distributing light to all microalgae. The experimental lab setup to test this idea is shown in **Figure 5**.

Figure 5 Acrylic rods distribute light to microalgae below the water's surface. If microalgae receive light, they can photosynthesize and eventually produce oils. Without light, microalgae are not productive.

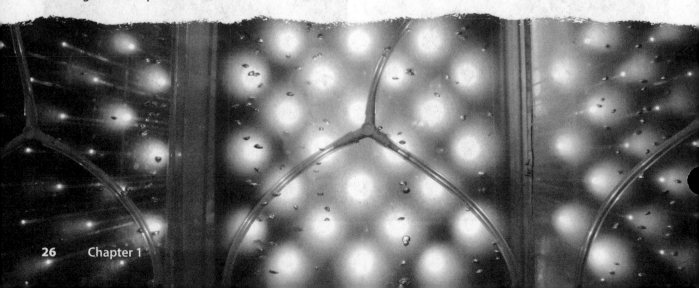

Bringing Light to Microalgae

Normally microalgae grow near the surface of a pond. Any microalgae about 5 cm below the pond's surface will grow less. Why is this? First, water blocks light from reaching deep into a pond. Second, microalgae at the top of a pond block light from reaching microalgae below them. Only the top part of a pond is productive.

Recognize

4 Highlight why microalgae grow at a pond's surface.

Experimental Group Researchers decided to assemble a team of engineers to design a light-distribution system. Light rods distribute artificial light to microalgae in a bioreactor. The bioreactor controls the environmental conditions that affect how the microalgae grow. These conditions include temperature, nutrient levels, carbon dioxide level, airflow, and light.

Data from their experiments showed scientists how microalgae in well-lit environments grow compared to how microalgae grow in dimmer environments. Using solar data for various parts of the country, the scientists concluded that the light rod would significantly increase microalgae growth and oil production in outdoor ponds. These scientists next plan to use the light-rod growing method in outdoor ponds.

Field Testing Scientists plan to take light to microalgae instead of moving microalgae to light. Dr. Jay Burns is chief microalgae scientist at a biofuel company. He said, "What we are proposing to do is to take the light from the surface of a pond and distribute it throughout the depth of the pond. Instead of only the top 5 cm being productive, the whole pond becomes productive."

Scientists tested their hypothesis, collected data, analyzed the data, and drew conclusions.

Analyze Results:
The experimental results showed that microalgae would produce more oil using a light-rod system than by using just sunlight.

Draw a Conclusion:
The researchers concluded that the light-rod system greatly increased microalgae oil production.

Connect

5. What conditions are held constant in a bioreactor? Why is this important in a controlled experiment? Write your responses in your interactive notebook.

Research scientists and scientists in the field rely on scientific methods and scientific inquiry to solve real-life problems. When a scientific investigation lasts for several years and involves many scientists, such as this study, many hypotheses can be tested. Some hypotheses are supported, and other hypotheses are not. However, information is gathered and lessons are learned. Hypotheses are refined and tested many times. This process of scientific inquiry results in a better understanding of the problem and possible solutions.

6. Based on **Figure 6,** microalgae can be used to make which products not listed in the text?

_____

_____

_____

_____

_____

Figure 6 There are many benefits to cultivating microalgae.

Another Way to Bring Light to Microalgae Light rods are not the only way to bring light to microalgae. Paddlewheels can be used to keep the microalgae's locations changing. Paddlewheels continuously rotate microalgae to the surface. This exposes the organisms to more light.

Why Grow Microalgae?

While the focus of this case study is microalgae growth for biodiesel production, there are other benefits of growing microalgae, as shown in **Figure 6.** Power plants that burn fossil fuels release carbon dioxide into the atmosphere. Evidence indicates that this contributes to global warming. During photosynthesis, microalgae use carbon dioxide and water, release oxygen, and produce sugar, which they convert to oil. Not only do microalgae produce a valuable fuel, they also remove pollutants from and add oxygen to the atmosphere. Harvested microalgae can be used to make different products, such as food for livestock and additives to cosmetics.

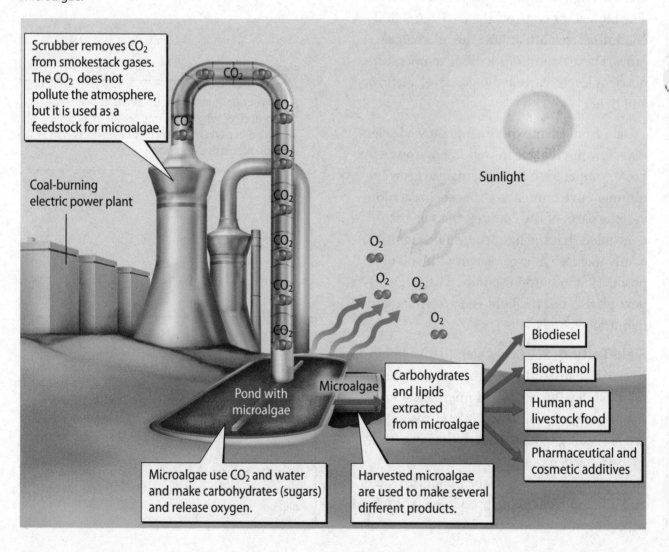

Scrubber removes CO_2 from smokestack gases. The CO_2 does not pollute the atmosphere, but it is used as a feedstock for microalgae.

Coal-burning electric power plant

Sunlight

Pond with microalgae

Microalgae

Carbohydrates and lipids extracted from microalgae

Biodiesel

Bioethanol

Human and livestock food

Pharmaceutical and cosmetic additives

Microalgae use CO_2 and water and make carbohydrates (sugars) and release oxygen.

Harvested microalgae are used to make several different products.

Are microalgae the future?

Scientists face many challenges in their quest to produce biodiesel from microalgae. For now, the costs of growing microalgae and extracting their oils are too high to compete with petroleum-based diesel. However, the combined efforts of government-funded programs and commercial biofuel companies might one day make microalgae-based biodiesel an affordable reality in the United States. In fact, a company in Israel has a successful test plant in operation, as shown in **Figure 7.** Plans are underway to build a large-scale industrial facility to convert carbon dioxide gases released from an Israeli coal-powered electrical plants into useful microalgae products. If this technology performs as expected, microalgae cultivation might occur near coal-fueled power plants in other parts of the world, too.

Currently, scientists have no final conclusions about using microalgae as a fuel source. As long as petroleum remains relatively inexpensive and available, it probably will remain the preferred source of diesel fuel. However, if petroleum prices increase or availability decreases, new sources of fuel will be needed. Biodiesel made from microalgae oils might be one of the alternative fuel sources used.

Figure 7 This microalgae test facility in Israel is reducing the amount of carbon dioxide pollution in the atmosphere.

LAB Manager

Skill Practice: *How can you build your own scientific instrument?*
TEKS 7.1(A); 7.2(A), (E); 7.4(A), (B)

LAB: *How can you design a bioreactor?*
TEKS 7.1(A); 7.2(A), (C), (D), (E); 7.3(A); 7.4(A), (B)

Evaluate

7. Identify one hypothesis that was supported and one hypothesis that was not supported throughout the scientific investigation of microalgae as a biodiesel food source. Explain your choices.

Use Vocabulary

1. **Contrast** the terms *dependent variable,* *independent variable,* and *constants.*
   TEKS 7.3(A)

Apply the Essential Questions

2. **Give an example** of a scientific inquiry used in a real-life scientific investigation that is not mentioned in this lesson.
   TEKS 7.3(A)

3. Which best describes how scientific thought was impacted by the research on protists? **TEKS** 7.3(D)

   A. Biodiesel made from microalgae oil is a possible future alternative fuel.

   B. Microalgae oil production increases under low light.

   C. Microalgae remove excess CO_2 from the atmosphere.

   D. Starving microalgae increases oil production.

🔥 H.O.T. Question (Higher Order Thinking)

4. **Evaluate** scientists' efforts to increase the oil content of microalgae and to grow microalgae more quickly. What would you do differently? **TEKS** 7.3(A)

Writing in Science

5. **Assess** Identify the experimental group, the control group, and controls in the following example. Explain your decisions on a separate sheet of paper.

   A scientist tests a new cough medicine by giving it to a group of people with colds. The scientist gives another group with colds a liquid and tells them it is cough medicine. The people in both groups are women between the ages of 20 and 30 who normally are in good health.
   TEKS 7.3(A)

Test-Taking Strategy

Interpret an Experiment The results of an experiment are often presented in graphics such as tables, graphs, photos, and diagrams. Though these types of graphics are each read in a different way, the same procedure can be used to understand the results of an experiment.

Example

Use the table below to answer question 1.

Length of Ramp (m)	Force Needed to Push Box Up Ramp (N)
2	2.50
3	1.67
4	1.25
5	1.00

1 ① Identify the variables in the experiment. In this experiment, the students changed the length of the ramp, so that is the independent variable. They measured the force it took to push the block up the ramp, so that is the dependent variable.

1 The table above shows the results of an experiment that students conducted to determine how the length of a ramp affects the amount of force needed to raise a box to a height of 0.5 m. Which graph best summarizes the data?

TEKS 7.7(A) *supporting;* 7.2(E)

② Determine how those variables changed in relation to one another. In this experiment, the force needed to push the box up the ramp decreased as the length of the ramp increased.

A Force / Distance

B Force / Distance

C Force / Distance

D Force / Distance

③ Examine the answer choices to find the one that matches the trend that you found. Carefully read the axis labels. The dependent variable is usually on the vertical axis. Start by eliminating choices with the trend shown in the wrong direction. A and B can be eliminated. Carefully examine the remaining choices. Graph the points on scratch paper. Choice D most accurately shows the trend.

TIP: Make sure you are marking your answer on the correct row of your answer sheet. Use a scrap piece of paper to keep yourself on track.

Multiple Choice

1 In some areas of science, scientists do fieldwork instead of laboratory work. For which investigation requiring fieldwork would a scientist need to make observations using this tool? **TEKS** 7.2(A)

A the study of atomic particles

B the study of nesting birds

C the study of plant distribution

D the study of tree growth rings

2

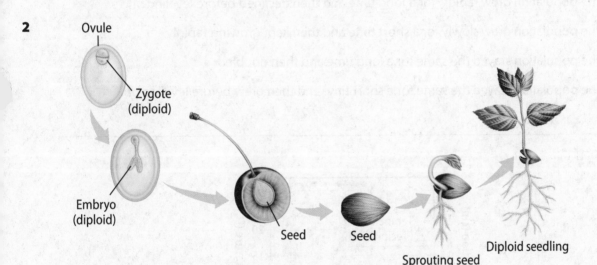

Daniel observes this diagram of a growing plant. He knows that plants need sunlight, water, and nutrients from the soil to enable them to make food and energy for growth. He also knows that seeds start to sprout from under the ground. Based on his knowledge and observations, what would be a likely question for Daniel to investigate? **TEKS** 7.2(B)

A How do plants grow if their roots stay within the soil?

B How do plants get the energy to break out of the seed coat?

C Why do plants grow larger as they get more sunlight?

D Why don't all parts of a plant grow under the ground?

3 Microalgae can convert used cooking oil into biodiesel fuel. Large amounts of microalgae can be produced by growing them in a nutrient liquid. Analyze the data in this graph showing the growth of a microalgae population. **TEKS** 7.2(E)

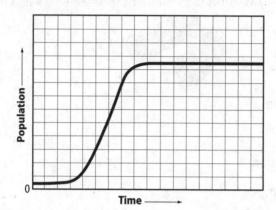

Which statement best explains what happened to the population of microalgae over time?

A The population grew rapidly for a long time and then declined before leveling off.

B The population grew slowly for a short time and then kept growing rapidly.

C The population stayed the same for a long time and then doubled.

D The population stayed the same for a short time and then grew before leveling off.

4

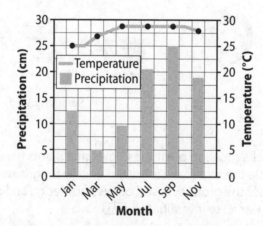

This graph shows temperature and precipitation data for one location. What best describes the weather conditions in this location during the month of September? **TEKS** 7.2(E)

A cool and dry

B cool and rainy

C warm and dry

D warm and rainy

5

> Your science lab group is designing an experiment to test the effectiveness of three different brands of fertilizer on plant growth. Your group plants seeds in three identical pots. Each pot contains the same amount of soil. You place the pots near a sunny window. Next, you add a different fertilizer to each of the three pots. You label each pot with the name of the fertilizer it contains. Every day you will add a measured amount of water to each pot. After several weeks you will measure the plants to see which fertilizer is more effective.

What is missing from this experiment? **TEKS** 7.2(B)

A a pot containing fertilizer, seeds, and soil placed in the shade as a control

B a pot containing fertilizer, seeds, and soil placed with the others, but not watered to act as a control

C a pot containing only seeds and fertilizer placed with the others to act as a control

D a pot containing only seeds and soil placed near the others to act as a control

---

6

> In the 1600s, Belgian scientist Jan Baptiste von Helmont wanted to know how plants gained matter as they grew. Many people thought that plants grew by taking in matter from the soil only. To test this idea von Helmont devised an experiment described as follows: He placed 200 pounds of soil in an earthen pot. The soil was dried in an oven. He then moistened the soil with rainwater and in it planted a branch of willow that weighed five pounds. He wet the soil whenever necessary with rain or distilled water only. After five years, the willow tree weighed 169 pounds and about three ounces. He again dried out the soil in the pot and found it weighed 199 pounds and 14 ounces.

After completing his experiment, van Helmont proposed another hypothesis. Which hypothesis is based on his results? **TEKS** 7.3(D)

A Plants grow by taking in matter from other plants.

B Plants grow by taking in matter from soil and rocks.

C Plants grow by taking in matter from themselves.

D Plants grow by taking in matter from water.

TEKS Strand 2
Matter and Energy

TEKS in this strand

✓ **7.5** The student knows that interactions occur between matter and energy.

✓ **7.6** The student knows matter has physical properties and can undergo physical and chemical changes.

✓ **7.13** The student knows that a living organism must be able to maintain balance in stable internal conditions in response to external and internal stimuli.

✓ Also includes the following Scientific Investigation and Reasoning strand TEKS: 7.1, 7.2, 7.3, 7.4

Texas Fun Fact

Did You Know? The horns on Texas Longhorn cattle can grow up to 2 meters in length. It takes a lot of energy to grow horns that large. Longhorns get their energy from the plants they consume. They are part of a food chain that allows energy from the Sun to flow through an ecosystem.

Interactions of Matter and Energy

The **BIG** Idea

Interactions occur between matter and energy, including the transformation of energy through the process of photosynthesis, the cycling of matter, and the flow of energy through living systems.

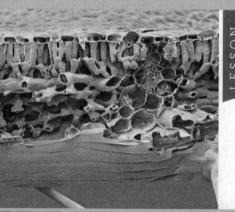

LESSON

2.1 Energy Processing in Plants

Plants use the processes of photosynthesis and cellular respiration to convert light energy into usable forms of chemical energy.

TEKS 7.5(A); 7.13(B); Also covers 7.1(A); 7.2(A), (C), (E); 7.4(A), (B)

LESSON

2.2 Cycles of Matter

Matter such as water, oxygen, nitrogen, and carbon cycles through ecosystems.

TEKS 7.5(B); Also covers 7.1(A); 7.2(A), (C), (E); 7.3(B); 7.4(A), (B)

LESSON

2.3 Energy in Ecosystems

Food chains, food webs, and energy pyramids model the flow of energy in ecosystems.

TEKS 7.5(A), (C); Also covers 7.1(A); 7.2(A), (C), (E); 7.4(A), (B)

2.2 Cycles of Matter

Where does water go?

All water, including the water in this waterfall, can move throughout an ecosystem in a cycle. It can also change forms. What other forms do you think water takes as it moves through an ecosystem?

Write your response in your interactive notebook.

◀ LAB Manager

Go to your Lab Manual or visit connectED.mcgraw-hill.com to perform the labs for this lesson.

MiniLAB: *Is your soil rich in nitrogen?*

TEKS 7.1(A); 7.2(A), (C), (E); 7.4(A), (B); 7.5(B)

How can you model raindrops?

Like all matter on Earth, water is recycled. It constantly moves between Earth and its atmosphere. You could be drinking the same water that a *Tyrannosaurus rex* drank 65 million years ago!

Procedure

1. Read and complete a lab safety form.

2. Half-fill a **plastic cup** with warm water.

3. Cover the cup with **plastic wrap**. Secure the plastic with a **rubber band**.

4. Place an **ice cube** on the plastic wrap. Observe the cup for several minutes. Record your observations in your Lab Manual.

Think About This

1. What did you observe on the underside of the plastic wrap? Why do you think this happened?

_____

_____

2. How does this activity model the formation of raindrops?

_____

_____

_____

3. Do you think other matter moves through the environment? Explain your answer.

_____

_____

_____

_____

TEKS in this Lesson

7.5(B) Demonstrate and explain the cycling of matter within living systems such as in the decay of biomass in a compost bin.

Also covers Process Standards: 7.1(A); 7.2(A), (C), (E); 7.3(B); 7.4(A), (B)

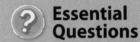 **Essential Questions**

- How does matter move in ecosystems?

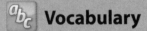 **Vocabulary**

evaporation
condensation
precipitation
nitrogen fixation

How does matter move in ecosystems?

TEKS 7.5(B)

The water that you used to wash your hands this morning might have once traveled through the roots of a tree in Africa, or it might have been part of an Antarctic glacier. How can this be? Water moves continuously through ecosystems. It is used over and over again. The same is true of carbon, oxygen, nitrogen, and other types of matter. Elements that move through one matter cycle may also play a role in another, such as oxygen's role in the water cycle.

Identify

1. List four materials that cycle through ecosystems.

_____

_____

_____

_____

The Water Cycle

Look at a globe or a map. Notice that water surrounds the landmasses. Water covers about 70 percent of Earth's surface.

Most of Earth's water—about 97 percent—is in oceans. Water is also in rivers and streams, lakes, and underground reservoirs. In addition, water is in the atmosphere, icy glaciers, and living things.

Water continually cycles from Earth to its atmosphere and back again. This movement of water is called the water cycle. It involves three processes: evaporation, condensation, and precipitation.

Identify

2. **Name** the source of energy that drives the water cycle.

_____

Figure 1 During the water cycle, the processes of evaporation, condensation, and precipitation move water from Earth's surface into the atmosphere and back again.

Evaporation

The Sun supplies the energy for the water cycle, as shown in **Figure 1**. As the Sun heats Earth's surface waters, evaporation occurs. **Evaporation** (ih va puh RAY shun) *is the process during which liquid water changes into a gas called water vapor.* This water vapor rises into the atmosphere. Temperature, humidity, and wind affect how quickly water evaporates.

Water is also released from living things. Transpiration is the release of water vapor from the leaves and stems of plants. Recall that cellular respiration is a process that occurs in many cells. A by-product of cellular respiration is water. This water leaves cells and enters the environment and atmosphere as water vapor.

Condensation

The higher in the atmosphere you are, the cooler the temperature is. As water vapor rises, it cools and condensation occurs.

Condensation (kahn den SAY shun) *is the process during which water vapor changes into liquid water.* Clouds form due to condensation.

Clouds are made of millions of tiny water droplets or crystals of ice. These form when water vapor condenses on particles of dust and other substances in the atmosphere.

Precipitation

Water that falls from clouds to Earth's surface is called **precipitation** (prih sih puh TAY shun). It enters bodies of water or soaks into soil. Precipitation can be rain, snow, sleet, or hail. It forms as water droplets or ice crystals join together in clouds. Eventually, these droplets or crystals become so large and heavy that they fall to Earth. Over time, living things use this precipitation, and the water cycle continues.

> **Select**
>
> 3. Highlight the process that releases water vapor from the leaves and stems of plants.

Organize it!

Draw a cycle diagram that shows how water moves through the water cycle. Include the terms *condensation, precipitation, transpiration,* and *evaporation*. Explain the water cycle.

Explanation:

_____

_____

_____

_____

_____

_____

_____

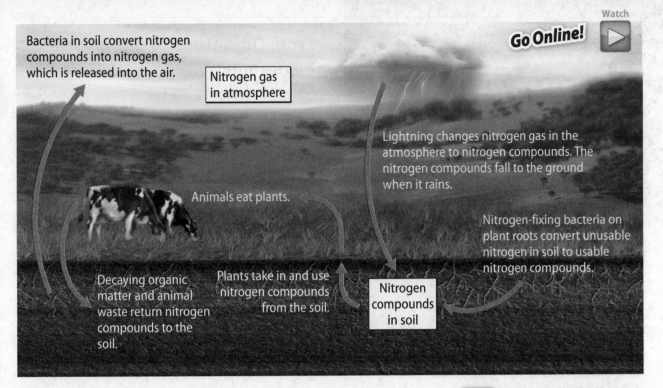

Bacteria in soil convert nitrogen compounds into nitrogen gas, which is released into the air.

Nitrogen gas in atmosphere

Lightning changes nitrogen gas in the atmosphere to nitrogen compounds. The nitrogen compounds fall to the ground when it rains.

Animals eat plants.

Nitrogen-fixing bacteria on plant roots convert unusable nitrogen in soil to usable nitrogen compounds.

Decaying organic matter and animal waste return nitrogen compounds to the soil.

Plants take in and use nitrogen compounds from the soil.

Nitrogen compounds in soil

Figure 2 Different forms of nitrogen are in the atmosphere, soil, and organisms.

The Nitrogen Cycle TEKS 7.5(B)

Just as water is necessary for life on Earth, so is the element nitrogen. It is an essential part of proteins, which all organisms need to stay alive. Nitrogen is also an important part of DNA, the molecule that contains genetic information. Nitrogen, like water, cycles between Earth and its atmosphere and back again as shown in **Figure 2**.

From the Environment to Organisms

Recall that the atmosphere is mostly nitrogen. However, this nitrogen is in a form that plants and animals cannot use. How do organisms get nitrogen into their bodies? The nitrogen must first be changed into a different form with the help of certain bacteria that live in soil and water. These bacteria take in nitrogen from the atmosphere and change it into nitrogen compounds that other living things can use. *The process that changes atmospheric nitrogen into nitrogen compounds that are usable by living things is called* **nitrogen fixation** (NI truh jun • fihk SAY shun). Nitrogen fixation is shown in **Figure 3**.

LAB Manager

Mini LAB: *Is your soil rich in nitrogen?*

TEKS 7.1(A); 7.2(A), (C), (E); 7.4(A), (B); 7.5(B)

Figure 3 Certain bacteria convert nitrogen in soil and water into a form usable by plants.

Figure 4 Bacteria break down the remains of dead plants and animals.

From Organisms to the Environment

Some types of bacteria can break down the tissues of dead organisms. When organisms die, these bacteria help return the nitrogen in the tissues of dead organisms to the environment. This process is shown in **Figure 4**.

Nitrogen also returns to the environment in the waste products of organisms. Farmers often spread animal wastes, called manure, on their fields during the growing season. The manure provides nitrogen to plants for better growth.

Organize

4. **Recall** information about the nitrogen cycle. Describe the role each part of the cycle plays by completing the table.

Parts of the Cycle	What It Does
Bacteria in soil	
Lightning	
Bacteria on plant roots	
Plants	
Animals	
Decaying matter and waste products	

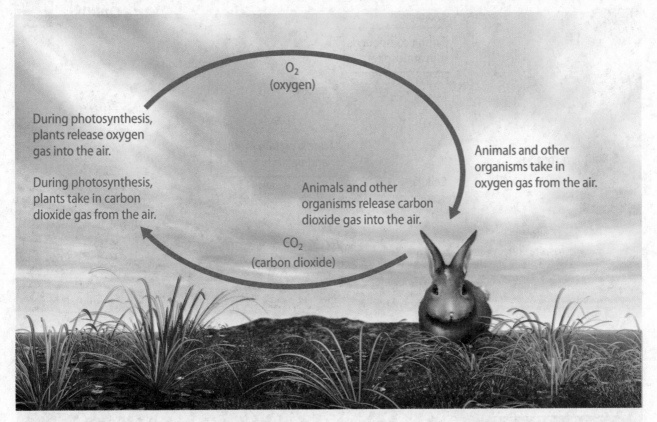

During photosynthesis, plants release oxygen gas into the air.

During photosynthesis, plants take in carbon dioxide gas from the air.

O₂ (oxygen)

Animals and other organisms release carbon dioxide gas into the air.

Animals and other organisms take in oxygen gas from the air.

CO₂ (carbon dioxide)

Figure 5 Most oxygen in the air comes from plants and algae.

The Oxygen Cycle **TEKS** 7.5(B)

Almost all living things need oxygen for cellular processes that release energy. Oxygen is also part of many substances that are important to life, such as carbon dioxide and water. Oxygen cycles through ecosystems, as shown in **Figure 5**.

Earth's early atmosphere probably did not contain oxygen gas. Oxygen might have entered the atmosphere when certain bacteria evolved that could carry out the process of photosynthesis and make their own food. A by-product of photosynthesis is oxygen gas. Over time, other photosynthetic organisms evolved and the amount of oxygen in Earth's atmosphere increased. Today, photosynthesis is the primary source of oxygen in Earth's atmosphere. Some scientists estimate that unicellular organisms in water, called phytoplankton, release more than 50 percent of the oxygen in Earth's atmosphere.

Many living things, including humans, take in the oxygen and release carbon dioxide. The interaction of the carbon and oxygen cycles is one example of a relationship between different types of matter in ecosystems. As the matter cycles through an ecosystem, the carbon and the oxygen take different forms and play a role in the other element's cycle.

Review Vocabulary

bacteria a group of microscopic unicellular organisms without a membrane-bound nucleus

Identify

5. What is currently the primary source of oxygen in Earth's atmosphere?

_____

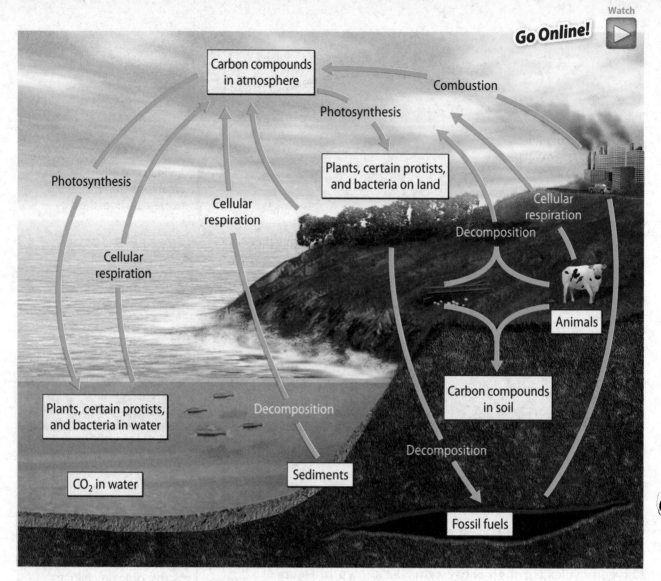

Carbon compounds
in atmosphere

Combustion

Photosynthesis

Photosynthesis

Cellular
respiration

Plants, certain protists,
and bacteria on land

Cellular
respiration

Cellular
respiration

Decomposition

Plants, certain protists,
and bacteria in water

Decomposition

Animals

CO₂ in water

Sediments

Carbon compounds
in soil

Decomposition

Fossil fuels

Figure 6 In the carbon cycle, all organisms return carbon to the environment.

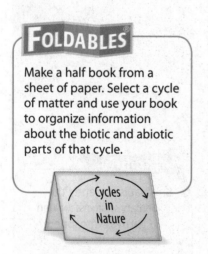

FOLDABLES®

Make a half book from a sheet of paper. Select a cycle of matter and use your book to organize information about the biotic and abiotic parts of that cycle.

Cycles
in
Nature

The Carbon Cycle TEKS 7.5(B)

All organisms contain carbon. It is part of proteins, sugars, fats, and DNA. Some organisms, including humans, get carbon from food. Other organisms, such as plants, get carbon from the atmosphere or bodies of water. Like other types of matter, carbon cycles through ecosystems, as shown in **Figure 6**.

Carbon in Soil

Like nitrogen, carbon can enter the environment when organisms die and decompose. This returns carbon compounds to the soil and releases carbon dioxide (CO_2) into the atmosphere for use by other organisms. Carbon is also found in fossil fuels, which formed when decomposing organisms were exposed to pressure, high temperatures, and bacteria over hundreds of millions of years.

Carbon in Air

Recall that carbon is found in the atmosphere as carbon dioxide. Plants and other photosynthetic organisms take in carbon dioxide and water and produce energy-rich sugars. These sugars are a source of carbon and energy for organisms that eat photosynthetic organisms. When the sugar is broken down by cells and its energy is released, carbon dioxide is released as a by-product. This carbon dioxide gas enters the atmosphere where it can be used again.

Academic Vocabulary

release *(verb)* to set free or let go

The Greenhouse Effect

Carbon dioxide is one of the gases in the atmosphere that absorbs thermal energy from the Sun and keeps Earth warm. This process is called the greenhouse effect. The Sun produces solar radiation, as shown in **Figure 7**. Some of this energy is reflected back into space, and some passes through Earth's atmosphere. Greenhouse gases in Earth's atmosphere absorb thermal energy that reflects off Earth's surface. The more greenhouse gases that are released, the greater the gas layer becomes and the more thermal energy is absorbed. These gases are one factor that keeps Earth from becoming too hot or too cold.

Although the greenhouse effect is essential for life, a steady increase in greenhouse gases can harm ecosystems. For example, carbon is stored in fossil fuels such as coal, oil, and natural gas. When people burn fossil fuels to heat homes, for transportation, or to provide electricity, carbon dioxide gas is released into the atmosphere. The amount of carbon dioxide in the air has increased due to natural and human activities.

Recognize

6. Highlight the definition of the greenhouse effect.

Figure 7 Some thermal energy remains close to the Earth due to greenhouse gases.

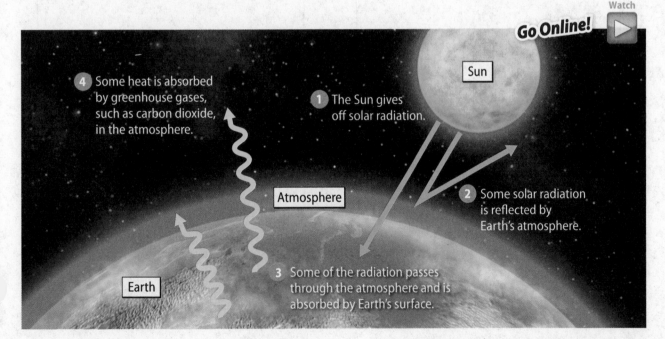

Watch

Go Online!

4 Some heat is absorbed by greenhouse gases, such as carbon dioxide, in the atmosphere.

1 The Sun gives off solar radiation.

Sun

Atmosphere

2 Some solar radiation is reflected by Earth's atmosphere.

Earth

3 Some of the radiation passes through the atmosphere and is absorbed by Earth's surface.

Organize it!

Model the carbon cycle. Identify the role of each item shown in the cycle. Draw arrows showing the flow of carbon through the system.

Air, water, and soil

Producers

Burning wood and fossil fuels and decomposition

Consumers

2.2 Review

Summarize it!

Explain the role of plants in the water, oxygen, nitrogen, and carbon cycles.

| Water Cycle | | Oxygen Cycle |

| Plants |

| Nitrogen Cycle | | Carbon Cycle |

Cycles of Matter

Apply the Essential Questions

1. What is the source of energy for the water cycle? **TEKS** 7.5(B)

   A. gravity

   B. plants

   C. sunlight

   D. wind

2. During the carbon cycle, _____ take in carbon dioxide from the atmosphere. **TEKS** 7.5(B)

   A. animals

   B. consumers

   C. decomposers

   D. plants

3. Which statement is true of the amount of matter in ecosystems? **TEKS** 7.5(B)

   A. It decreases over time.

   B. It increases over time.

   C. It remains constant.

   D. Scientists cannot determine how it changes.

4. **Define** nitrogen fixation in your own words. **TEKS** 7.5(B)

   _____

   _____

   _____

   _____

   _____

🔥 H.O.T. Questions (Higher Order Thinking)

5. **Infer** Farmers add nitrogen to their fields every year to help their crops grow. Why must farmers continually add nitrogen when this element recycles naturally? **TEKS** 7.5(B)

   _____

   _____

   _____

   _____

   _____

6. **Explain** how oxygen cycles through the ecosystem in which you live. **TEKS** 7.5(B)

   _____

   _____

   _____

   _____

   _____

   _____

7. **Predict** How might ecosystems be affected if levels of atmospheric CO_2 continue to rise? **TEKS** 7.5(B)

   _____

   _____

   _____

   _____

   _____

AMERICAN MUSEUM
of NATURAL HISTORY

Tracking Carbon Among Earth Systems

How the Biosphere Affects Levels of Atmospheric Carbon Dioxide

Scientists study Earth systems—atmosphere, hydrosphere, geosphere, and biosphere—to understand how our planet works and changes over time. These studies help scientists predict climate, weather, and natural disasters. They also explore the effects of human actions on the environment.

The National Oceanic and Atmospheric Administration (NOAA) has a research group called the Earth System Research Laboratory (ESRL). This group investigates how weather, air quality, and climate are affected by interactions among Earth systems. Data show that the average temperature in the atmosphere near Earth's surface is increasing. ESRL scientists relate this trend to the increase in carbon dioxide in the atmosphere. How do they know this increase is occurring?

Trees and the Carbon Cycle

Trees absorb and transfer carbon dioxide from the atmosphere.

Trees take in carbon dioxide through photosynthesis.

Trees release carbon dioxide into the atmosphere through cellular respiration.

The trunk, leaves, and branches store carbon.

Some carbon is carried down to the roots.

Fallen leaves and branches add carbon to the soil.

Carbon is stored in the roots.

When a tree dies, some carbon moves from the roots to the soil.

ESRL scientists analyze tens of thousands of air samples collected from eight tall towers across the United States. They analyze samples for levels of carbon dioxide and other greenhouse gases. Using data such as these, scientists have confirmed that carbon dioxide levels are increasing.

But ESRL scientists also discovered good news! Forests and farms are slowing the process. Analyses of air samples collected worldwide show that trees and crops absorb about one-third of the carbon dioxide produced by burning fossil fuels. This shows the interaction between the biosphere and the atmosphere. It also shows that protecting trees and planting new ones can help reduce carbon in the atmosphere.

◄ **The ESRL mounts air-sample collection tubes on existing television, radio, and cell phone towers. The narrow tubes carry the samples from the towers to nearby analysts.**

It's Your Turn!

RESEARCH The ocean is a carbon reservoir that soaks up and stores carbon dioxide. Research the role of ocean organisms in reducing atmospheric carbon dioxide. Share your findings with the class.

INQUIRY

Time for a snack? All organisms need energy, and many get it from eating other organisms. Can you guess how each of the living things in this picture gets the energy it needs?

Write your response in your interactive notebook.

🦶 LAB Manager

Go to your Lab Manual or visit connectED.mcgraw-hill.com to perform the labs for this lesson.

MiniLAB: *How can you classify organisms?*
TEKS 7.2(A), (E)

LAB: *Photosynthesis and Light*
TEKS 7.1(A); 7.2(A), (C), (E); 7.4(A), (B); 7.5(A)

Explore Activity

TEKS 7.1(A); 7.2(A), (C), (E)

How does energy change form?

Every day, sunlight travels hundreds of millions of kilometers and brings warmth and light to Earth. Energy from the Sun is necessary for nearly all life on Earth. Without it, most life could not exist.

Procedure

1. Read and complete a lab safety form.

2. Obtain **UV-sensitive beads** from your teacher. Write a description of them in your Lab Manual or interactive notebook.

3. Place half the beads in a sunny place. Place the other half in a dark place.

4. Wait a few minutes, and then observe both sets of beads. Record your observations.

Think About This

1. Compare and contrast the two sets of beads after a few minutes. How are they different? How are they the same?

2. Hypothesize why the beads looked different.

3. How do you think living things use energy?

TEKS in this Lesson

7.5(A) Recognize that radiant energy from the Sun is transformed into chemical energy through the process of photosynthesis.

7.5(C) Diagram the flow of energy through living systems, including food chains, food webs, and energy pyramids.

Also covers Process Standards: 7.1(A); 7.2(A), (C), (E); 7.4(A), (B)

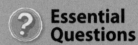

? Essential Questions

- How does energy move in ecosystems?
- How is the movement of energy in an ecosystem modeled?

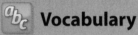

abc Vocabulary

chemosynthesis
food chain
food web
energy pyramid

How does energy move in ecosystems?

When you see a picture of an ecosystem, it often looks quiet and peaceful. However, ecosystems are actually full of movement. Birds squawk and beat their wings, plants sway in the breeze, and insects buzz.

Each movement made by a living thing requires energy. All life's functions, including growth and reproduction, require energy. The main source of energy for most life on Earth is the Sun. Unlike other resources such as water and carbon, energy does not cycle through ecosystems. Instead, energy flows in one direction. In most cases, energy flow begins with the Sun and moves from one organism to another. Many organisms get energy by eating other organisms. Sometimes organisms change energy into different forms as it moves through an ecosystem. Not all the energy an organism gets is used for life processes. Some is released to the environment as thermal energy. You might have read that energy cannot be created or destroyed, but it can change form. This idea is called the law of conservation of energy.

Identify

1. **Label** the patterns below and the type of material that moves through each one.

Type of pattern: _____   Type of pattern: _____

Type of material: _____   Type of material: _____

Producers

People who make things or products are often called producers. Similarly, living things that make their own food are called producers. Producers make their food from materials found in their environments. Most producers are photosynthetic (foh toh sihn THEH tihk). They use the process of photosynthesis (foh toh SIHN thuh sus), which is described below. Grasses, trees and other plants, algae and some other protists, and certain bacteria are photosynthetic. Other producers, including some bacteria, are chemosynthetic (kee moh sihn THEH tihk). They make their food using chemosynthesis (kee moh SIHN thuh sus).

Photosynthesis In the carbon cycle, carbon in the atmosphere cycles through producers such as plants into other organisms and back into the atmosphere. This and other matter cycles involve photosynthesis, like in **Figure 1.** Photosynthesis is a series of chemical reactions that convert light energy, water, and carbon dioxide into the food-energy molecule glucose and give off oxygen.

Chemosynthesis As you read earlier, some producers make food using chemosynthesis. **Chemosynthesis** *is the process during which producers use chemical energy in matter rather than light energy and make food.* One place where chemosynthesis can occur is on the deep ocean floor. There, inorganic compounds that contain hydrogen and sulfur, along with thermal energy from Earth's interior, flow from cracks in the ocean floor. These cracks are called hydrothermal vents. These vents, such as the one shown in **Figure 2,** are home to chemosynthetic bacteria. These bacteria use the chemical energy contained in inorganic compounds in the water to produce food.

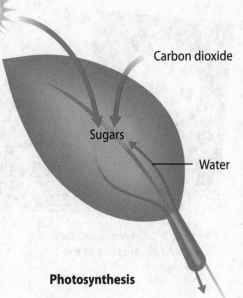

Light energy

Carbon dioxide

Sugars

Water

Photosynthesis

Figure 1 Most producers make their food through the process of photosynthesis.

Figure 2 The producers at a hydrothermal vent make their food using chemosynthesis.

Describe

2. Organize information about photosynthesis and chemosynthesis.

Photosynthesis	Process by which producers make food from materials in the environment	Chemosynthesis
• converts _____ _____ into food-energy molecule _____ • gives off _____		• occurs when producers use _____ in matter to make food • can take place on the _____

Herbivore

Carnivore

Omnivore

Detritivore

Detritivore—
Decomposer

Figure 3 Organisms can be classified by the type of food they eat.

Consumers

Some consumers are shown in **Figure 3.** Consumers do not produce their own energy-rich food as producers do. Instead, they get the energy they need to survive by consuming other organisms.

Consumers can be classified by the type of food that they eat. Herbivores feed on only producers. For example, a deer is an herbivore because it eats only plants. Carnivores eat other animals. They are usually predators such as lions and wolves. Omnivores eat producers and other consumers. A bird that eats berries and insects is an omnivore.

Another group of consumers is detritivores (dih TRI tuh vorz). They get their energy by eating the remains of other organisms. Some detritivores such as insects eat dead organisms. Other detritivores such as bacteria and mushrooms feed on dead organisms and help decompose them. For this reason, these organisms often are called decomposers. During decomposition, decomposers produce carbon dioxide that enters the atmosphere. Some of the decayed matter enters the soil. In this way, detritivores help recycle nutrients through ecosystems. They also help keep ecosystems clean. Without decomposers, dead organisms would pile up in an ecosystem.

Type of Consumer	What It Does
Herbivore	
Carnivore	
Omnivore	
Detritivore	
Detritivore/decomposer	

Modeling Energy in Ecosystems TEKS 7.5(C)

Unlike matter, energy does not cycle through ecosystems because it does not return to the Sun. Instead, energy flows through ecosystems. Organisms use some energy for life processes. In addition, organisms store some energy in their bodies as chemical energy. When consumers eat these organisms, this chemical energy moves into the bodies of consumers. However, with each transfer of energy from organism to organism, some energy changes to thermal energy. The bodies of consumers emit excess thermal energy, which then enters the environment. Scientists use models to study this flow of energy through an ecosystem. They use different models depending on how many organisms they are studying.

Food Chains

A **food chain** *is a model that shows how energy flows in an ecosystem through feeding relationships.* In a food chain, arrows show the transfer of energy. A typical food chain is shown in **Figure 4.** Notice that there are not many links in this food chain. That is because the amount of available energy decreases every time it is transferred from one organism to another.

Figure 4 Energy moves from the Sun to a plant, a mouse, a snake, and a hawk in this food chain.

FOLDABLES

Make a pyramid book from a sheet of paper. Use each side to organize information about one of the ways energy flows in an ecosystem. You can add additional information on the inside of your pyramid book.

Connect

4. **Highlight** what happens to some energy as it is transferred from organism to organism.

1 The Sun emits energy.

5 The hawk obtains energy by eating the snake.

2 Plants make energy-rich food using sunlight.

3 The mouse obtains energy by eating the plant.

4 The snake obtains energy by eating the mouse.

Food Webs TEKS 7.5(C)

Imagine you have a jigsaw puzzle of a tropical rain forest. Each piece of the puzzle shows only one small part of the forest. A food chain is like one piece of an ecosystem jigsaw puzzle. It is helpful when studying certain parts of an ecosystem, but it does not show the whole picture.

In the previous food chain, the mouse might also eat the seeds of several producers, such as corn, berries, or grass. The snake might eat other organisms such as frogs, crickets, lizards, or earthworms too.

The hawk hunts mice, squirrels, rabbits, and fish, as well as snakes. Scientists use a model of energy transfer called a **food web** *to show how food chains in a community are interconnected,* as shown in **Figure 5.** You can think of a food web as many overlapping food chains. Like in a food chain, arrows show how energy flows in a food web. Some organisms in the food web might be part of more than one food chain in that web.

Go Online! Watch Tutor

Figure 5 A food web shows the complex feeding relationships among organisms in an ecosystem.

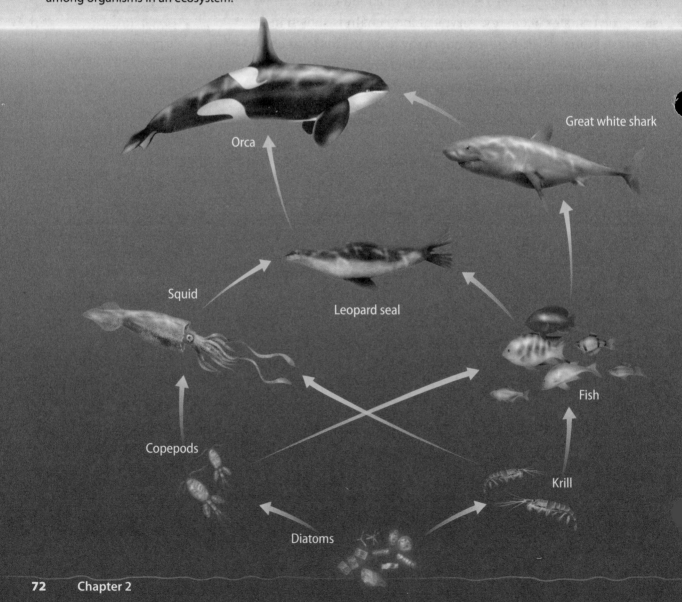

Orca

Great white shark

Squid

Leopard seal

Fish

Copepods

Krill

Diatoms

Energy Pyramids TEKS 7.5(C)

Food chains and food webs show how energy moves in an ecosystem. However, they do not show how the amount of energy in an ecosystem changes. *Scientists use a model called an* **energy pyramid** *to show the amount of energy available in each step of a food chain, as shown in* **Figure 6.** The steps of an energy pyramid are also called trophic (TROH fihk) levels.

Producers, such as plants, make up the trophic level at the bottom of the pyramid. Consumers that eat producers, such as squirrels, make up the next trophic level. Consumers such as hawks that eat other consumers make up the highest trophic level. Notice that less energy is available for consumers at each higher trophic level. As you read earlier, organisms use some of the energy they get from food for life processes. During life processes, some energy is changed to thermal energy and is transferred to the environment. Only about 10 percent of the energy available at one trophic level transfers to the next trophic level.

Figure 6 An energy pyramid shows the amount of energy available at each trophic level.

Go Online! Watch

Explain

5. **Summarize** why only 10 percent of energy is available at each successive trophic level.

_____

_____

_____

_____

_____

_____

_____

_____

_____

Available energy decreases.

Trophic level 3
(1 percent of energy available)

Trophic level 2
(10 percent of energy available)

Trophic level 1
(100 percent of energy available)

2.3 Review

Go Online! Check ✓

Summarize it!

Some of the feeding relationships among organisms that live on the Gulf Coast of Texas are described below. **TEKS** 7.5(C)

- Clover grass and algae are producers.

- Muskrats, whistling swans, hermit crabs, sea urchins, and Gulf pipefish eat clover grass.

- Muskrats, hermit crabs, sea urchins, and Gulf pipefish eat algae.

- Raccoons, bald eagles, and American alligators eat muskrats and whistling swans.

- Blue crabs and snowy egrets eat hermit crabs and sea urchins.

- Loggerhead sea turtles and catfish eat Gulf pipefish.

- Snowy egrets eat blue crabs, loggerhead sea turtles, and catfish.

- Bald eagles and American alligators eat raccoons, whistling swans, loggerhead sea turtles, and catfish.

Procedure

1. Diagram three food chains in the Gulf Coast ecosystem on another sheet of paper. Remember that each food chain should begin with a producer.

2. Use the food chains from step 1 to create a food web of the Gulf Coast ecosystem.

3. Create an energy pyramid using the following organisms: American alligators, clover grass, whistling swans.

Apply the Essential Questions

1. Which best represents the flow of energy through a food chain? **TEKS** 7.5(C) *supporting*

   A. Sun ⟶ rabbit ⟶ fox ⟶ grass

   B. Sun ⟶ grass ⟶ rabbit ⟶ fox

   C. fox ⟶ grass ⟶ rabbit ⟶ Sun

   D. grass ⟶ rabbit ⟶ fox ⟶ Sun

Trophic level 3

Trophic level 2

Trophic level 1

2. Which organism might you expect to find at trophic level 1 in the image above?
   TEKS 7.5(C) *supporting*

   A. fox

   B. frog

   C. grass

   D. grasshopper

 H.O.T. Questions (Higher Order Thinking)

3. **Recommend** Which model would you recommend to show how energy flows through ecosystems? Explain.
   TEKS 7.5(C) *supporting*

   _____

   _____

   _____

4. **Diagram** a food web showing the flow of energy through the living systems in this ecosystem. Algae is floating in a pond ecosystem. Stoneflies and minnows eat the algae. Sunfish and bats eat the stoneflies. Walleye eat the sunfish and minnows. Great blue heron eat the sunfish and minnows. **TEKS** 7.5(C) *supporting*

Writing in Science

5. **Write** an argument for or against the following statement. The energy humans use in cars originally came from the Sun.
   TEKS 7.5(C) *supporting*

   _____

   _____

   _____

   _____

   _____

Test-Taking Strategy

Key Words Key words are used to identify exactly what is being asked in a question. These words help to clarify what information you need to use in order to correctly answer the question.

1 After reviewing the diagram, you'll notice that water, carbon dioxide and sunlight are all going into the leaf to be used for photosynthesis. Sugar is one of the materials produced by photosynthesis.

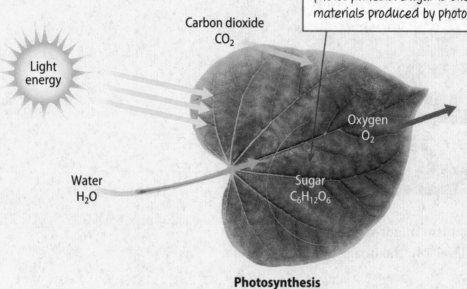

Photosynthesis

Carbon dioxide + Water ⟶ Sugar + Oxygen

$$6CO_2 + 6H_2O \xrightarrow[\text{Chlorophyll}]{\text{Light energy}} C_6H_{12}O_6 + 6O_2$$

Example

Use the diagram to answer question 1.

1 Which of the following is not used by plants during photosynthesis? **TEKS** 7.5(A)

A water

B carbon dioxide

C sunlight

2 Sugar is NOT used to photosynthesize. The correct answer is choice **D**.

D sugar ⟵

TIP: Each question will have key words that will tell you exactly what information you need. Other important words include *not*, *no*, *never*, *now*, *always*, *only*, *best*, *except*, *most* and *least*.

Multiple Choice

1

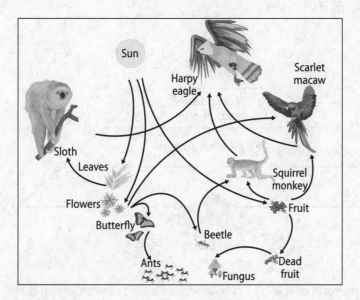

Analyze the positions of the harpy eagle and the scarlet macaw in the food web diagram. Which statement is correct? **TEKS** 7.2(E); 7.5(C) *Supporting*

A The harpy eagle eats more types of organisms in the food web than the scarlet macaw does.

B The harpy eagle eats the same type of organisms as the scarlet macaw does.

C The scarlet macaw eats more types of organisms in the food web than the harpy eagle does.

D The scarlet macaw is eaten by the same type of organisms as the harpy eagle is.

---

2 This equation shows the reaction involved in photosynthesis. **TEKS** 7.5(A)

$$6CO_2 + 6H_2O \rightarrow C_6H_{12}O_6 + 6O_2$$

If you were to place the label "Energy from Sunlight" on this equation, where would you place it?

A above the arrow to indicate that the energy drives the reactions of photosynthesis

B above the second plus sign to indicate that energy is created during photosynthesis

C at the end of the equation because energy goes back to the Sun after photosynthesis

D next to the six carbon dioxide molecules because the Sun's energy is stored there

3 An energy pyramid shows how much energy is available at each trophic level. Observe the shape of the diagram below. **TEKS** 7.5(C) *Supporting*

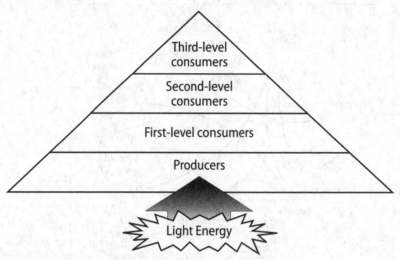

Is there a limit to the number of levels of consumers an energy pyramid can have? Which statement justifies your conclusion?

A No, because as you go up the food pyramid the amount of energy increases.

B No, because predators can also be prey so there would always be an ample food supply.

C Yes, because each level receives only a small percentage of the energy in the level below it.

D Yes, because there is no energy above the level of producers.

---

4 In an energy pyramid, approximately 10 percent of the energy available in one trophic level is transferred to the next level. Which statement helps explain why this occurs? **TEKS** 7.5(C) *Supporting*

A Consumers eat both producers and other consumers.

B Organisms use most of the available energy to fuel their own life processes.

C Predators eat more organisms in their own level than organisms in other levels.

D Producers exist only in the lowest level of the pyramid.

5 In recent decades, average global temperatures have increased significantly. The cause or causes of these increases are being investigated. Some people say that widespread destruction of the Amazon rain forest contributes to global warming. Which mechanism might be cited in support of that hypothesis? **TEKS** 7.5(B)

  A Deforestation causes water on the ground to reflect sunlight.

  B Deforestation reduces the number of plants able to absorb carbon dioxide.

  C Photosynthesis produces energy which gives off heat.

  D Plants produce energy during cellular respiration.

---

6 Keshia and her classmates created a model of the nitrogen cycle. Their diagram is shown below. **TEKS** 7.2(E); 7.5(B)

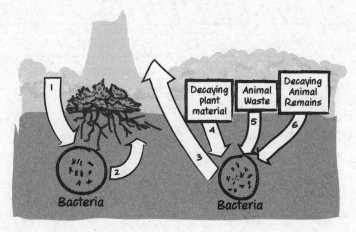

What is the function of the bacteria?

  A They prevent the nitrogen from harming the plants.

  B They remove the nitrogen from the soil.

  C They remove the oxygen from the soil.

  D They return nitrogen to the system.

My Notes

Carbon Chemistry

The BIG Idea

Carbon is the foundation of life because of its ability to bond easily to other atoms and to other carbon atoms.

LESSON

3.1 Elemental Carbon and Simple Organic Compounds

Organic compounds contain carbon bonded to at least one hydrogen atom.

TEKS 7.6(A); Also covers 7.1(A); 7.2(A), (C), (E); 7.3(B), (D); 7.4(A), (B)

LESSON

3.2 Other Organic Compounds

Organic compounds bonded to elements, such as oxygen, nitrogen, phosphorus, or sulfur, create compounds with different properties.

TEKS 7.6(A); Also covers 7.1(A), (B); 7.2(A), (C), (E); 7.4(A), (B)

LESSON

3.3 Compounds of Life

Proteins, carbohydrates, nucleic acids, and lipids are organic compounds in organisms.

TEKS 7.6(A), (C); Also covers 7.1(A), (B); 7.2(A), (C), (E); 7.3(A); 7.4(A), (B)

Atom of Life

When you walk through an ecosystem, there are several different atoms that make up the living things in the ecosystem. Of all these different atoms, which atom do you think forms the basis of the molecules that make up living things?

A. Hydrogen

B. Oxygen

C. Carbon

D. Nitrogen

E. Sulfur

F. Phosphorus

G. Water

Explain your thinking. Why do you think that atom is considered the basis of the molecules that make up living things?

A Diamond? The yellow rock probably does not look like a diamond that you have seen. It lacks sparkle because it is rough and uncut. What do you think diamonds are made of? How are diamonds formed?

 Write your response in your interactive notebook.

 LAB Manager

Go to your Lab Manual or visit connectED.mcgraw-hill.com to perform the lab for this lesson.

MiniLAB: *How do carbon atoms bond with carbon and hydrogen atoms?*

TEKS 7.1(A); 7.2(A), (C), (E); 7.3(B); 7.4(B); 7.6(A)

Explore Activity

TEKS 7.1(A); 7.2(A), (E); 7.3(B); 7.4(A), (B); 7.6(A)

Why is carbon a unique element?

A carbon atom is unique because it can easily form four bonds with other atoms, including other carbon atoms. Because of this property, carbon forms many different compounds.

Procedure 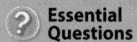 *Do not eat the gumdrops.*

1. Read and complete a lab safety form.

2. Use **gumdrops** and **toothpicks** to make models of as many different carbon molecules as you can. Keep these rules in mind.

   • Each gumdrop represents one carbon atom.
   • Each toothpick represents one chemical bond.
   • Each molecule must contain four carbon atoms (gumdrops).
   • Each carbon atom must have four chemical bonds (toothpicks).
   • One carbon atom can share up to three bonds with another carbon atom.

3. Sketch each molecule in your Lab Manual or interactive notebook.

Think About This

1. How many different molecules were you able to build?

   _____

   _____

   _____

2. If you had five gumdrops, would you be able to build more molecules? Explain your answer.

   _____

   _____

   _____

3. How do you think a carbon atom bonds with other carbon atoms?

   _____

   _____

   _____

TEKS in this Lesson

7.3(D) Relate the impact of research on scientific thought and society, including the history of science and contribution of scientists as related to content

7.6(A) Identify that organic compounds contain carbon and other elements such as hydrogen, oxygen, phosphorus, nitrogen, or sulfur

Also covers Process Standards: 7.1(A); 7.2(A), (C), (E); 7.3(B); 7.4(A), (B)

 Essential Questions

• What is an organic compound?

• How is carbon unique compared to other elements?

• What elements can be found in organic compounds?

Vocabulary

organic compound
hydrocarbon
isomer
saturated hydrocarbon
unsaturated
  hydrocarbon

Elements in Living Things

What do you have in common with the fish and corals in **Figure 1?** You might be surprised to learn that you, a fish, and a coral have several things in common. Each living organism is made of cells that contain carbon, hydrogen, oxygen, nitrogen, and a few other elements. In fact, the masses of all living organisms contain about 18 percent carbon compounds.

Except for water and some salts, most things you put in or on your body—food, clothing, cosmetics, and medicines—consist of compounds that contain carbon. This lesson explores various types of carbon compounds that make up living things.

Figure 1 All living things are made of similar carbon-containing compounds.

Organic Compounds TEKS 7.3(D); 7.6(A)

Scientists once thought that all carbon compounds came from living or once-living organisms, and they called these compounds organic. Scientists now know that carbon is also in many nonliving things. Today, scientists define an **organic compound** *as a chemical compound that contains carbon atoms usually bonded to at least one hydrogen atom.* Organic compounds can also contain other elements such as oxygen, nitrogen, phosphorus, or sulfur. However, compounds such as carbon dioxide (CO_2) and carbon monoxide (CO) are not organic because they do not have a carbon-hydrogen bond.

Understanding Carbon

A carbon atom is unique because it can easily combine with other atoms and form millions of compounds. Find carbon on the periodic table in the back of your book. Carbon has an atomic number of 6. Therefore, a neutral carbon atom has six protons and six electrons. Four of these electrons are valence electrons, or are in the outermost energy level. Recall that many atoms are chemically stable when they have eight valence electrons. Carbon atoms become more chemically stable through **covalent bonding,** as shown in **Figure 2.** In a covalent bond, carbon atoms have eight valence electrons, like a stable, unreactive noble gas.

The Carbon Group

Look again at the periodic table. Notice that silicon and germanium are in the same group as carbon. They each have four valence electrons. Silicon and germanium atoms also become stable by forming four covalent bonds. However, it takes more energy for them to do this. The more energy it takes, the less likely it is that bonding will occur.

Identify

1. Organic compounds usually contain which two elements?

   a. _____

   b. _____

   List three other elements that can be found in organic compounds.

   a. _____

   b. _____

   c. _____

   List one example of a compound that is not an organic compound.

   _____

Review Vocabulary

covalent bond a chemical bond formed by sharing one or more pairs of electrons between atoms

Figure 2 Carbon often bonds with four hydrogen atoms and forms a stable compound.

Bonding with Carbon

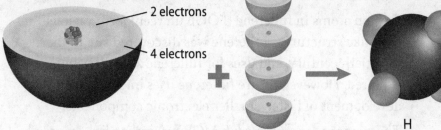

2 electrons

4 electrons

1 electron

$\cdot \overset{\cdot}{\underset{\cdot}{C}} \cdot$

4H·

$H \overset{\overset{\displaystyle H}{\cdot\cdot}}{\underset{\overset{\cdot\cdot}{\displaystyle H}}{:C:}} H$

For each carbon-hydrogen covalent bond, the hydrogen atom and the carbon atom share a pair of electrons.

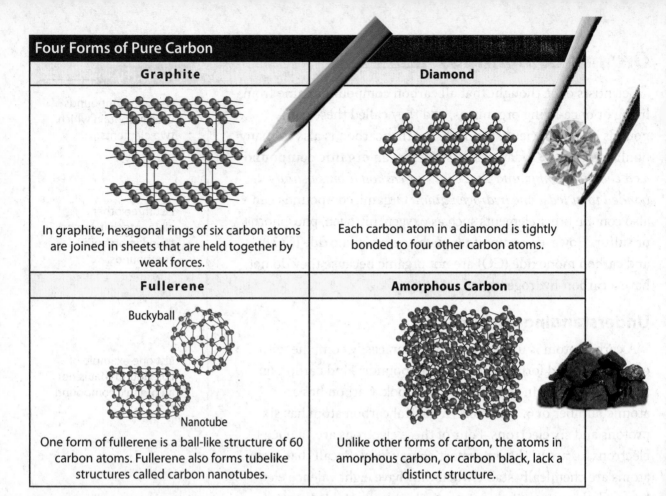

Four Forms of Pure Carbon

Graphite	Diamond
In graphite, hexagonal rings of six carbon atoms are joined in sheets that are held together by weak forces.	Each carbon atom in a diamond is tightly bonded to four other carbon atoms.
Fullerene	**Amorphous Carbon**
One form of fullerene is a ball-like structure of 60 carbon atoms. Fullerene also forms tubelike structures called carbon nanotubes.	Unlike other forms of carbon, the atoms in amorphous carbon, or carbon black, lack a distinct structure.

Figure 3 Four common forms of pure carbon are graphite, diamond, fullerene, and amorphous.

Infer

2. Compare, in your interactive notebook, the structures of graphite and diamond and explain why graphite is used in pencil lead but diamonds are not.

Word Origin

amorphous from *a-* and Greek *morphe,* means "without form"

The Forms of Pure Carbon

When carbon atoms bond together, they form one of several different arrangements, such as those shown in **Figure 3.** Forms of carbon are described below.

- One form of carbon is graphite (GRA fite). In graphite, carbon atoms form thin sheets that can slide over one another or bend. Graphite is used as a lubricant and in pencil lead and other items.

- Diamonds, another form of carbon, are used in jewelry, on the tips of drill bits, and on the edges of some saw blades. The carbon atoms bond to one another in a rigid and orderly structure, making diamonds extremely strong. This makes diamonds one of the hardest materials known.

- Carbon atoms in fullerene (FOOL uh reen) form various cage-like structures. Fullerene was discovered late in the twentieth century, and uses for fullerene are still being explored. However, future fullerene uses might include the development of faster, smaller electronic components.

- The atoms in amorphous (uh MOR fus) carbon lack an orderly arrangement. Amorphous carbon is found in coal and charcoal.

Organize it!

Define organic compound by telling how the definition has changed over time. **TEKS** 7.6(A)

Organic compound
- In the past: _____
  _____
- Today: _____
  _____
  _____

Explain why carbon easily combines with other elements.

| Carbon has _____ valence electrons. | → | To be stable, carbon needs _____ valence electrons. | → | Carbon becomes stable by sharing electrons with other _____ through _____. |

Hydrocarbons TEKS 7.6(A)

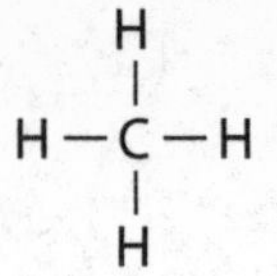

Many organic compounds contain only carbon and hydrogen atoms. However, organic compounds can also contain other elements such as oxygen, phosphorus, nitrogen, or sulfur. *A compound that contains only carbon and hydrogen atoms is called a* **hydrocarbon.** There are many different hydrocarbons. The simplest is methane (CH_4), shown in **Figure 4.**

Hydrocarbon Chains

When carbon atoms form hydrocarbons, the carbon atoms can link together in different ways. They can form straight chains, branched chains, or rings. **Table 1** shows examples of each type of arrangement. Look closely at the molecular formula for each compound. Notice that butane and isobutane have the same molecular formula. They have the same ratio of carbon atoms to hydrogen atoms. *Compounds that have the same molecular formula but different structural arrangements are called* **isomers** (I suh murz). Each isomer is a different molecule with its own unique name and properties.

Methane
CH₄

Structural formula

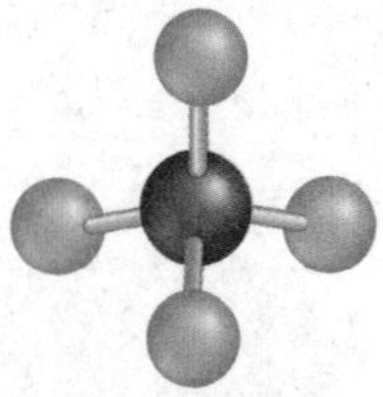

Ball-and-stick model

Figure 4 Methane consists of one carbon atom bonded to four hydrogen atoms. Methane is the main component in natural gas.

Table 1 Carbon atoms can form straight chains, branched chains, or rings.

Identify

3. (Circle) the three ways carbon can link together when forming hydrocarbons chains.

Watch

Table 1 Hydrocarbon Arrangements		Go Online! ▶
Butane	**Isobutane**	**Cyclobutane**
Molecular formula : C_4H_{10}	**Molecular formula : C_4H_{10}**	**Molecular formula : C_4H_8**
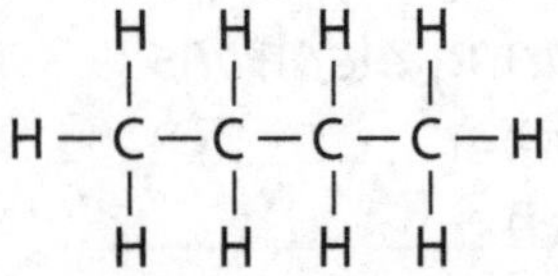 Structural formula	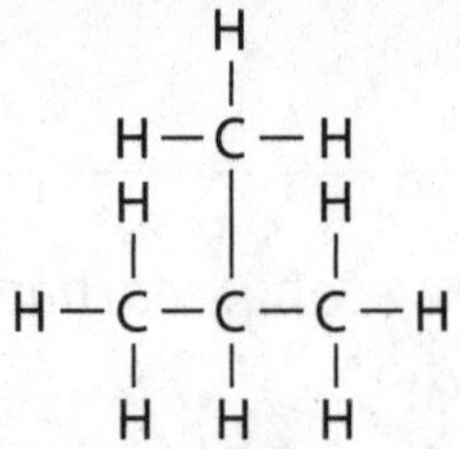 Structural formula	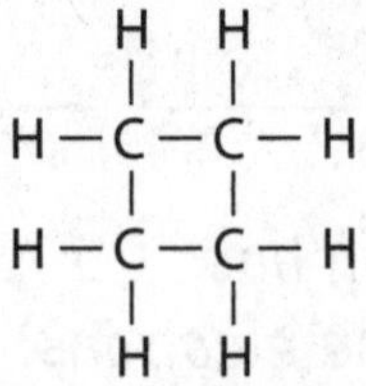 Structural formula
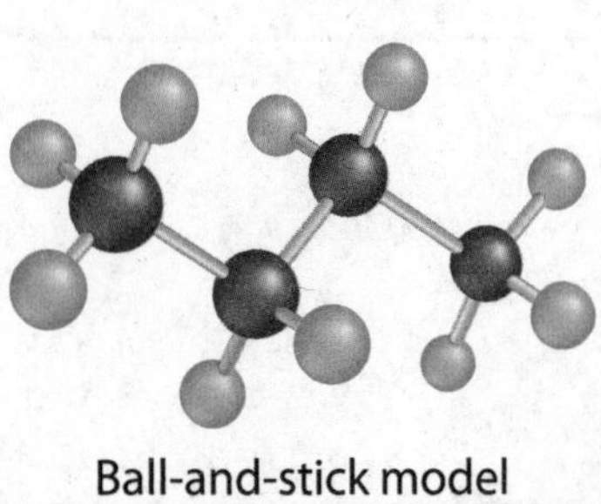 Ball-and-stick model	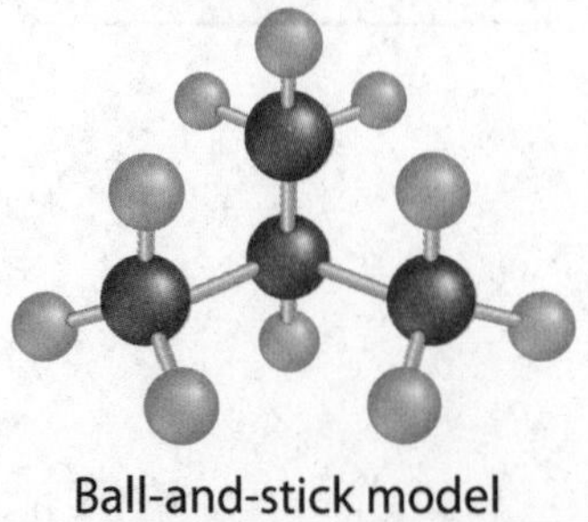 Ball-and-stick model	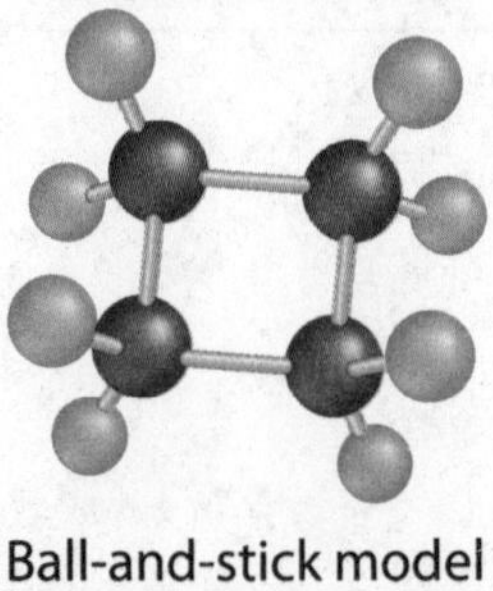 Ball-and-stick model

Carbon-to-Carbon Bonding

When a carbon atom bonds to another carbon atom, the two atoms can share two, four, or six electrons, as shown in **Figure 5.** In all cases, the carbon atoms in each molecule have eight valence electrons and are stable. When two carbon atoms share two electrons, it is called a single bond. A hydrocarbon that contains only single bonds is called an alkane. When two carbon atoms share four electrons, it is called a double bond. A hydrocarbon that contains at least one double bond is called an alkene. If two carbon atoms share six electrons, it is called a triple bond. A hydrocarbon that contains at least one triple bond is called an alkyne.

Saturated Hydrocarbons Hydrocarbons are often classified by the type of bonds the carbon atoms share. *A hydrocarbon that contains only single bonds is called a* **saturated hydrocarbon.** It is called saturated because no more hydrogen atoms can be added to the molecule. Look at the top image in **Figure 5.** Notice that three of the valence electrons in each carbon atom bond with hydrogen atoms. The carbon atoms are saturated with hydrogen atoms.

Unsaturated Hydrocarbons *A hydrocarbon that contains one or more double or triple bonds is called an* **unsaturated hydrocarbon.** Look at the double bond and triple bond examples in **Figure 5.** If the double and triple bonds are broken, additional hydrogen atoms could bond to the carbon atoms. Therefore, molecules containing double and triple bonds are not saturated with hydrogen atoms.

Analyze

4. Two carbon atoms in a five-carbon hydrocarbon share four electrons. What type of bond is formed? What type of hydrocarbon is formed? Is the hydrocarbon saturated or unsaturated? Write your response in your interactive notebook.

Carbon-to-Carbon Bonding

Figure 5 Two carbon atoms can form a single, double, or triple bond.

Alkane
- single bond
- two electrons shared between two carbon atoms

Single line indicates a single bond. — $CH_3 — CH_3$

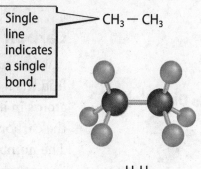

$$H \quad H$$
$$H : \overset{..}{\underset{..}{C}} : \overset{..}{\underset{..}{C}} : H$$
$$H \quad H$$

Alkene
- double bond
- four electrons shared between two carbon atoms

Double line indicates a double bond. — $CH_2 = CH_2$

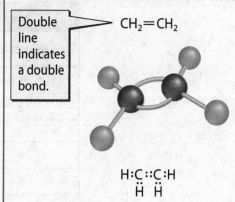

$$H : \overset{..}{C} :: \overset{..}{C} : H$$
$$\overset{..}{H} \quad \overset{..}{H}$$

Alkyne
- triple bond
- six electrons shared between two carbon atoms

Triple line indicates a triple bond. — $CH \equiv CH$

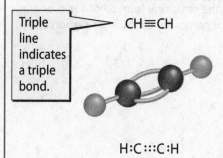

$$H : C ::: C : H$$

Naming Hydrocarbons

What type of shape is a stop sign? It is an octagon. An octagon is a figure with eight sides. Its name comes from the root *oct–*, which means "eight." Most geometric shapes have names that refer to the number of sides they have, such as a triangle. Similarly, hydrocarbons have names that indicate how many carbon atoms are in each molecule.

Carbon Chains

When naming a hydrocarbon, the first thing you need to do is find the longest carbon chain and count the number of carbon atoms in it. Look at **Figure 6.** Find the carbon chain and count the carbon atoms. In this molecule, there are four carbon atoms. The number of carbon atoms gives you the root word of the name. Now look at **Table 2.** This table shows the root word for any hydrocarbon that has one through ten carbon atoms. What is the root name for the molecule in **Figure 6?** The root name is *but–* (BYEWT). What would be the root name if the carbon chain had eight carbon atoms like a stop sign? The root name is *oct–*.

Watch

Go Online!

Figure 6 This hydrocarbon has four carbon atoms in its chain.

Table 2	Root Words		
Carbon Atoms	**Root Name**	**Carbon Atoms**	**Root Name**
1	*meth–*	6	*hex–*
2	*eth–*	7	*hept–*
3	*prop–*	8	*oct–*
4	*but–*	9	*non–*
5	*pent–*	10	*dec–*

Table 2 The number of carbon atoms in the longest continuous chain determines the root word for the name of the hydrocarbon.

Classify

5. Draw the structural formula of a hydrocarbon with three atoms in its chain. Label the hydrocarbon with its root name. Repeat for a six-carbon chain.

Determine the Suffix

Now that you know how to find the root word of a hydrocarbon, you must also find the suffix, or end, of the name. Recall that carbon atoms bond to other carbon atoms by single bonds, double bonds, or triple bonds. **Table 3** shows which suffix to use based on the types of bonds in the molecule. Look at **Figure 6** again. The molecule has all single bonds and should have the suffix *–ane*. Put the root and the suffix together, and you get *butane*.

Determine the Prefix

Sometimes hydrocarbons have a prefix, and sometimes they do not. Recall that hydrocarbons form chains, branched chains, and rings. If a hydrocarbon contains a ring structure, the prefix *cyclo–* is added before the root name. Hydrocarbons sometimes have other prefixes and numbers added before their names. You might read about this naming system in more advanced chemistry courses. For this lesson, only hydrocarbons in the form of a ring will get a prefix. **Table 4** summarizes the steps used to name a hydrocarbon.

Table 3 The types of bonds in the hydrocarbon chain determine the suffix in the name.

Table 3	Bond Type and Hydrocarbon Suffix	
Bond Type		**Suffix**
All single bonds $-C-C-$		-ane
At least one double bond $-C=C-$		-ene
At least one triple bond $-C\equiv C-$		-yne

Table 4   Naming Hydrocarbons

Go Online!

Watch ▶

Steps for Naming Hydrocarbons	Example A	Example B
❶ Examine the compound.	H–C≡C–C–C–H (with H, H above and H, H below middle carbons)	CH₂ ring of CH₂ groups
❷ Count the number of carbon atoms in the longest continuous chain.	There are four carbon atoms in the longest chain.	There are six carbon atoms in the longest chain.
❸ Determine the root name of the hydrocarbon using **Table 2.**	The root name is *but–*.	The root name is *hex–*.
❹ Determine the types of bonds in the hydrocarbon, and then use **Table 3** to find the suffix.	There is a triple bond, so add the suffix *–yne*.	There are only single bonds, so add the suffix *–ane*.
❺ Put the root and suffix together to name the hydrocarbon.	Combining the root and suffix gives the name *butyne*.	Combining the root and suffix gives the name *hexane*.
❻ If the hydrocarbon is a ring, add *cyclo-* to the beginning of the name.	No prefix is needed because the structure is not a ring. The name of the hydrocarbon is *butyne*.	The structure is a ring, so the prefix *cyclo–* is added to the name. The name of the hydrocarbon is *cyclohexane*.

Summarize it!

Draw the hydrocarbon molecules listed below. For each one, list the number of carbon atoms, the number of hydrogen atoms, and the types of bonds the molecule contains. **TEKS** 7.6(A)

Ethane   This molecule looks like:

Number of carbon atoms: _____

Number of hydrogen atoms: _____

Types of bonds: _____

Pentyne   This molecule looks like:

Number of carbon atoms: _____

Number of hydrogen atoms: _____

Types of bonds: _____

Octene   This molecule looks like:

Number of carbon atoms: _____

Number of hydrogen atoms: _____

Types of bonds: _____

Cycloheptane   This molecule looks like:

Number of carbon atoms: _____

Number of hydrogen atoms: _____

Types of bonds: _____

Elemental Carbon and Simple Organic Compounds

Apply the Essential Questions

1. **Define** *organic compound*. How has the definition changed as scientific thought has changed? Where can organic compounds be found? **TEKS** 7.3(D); 7.6(A) *supporting*

2. **Explain** why carbon is unique compared to other elements. **TEKS** 7.6(A) *supporting*

3. **List** Besides carbon, what other elements can organic compounds contain? **TEKS** 7.6(A) *supporting*

H.O.T. Questions (Higher Order Thinking)

4. **Draw** three isomers for pentane on a separate sheet of paper. **TEKS** 7.6(A) *supporting*

5. **Explain** why so many different compounds are made from carbon. **TEKS** 7.6(A) *supporting*

6. **Create** a poster, on a separate sheet of paper, that illustrates why hydrocarbons are present in so many different compounds. **TEKS** 7.6(A) *supporting*

7. **Critique** Certain produce in the grocery store is labeled *organic*. Based on what you read in this lesson, should only some foods be labeled *organic*? Explain your reasoning **TEKS** 7.6(A) *supporting*

Carbon

Will it replace the silicon in your computer?

You have something like a computer inside your head—your brain. Your brain has 100 billion tiny "switches" that allow you to process information every day. Those "switches" are your brain cells. Like your brain, computers have billions of tiny "brain cells" called silicon transistors. These tiny electronic components have been changing society since they were first developed in the 1950s.

Transistors are devices that can strengthen an electronic signal. Transistors can rapidly turn computer circuits off and on. They are efficient and produce very little heat, which makes them useful in cellular phones, radios, and computers. Silicon transistors first were used in computers in 1955. At the time, computers were about the size of three or four adults put together. Now, of course, computers are much smaller.

Scientists developed the first miniature silicon transistor in 1965. They attached several of the tiny transistors, along with other electronic components, to a piece of plastic. This was the invention of the circuit board. The circuit board allowed designers to fit many more transistors into a computer. This also allowed computers to be made much smaller.

The number of transistors that can be placed on a single circuit board has doubled every two years since 1965. Computers have become smaller, faster, and more powerful. However, silicon transistors cannot be made much smaller. How might scientists create smaller transistors? The answer is to use carbon instead of silicon. Carbon nanotubes are cylindrical structures made of pure carbon. They conduct both heat and electricity and are many times faster and more efficient than silicon transistors. In addition, nanotubes are tiny—100,000 of them side by side would be about as thick as a human hair. As if that were not enough, the tubes are ten times stronger than steel. Once again, society will change as electronics you cannot even imagine today become everyday items of the future.

The first silicon transistor, shown here on top of a postage stamp, was small for its time but huge by today's standards.

TRIDAC was the first fully transistorized computer.

Carbon nanotube

By the 1980s, computers had become small enough to fit on a desktop.

It's Your Turn!

RESEARCH AND REPORT What do scientists think is the next step in using carbon nanotube transistors? If nanotube transistors lead to even faster and more powerful devices, how might those devices impact your everyday life? Share your research with your class.

INQUIRY

Does it bite? This interesting caterpillar is not feared because of its bite. It shoots an organic compound called formic acid at its enemies. What other organisms use acids for defense? What elements do you think make up formic acid?

Write your responses in your interactive notebook.

LAB Manager

Go to your Lab Manual or visit connectED.mcgraw-hill.com to perform the labs for this lesson.

MiniLAB: *How can you make a polymer?*
TEKS 7.1(A), (B); 7.2(A), (C), (E); 7.4(A), (B); 7.6(A)

Skill Practice: *How do you test for vitamin C?*
TEKS 7.1(A), (B); 7.2(A), (C), (E); 7.4(A), (B); 7.6(A)

Explore Activity

TEKS 7.1(A), (B); 7.2(A), (C), (E); 7.4(A), (B); 7.6(A)

How do functional groups affect compounds?

In some hydrocarbons, a hydrogen atom is removed and another atom takes its place. Rubbing alcohol and glycerin are two examples.

Procedure

1. Read and complete a lab safety form.

2. Use a **plastic spoon** to measure two spoons of **rubbing alcohol** and pour the liquid into a **clear plastic cup.** Observe the properties of the alcohol. Use the wafting method to check the odor. Record your observations in your Lab Manual or interactive notebook.

3. Repeat step 2 with **glycerin** using a clean spoon and cup. Add **distilled water** to both cups until they are one-third full. Stir gently using the same spoon in each cup that you used before.

4. Twist three **chenille stems** to make bubble wands. Dip a clean bubble wand into each cup. Check to see if a film forms within the circle for each mixture. Record your observations.

5. Dispose of the materials as instructed by your teacher.

Think About This

1. Compare and contrast the properties and structural diagrams of rubbing alcohol and glycerin. Structural diagrams are found in your Lab Manual.

   _____

   _____

   _____

   _____

2. When a hydrogen atom in propane is replaced by an oxygen atom and a hydrogen atom, rubbing alcohol forms. What changes occur when this happens?

   _____

   _____

   _____

   _____

TEKS in this Lesson

7.6(A) Identify that organic compounds contain carbon and other elements such as hydrogen, oxygen, phosphorus, nitrogen, or sulfur

Also covers Process Standards: 7.1(A), (B); 7.2(A), (C), (E); 7.4(A), (B)

Essential Question

What elements are in the four common functional groups of organic compounds?

Vocabulary

substituted hydrocarbon
functional group
hydroxyl group
halide group
carboxyl group
amino group
polymer
monomer
polymerization

Substituted Hydrocarbons TEKS 7.6(A)

Think for a moment about any sports team. Teams often substitute players in and out of a game. In a similar way, other atoms can be substituted for a hydrogen atom in a hydrocarbon. *A **substituted hydrocarbon** is an organic compound in which a carbon atom is bonded to an atom, or group of atoms, other than hydrogen.* Just as a team might function differently when new players are substituted into the game, organic compounds function differently when hydrogen atoms are substituted with other atoms, such as oxygen, nitrogen, phosphorus, and sulfur.

You might be familiar with the substituted hydrocarbon ethanol. It is often mixed with gasoline and used as a fuel for cars. Ethanol is also in food flavorings, such as vanilla extract. The chemical formula for ethanol is CH_3CH_2OH. In this compound, one hydrogen atom of ethane (CH_3CH_3) has been replaced with $-OH$. This is just one type of substituted hydrocarbon that you will read about in this lesson.

Explain

1. Similar to substituting players in a game, how does substituting a hydrocarbon change its properties?

Math Skills

Use Ratios

A ratio expresses the relationship between two or more things. For example, in the formula for methane, CH_4, the ratio of carbon atoms to hydrogen atoms is 1:4, read as "1 to 4." Ethanol is written CH_3CH_2OH. One molecule contains **2** carbon atoms, **6** hydrogen atoms, and **1** oxygen atom. The ratio is: C:H:O = **2:6:1**

Practice

What is the ratio of carbon to hydrogen to oxygen atoms in table sugar, $C_{12}H_{22}O_{11}$?

Check Tutor

Go Online!

Functional Groups **TEKS** 7.6(A)

You just read that a hydrogen atom in an organic compound can be substituted with other atoms. This causes the substituted hydrocarbon to have new properties. *A **functional group** is an atom or group of atoms that determine the function and properties of the compound.* The substituted hydrocarbon is renamed to indicate which functional group has been substituted. There are many functional groups, each with specific characteristics. Four functional groups are discussed in this lesson.

Hydroxyl Group

Have you ever used rubbing alcohol to clean a cut or a scrape? It is often used to soothe and disinfect the skin. Rubbing alcohol is the common name for the compound 2-propanol. 2-Propanol is a substituted hydrocarbon of propane and contains the hydroxyl (hi DRAHK sul) functional group, as shown in **Figure 1.** *The* **hydroxyl group** *contains two atoms—oxygen and hydrogen. Its formula is –OH.* Organic compounds that contain the hydroxyl group are called alcohols. Alcohols are polar compounds and can dissolve in water. They have high melting and boiling points and are commonly used as disinfectants, fuel, and solvents. **Figure 1** also shows how the substituted hydrocarbon ethanol differs from ethane. Larger alcohols form when the hydroxyl group is substituted in larger hydrocarbons.

Infer

2. Using **Figure 1** as a guide, what does the *2-* indicate on the 2-propanol?

Figure 1 Substituting a H atom for a functional group in a hydrocarbon changes its properties.

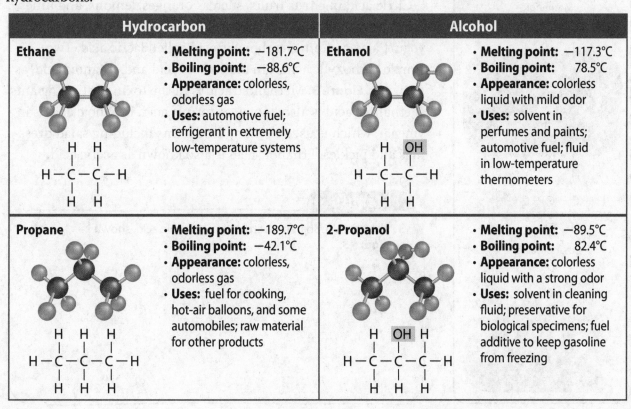

Hydrocarbon		Alcohol	
Ethane	• **Melting point:** −181.7°C • **Boiling point:** −88.6°C • **Appearance:** colorless, odorless gas • **Uses:** automotive fuel; refrigerant in extremely low-temperature systems	**Ethanol**	• **Melting point:** −117.3°C • **Boiling point:** 78.5°C • **Appearance:** colorless liquid with mild odor • **Uses:** solvent in perfumes and paints; automotive fuel; fluid in low-temperature thermometers
Propane	• **Melting point:** −189.7°C • **Boiling point:** −42.1°C • **Appearance:** colorless, odorless gas • **Uses:** fuel for cooking, hot-air balloons, and some automobiles; raw material for other products	**2-Propanol**	• **Melting point:** −89.5°C • **Boiling point:** 82.4°C • **Appearance:** colorless liquid with a strong odor • **Uses:** solvent in cleaning fluid; preservative for biological specimens; fuel additive to keep gasoline from freezing

Halide Group

Group 17 elements—the halogens—can also be substitutions in hydrocarbons. This functional group is called the halide group. *The* **halide group** *contains group 17 halogens—fluorine, chlorine, bromine, and iodine.* Bromomethane (broh moh MEH thayn) is an example of a substance with halide substitution. In bromomethane, a bromine atom replaces one of the hydrogen atoms in methane. This process is similar to the one shown in **Figure 1.** Notice the prefix *bromo–* is before the hydrocarbon name to form the name bromomethane, as illustrated in **Figure 2.**

As shown in **Figure 2,** bromomethane is a pesticide. It can be used to kill pests in the soil before strawberries are planted. Its use is strictly regulated because of its environmental hazards. Some countries have banned its use or are phasing out its use.

Carboxyl Group

If you had orange juice for breakfast or a salad for lunch, you ate compounds containing one or more carboxyl (kar BAHK sul) functional groups. *A* **carboxyl group** *consists of a carbon atom with a single bond to a hydroxyl group and a double bond to an oxygen atom. Its formula is* $-COOH$. When a carboxyl group replaces a hydrogen atom in a hydrocarbon, the result is a carboxylic acid.

Citric acid in citrus fruits, such as oranges, lemons, and limes, is a carboxylic acid. Dairy products such as buttermilk and yogurt also contain a carboxylic acid called lactic acid. Two simple carboxylic acids are methanoic acid and ethanoic acid, as shown in **Figure 3.** Methanoic acid is in the toxin of stinging ants. Methanoic acid is also known as formic acid. Ethanoic acid is in vinegar, which is used in many food items including salad dressings and pickles. Ethanoic acid is also known as acetic acid.

Figure 2 Bromomethane, sometimes called methyl bromide, contains one carbon atom, three hydrogen atoms, and one bromine atom. It is used for rodent control.

Bromomethane, CH_3Br

Figure 3 Methanoic and ethanoic acid are simple carboxylic acids.

Methanoic acid, HCOOH

Ethanoic acid, CH_3COOH

Identify

3. Illustrate the shared electrons for ethanoic acid, shown in **Figure 3.**

Amino Group

Have you ever smelled cheese with a strong odor? The strong odor is due to the presence of an amino (uh MEE noh) group. *The **amino group** consists of a nitrogen atom covalently bonded to two hydrogen atoms, and its formula is $-NH_2$.* The suffix *–amine* is added to the end of each root name to indicate that the amino group is in the compound. The amine, methylamine (meh thuh luh MEEN), forms when an amino group is substituted for a hydrogen in methane. **Figure 4** illustrates the structure and chemical formula of methylamine.

Notice that *–yl* follows the root name *meth-*. If a hydrocarbon, such as methane, loses a hydrogen atom, its name changes to methyl. If ethane loses a hydrogen atom, its name becomes ethyl.

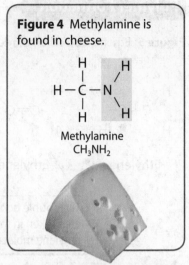

Figure 4 Methylamine is found in cheese.

Methylamine
CH_3NH_2

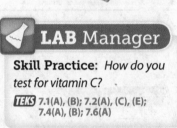

LAB Manager

Skill Practice: *How do you test for vitamin C?*

TEKS 7.1(A), (B); 7.2(A), (C), (E); 7.4(A), (B); 7.6(A)

Identify

4. Classify the elements commonly found in organic compounds by matching them with their functional group names.

Amino Group	–OH
Carboxyl Group	–Cl, Br, I or F
Hydroxyl Group	–COOH
Halide Group	–NH₂

Shapes of Molecules

Molecules come in different shapes and sizes. Scientists often make three-dimensional models of molecules to study their shapes. Knowing a molecule's shape helps scientists understand how it interacts with other molecules, how strong the bonds are between atoms, and what types of bonds are in the molecule. The molecular shapes in **Table 1** show you how some molecules might look in three dimensions.

1. **Tetrahedral**—Methane is an example of a tetrahedral molecule. The atoms in a tetrahedral molecule form a pyramid.

2. **Planar**—Ethene is an example of a planar molecule. The atoms in a planar molecule are all on the same plane.

3. **Linear**—Ethyne is an example of a linear molecule. The atoms in a linear molecule form a straight line.

Table 1 Molecules are not flat. They are three-dimensional.

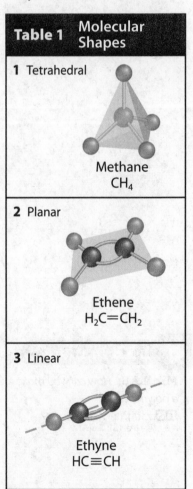

Table 1	Molecular Shapes
1 Tetrahedral	Methane CH_4
2 Planar	Ethene $H_2C=CH_2$
3 Linear	Ethyne $HC\equiv CH$

Figure 5 Ethene, also called ethylene, molecules form polyethylene during polymerization.

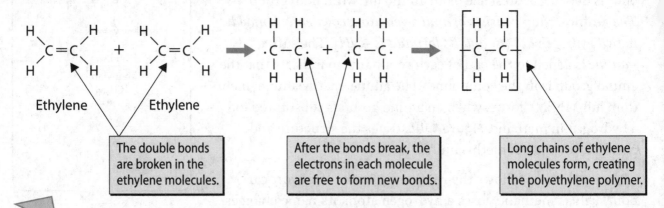

Ethylene Ethylene

The double bonds are broken in the ethylene molecules.

After the bonds break, the electrons in each molecule are free to form new bonds.

Long chains of ethylene molecules form, creating the polyethylene polymer.

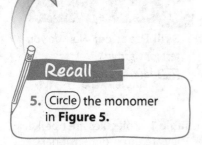

Recall

5. Circle the monomer in **Figure 5.**

Polymers **TEKS** 7.6(A)

What do a bottle of water, a toy car, a marker, and a video game have in common? They all contain some amount of plastic. The word *plastic* is a common term that refers to a type of substance called a polymer (PAH luh mur). *A **polymer** is a molecule made up of many of the same small organic molecules covalently bonded together, forming a long chain. A **monomer** (MAH nuh mur) is one of the small organic molecules that makes up the long chain of a polymer.* Some polymers occur naturally, but many are made in laboratories. Polymers occurring in nature are called natural polymers. Polymers made in laboratories are called synthetic polymers.

*Many synthetic polymers are made from simple hydrocarbons by a process called **polymerization*** (pah luh muh ruh ZAY shun). Polymerization is the chemical process in which small organic molecules, or monomers, bond together to form a chain. Polyethylene is a polymer used to make shampoo bottles, grocery bags, and toys. It is made by the polymerization of ethene, also known as ethylene. As shown in **Figure 5,** first the double bonds are broken in the ethene molecules. Then the carbon atoms bond and form long chains.

Synthetic Polymers **TEKS** 7.6(A)

Polyethylene and many other synthetic polymers are made from petroleum. Petroleum is a thick, oily, flammable mixture of solid, liquid, and gaseous hydrocarbons. Petroleum, an example of a fossil fuel, occurs naturally beneath Earth's surface. It formed from the remains of ancient, microscopic marine organisms.

Examples of polymers and some of their applications are shown in **Table 2** on the next page. This is only a small sample of the many polymers and polymer applications that are used today.

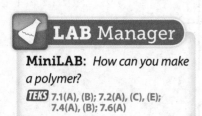

LAB Manager

MiniLAB: *How can you make a polymer?*

TEKS 7.1(A), (B); 7.2(A), (C), (E); 7.4(A), (B); 7.6(A)

Table 2   Sample Polymers and Applications

Polymers	Examples	
 Polyethylene (PE)		Bales of hay are rolled in polyethylene to protect them from rain. The hay is used to feed farm animals such as cows, horses, and sheep.
 Polyvinyl chloride (PVC)		Pipes made of polyvinyl chloride, or PVC, are used for plumbing. Some rainwear, home siding, and garden hoses are also made of polyvinyl chloride.
 Polytetrafluoroethylene (PTFE)		Polytetrafluoroethylene (pah lee teh truh flor oh ETH uh leen) is used for nonstick coating on cookware.
 Polypropylene (PP)		Polymer bank notes are made of polypropylene. These bank notes last longer than traditional paper notes. Also, many ropes are made of polypropylene.

Table 2 Many common objects are made of synthetic polymers.

Analyze

6. Petroleum is a nonrenewable resource. Because of this, scientists predict that someday there will be no more oil. What effect will this have on the plastics industry and the production of synthetic polymers? Explain your answer.

_____

_____

_____

_____

Summarize it!

Create your own graphic organizer summarizing the structures and elements of the four functional groups discussed in this lesson. *TEKS* 7.6(A)

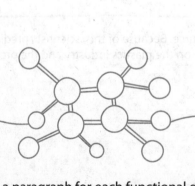

 Connect it! **Write** a paragraph for each functional group describing at least one practical use of each group of organic compounds. Write your response in your interactive notebook.

Other Organic Compounds

Use Vocabulary

1. When a hydrogen atom is replaced by a

_____ _____, it forms a

_____ _____.

TEKS 7.6(A) *supporting*

Apply the Essential Questions

2. **List** the elements in each of the four common functional groups.

TEKS 7.6(A) *supporting*

_____

_____

_____

_____

3. Select the correct formula for an example of the halide group. **TEKS** 7.6(A) *supporting*

   A. –Cl

   B. –COOH

   C. –H

   D. –OH

4. Which functional group does this molecule contain? **TEKS** 7.6(A) *supporting*

$$\begin{array}{c} H \\ | \\ H-C-C-O-H \\ | \quad \| \\ H \quad O \end{array}$$

   A. amino

   B. carboxyl

   C. halide

   D. hydroxyl

H.O.T. Questions (Higher Order Thinking)

5. **Compare and contrast** the structures of butane and butanol. **TEKS** 7.6(A) *supporting*

_____

_____

_____

_____

_____

_____

Writing in Science

6. **Research** Laboratories are not the only place polymers are created. Research natural polymers and where they are found in nature. On a separate sheet of paper, record your research findings. Be sure to give examples of natural polymers, and draw structures and label elements in each example. **TEKS** 7.6(A) *supporting*

Math Skills

Use Ratios

7. Isopropyl alcohol, or rubbing alcohol, has the formula $CH_3CH_2CH_2OH$. What is the ratio of carbon to hydrogen to oxygen atoms in this compound?

Check Tutor

Go Online!

INQUIRY

Healthful Diet? The man and the dog get their energy from the foods they eat. Foods contain carbon compounds that the body uses to function. What carbon compounds are known as the compounds of life?

Write your response in your interactive notebook.

LAB Manager

Go to your Lab Manual or visit connectED.mcgraw-hill.com to perform the labs for this lesson.

LAB: *Testing for Carbon Compounds*

TEKS 7.1(A), (B); 7.2(A), (C), (E); 7.3(A); 7.4(A), (B); 7.6(A)

Explore Activity

TEKS 7.1(A), (B); 7.2(A), (C), (E); 7.3(A); 7.4(A), (B); 7.6(A)

What does a carbon compound look like when its structure changes?

Proteins are carbon compounds that are in many living things. They are also in products made by living things, such as milk. Like all proteins, the proteins in milk have a three-dimensional structure. You can observe the result of a structural change of one protein when acid is added to milk.

Procedure

1. Read and complete a lab safety form.

2. Add **skim milk** to a **clear plastic cup** until it is one-third full. Observe the milk with a **magnifying lens.** Record your observations in your Lab Manual or interactive notebook.

3. Use a **plastic spoon** to add two spoonfuls of **white vinegar (acetic acid)** to the skim milk. After 1 min, observe the mixture with the magnifying lens. Record your observations.

4. Place a **coffee filter** in a **funnel**. Hold the funnel over another **clear plastic cup** and pour the milk-vinegar mixture into the filter-lined funnel. Observe the contents of the cup and funnel. Record your observations.

Think About This

1. Compare and contrast the milk before and after the vinegar was added.

_____

_____

2. What caused the protein to clump when the vinegar was added?

_____

_____

_____

3. Based on your knowledge of organic compounds, what elements must proteins contain? Vinegar is also called ethanoic acid. What functional group does it contain?

_____

_____

TEKS in this Lesson

7.6(A) Identify that organic compounds contain carbon and other elements such as hydrogen, oxygen, phosphorus, nitrogen, or sulfur

7.6(C) Recognize that large molecules are broken down into smaller molecules such as carbohydrates broken down into sugars

Also covers Process Standards: 7.1(A), (B); 7.2(A), (C), (E); 7.3(A); 7.4(A), (B)

 ### Essential Questions

- What are some groups of carbon compounds found in living organisms?

- How are large biological molecules broken down into smaller molecules?

 ### Vocabulary

biological molecule
protein
amino acid
carbohydrate
nucleic acid
lipid

Biological Molecules

Many of the objects you use, such as CDs, DVDs, sandwich bags, plastic bowls, combs, and hairbrushes, are made of synthetic polymers. The bodies of the man and the dog in the photograph also contain polymers. Recall that polymers in nature are called natural polymers. Cells, tissues, and organs in your body and in the bodies of other living things contain natural polymers.

Individual cells of a living thing contain polymers that carry **genetic information** and pass this information to new cells. The chemical energy stored in your muscles is a polymer, too. All of these natural polymers are called biological molecules. *A* **biological molecule** *is a large organic molecule in any living organism.* Biological molecules help determine the structure and function of many different body parts. They also provide the energy needed to run, to pedal a bicycle, and to do the many other activities you do. The chemical elements that make up these molecules come from the variety of foods you eat and the air you breathe.

FOLDABLES®

Fold a sheet of paper into a four column chart. Label it as shown. Use it to record information about the four biological molecules and their functions.

| Biological Molecules | | | |
| Proteins | Carbohydrates | Nucleic Acids | Lipids |

Review Vocabulary

genetic information a set of instructions—passed from one generation to the next by genes—that defines how biological processes will occur and determines physical characteristics

Characterize

1. Identify information about biological molecules.

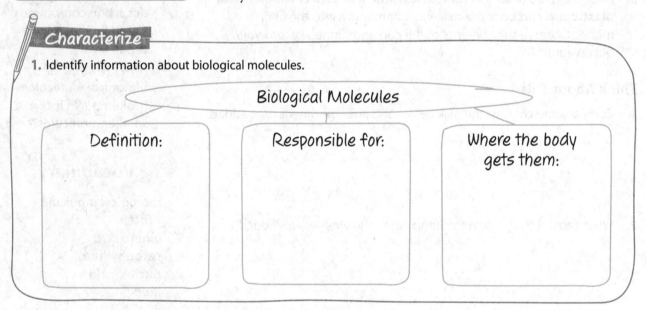

Biological Molecules

Definition:

Responsible for:

Where the body gets them:

Proteins TEKS 7.6(A), (C)

What do spiderwebs, plant leaves and roots, and the feathers of a peacock have in common? They contain natural polymers called proteins. Much of your body is made of proteins, too, including your hair, muscles, blood, organs, and fingernails. *A* **protein** (PROH teen) *is a biological polymer made of amino acid monomers. An* **amino acid** (uh MEE noh • A sud) *is a carbon compound that contains two functional groups—amino and carboxyl.*

Amino-Acid Chains

Amino acids link together and form long chains. **Figure 1** shows the basic chemical structure of an amino acid. The *R* represents a side chain of molecules that can differ. There are 20 different side chains. Therefore, 20 different amino acids can link and form proteins, as shown in **Figure 2**.

Proteins and the Human Body

Proteins are important to the body. Of the 20 different amino acids, the human body can make 11 of them. The other nine must be included in the foods that you eat. These nine amino acids are often referred to as essential amino acids. They are in a variety of foods, including fish, dairy products, beans, and meat.

Enzymes

An enzyme is a special kind of protein molecule made of hydrogen and carbon atoms with some other atoms as well. An enzyme's purpose is to help chemical reactions in cells occur faster. Many chemical reactions occur within cells, but without enzymes, most would happen too slowly to be useful to the body.

Some enzymes help digest food by breaking large food molecules into small molecules that can get into a cell. Enzymes break down other proteins, carbohydrates, nucleic acids, and lipids. For example, digestive enzymes in saliva break starch molecules into sugar molecules that can easily pass into your body's cells and turn into energy.

Each type of enzyme has a unique shape. An enzyme molecule will work only with molecules that it fits exactly, like the correct key for a lock. That way each type of enzyme can function without disrupting other chemical reactions in the cell.

Amino acid

Amino group   Variable side chain

Hydrogen atom   Carboxyl group

Figure 1 Amino acids are the monomers that form proteins.

Some proteins form helical, or spiral, shapes.

Figure 2 Proteins are polymers that contain hundreds of amino acids linked together in a chain.

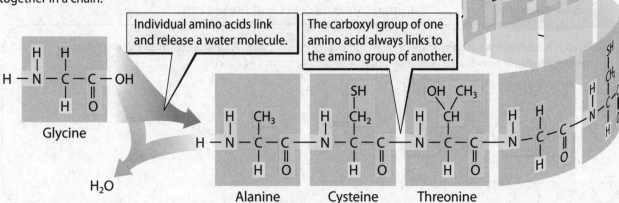

Individual amino acids link and release a water molecule.

The carboxyl group of one amino acid always links to the amino group of another.

Glycine

H₂O

Alanine   Cysteine   Threonine

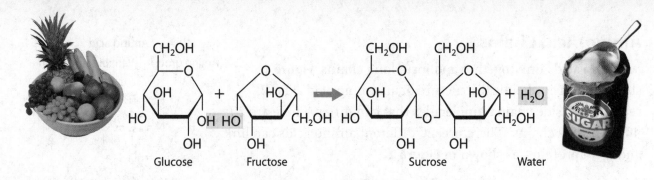

Figure 3 Glucose and fructose are simple sugars in fruits. Sucrose, also known as table sugar, forms from the chemical reaction between glucose and fructose.

Carbohydrates TEKS 7.6(A), (C)

When you eat pasta or sugary snacks, you probably do not think about the carbohydrates in your food. A **carbohydrate** (kar boh HI drayt) *is a group of organic molecules that includes sugars, starches, and cellulose.* Carbohydrates are natural polymers that contain carbon, hydrogen, and oxygen atoms. They are a source of energy in cells.

Sugars

Simple sugars, such as glucose and fructose, usually contain five or six carbon atoms. The carbon atoms can be arranged in a ring, as shown in **Figure 3,** or in a straight chain. Your cells can easily break apart these large moleclues into smaller simple sugars, which provide quick energy. Glucose is in foods such as fruits and honey. It is also in your blood. Glucose and fructose combine and form a sugar called sucrose, also shown in **Figure 3.** Sucrose is used to sweeten many foods.

Starch and Cellulose

When simple sugar molecules form chains, they form polymers called complex carbohydrates. Starch and cellulose are complex carbohydrates made of glucose monomers. The chemical bonds in starches take longer to break apart than simple sugars. They provide energy over a longer period. Human digestive systems cannot break the bonds in cellulose, but the digestive systems of animals such as cows and horses can.

Draw

2. Starch is a complex carbohydrate of over 300 glucose molecules. A small section of starch is shown below. Illustrate how starch is broken apart into simple sugars of glucose.

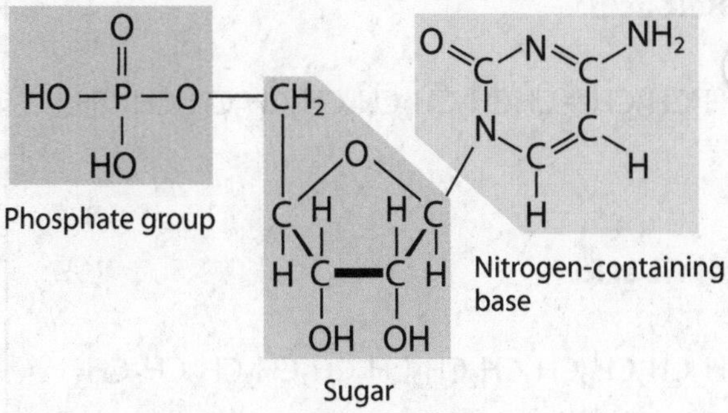

Figure 4 Nucleotide monomers make up nucleic-acid polymers.

Phosphate group

Sugar

Nitrogen-containing base

Go Online!

Tutor

Nucleic Acids **TEKS** 7.6(A)

A biological polymer that stores and transmits genetic information is a **nucleic acid** (new KLEE ihk • A sud). Genetic information includes instructions for cells on how to make proteins, produce new cells, and transfer genetic information. It is genetic information that determines how you look and how your body functions.

The monomer in a nucleic-acid polymer is called a nucleotide, as shown in **Figure 4.** Each nucleotide monomer contains a phosphate group, a sugar, and a nitrogen-containing base. All nucleotides contain the same phosphate group. However, the sugar and nitrogen base can vary in nucleic acids. The elements needed by your body to make nucleic acids come from the foods that you eat.

DNA

Two common nucleic acids, DNA and RNA, control cellular function and heredity. DNA is deoxyribonucleic acid (dee AHK sih rib oh noo klay ihk • A sud). DNA is a spiral-shaped molecule that resembles a twisted zipper, as shown in **Figure 5.** Each DNA monomer contains the five-carbon sugar deoxyribose. Deoxyribose and phosphate groups form the outside of the zipper. Pairs of nitrogen-containing bases—adenine (A) and thymine (T) or cytosine (C) and guanine (G)—form the teeth of the zipper.

RNA

RNA is ribonucleic acid. It contains the five-carbon sugar ribose. RNA is usually single-stranded, not double-stranded like DNA. It contains the nitrogen bases adenine, cytosine, guanine, and uracil. DNA provides information to make RNA, and then RNA makes the proteins that a cell needs to function.

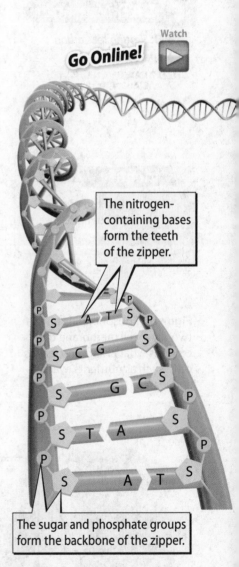

Go Online! Watch

The nitrogen-containing bases form the teeth of the zipper.

The sugar and phosphate groups form the backbone of the zipper.

Figure 5 DNA is a spiral-shaped molecule which is often called a double helix.

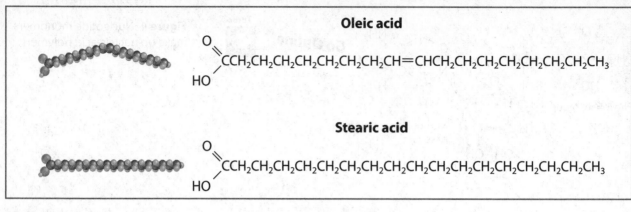

Oleic acid

$\overset{O}{\underset{HO}{\parallel}}CCH_2CH_2CH_2CH_2CH_2CH_2CH_2CH=CHCH_2CH_2CH_2CH_2CH_2CH_2CH_2CH_3$

Stearic acid

$\overset{O}{\underset{HO}{\parallel}}CCH_2CH_2CH_2CH_2CH_2CH_2CH_2CH_2CH_2CH_2CH_2CH_2CH_2CH_2CH_2CH_2CH_3$

Figure 6 Oleic acid is an unsaturated lipid found in olive oil. Stearic acid is a saturated lipid found in bacon.

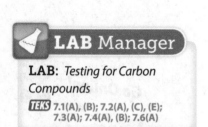

LAB Manager

LAB: *Testing for Carbon Compounds*

TEKS 7.1(A), (B); 7.2(A), (C), (E); 7.3(A); 7.4(A), (B); 7.6(A)

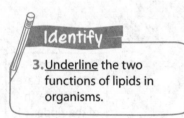

Identify

3. Underline the two functions of lipids in organisms.

Figure 7 Phospholipids form a two-layer cell membrane that controls what enters and leaves cells, such as nutrients, waste, and water.

Lipids **TEKS** 7.6(A), (C)

Examples of lipids are shown in **Figure 6.** Lipids are biological molecules, but they are not polymers. A lipid molecule is a long hydrocarbon chain with a carboxyl group on the end. *A **lipid** is a type of biological molecule that includes fats, oils, hormones, waxes, and components of cellular membranes.* Lipids have two major functions—storing energy and making up cell membranes.

Saturated and Unsaturated Lipids

There are two main groups of lipids—saturated and unsaturated. Saturated lipids contain only single bonds. Unsaturated lipids contain at least one double bond. If an unsaturated lipid has one double bond, it is called monounsaturated. If it has more than one double bond, it is called polyunsaturated.

Lipids in Organisms

Lipids, such as fats and oils, store energy for organisms. Enzymes from the pancreas help break lipids into smaller pieces to aid in digestion and energy use. Another function of lipids is to control what enters and leaves individual cells. These lipids are called phospholipids because they contain a phosphate functional group in their structure. Phospholipids form the cell membrane around individual cells, as shown in **Figure 7.**

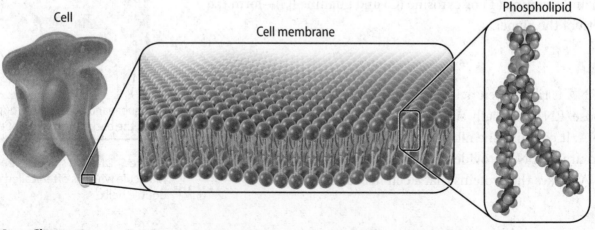

Cell

Cell membrane

Phospholipid

Summarize it!

Explain why all living things contain carbon, oxygen, and hydrogen. **TEKS** 7.6(A)

_____

_____

_____

_____

_____

_____

_____

_____

_____

_____

_____

_____

_____

_____

 Connect it! **Research** the disorder lactose intolerance. What causes this problem? What can people do to reduce their symptoms? Write your research findings in your interactive notebook. Discuss your findings with a partner. **TEKS** 7.6(C)

Compounds of Life

Apply the Essential Questions

1. **Explain** What are the four types of biological molecules and their main function in the human body?
   TEKS 7.6(A) *supporting*

   _____

   _____

   _____

   _____

   _____

2. Carbohydrates are broken down into smaller molecules for what purpose?
   TEKS 7.6(C)

   A. to form cell membranes

   B. to form muscle

   C. to transmit genetic information

   D. to provide energy

H.O.T. Questions (Higher Order Thinking)

3. **Explain** how enzymes aid in food digestion. **TEKS** 7.6(C)

   _____

   _____

   _____

   _____

   _____

   _____

   _____

4. **Evaluate** Many weight-loss diets stress eliminating carbohydrates and fats from the diet. Explain why eliminating these foods completely from the diet over long periods of time might not be a good idea.
   TEKS 7.6(C)

   _____

   _____

   _____

   _____

   _____

5. **Infer** The odor produced by burning hair is due to large amounts of the amino acid cysteine in keratin, the major protein in hair. What elements make up the variable side chain of cysteine? What element causes this smell? **TEKS** 7.6(A) *supporting*

   _____

   _____

   _____

   _____

   _____

Writing in Science

6. Spider webs, fingernails, and muscles are just a few examples of proteins. **Analyze** why there are so many proteins, each with different properties. Write your response on a separate sheet of paper.
   TEKS 7.6(A) *supporting*

7. **Design** a brochure, on a separate sheet of paper, that explains information about each biological molecule discussed in this lesson. **TEKS** 7.6(A) *supporting*

The Need for Proper
NUTRITION

You've just learned about the compounds of life. So what? What do these different compounds mean to you? How can they affect your life?

Did you know that your body needs a balance of proteins, carbohydrates, and fats to function properly? Think of your body like a car. Carbohydrates are like the fuel that gives the car the energy to go. Lipids, or fats, are like the oil of the car. They maintain the engine and keep things running smoothly. Proteins are like mechanics that build and repair the car. If you remove any of these critical components, the car will not run properly.

When trying to reach a healthy weight, some people follow "fad diets" that have you avoid certain food groups, such as the "no carb" or "no fat" diets, or eat only one type of food, like the "only grapefruit" diet. The truth is, these diets generally do not work in the long run and can come with some risk.

Avoiding all carbohydrates, such as starches, sugars, and fiber, means that your body loses out on its main source of energy, and you may experience exhaustion. Secondarily, you could increase your risk of heart disease and cancer by consuming only protein and fat.

By avoiding all fats, your body misses important lipids used in cell membrane maintenance, vitamin transport, and lowering cholesterol.

Avoiding all proteins prevents your body from receiving all the amino acids it needs to build and repair muscle and tissue. By consuming only one type of food all the time, you will miss out on all the different vitamins, minerals, antioxidants, and amino acids your body requires to function properly. A properly portioned, well-balanced approach is the way to go!

So WHAT?!

Nutrition **does** have a major impact on your life! A balanced diet is vital to keep the human body running like a finely-tuned machine.

THAT'S
what!!

Test-Taking Strategy

Analyze a Table Sometimes a question will ask you to analyze a table in order to answer a question. In these questions, you need to break down and interpret the information supplied in the table, then apply it to what the question is asking.

Example

Use the table below to answer question 1.

Root Words of Carbon Chains			
Carbon Atoms	Name	Carbon Atoms	Name
1	meth–	6	hex–
2	eth–	7	hept–
3	prop–	8	oct–
4	but–	9	non–
5	pent–	10	dec–

2 Next, analyze the table. What information does this table display? According to the table name, this table describes information about the root words of carbon chains. Find the root name for heptane on the table.

1 How many carbon atoms are found in one molecule of heptane?

TEKS 7.6(A) supporting

1 Carefully read the question to understand what the question is asking. With this question, we know we're trying to find the number of carbon atoms in heptane.

A 2

B 5

C 6

3 Heptane contains seven carbon atoms. The correct answer is choice **D**.

D 7

TIP: Carefully read the information provided by the table. The name of the table should describe what information the table is providing. Each column and row will also have a label describing what it is displaying. Track the columns and rows with your pencil or fingers to ensure that you're reading the correct line.

Multiple Choice

1   The two chemicals shown below formed from the breakdown of a larger
    compound in the presence of water. **TEKS** 7.6(C); 7.2(E)

Which compound could breakdown to form these chemicals?

A

B

C

D

2   A class has been divided into groups. Each group will be assigned a chemical compound to research. Students are to discover the name of their chemical and the chemical's uses and properties. The chemical formulas for the compounds are shown in the table.

TEKS 7.6(A), *supporting*; 7.2(E)

Group Number	Chemical Formula of Compound
Group 1	N_2O
Group 2	Na_2CrO_4
Group 3	HCl
Group 4	C_3H_8O
Group 5	CO_2

Which group was assigned an organic compound to research? Record and bubble in your answer in the answer document.

3

> Proteins are biological molecules that form much of the body's organs and cells. They are involved in just about every process carried out by the cells and are essential to life. Proteins consist of one or more chains of amino acids. Some proteins are simple, consisting of no more than two or three amino acids. Other proteins are quite complex and comprise hundreds of amino acids that are folded into an intricate shape. No matter the size or complexity, the body builds the proteins it needs to sustain life. To do this, it first breaks down proteins from food through digestion. This yields the amino acid building blocks from which new proteins can be formed.

Which conclusion can you draw about proteins and amino acids? **TEKS** 7.6(C); 7.3(A)

A   All amino acids are produced in the human body.

B   Amino acids are large molecules that can be broken down into simple proteins.

C   Amino acids are produced from the stomach's gastric juices and used to build proteins.

D   Proteins are large molecules that can be broken down into simple amino acids.

4 The diagram shows the structural formula for starch, a carbohydrate found in many foods including wheat, potatoes, and rice. During digestion, carbohydrates are broken down into simpler sugars. **TEKS** 7.6(C); 7.2(E)

Starch

Into which sugar would starch likely be broken down in the body?

A   Fructose

B   Glucose

C   Ribose

D   Sucrose

My Notes

My Notes

TEKS Strand 3
Force, Motion, and Energy

TEKS in this strand

✓ **7.7** The student knows that there is a relationship among force, motion, and energy.

✓ Also includes the following Scientific Investigation and Reasoning strand TEKS: **7.1, 7.2, 7.3, 7.4**

Texas Fun Fact

Did You Know? The Plano Balloon Festival is held each September. This festival is one of the city's largest celebrations. Hot-air balloons work by transforming chemical energy into thermal energy to heat the air inside the balloon. The rainbow of balloons is an amazing sight across the skies of Plano.

Forces, Energy, and Work

The **BIG** Idea

Energy transformations and work can occur in living and nonliving systems.

Lifting Weights

Two friends were at the gym. One friend tried to lift 100 kilograms. He pulled up with all his strength, but the weight would not budge. This is what the two friends said to each other:

Todd: I did a lot of work to try and lift this weight.

Matt: I don't think you did any work to try and lift the weight.

Which friend do you agree with the most? _____ Explain why you agree with that friend.

Why is one side of the ball flat?

A ball, such as this tennis ball, is usually round. Its shape lets it roll farther and travel farther in the air. What could cause part of a ball to become flat like this one? Does the same thing happen when a baseball hits a bat? Or when a golf club hits a golf ball?

Write your responses in your interactive notebook.

LAB Manager

Go to your Lab Manual or visit connectED.mcgraw-hill.com to perform the labs for this lesson.

MiniLAB: *How does friction affect an object's motion?*

TEKS 7.1(A); 7.2(A), (C), (D), (E); 7.3(A); 7.4(A), (B); 7.7(C)

Explore Activity

TEKS 7.1(A); 7.2(A), (C), (E); 7.4(A), (B); 7.7(C)

How can you change an object's shape and motion?

You probably can think of many ways that things change. For example, paper can change from a flat sheet to a crumpled ball. A sailboat changes its location as it moves across a lake. How can you change an object's shape and motion?

Procedure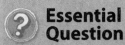

1. Read and complete a lab safety form.

2. Observe and record in your Lab Manual or interactive notebook how you make the changes described below. Change the shape of a handful of **clay** several times.

3. Mold the clay into a log. Cause the log to roll and then cause it to stop rolling.

4. Cause the log to roll so its speed changes. Then change the log's direction of motion. Observe and record how you made these changes.

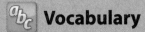

Think About This

1. Describe what you did to change the shape of the clay.

_____

_____

2. Explain how you changed the motion of the clay.

_____

_____

3. How was your interaction with the clay similar when you changed its shape and when you changed its motion?

_____

_____

TEKS in this Lesson

7.7(C) Demonstrate and illustrate forces that affect motion in everyday life, such as emergence of seedlings, turgor pressure, and geotropism.

Also covers 7.1(A); 7.2(A), (C), (D), (E); 7.3(A); 7.4(A), (B)

? Essential Question

- How do forces affect motion in everyday life?

abc Vocabulary

force
noncontact force
contact force
friction
gravity
balanced forces
unbalanced forces

Figure 1 The arrows show forces with very different sizes acting in opposite directions.

What are forces? **TEKS** 7.7(C)

What do typing on a computer, lifting a bike, and putting on a sweater have in common? Each involves an interaction between you and another object. You push on the keys. You push or pull on the bike. You pull on the sweater. *A push or pull on an object is a* **force.**

Forces affect motion of everyday life. Seedlings emerging through soil or growing toward the sun are examples of how objects around us are affected by forces. You are sitting on Earth due to a force—gravity!

A force has size and direction. As shown in **Figure 1,** the length of the arrow represents the size of the force. The direction in which the arrow points represents the direction of the force. The unit of force is the newton (N). It takes about 4 N of force to lift a can of soda.

There are two ways a force can affect an object. A force can change an object's speed. It also can change the direction in which the object is moving. In other words, a force can cause acceleration. Recall that acceleration is a change in an object's velocity—its speed and/or its direction in a given time. When you apply a force to a tennis ball like the one shown at the beginning of this lesson, the force first stops the motion of the ball. The force then causes the ball to accelerate in the opposite direction, changing its speed and direction.

Summarize

1. Characterize forces.

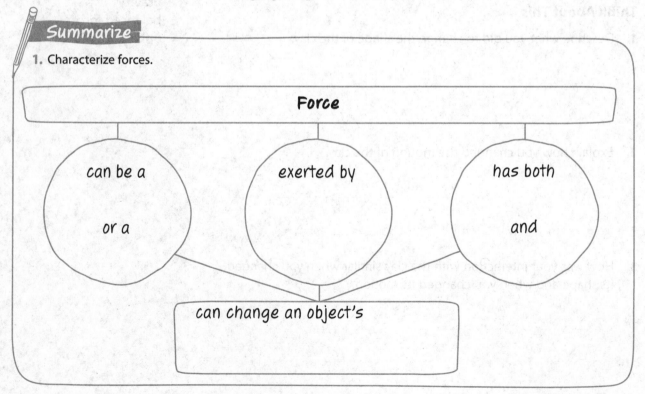

Force

can be a

or a

exerted by

has both

and

can change an object's

Types of Forces TEKS 7.7(C)

Some forces are easy to recognize. You can watch a hammer apply a force as it hits a nail. Other forces seem to act on objects without touching them. For example, what force causes your ice cream to fall toward the ground if it slips out of the cone?

Noncontact Forces

The top left image of **Figure 2** shows a girl's hair being pulled toward the slide even though it isn't touching the slide. *A force that pushes or pulls an object without touching it is a* **noncontact force.** The force that pulls the girl's hair is an electric force. The top half of **Figure 2** shows other noncontact forces—magnetism and gravity.

Noncontact forces affect all motion in everyday life. For example, a plant growing in soil is affected by gravity. The root system of a plant grows toward gravity. The response of a plant to gravity is called geotropism.

Contact Forces

The bottom left image of **Figure 2** shows a baker pushing his hand into dough, causing the top of the dough to accelerate downward. You can see the baker's hand and the dough come into contact with each other. A **contact force** *is a push or a pull applied by one object to another object that is touching it.* Contact forces also are called mechanical forces. The bottom half of **Figure 2** also shows other types of contact forces.

A growing seedling is an example of an applied force. As the plant pushes on the seed walls, the walls begin to crack and the seedling emerges from the seed pod.

Figure 2 The pictures in the top row show examples of various types of noncontact forces. The ones in the bottom row show examples of several types of contact forces.

A **noncontact**, or field, force is a force exerted when there is no visible object exerting the force.

Electric forces cause the girl's hair to stick out.

Magnetic forces hold these magnets apart.

Gravity is the force that pulls these divers toward the water.

A **contact**, or mechanical, force is a force exerted by a physical object that touches another object.

An **applied force** is a force in which one object directly pushes or pulls on another object.

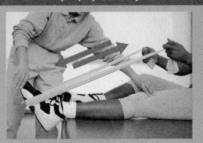
An **elastic** or spring force is the force exerted by a compressed or stretched object.

A **normal force** is the support force exerted on an object that touches another stable object.

Figure 3 The player must overcome friction or he won't reach the base.

Friction

Why does the baseball player in **Figure 3** slow down as he slides toward the base? **Friction** *is a contact force that resists the sliding motion between two objects that are touching.* The force of friction acts in the opposite direction of the motion, as shown by the blue arrow. Rougher surfaces produce greater friction than smooth surfaces. Other factors such as the weight of an object also affect the force of friction.

Gravity **TEKS** 7.7(C)

Is there anywhere on Earth where you could drop a pencil and not have it fall? No! **Gravity** *is a noncontact attractive force that exists between all objects that have mass.*

Mass is the amount of matter in an object. Your pencil and Earth have mass. They exert a gravitational pull on each other. In fact, they exert the same gravitational force on each other. Why doesn't your pencil pull Earth toward it? It actually does! The pencil has very little mass, so the force of gravity causes it to rapidly accelerate downward toward Earth's surface. Earth "falls" upward toward the pencil at the same time, but because of its mass, Earth's motion is too small to see.

LAB Manager

MiniLAB: *How does friction affect an object's motion?*

TEKS 7.1(A); 7.2(A), (C), (D), (E); 7.3(A); 7.4(A), (B); 7.7(C)

FOLDABLES®

Cut out the Lesson 4.1 Foldable in the back of the book. Use it to organize your notes on forces.

Tape here

Force is a push or a pull on an object.

Notes on Noncontact Forces

Notes on Contact Forces

Distance and Gravity

You might have heard that astronauts become weightless in space. This is not true. Astronauts have some weight in space, but it is much less in space than their weight on Earth. Weight is a measure of the force of gravity acting on an object. As two objects get farther apart, the gravitational force between the objects decreases. **Figure 4** shows how the weight of an astronaut changes as he or she moves farther from Earth.

You know that all objects exert a force of gravity on all other objects. If the astronaut drops a hammer on the Moon, will it fall toward Earth? No the attraction between the Moon and the hammer is stronger than the attraction between Earth and the hammer because the hammer is very close to the Moon and very far from Earth. The hammer will fall down toward the Moon.

Mass and Gravity

Another factor that affects the force of gravity between two objects is the mass of the objects. As the mass of one or both objects increases, the gravitational force between them increases. For example, in **Figure 5,** F stands for the gravitational force. As the figure shows, doubling the mass of one of the objects doubles the force of attraction.

The effect of mass on the force of gravity is most noticeable when one object is very massive, such as a planet, and the other object has much less mass, such as a person. Even though the force of gravity acts equally on both objects, the less massive object accelerates more quickly due to its smaller mass. Because the planet accelerates so slowly, all you observe is the object with less mass "falling" toward the object with greater mass.

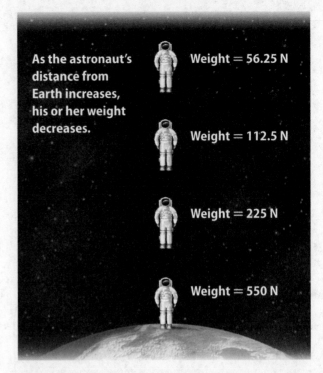

As the astronaut's distance from Earth increases, his or her weight decreases.

Weight = 56.25 N

Weight = 112.5 N

Weight = 225 N

Weight = 550 N

Figure 4 Gravitational force (weight) decreases as the distance between the centers of the objects increases.

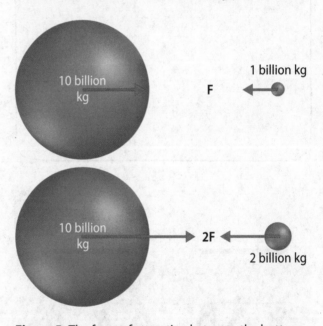

10 billion kg

1 billion kg

F

10 billion kg

2F

2 billion kg

Figure 5 The force of attraction between the bottom two objects is twice as much as between the top two objects.

Go Online!

Tutor

Identify

2. Highlight in the text how mass and distance affect the way gravity acts on objects.

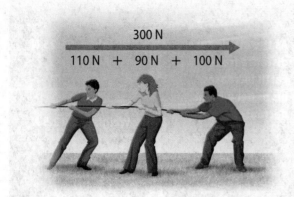

Figure 6 Forces in the same direction act as a single force.

✏️ Infer

3. A car begins to move after having stopped at a traffic light. What must be true about all the forces acting on the car?

Go Online!

Tutor 💬

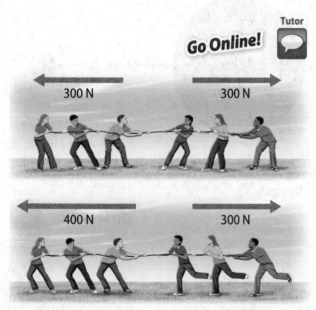

Figure 7 No change in motion takes place when forces on an object are balanced. Unbalanced forces cause the team on the right to accelerate to the left.

Combining Forces **TEKS** 7.7(C)

Have you ever played tug-of-war? If you alone pull against a team, you will probably be pulled over the line. However, if you are on a team, your team might pull the rope hard enough to cause the other team to move in your direction. When several forces act on an object, the forces combine to act as a single force. The sum of the forces acting on an object is called the net force.

Forces in the Same Direction

When different forces act on an object in the same direction, you can find the net force by adding the forces together. In **Figure 6,** each team member pulls in the same direction. The net force on the rope is 110 N + 90 N + 100 N = 300 N.

Forces in Opposite Directions

When forces act in opposite directions, you must include the direction of the force when you add them. Like numbers on a number line, forces in the direction to the right are normally considered to be positive values. Forces to the left are negative values. In the first panel of **Figure 7,** the team on the right pulls with a force of 300 N. The team on the left pulls with a force of −300 N. The net force is 300 N + (−300 N) = 0.

Balanced and Unbalanced Forces

The net force on the rope in the top of **Figure 7** is 0. *When the net force on an object is 0 N, the forces acting on it are* **balanced forces.** If the forces acting on an object are balanced, the object's motion does not change. *When the net force acting on an object is not 0, the forces acting on the object are* **unbalanced forces.** The forces acting on the rope in the bottom of **Figure 7** are unbalanced. Unbalanced forces cause objects to change their motion, or accelerate.

4.1 Review

Go Online!  Check

Assess how distance and mass affect the force of gravity between two objects.
TEKS 7.7(C)

Distance	Mass

Calculate net forces. Draw an arrow to show direction. **TEKS** 7.7(C)

Combined Forces	Net Force
→ 30 N → 70 N	
→ 30 N ← 40 N	
→ 60 N ← 60 N	
→ 18 N → 12 N ← 30 N	

 Connect It! Suppose you want to build a machine to perform some task. Why must you understand forces to complete your mission? Write your response in your interactive notebook.

Forces

Use Vocabulary

1. **Describe** an example when friction has affected your life. **TEKS** 7.7(C)

_____

_____

_____

Apply the Essential Question

2. **Demonstrate** using words how forces affect motion in everyday life.
   TEKS 7.7(C)

_____

_____

_____

_____

3. **Describe** any balanced and unbalanced forces acting on a book resting on a table.
   TEKS 7.7(C)

_____

_____

_____

_____

🔥 **H.O.T. Questions** (Higher Order Thinking)

4. **Rank** the force of gravity between these pairs of objects: a 1-kg mass and a 2-kg mass that are 1 m apart; a 1-kg mass and a 2-kg mass that are 2 m apart; and two 2-kg masses that are 1 m apart.
   TEKS 7.7(C)

_____

_____

Use the figure below to answer question 5.

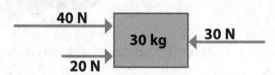

5. **Interpret Graphics** What is the net force on the object? Include the size of the force and its direction.

_____

_____

6. **Research** the contact and noncontact forces that affect a plant. **Illustrate** in the space below a plant growing in a pot. Label the forces that affect the plant.
   TEKS 7.7(C)

Writing in Science

7. **Demonstrate** how forces affect a moving car. Make a diagram on a separate sheet of paper. Draw one force acting on a car in one direction and two forces acting in the opposite direction. **TEKS** 7.7(C)

My Notes

INQUIRY

Robots? What do energy and this production line have in common? The robotic arms use energy when they move. The robots transform electric energy to thermal energy when they weld parts together. Can you identify other energy transformations in the photo?

Write your response in your interactive notebook.

LAB Manager

Go to your Lab Manual or visit connectED.mcgraw-hill.com to perform the labs for this lesson.

MiniLAB: *What affects an object's potential energy?*

TEKS 7.1(A); 7.2(A), (C), (E); 7.3(A); 7.4(A), (B)

Explore Activity

TEKS 7.1(A); 7.2(A), (C), (E); 7.4(A), (B)

Where does energy come from?

How can you heat your hands when they are cold? You could rub them together, put them in your pockets, or hold them near a heater. What makes your hands get warmer?

Procedure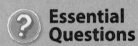

1. Read and complete a lab safety form.

2. As you complete each of the following steps, observe and record any changes in your Lab Manual or interactive notebook. Discuss the changes with your lab group. In each case, ask: What caused this change to occur? Record your ideas.

3. Rub your hands together. What do you feel?

4. Use a **match** to light a **candle.** Holding your hands near the flame, what do you see and feel?

    ⚠ *Use caution around an open flame.*

5. Turn on a **flashlight.** Where did the light come from?

6. Observe the overhead lights in your classroom. What is the source of the light?

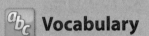

Think About This

1. Where did the light and the heat come from in steps 3, 4, 5, and 6?

    _____

    _____

    _____

2. How many different sources of energy can you recall? Briefly explain each one and tell how they differ from one another.

    _____

    _____

    _____

TEKS in this Lesson

This lesson provides background information for the following TEKS:

7.7(B) Illustrate the transformation of energy within an organism, such as the transfer from chemical energy to heat and thermal energy in digestion.

Also covers Process Standards: 7.1(A); 7.2(A), (C), (E); 7.3(A); 7.4(A), (B)

? Essential Questions

- What is energy?
- What are the different forms of energy?
- How is energy used?

ᵃᵇᵼ Vocabulary

energy
kinetic energy
electric energy
potential energy
chemical energy
nuclear energy
mechanical energy
thermal energy
sound energy
seismic energy
radiant energy

Figure 1 Satellites need a source of energy to run their systems and to stay in orbit. The *International Space Station* uses solar panels to generate energy.

What is energy?

You probably have heard the word *energy* used on the television, the radio, or the Internet. Commercials claim that the newest models of cars are energy efficient. What is energy? Scientists define **energy** *as the ability to cause a change.*

Using this definition, how do cars use energy? Most cars use some type of fuel such as gasoline or diesel as their energy source. The car's engine transforms the energy stored in the fuel to a form of energy that moves the car. Compared to other cars, an energy-efficient car uses less fuel to move the car a certain distance.

Gasoline and diesel fuel are not the only sources of energy. Food is an energy source for your body. The solar panels shown in **Figure 1** provide energy for the *International Space Station*. As you will read, wind, coal, nuclear fuel, Earth's interior, and the Sun also are sources of energy. Energy from each of these sources can be transformed into other forms of energy such as electric energy. Every time you turn on a light, you use energy that was transformed from one form to another.

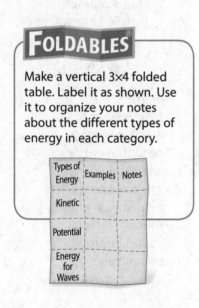

FOLDABLES

Make a vertical 3×4 folded table. Label it as shown. Use it to organize your notes about the different types of energy in each category.

Types of Energy	Examples	Notes
Kinetic		
Potential		
Energy for Waves		

Organize

1. Determine sources of energy for different objects.

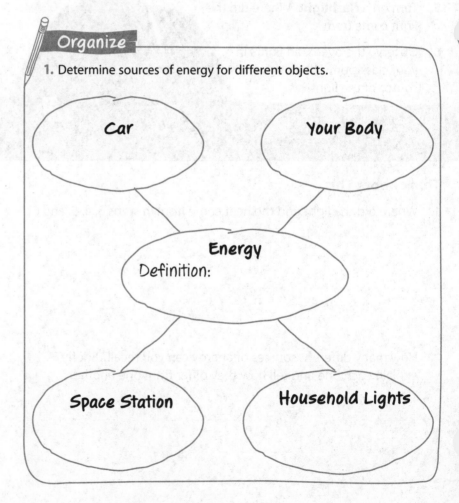

Kinetic Energy

Think about turning a page of a book. As the page moves, it has **kinetic energy**—*the energy an object has because it is in motion.* Anything that is in motion has kinetic energy, including large objects that you can see as well as small particles such as molecules, ions, atoms, and electrons.

Kinetic Energy of Objects

When the wind blows, the blades of the wind turbines in **Figure 2** turn. Because they are moving, they have kinetic energy. Kinetic energy depends on mass. If the turbine blades were smaller and had less mass, they would have less kinetic energy. Kinetic energy also depends on speed. When the wind blows harder, the blades move faster and have more kinetic energy. When the wind stops, the blades stop. When the blades are not moving, the kinetic energy of the blades is zero. One of the drawbacks of using wind-generated energy is that wind does not always blow, which makes the supply of energy inconsistent.

Electric Energy

When you turn on a lamp or use a cell phone, you are using a type of kinetic energy—**electric** energy. Recall that all objects are composed of atoms. Electrons move around the nucleus of an atom, and they move from one atom to another. When electrons move, they have kinetic energy and create an electric current. *The energy that an electric current carries is a form of kinetic energy called* **electric energy.**

Electric energy can be produced by moving objects. When the blades of wind turbines rotate, they turn a generator that changes the kinetic energy of the moving blades into electric energy. Electric energy generated from the kinetic energy of wind creates no waste products.

Explain

2. Why does the kinetic energy of the wind turbines in **Figure 2** change?

_____

_____

_____

_____

_____

_____

_____

Word Origin

electric from Greek *electrum*, means "amber"; because electricity was first generated by rubbing pieces of amber together

Figure 2 Wind turbines convert kinetic energy in the wind to electric energy.

Potential Energy

Suppose you hold up a piece of paper. When the paper is held above the ground, it has potential energy. **Potential energy** *is stored energy that depends on the interaction of objects, particles, or atoms.*

Gravitational Potential Energy

Gravitational potential energy is a type of potential energy stored in an object due to its height above Earth's surface. The water at the top of the dam in **Figure 3** has gravitational potential energy. Gravitational potential energy depends on the mass of an object and its distance from Earth's surface. The more mass an object has and the greater its distance from Earth is, the greater its gravitational potential energy will be.

In a hydroelectric energy plant, water above a dam flows through turbines as it falls. Generators connected to the spinning turbines convert the gravitational potential energy of the water into electric energy.

Hydroelectric power plants are a very clean source of energy. About 7 percent of all electric power in the United States is produced from hydroelectric energy. However, hydroelectric plants can interrupt the movement of animals in streams and rivers.

Word Origin

potential from Latin *potens*, means "power"

LAB Manager

MiniLAB: *What affects an object's potential energy?*

TEKS 7.1(A); 7.2(A), (C), (E); 7.3(A); 7.4(A), (B)

Define

3. In the text above, highlight the definition of *gravitational potential energy.*

Coal contains potential energy stored in the chemical bonds between atoms.

Nuclear fuel pellets contain potential energy stored in the nuclei of atoms.

Figure 4 Chemical energy and nuclear energy are two forms of potential energy.

Chemical Energy

Most electric energy in the United States comes from fossil fuels such as petroleum, natural gas, and coal. The atoms that make up these fossil fuels are joined by chemical bonds. Chemical bonds have the potential to break apart. Therefore, chemical bonds have a form of potential energy called chemical energy. **Chemical energy** *is energy that is stored in and released from the bonds between atoms.*

When fossil fuels burn, the chemical bonds between the atoms that make up the fossil fuel break apart. When this happens, chemical energy transforms to thermal energy. This energy is used to heat water and to form steam. The steam is used to turn a turbine, which is connected to a generator that generates electric energy.

A drawback of fossil fuels is that they introduce harmful waste products such as sulfur dioxide and carbon dioxide into the environment. Sulfur dioxide in the air creates acid rain. Scientists are searching for replacement fuels that do not harm the environment.

Fossil fuels are not the only source of chemical energy. Chemical energy also is stored in the foods you eat. Your body converts the energy stored in chemical bonds in food into the kinetic energy of your moving muscles and into the electric energy that sends signals through your nerves to your brain.

Nuclear Energy

The majority of energy on Earth comes from the Sun. A process that occurs in the Sun, called nuclear fission, joins the nuclei of atoms, releasing large amounts of energy. On Earth, nuclear energy plants such as the one shown in **Figure 4** break apart the nuclei of certain atoms using a process called nuclear fission. Nuclear fusion and nuclear fission release **nuclear energy**—*energy stored in and released from the nucleus of an atom.*

Nuclear fission produces a large amount of energy from just a small amount of fuel. However, the process produces radioactive waste that is hazardous and difficult to dispose of safely.

Potential and Kinetic Energy Combined

Moving objects have kinetic energy. Objects such as wind turbine blades and particles such as molecules, ions, atoms, and electrons often have kinetic and potential energies.

Mechanical Energy

The sum of potential energy and kinetic energy in a system of objects is **mechanical energy.** Mechanical energy is the energy a system has because of the movement of its parts (kinetic energy) and because of the position of its parts (potential energy). An object such as the wind turbine shown in **Figure 5** has mechanical energy because the parts that make up the system have potential energy and kinetic energy. A rotating blade has kinetic energy because of its motion, and it has gravitational potential energy because of its distance from Earth's surface.

Thermal Energy

The particles that make up the wind turbine also have thermal energy. **Thermal energy** *is the sum of the kinetic energy and potential energy of the particles that make up an object.* Although you cannot see the individual particles move, they vibrate back and forth in place. This movement gives the particles kinetic energy. The particles also have potential energy because of the distance between particles and the charge of the particles.

Geothermal Energy

The particles in Earth's interior contain great amounts of thermal energy—geothermal energy. In geothermal energy plants such as the one shown in **Figure 6,** thermal energy is used to heat water and to turn it into steam. The steam turns turbines in electric generators, converting the geothermal energy to electric energy. Geothermal energy produces almost no pollution.

Figure 5 The entire wind turbine has mechanical energy. The particles that make up the wind turbine have thermal energy.

Figure 6 Geothermal energy plants convert thermal energy of the particles deep inside Earth to electric energy. Geothermal plants must be built in places where molton rock is close to Earth's surface. The states with the most geothermal plants are Alaska, Hawaii, and California.

Plan Imagine you are an engineer who designs electric power plants. Choose one of the following sequence of events that produces electricity: 1) geothermal energy, 2) gravitational potential energy, or 3) mechanical energy. In the space below, draw a diagram that illustrates the equipment needed to produce electricity. Label each device and briefly describe its function. Use other books or the Internet to research your plans.

Energy from Waves

Have you ever seen waves crash on a beach? When a big wave crashes, you hear the sound of the impact. The movement and the sound result from the energy carried by the wave. Waves are disturbances that carry energy from one place to another. Waves move only energy, not matter.

Sound Energy

If you clap your hands together, you create a sound wave in the air. Sound waves move through matter. **Sound energy** *is energy carried by sound waves.* Some animals such as the bat shown in **Figure 7** emit sound waves to find their prey. The length of time it takes sound waves to travel to their prey and echo back tells the bat the location of the prey it is hunting.

Seismic Energy

You probably have seen news reports showing photographs of damage caused by earthquakes that is similar to the damage shown in **Figure 8.** Earthquakes occur when Earth's tectonic plates, or large portions of Earth's crust, suddenly shift position. The kinetic energy of the plate movement is carried through the ground by seismic waves. **Seismic energy** *is the energy transferred by waves moving through the ground.* Seismic energy can destroy buildings and roads.

Figure 7 Bats use sound energy to detect the location of their prey.

Figure 8 The seismic energy of a large earthquake caused severe damage to this building in San Francisco, California. In some locations, newly constructed homes and buildings are built to withstand many earthquakes.

Radiant Energy

When you listen to the radio, use a lamp to read, or call someone on your cell phone, do you think of waves? Electromagnetic waves are electric and magnetic waves that move perpendicular to each other, as shown in **Figure 9.** Radio waves, light waves, and microwaves are electromagnetic waves, as shown in **Figure 10.** Some electromagnetic waves can travel through solids, liquids, gases, and vacuums. *The energy carried by electromagnetic waves is* **radiant energy.**

The Sun's energy is transmitted to Earth by electromagnetic waves. Photovoltaic (foh toh vohl TAY ihk) cells, also called solar cells, are made of a special material that transforms the radiant energy of light into electric energy. You might have used a solar calculator. It does not need batteries because it has a photovoltaic cell. Photovoltaic cells also are used to provide energy to satellites, offices, and homes. Because so much sunlight hits the surface of Earth, the supply of solar energy is plentiful. Also, using solar energy as a source for electric energy produces almost no waste or pollution. However, only about 1 percent of the electric energy used in the United States comes directly from the Sun.

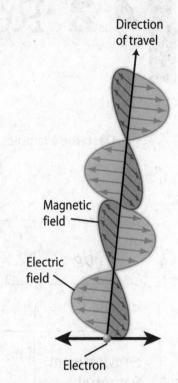

Direction of travel

Magnetic field

Electric field

Electron

Figure 9 Electromagnetic waves carry radiant energy.

Go Online!   Tutor

Figure 10 Radiant energy is carried by different forms of electromagnetic waves.

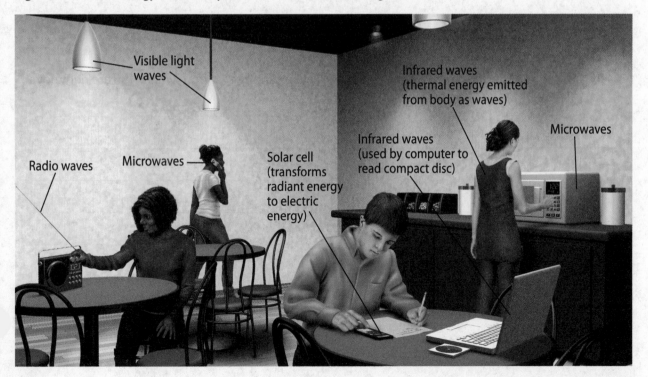

Visible light waves

Infrared waves (thermal energy emitted from body as waves)

Microwaves

Radio waves

Microwaves

Solar cell (transforms radiant energy to electric energy)

Infrared waves (used by computer to read compact disc)

4.2 Review

Describe examples of each type of energy listed below. Review the lesson if you need help.

Type	Example of Use
Kinetic	
Gravitational Potential	
Chemical	
Sound	
Radiant	

Connect it! **Identify** three examples of energy you can observe from where you are right now.

_____

_____

_____

_____

_____

_____

Use Vocabulary

1. **Distinguish** between kinetic energy and potential energy.

Apply the Essential Questions

2. **Compare** seismic and sound energies.

3. **Explain** how hydroelectric energy plants convert potential energy into kinetic energy.

4. **Interpret Graphics** In the graphic organizer below, what word or phrase could replace the question mark?

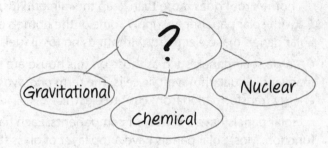

Gravitational

Chemical

Nuclear

 H.O.T. Questions (Higher Order Thinking)

5. **Critique** You overhear someone say, "I'm going to nuke it" when referring to cooking food in a microwave oven. Explain why this terminology is incorrect.

6. **Assess** Which forms of energy are involved when you turn on a desk lamp and the bulb becomes hot?

Using Solar Panels

Energy from Sunlight

A home's roof does more than keep the rain out! It's equipped with solar panels that supply some of the home's energy needs. Solar panels make electricity without using fossil fuels.

Large solar panels such as those on this house are made up of many individual photovoltaic cells. The term *photovoltaic* refers to an energy transformation from light to electricity.

Solar panels have a variety of components. Each has an important function. Most solar panels have a top layer of glass that protects the parts inside the panel. Under the glass is an anti-reflective layer that helps the panel absorb sunlight rather than reflect it. On the back is a layer that keeps the solar panel from getting too hot.

These solar panels contain materials that can transform energy from one form to another.

Sunlight

Anti-reflection coating

Doped semiconductor

Electric current

Cover glass

Back layer

Electric current flows from the solar panel to objects in the home that use electricity, such as lightbulbs, and back to the solar panel in a complete circuit.

The middle of the solar panel contains a large number of individual photovoltaic cells. That's where the energy occurs! In a photovoltaic cell, sunlight strikes a doped semiconductor, or a semiconductor with atoms of other elements that increase conductivity. The energy in the sunlight knocks electrons in the doped semiconductor out of their positions and gives them energy to move. When electrons move, they create an electric current. Wires attached to the doped semiconductor allow the flowing electrons, or electric current, to travel to the electric circuits within the home and back again.

It's Your Turn!

RESEARCH AND REPORT How might solar panels affect your life? How is new technology making solar panels less expensive to make and more efficient to use? Research to find out and then share what you learn with the rest of your class.

Space Aliens? It might look like an invasion from space, but these solar-powered cars are in a race. Large solar panels across the width of the cars transform radiant energy from the Sun into electric energy that moves the cars. Using this photo, discuss with a partner why most of the cars look so similar.

Write your response in your interactive notebook.

 LAB Manager

Go to your Lab Manual or visit connectED.mcgraw-hill.com to perform the labs for this lesson.

MiniLAB: *How do energy transformations work for you?*
TEKS 7.4(A)

Skill Practice: *How can you transfer energy to make a vehicle move?*
TEKS 7.1(A); 7.2(A), (E); 7.4(A), (B); 7.7(A)

Explore Activity

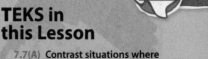

How far will it go?

Suppose you are hired to design a roller coaster. Could you make it any shape you wanted? Could a hill in the middle of the ride be higher than the starting point?

Procedure

1. Read and complete a lab safety form.

2. **Tape** one end of a **foam track** to the wall or other vertical object so the end is 70–100 cm above the floor.

3. Tape the other end of the track to a chair so the track forms a *U* shape. Predict how far a **marble** will travel if you release it at the top of the track on the wall side. Record your prediction in your Lab Manual or interactive notebook. Then test your prediction. Use a **meterstick** to measure the height from which you drop the marble and the height to which it rises.

4. Repeat step 3 several times using different heights above and below the starting point. Record your observations.

Think About This

1. How does the height to which the marble rises relate to the height at which it started?

2. Do you think a hill at the end of the roller coaster ride could be higher than the starting point of the coaster car? Why or why not? Explain in terms of potential and kinetic energy.

TEKS in this Lesson

7.7(A) Contrast situations where work is done with different amounts of force to situations where no work is done, such as moving a box with a ramp and without a ramp or standing still.

7.7(B) Illustrate the transformation of energy within an organism, such as the transfer from chemical energy to heat and thermal energy in digestion.

Also covers Process Standards: 7.1(A); 7.2(A), (C), (E); 7.3(A); 7.4(A), (B)

? Essential Questions

- What is work, and what is needed to do work?
- In what ways can energy be transformed in an organism?

abc Vocabulary

energy transformation
law of conservation of energy
work

Figure 1 Electric energy is transformed into thermal energy in the heat lamp. Thermal energy from the lamp is transferred to the zebra.

Go Online! Tutor

Energy Transformations TEKS 7.7(B)

Different types of electric energy plants supply the energy you use in your home and school. **Energy transformation** *is the conversion of one form of energy to another,* as shown in **Figure 1.** The electric energy in the wiring of the heat lamp is transformed into thermal energy.

Energy also is transferred when it moves from one object to another. When energy is transferred, the form of energy does not have to change. For example, the radiant energy from the heat lamp is transferred to the zebra where the energy is transformed to thermal energy.

Energy Conservation

Suppose you turn on a light switch. The radiant energy coming from the bulb had many other forms before it shined in your eyes. It was electric energy in the lamp's wiring and chemical energy in the fuel at the electric energy plant. **The law of conservation of energy** *says that energy can be transformed from one form to another, but it cannot be created or destroyed.* Even though energy can change forms, the total amount of energy in the universe does not change. It just changes form.

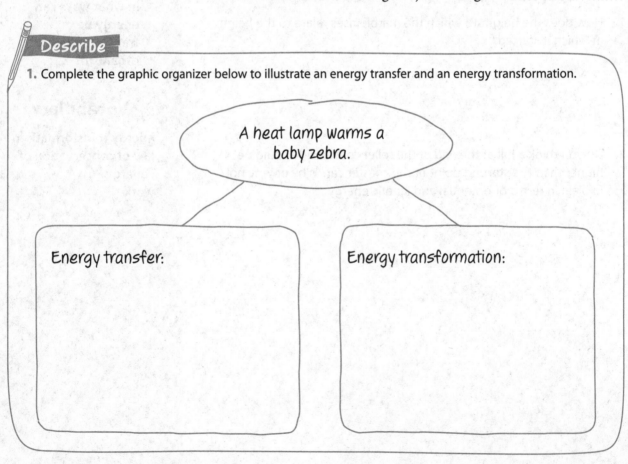

Describe

1. Complete the graphic organizer below to illustrate an energy transfer and an energy transformation.

A heat lamp warms a baby zebra.

Energy transfer:

Energy transformation:

GPE high
KE low

KE high
GPE low

GPE = gravitational potential energy
KE = kinetic energy

Roller Coasters

Have you ever thought about the energy transformations that occur on a roller coaster such as the one shown in **Figure 2?** Most roller coasters start by pulling you to the top of a big hill. When you go up a hill, the distance between you and Earth increases and so does your potential energy. Next, you race down the hill. You move faster and faster. The gravitational potential energy is transformed into kinetic energy. At the bottom of the hill, your gravitational potential energy is small, but you have a lot of kinetic energy. This kinetic energy is transformed back into gravitational potential energy as you move up the next hill.

Figure 2 When you ride a roller coaster, your gravitational potential energy is transformed into kinetic energy and back into gravitational potential energy.

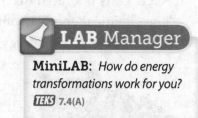

LAB Manager

MiniLAB: *How do energy transformations work for you?*
TEKS 7.4(A)

Describe

2. **Contrast** the energy present at different points of a roller-coaster ride.

At the top of the hill	Near the bottom of the hill
Gravitational potential energy:	Gravitational potential energy:
Kinetic energy:	Kinetic energy:

Figure 3 To carry out life processes, humans and other animals transform the chemical energy of plants into other forms of energy.

Radiant energy (Sun)

Chemical energy (plant molecules)

Electric Energy Plants

About 300 million years ago, plants carried out photosynthesis, just like plants do today. These ancient plants stored radiant energy from the Sun as chemical energy in their molecular bonds. After they died, the plants became buried under sediment. After much time and pressure from the sediments above them, these plants changed into fossil fuels. When electric energy plants burn fossil fuels, they transform the chemical energy from the molecules that were made by plants that lived millions of years ago. That chemical energy is transformed into the electric energy that you use in your home and school.

Electric energy plants also transform solar, wind, geothermal, and hydroelectric energy in electric energy.

Plants and the Body

When a plant carries on photosynthesis as shown in **Figure 3**, it transforms radiant energy from the Sun into chemical energy. The chemical energy is stored in the bonds of the plant's molecules. When you eat the broccoli, your body breaks the chemical bonds in the molecules that make up the broccoli. This releases chemical energy that your body transforms into energy your body needs, such as energy for movement, temperature control, and other life processes.

A *Closer* Look > at Energy Transformations in Organisms

You might not think of yourself as an electrically operated machine, but you are. The chemical energy from your food transforms into electric energy, which your body uses to control the function of your body's cells. Nerve cells also transform electrical energy. Nerves generate electric impulses that communicate information to your brain or carry a signal from your brain to a muscle to initiate its movement. Electric energy transformation is essential for sensing your environment as well as for reacting to that environment.

Movement is essential to life and requires energy. Muscle movements occur when chemical energy transforms into mechanical energy. This muscle movement is important and requires a great deal of energy. Special molecules within cells store chemical energy, then release it as thermal energy when needed. Muscle cells function by converting thermal energy into mechanical energy. This mechanical energy allows organisms to move, walk, and run.

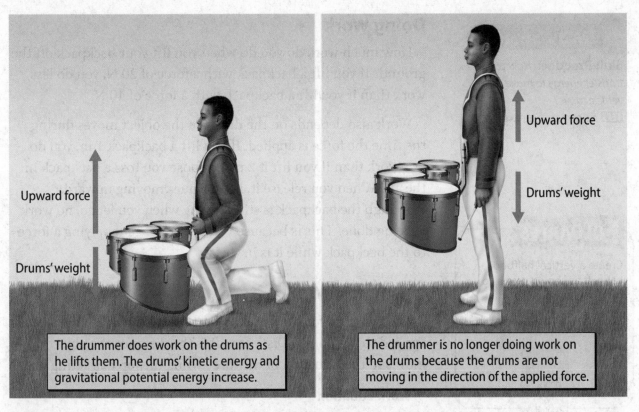

The drummer does work on the drums as he lifts them. The drums' kinetic energy and gravitational potential energy increase.

Upward force

Drums' weight

The drummer is no longer doing work on the drums because the drums are not moving in the direction of the applied force.

Upward force

Drums' weight

Figure 4 The boy does work on the drums when he lifts them. After the drums are in place, no work is being done.

Energy and Work TEKS 7.7 (A)

When you study for a test, do you do work? It might seem like it, but it would not be work as defined by science. **Work** *is the transfer of energy that occurs when a force makes an object move in the direction of the force while the force acts on the object.* Recall that forces are pushes or pulls. When you lift an object, you transfer energy from your body to the object. As the boy lifts the drums in **Figure 4,** they move and have kinetic energy. As the drums get higher off the ground, they gain gravitational potential energy. The boy has done work on the drums.

On the right in **Figure 4,** the boy is standing still with his drums lifted in place. Because he is not moving the drums, he is not doing work. To do work on an object, an object must move in the direction of the force. Work is done only while the force is moving the object.

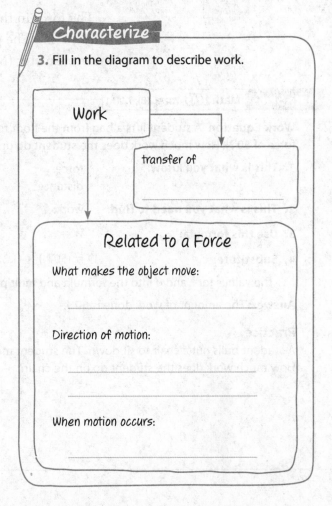

Characterize

3. Fill in the diagram to describe work.

Work

transfer of
_____

Related to a Force

What makes the object move:

_____

Direction of motion:

_____

_____

When motion occurs:

_____

FOLDABLES®

Create a vertical halfbook. Label it as shown. Use it to summarize in your own words the relationship between work and energy.

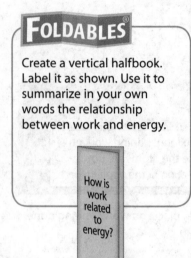

How is work related to energy?

Doing Work

How much work do you do when you lift your backpack off the ground? If you lift a backpack with a force of 20 N, you do less work than if you lift a backpack with a force of 40 N.

Work also depends on the distance the object moves during the time the force is applied. If you lift a backpack 1 m, you do less work than if you lift it 2 m. Suppose you toss a backpack in the air. When you release it, it continues moving upward. Although the backpack is still moving when you let go, no work is being done. This is because you are no longer applying a force to the backpack while it is in the air.

Calculating Work

The equation for work is shown below. *Force* (*F*) is the force applied to the object. *Distance* (*d*) is the distance the object moves in the direction of the force while the force is acting on it.

Work Equation

work (in joules) = force (in newtons) × distance (in meters)

$$W = Fd$$

The force in the equation is in newtons (N), and distance is in meters (m). The product of newtons and meters is a newton-meter (N•m). A newton-meter is a joule (J).

Math Skills   **Math TEKS** 7.1(A), (B); 7.3(A)

Work Equation A student lifts a bag from the floor to his or her shoulder 1.2 m above the floor, using a force of 50 N. How much work does the student do on the bag?

1. **This is what you know:**
   force: $F = 50$ N
   distance: $d = 1.2$ m

2. **This is what you need to find:** work: W

3. **Use this formula:** $W = Fd$

4. **Substitute:** $W = (50$ N$) \times (1.2$ m$) =$ **60 N•m 60 J**

   the values for F and d into the formula and multiply

Answer: The amount of work done is **60 J**.

Practice

A student pulls out a chair to sit down. The student moves the chair 0.75 m with a force of 20 N. How much work does the student do on the chair?

Check   Tutor

Go Online! ✓ 💬

Energy and Heat

Have you ever heard the phrase burning rubber? The tires of race cars are made of rubber. The tires and the road are in contact, and they move past each other very fast. Recall that friction is a force between two surfaces that are in contact with each other. The direction of friction is in the opposite direction of the motion.

Friction between a car's tires and the road causes some of the kinetic energy of the tires to transform into thermal energy. If race cars are going really fast, thermal energy in the tires causes the rubber to give off a burnt odor.

In every energy transformation and every energy transfer, some energy is transformed into thermal energy, as shown in **Figure 5.** This thermal energy is transferred to the surroundings. Thermal energy moving from a region of higher temperature to a region of lower temperature is called heat. Scientists sometimes call this heat waste energy because it is not easily used to do useful work.

Figure 5 Thermal energy is released to the surroundings during energy transformations and energy transfers in the engines of race cars.

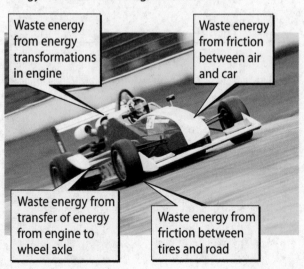

Waste energy from energy transformations in engine

Waste energy from friction between air and car

Waste energy from transfer of energy from engine to wheel axle

Waste energy from friction between tires and road

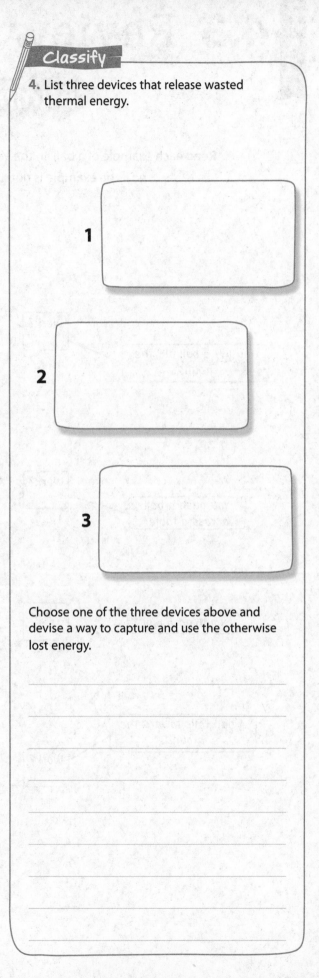

Classify

4. List three devices that release wasted thermal energy.

1

2

3

Choose one of the three devices above and devise a way to capture and use the otherwise lost energy.

4.3 Review

Summarize it!

Read each example of a ball. In the *Work* box, write *yes* if the example is work and *no* if the example is not. Explain your answers. **TEKS** 7.7(A)

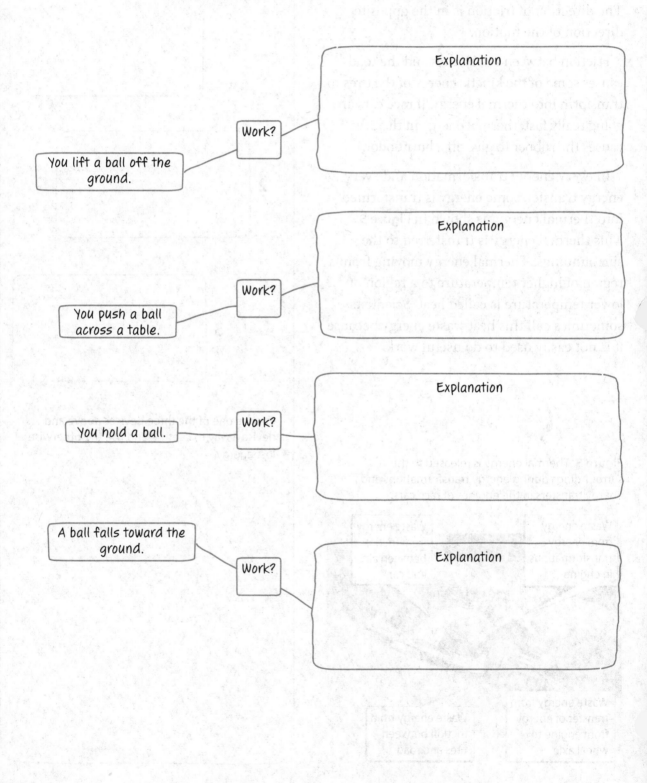

You lift a ball off the ground. — Work? — Explanation

You push a ball across a table. — Work? — Explanation

You hold a ball. — Work? — Explanation

A ball falls toward the ground. — Work? — Explanation

Energy Transformations and Work

Use Vocabulary

1. A(n) _____ occurs when energy is converted from one form into another. **TEKS** 7.7(B)

Apply the Essential Questions

2. **Describe** the energy transformations that occur during digestion. **TEKS** 7.7(B)

_____

_____

_____

3. **Contrast** a situation where work is done and a situation where work is not done. **TEKS** 7.7(A) supporting

_____

_____

_____

H.O.T. Questions (Higher Order Thinking)

4. **Interpret Graphics** Complete the graphic organizer below.

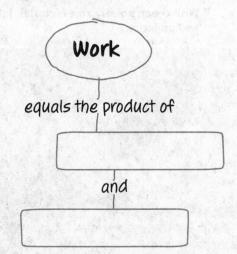

5. **Compare** Describe the energy transformations that are similar in the human body and in fossil fuel electric energy plants. **TEKS** 7.7(B)

_____

_____

_____

_____

6. **Explain** A coach sets up a tug-of-war between two evenly matched teams, Team A and Team B. Both teams pull against the rope as hard as they can, but the rope does not move. Is any work being done? Why or why not? **TEKS** 7.7(A) supporting

_____

_____

_____

_____

| Math Skills | Math **TEKS** 7.1(A), (B); 7.3(A) |

Work Equation

7. Humpty Dumpty weighs 400 N. He falls off a wall 3 m high. How much work was done by gravity on Humpty Dumpty?

Go Online! Check ✓ Tutor 💬

What is horsepower?

You might be surprised to learn that there is a connection between a horse and a steam engine.

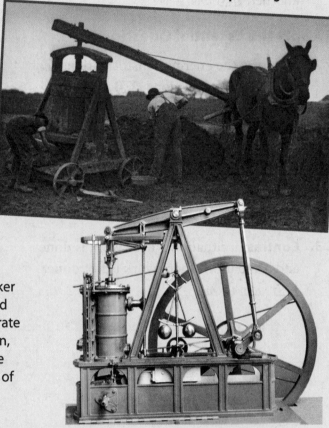

▼ A draft horse powering a mill

In the early 1700s, horses did work on farms, powered factories, and moved vehicles. When people spoke of power, they literally were referring to horsepower. It was natural, then, for James Watt to think in terms of horsepower when he set out to improve the steam engine.

Watt did not invent the steam engine, but he realized its potential. He also realized that he needed a way to measure the power produced by steam engines. Watt knew that fabric mills used horses to power machinery. A worker attached a horse to a power wheel. The horse turned the wheel by walking in a 24-ft diameter circle at a rate of two revolutions per minute. From this information, Watt calculated the power supplied by a horse to be about 33,000 foot-pounds per minute. This amount of power became known as 1 horsepower (1 hp).

Watt succeeded in making better steam engines. Eventually, some steam engines produced more than 200 hp. Something unexpected happened as a result of all this power—life changed. More work was done, and it was done faster. The mills expanded. People moved to the cities to work in the mills. Populations of cities in industrialized countries increased. The world changed because steam engines easily could produce more horsepower than horses.

▲ An early steam engine developed by James Watt

▼ With cheap power came factories, jobs, and pollution.

It's Your Turn!

RESEARCH Steam engines are seldom used today. Research steam engines to determine why the power source that was key to the Industrial Revolution is no longer used.

INQUIRY

A machine? When you look at a unicycle, you probably don't see a collection of simple machines. However, just like the bicycle that you will read about in this lesson, a unicycle contains simple machines. How many simple machines are there? What can they do?

Write your responses in your interactive notebook.

🧪 **LAB** Manager

Go to your Lab Manual or visit connectED.mcgraw-hill.com to perform the labs for this lesson.

MiniLAB: *Does a wheel and axle make work easier?*
TEKS 7.1(A); 7.2(A), (C), (E); 7.4(A), (B); 7.7(A)

Lab: *Build a Powered Vehicle.*
TEKS 7.1(A); 7.2(B), (E); 7.4(A), (B); 7.7(A)

Explore Activity

TEKS 7.1(A); 7.2(A), (C), (E); 7.3 (A); 7.4(A), (B); 7.7(A)

Can you make work easier?

Have you ever tried to pull a nail from a board without a claw hammer? The claw hammer makes an impossible task quite easy. What are some other ways to make work easier?

Procedure

1. Read and complete a lab safety form.

2. Try to press the tip of a piece of **wire** into a **pine block** with your fingers. Then press a **thumbtack** with the same diameter into the block. Describe in your Lab Manual or interactive notebook how the amount of force you used differed in each case.

3. Screw an **eyehook** into the block as far as it will go. Start a **second eyehook** and then run your **pencil** through the hole in the eyehook. Use the pencil to screw in the eyehook. Compare the force you used in each case.

4. Tie a length of **string** around a **book.** Hook a **spring scale** through the string and lift the book to a height of 30 cm. Record the reading on the scale. Then use the spring scale to slide the book along a **ramp** to a height of 30 cm. Record the reading on the scale as you pull the book.

Think About This

1. How did the force needed in the first attempt of each task differ from the second attempt? What caused this difference?

_____

_____

_____

2. How did the amount of work you did using the two methods in each step compare and contrast? What was the same? What was different? Explain.

_____

_____

_____

_____

TEKS in this Lesson

7.7(A) Contrast situations where work is done with different amounts of force to situations where no work is done, such as moving a box with a ramp and without a ramp or standing still.

Also covers Process Standards: 7.1(A); 7.2(A), (B), (C), (E); 7.3(A); 7.4(A), (B)

 Essential Question

- In what ways can machines make work easier?

 Vocabulary

simple machine
inclined plane
wedge
screw
lever
wheel and axle
pulley
complex machine
efficiency

Figure 1 The bottle opener is a machine that transfers energy from your hand to the bottle cap.

Watch

Go Online!

> **Review Vocabulary**
>
> **plane** a flat, level surface

Figure 2 Simple machines do work using one movement. They can change the direction of a force or the amount of force required to perform a task.

Machines Transfer Mechanical Energy

TEKS 7.7(A)

Suppose you want to open a bottle like the one in **Figure 1.** If you use a bottle opener, you can easily pry off the top. A bottle opener is a machine. Many machines transfer mechanical energy from one object to another. The bottle opener transfers mechanical energy from your hand to the bottle cap. In this lesson, you will read about the ways in which machines transfer mechanical energy to other objects.

Simple Machines

Did you walk up a ramp this morning? Did you cut food with a knife? If you did, you used a simple machine. **Simple machines** *are machines that do work using one movement.* As shown in **Figure 2,** a simple machine can be an inclined plane, a screw, a wedge, a lever, a pulley, or a wheel and axle. Simple machines do not change the amount of work required to do a task; they only change the way work is done.

Inclined Plane Furniture movers often use ramps to move furniture into a truck. It is easier to slide a sofa up a ramp than to lift it straight up into the truck. An **inclined plane,** such as the ramp shown in **Figure 2,** *is a flat, sloped surface.* Ramps with gentle slopes require less force to move an object than steeper ramps, but you have to move the object a greater distance.

Wedge Like all knives, pizza cutters are a special type of inclined plane. A **wedge** *is an inclined plane that moves.* Notice how the wedge changes the direction of the input force.

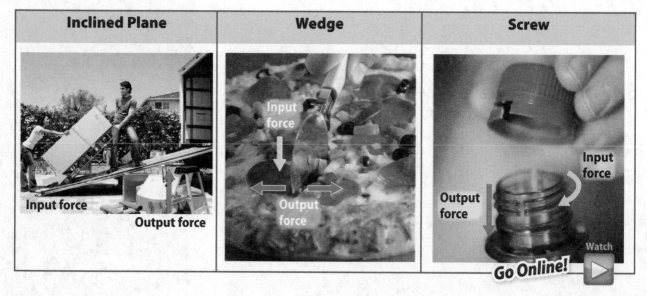

Inclined Plane	Wedge	Screw

Inclined Plane: Input force / Output force

Wedge: Input force / Output force

Screw: Input force / Output force

Watch

Go Online!

Screw A screw, such as a screw-top bottle, is a another special type of inclined plane. A **screw** *is an inclined plane wrapped around a cylinder.* A screw changes the direction of the force from one that acts in a straight line to one that rotates.

Lever The tab in **Figure 2** is a **lever,** *which is a simple machine that pivots around a fixed point.* The fixed point on a beverage can is where the finger tab attaches to the can. Bottle openers, scissors, seesaws, tennis racquets, and wheel barrows are other examples of levers. Levers decrease the amount of force required to complete a task, but the force must be applied over a longer distance.

Wheel and Axle A doorknob, a car's steering wheel, and a screwdriver are a type of simple machine called a **wheel and axle**—*a shaft attached to a wheel of a larger diameter so both rotate together.* The wheel and the axle are usually circular objects. The object with the larger diameter is the wheel, and the object with the smaller diameter is the axle. When you use a wheel and axle such as a screwdriver, you apply a small input force over a large distance to the wheel (screwdriver handle). This causes the axle (screwdriver shaft) to rotate a smaller distance with a greater output force.

Pulley Have you ever raised a flag on a flagpole or watched someone raise a flag? The rope that you pull goes through a **pulley,** *which is a grooved wheel with a rope or cable wrapped around it.* A single pulley, such as the kind on a flagpole, changes the direction of a force. A series of pulleys decreases the force you need to lift an object because the number of ropes or cables supporting the object increases.

LAB Manager

MiniLAB: *Does a wheel and axle make work easier?*

TEKS 7.1(A); 7.2(A), (C), (E); 7.4(A), (B); 7.7(A)

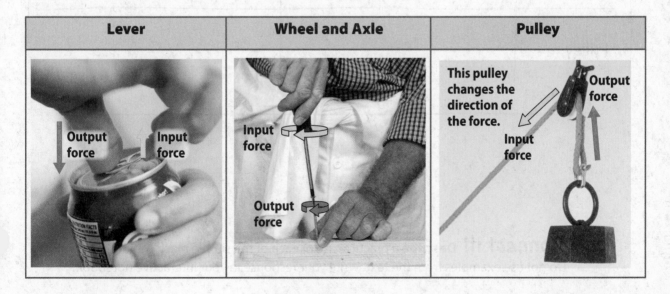

Lever	Wheel and Axle	Pulley

Lever: Output force / Input force

Wheel and Axle: Input force / Output force

Pulley: This pulley changes the direction of the force. Output force / Input force

Organize it!

Differentiate simple machines. **TEKS** 7.7(A)

Machine	Description	How It Makes Work Easier
Inclined plane		
Wedge		
Screw		
Lever		
Wheel and axle		
Pulley		

Connect it! **Describe** a practical use of each of the simple machine in the table above. Do not use examples from the text. Write your response in your interactive notebook.

Complex Machines

Bicycles such as the one in **Figure 3** are made up of many different simple machines. The pedal stem is a lever. The pedal and gears together act as a wheel and axle. The chain around the gear acts as a pulley system. *Two or more simple machines working together are a* **complex machine.** Complex machines such as bicycles use more than one motion to accomplish tasks.

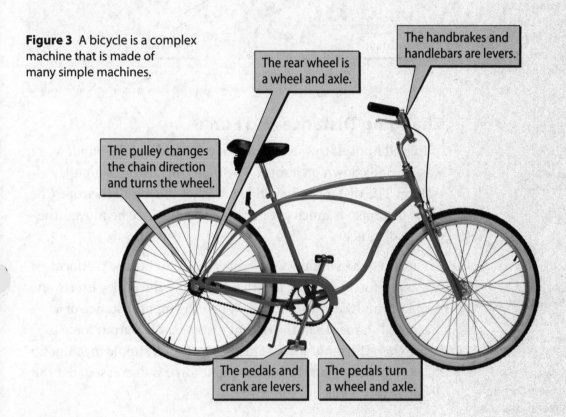

Figure 3 A bicycle is a complex machine that is made of many simple machines.

The handbrakes and handlebars are levers.

The rear wheel is a wheel and axle.

The pulley changes the chain direction and turns the wheel.

The pedals and crank are levers.

The pedals turn a wheel and axle.

Machines and Work [TEKS] 7.7(A)

Think of a window washer like the one in **Figure 4.** It takes a great amount of work to lift the washer's weight plus the weight of buckets of water, window-washing tools, and the platform into the air. The window washer is able to do this work because the pulley system that lifts him makes the work easier. Because two ropes are supporting the platform, the force required is half.

The work you do on a machine is called the input work. The work the machine does on an object is the output work. Recall that work is the product of force and distance. Machines make work easier by changing the distance the object moves or the force required to do work on an object.

LAB Manager

Lab: *Build a Powered Vehicle.*
[TEKS] 7.1(A); 7.2(B), (E); 7.4(A), (B); 7.7(A)

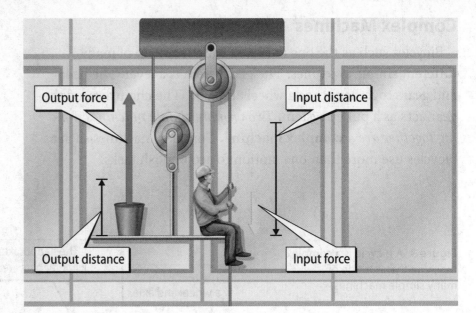

Figure 4 The window washer lifts his platform using a pulley system that increases the distance over which the force is exerted, decreases the input force needed, and changes the direction of the force.

Output force

Input distance

Output distance

Input force

Changing Distance and Force

To pull himself toward the top of the building, the window washer pulls down on a rope. The rope runs through a pulley system. The distance the window washer must pull the rope (the input distance) is much greater than the distance he moves (the output distance).

The force the window washer has to use to lift the platform (the input force) is much less than the force the pulley exerts on the platform (the output force). When the input distance of a machine is larger than the output distance, the output force is larger than the input force. This is true for all simple machines. Like other simple machines, the input force is decreased, but the distance it is applied is increased.

Changing Direction

Machines also can change the direction of a force. A window washer pulls down on the rope. The pulley system changes the direction of the force, which pulls the platform up.

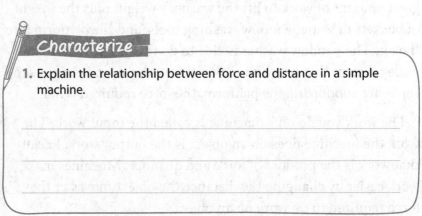

Characterize

1. Explain the relationship between force and distance in a simple machine.

STEMonline

Design and build a model transport system that uses simple and complex machines. Visit ConnectED for the **STEM** activity **Design a Transport System.** Resources

Go Online!

Efficiency

Suppose the window washer wants to buy a new pulley system. One way to compare machines is to calculate each machine's efficiency. **Efficiency** *is the ratio of output work to input work.* In other words, it is a measure of how much work put into the machine is changed into useful output work. Input and output work are measured in joules (J). Efficiency is expressed as a percentage by multiplying the ratio by 100%.

Word Origin

efficiency from Latin *efficere,* means "work out, accomplish"

Efficiency Equation

$$\text{efficiency (in \%)} = \frac{\text{output work (in J)}}{\text{input work (in J)}} \times 100\% = \frac{W_{out}}{W_{in}} \times 100\%$$

The window washer considers two systems that require 100 J of input work. The first pulley system does 90 J of output work on his platform. The other system does 95 J of output work. The efficiency of the first pulley system is (90 J/100 J) × 100% = 90%. The efficiency of the second one is (95 J/100 J) × 100% = 95%. The window washer decides to buy the second pulley system.

The efficiency of a machine is never 100%. Some work is always transformed into wasted thermal energy because of friction. The cars in **Figure 5** release most of the energy from their fuel as wasted thermal energy. One way to improve the efficiency of a machine is to lubricate the moving parts by applying a substance, such as oil, to them. This reduces the friction between the moving parts so less input work is transformed to waste energy.

Figure 5 No machine can be 100% efficient. A typical automobile engine is only about 30% efficient.

Infer

2. Using a lever, a person applies 70 N of force and moves the lever 1 m. This moves a 300 N rock at the other end by 0.25 m. What is the efficiency of the lever? In the space below, calculate your answer. Is your answer reasonable? Explain.

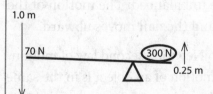

1.0 m

70 N   300 N

0.25 m

Figure 6 Newton's laws of motion help explain the forces applied by machines.

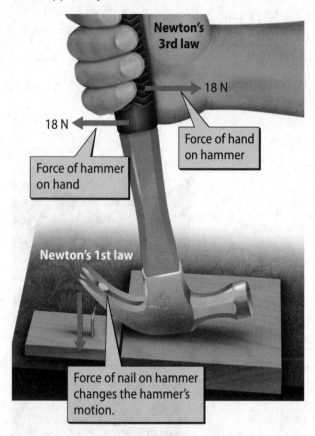

Newton's 3rd law

18 N

Force of hand on hammer

18 N

Force of hammer on hand

Newton's 1st law

Force of nail on hammer changes the hammer's motion.

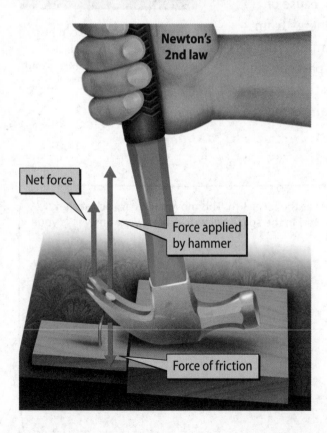

Newton's 2nd law

Net force

Force applied by hammer

Force of friction

Newton's Laws and Simple Machines

Newton's laws of motion explain how forces change the motion of objects. As you have read, machines apply forces on objects. For example, Newton's third law says that if one object applies a force on a second object, the second object applies an equal and opposite force on the first object.

As shown in the top part of **Figure 6,** when you use a hammer as a lever to pull out a nail, you apply a force on the hammer. The hammer applies an equal force in the opposite direction on your hand.

According to Newton's first law, the motion of an object changes when the forces that act on the object are unbalanced. When you pull on the hammer handle, the claws of the hammer apply a force on the nail. However, unless you pull hard enough, the nail does not move.

The nail does not move because there is another force acting on the nail—the force due to friction between the nail and the wood. Unless you pull hard enough, the force of friction balances the force the hammer exerts on the nail. As a result, the motion of the nail does not change, and the nail does not move.

If you pull hard enough, then the upward force the hammer applies on the nail is greater than the force of friction on the nail, as shown in the bottom part of **Figure 6**. Then the forces on the nail are unbalanced. The motion of the nail changes, and the nail moves upward.

According to Newton's second law of motion, the change in motion of an object is in the same direction as the total, or net, force on the object. The nail moves upward because the net force on the nail is upward.

4.4 Review

Go Online! 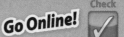 Check Virtual

Summarize it!

Think back to the Explore Activity, Step 3. **Contrast** how adding the pencil to the eyehook made the task easier. Did the amount of work change? **TEKS** 7.7(A)

_____

_____

_____

_____

_____

_____

_____

Illustrate picking up a box to the height of 1 m with and without a simple machine. Label how force and distance changes when a simple machine is used. **TEKS** 7.7(A)

Machines

Use Vocabulary

1. Contrast simple and complex machines.

_____

_____

_____

_____

Apply the Essential Question

2. Explain how machines make work easier.

TEKS 7.7(A) supporting

_____

_____

_____

_____

_____

3. Which is NOT a simple machine?

   A. inclined plane

   B. lever

   C. loop and hook

   D. wheel and axle

4. How does an inclined plane affect the work that is done on an object?

TEKS 7.7(A) supporting

   A. It decreases the input distance.

   B. It increases the input distance.

   C. It changes the direction of the input force.

   D. It changes the direction of the output force.

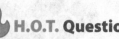 **H.O.T. Questions** (Higher Order Thinking)

5. Draw a machine that you could use to lift a bag of groceries from the floor to the counter using less force than if you lifted the bag with just your hands. Which simple machine(s) would you use? Does the machine change the amount of work?

TEKS 7.7(A) supporting

_____

_____

_____

6. Consider turning a bolt using a wrench. Will the work you do on the wrench be more or less than the work done by the wrench on the bolt? Explain.

TEKS 7.7(A) supporting

_____

_____

_____

_____

_____

Working Without Gravity

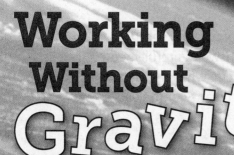

While doing repair work in space, astronauts face some unusual challenges. They wear bulky spacesuits and gloves that limit mobility and grip. They are also in a weightless environment where things don't react the same way they do on Earth.

To assist astronauts in conducting repairs, NASA designed special tools. These tools have handles and triggers that make them easier to grip. Some tools are specific to the task, while others are modified versions of tools you are probably familiar with.

To train astronauts for working in the microgravity environment of space, NASA built the Neutral Buoyancy Laboratory at Houston's Johnson Space Center. The laboratory, which simulates the weightless environment of space, is the world's largest indoor pool. The pool is 60 m long, 12 m deep, and contains 32.5 million L of water. Underwater at the Neutral Buoyancy Laboratory is where astronauts learn to use their special tools.

An astronaut on a space walk uses special tools developed by NASA.

An astronaut practices in the simulated microgravity environment in the Neutral Buoyancy Laboratory.

It's Your Turn!

RESEARCH a tool developed by NASA for use in space. What problem was the tool designed to overcome? Present your findings to your class.

Test-Taking Strategy

Calculations Some questions ask you to add, subtract, multiply, or divide in order to find an answer. Carefully read the question so that you will know exactly what calculation you need to perform in order to correctly answer the question.

Example

2 Since we are solving for "X", we should set up a simple equation as follows:

$$110 \text{ N} + X \text{ N} + 100 \text{ N} = 300 \text{ N}$$
$$X \text{ N} = 300 \text{ N} - 110 \text{ N} - 100 \text{ N}$$
$$X \text{ N} = 300 \text{ N} - 210 \text{N}$$
$$X \text{ N} = 90 \text{ N}$$

2 With how many newtons of force is the middle person pulling in the picture above? **TEKS** 7.7(C)

1 Carefully read the question. The question is asking us to find the force the middle person is pulling.

A 10 N

B 80 N

3 Find 90 N in the choices. The correct answer is choice **C**.

C 90 N

D 190 N

TIP: Feel free to write and work on calculations in the question columns of your test booklet or on a separate sheet of paper whenever you are allowed. Take your time and double check your steps to ensure you have performed your calculations correctly.

Multiple Choice

1

> Josh and Steven each have a box of books. Josh pushes his box of books 15 m along a straight hallway using a force of 10 N. Steven wants to push his box of books 25 m along the same hallway.

How much force, in Newtons, would Steven have to use in order to do the same amount of work as Josh? Record and bubble in your answer on the answer document. **TEKS** 7.7(A) *supporting*

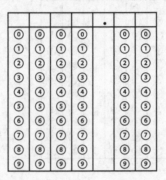

2

> Alicia and Taj are conducting an investigation to determine how much work is done when lifting a box. Alicia uses a force of 20 N to hold a box at a height of 2 m for 10 min. Taj uses a force of 20 Ns to lift a box to a height of 1 m in 10 s.

What was the total amount of work done by both students? Record and bubble in your answer on the answer document. **TEKS** 7.7(A) *supporting*; 7.2(C)

3

> The food you eat is made of complex and simple molecules. In digestion, food is broken down into simpler substances. The potential chemical energy of food is transformed into the energy used by the body to do work.

What evidence exists that shows that in the human body, during digestion, chemical energy is transformed into another form of energy? **TEKS** 7.7(B); 7.3(A)

A Heat is released that keeps the body warm.

B Waste materials are eliminated.

C Respiration or breathing takes place.

D Food is chewed into smaller pieces.

4 A tropism is the turning motion of a plant. This motion is a response to force or stimulus. Jake designed an experiment to demonstrate a tropism. To safely conduct the experiment, Jake wore goggles, apron, and gloves. He placed moist cotton in a petri dish. He then placed three bean seedlings on the cotton and covered the dish. Three days later he observed the results and made a report. In his report, he made the diagram below that shows two petri dishes containing damp cotton and bean seeds. When his experiment was finished, he disposed of his materials according to the direction of his teacher. **TEKS** 7.7(C); 7.4(B)

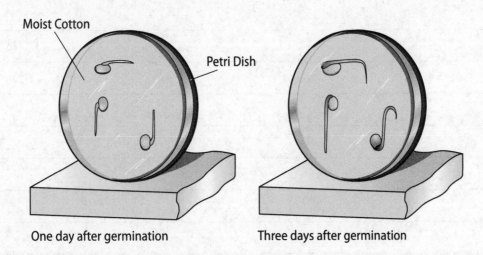

One day after germination   Three days after germination

Three days after germination, what did Jake's experiment illustrate?

A a tropism caused by chemical fertilizers

B a tropism caused by touch

C a tropism caused by the force of gravity

D a tropism caused by the light

My Notes

TEKS Strand 4
Earth and Space

Texas Fun Fact

Did You Know? Big Bend National Park is home to some BIG fossils! In 1971, Douglas Lawson, a graduate student from the University of Texas, discovered a new fossil, the Quetzalcoatlus (KWET-zal-koh-AT-lus), at Big Bend National Park. The Quetzalcoatlus is considered to be one of the largest known flying reptiles of all time. It had a wingspan nearly 30 feet from tip to tip making it about the size of a small jet! This giant reptile soared over Texas about 65 million years ago. Thanks to fossil discoveries like the Quetzalcoatlus, scientists continue to get a better, more accurate glimpse into Earth's past!

CHAPTER 5

Weather and Its Impacts

The **BIG** Idea

Earth's systems are impacted by slow processes as well as catastrophic events.

Clouds

Four friends talked about the clouds over the ocean. They each had different ideas about what makes up clouds over the ocean. This is what they said:

Jess: I think clouds over the ocean are made up of tiny droplets of freshwater.

Max: I think clouds over the ocean are made up of tiny droplets of salt water.

Raul: I think clouds over the ocean are made up of freshwater in the form of water vapor.

Mika: I think clouds over the ocean are made up of freshwater in the form of water vapor and evaporated salt.

Which friend do you agree with the most? _____ Explain your ideas about clouds that form over the ocean.

The Atmosphere

What is happening here? On a day like this, it might seem as though the atmosphere is calm. There does not seem to be much movement, and nothing seems to be changing. Actually, there is more happening than you can see. What is happening?

 Write your response in your interactive notebook.

 LAB Manager

Go to your Lab Manual or visit connectED.mcgraw-hill.com to perform the labs for this lesson.

MiniLAB: *What does it take to make a cloud?*

TEKS 7.1(A); 7.2(A), (C), (E); 7.4(A), (B)

Explore Activity

TEKS 7.2(A), (C); 7.4(A)

Can you keep it straight?

Although you cannot feel it, Earth is spinning. A person at the equator is moving at nearly 1,600 km per hour! This rotation affects the ocean, the atmosphere, and wind. How can drawing a line illustrate how Earth's rotation affects water and air movement?

Procedure

1. Use **tape** and **paper** to cover the top of a **turntable.**

2. In your Lab Manual or interactive notebook, predict what type of line you will be able to draw on the paper as the turntable rotates.

3. Have your partner spin the turntable in a counterclockwise direction. Use a **pencil** to draw a line from the center of the paper to its edge.

4. Observe, then record in your Lab Manual or interactive notebook, what happens as you draw the line.

Think About This

1. How does your prediction compare to your observation?

_____

_____

2. What does the pencil line represent?

_____

_____

3. What do you think is one thing that affects how air moves?

_____

_____

_____

TEKS in this Lesson

This lesson provides background support for the following TEKS:

7.8(A) Predict and describe how different types of catastrophic events impact ecosystems such as floods, hurricanes, or tornadoes

7.8(B) Analyze the effects of weathering, erosion, and deposition on the environment in ecoregions of Texas

Also covers Process Standards: 7.1(A); 7.2(A), (C), (E); 7.4(A), (B)

? Essential Questions

- What are the composition and structure of the atmosphere?
- What causes air to move?
- How do clouds form, and what are the three main types of clouds?

abc Vocabulary

air pressure
troposphere
convection
evaporation
condensation

1. Before you read this lesson, think about what you know about the atmosphere and weather. Record what you know about the atmosphere and weather in the first column. Then write what you want to learn about in the second column. After you have finished reading this lesson, fill in the final column with what you have learned.

What I Know	What I Want to Learn	What I Learned

Air's Composition

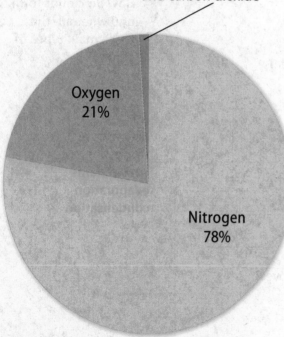

1% Other—including argon and carbon dioxide

Oxygen 21%

Nitrogen 78%

Figure 1 Air is made mostly of nitrogen and oxygen. There are also small amounts of other gases in the air.

Composition and Structure of the Atmosphere

What do you see when you look at the sky? You might see clouds, blue sky, lightning, or even a haze of air pollution. All of these things are in the atmosphere, a layer of gases that surrounds Earth.

What is in the air?

The atmosphere is mostly air, which is made of gas molecules. As shown in **Figure 1,** about four out of five molecules in the air are nitrogen gas (N_2). About one molecule out of five is oxygen gas (O_2). There are also small amounts of other gases, such as water vapor, argon (Ar) and carbon dioxide (CO_2). In addition to air, the atmosphere also contains tiny solid particles, such as dust and pollen. Some of the particles in the atmosphere even come from volcanic eruptions.

Layers of the Atmosphere

The characteristics and composition of Earth's atmosphere change with altitude. Molecules at the bottom of the atmosphere are packed together more closely than molecules higher in the atmosphere. This is because the weight of all the molecules above pushes down on the molecules at the bottom of the atmosphere. **Air pressure** *is the pressure that a column of air exerts on the air or surface below it.* When molecules in the air are packed closely together, it has high pressure. When molecules in the air are more spread out, it has low pressure.

Scientists divide the atmosphere into layers that have distinct characteristics. You can see these layers in **Figure 2.** *The* **troposphere** (TRO puh sfihr) *is the atmospheric layer closest to the Earth, extending from Earth's surface to about 10 km above it.*

Describe

2. What is the structure of Earth's atmosphere?

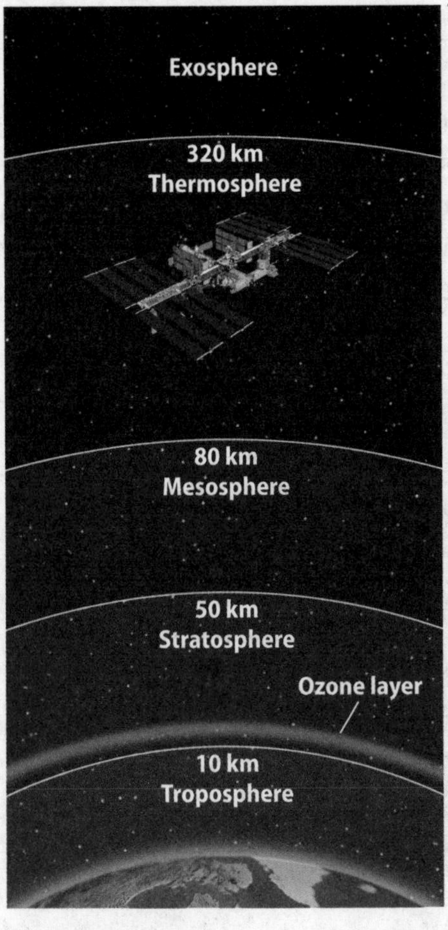

_____

_____

Figure 2 Scientists divide the atmosphere into five layers that have special characteristics. In some layers, temperature increases with altitude, but temperature decreases in other layers.

Go Online!   Watch

Exosphere

320 km
Thermosphere

80 km
Mesosphere

50 km
Stratosphere

Ozone layer

10 km
Troposphere

Upper layers The exosphere is thought of as outer space. It is the hottest layer of the atmosphere. The thermosphere is where the *International Space Station* orbits. As the altitude increases, so does the temperature in the thermosphere. In the mesosphere, temperature decreases with altitude. Meteors burn up in this layer. The upper layers contain very few molecules.

Stratosphere This layer extends to about 50 km above Earth's surface. Temperature increases with altitude. The ozone layer is a part of the stratosphere. It absorbs some of the Sun's most harmful rays, protecting living things on Earth.

Troposphere This is where you live and where weather happens. The majority of the atmosphere's molecules are in this layer. It's also where almost all types of clouds form. Air temperature decreases with altitude.

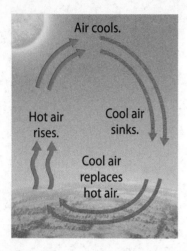

Figure 3 Cool air flows into a lower-pressure area, forcing the warmer air upward. After the air cools, it sinks toward Earth. As hot air rises, cool air replaces it.

Moving Air

Air pressure in the troposphere is always changing because air in the troposphere is always moving. Changing air pressures create wind patterns and cause weather events.

The Importance of the Sun

The Sun warms the rocks, soil, and water at Earth's surface. In turn, the Earth warms the air in the troposphere. Because warm air is less dense than cool air, it rises high in the troposphere. As the air moves higher, it cools. Denser, cooled air sinks. It flows toward the low-pressure area left by the rising warm air. The cooled air then warms and rises again. *The circulation of rising, less dense, warm air and sinking, more dense, cool air is called* **convection.** As illustrated in **Figure 3,** convection is responsible for the movement of air in the troposphere.

Local Winds

Some winds blow over short distances. A local wind results from air flowing from an area of higher air pressure to an area of lower air pressure. Differences in pressure result when the atmosphere is warmer in one area than in another.

Global Winds

At Earth's surface, atmospheric convection makes giant bands of winds, as shown in **Figure 4.** The westerlies generally blow from west to east, but Earth's rotation causes them to turn away from the equator. The trade winds generally blow east to west, but Earth's rotation causes them to turn toward the equator.

Word Origin

convection from Latin *convectionem,* means "the act of carrying"

Figure 4 Earth's rotation affects the direction of global winds. The westerlies blow from southwest to northeast in the northern hemisphere and from northwest to southeast in the southern hemisphere.

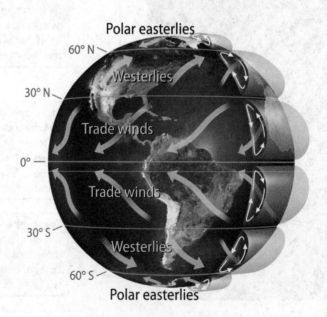

Clouds

Have you ever driven up a mountain into a cloud? A cloud is a group of water droplets or ice crystals so small that they float in the air. Clouds are important because they transport water to different areas of Earth.

Cloud Formation

How does the water vapor that makes clouds get into the sky? Most of it gets there by evaporation. Then, through the process of condensation, water vapor turns into clouds.

Evaporation *The process of a liquid, such as water, changing into a gas, such as water vapor, is called* **evaporation.** Thermal energy, usually from sunlight, heats water and causes it to evaporate. Water evaporates from the surfaces of bodies of water, such as oceans, lakes, and rivers, and from organisms, such as trees and humans.

Condensation *The process of water-vapor gas changing into liquid water is* **condensation.** Water vapor condenses around tiny particles of dust, pollen, or other air pollution. These water droplets are so small that they are able to float in the air. Many billions of these little water droplets make up a cloud. As more water condenses and the droplets increase in size, they can become so large that they fall from the sky as rain or snow.

LAB Manager

MiniLAB: *What does it take to make a cloud?*

TEKS 7.1(A); 7.2(A), (C), (E); 7.4(A), (B)

Science Use v. Common Use

condense

Science Use to change from vapor to liquid

Common Use to make smaller by compacting

Sequence

3. Complete the chart below with information about cloud formation.

Thermal energy from sunlight ⟩ ⟩

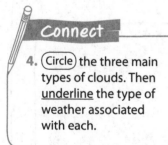

Cumulus clouds

Stratus clouds

Cirrus clouds

Figure 5 Cumulus, cirrus, and stratus clouds are recognizable by their different shapes. Can you find any of these cloud types in the sky today?

Connect

4. Circle the three main types of clouds. Then underline the type of weather associated with each.

Types of Clouds

There are many types of clouds. Each type has a specific appearance and forms at a specific height in the troposphere. The three main cloud types are shown in **Figure 5.**

Cumulus Clouds Puffy clouds that look like cotton balls are called cumulus (KYEW myuh lus) clouds. Some cumulus clouds are small and low with flat bases. These clouds indicate fair weather. Others grow taller and larger until they reach the top of the troposphere. They are called cumulonimbus (kyew myuh loh NIHM bus) clouds. These are the kind of clouds that make thunderstorms.

Stratus Clouds It might be hard for you to see individual stratus clouds or find the edges of them. They usually spread across most or all of the visible sky. Stratus clouds are low in the sky and can produce drizzle or light rain.

Cirrus Clouds High in the troposphere is where cirrus (SIHR us) clouds form. They are made of ice crystals that fan out in the wind and create long, wispy shapes. Cirrus clouds sometimes are called mare's tails because they look like a horse's tail. Cirrus clouds do not produce rain or snow.

Summarize it!

Summarize your understanding of Earth's atmosphere using the chart below. The topic is *Earth's Atmosphere*. Choose three main ideas you learned about in this lesson and provide specific details that explain each main idea.

Topic: _____

Main Ideas	Specific Details
	1. _____
	2. _____
	3. _____
	1. _____
	2. _____
	3. _____
	1. _____
	2. _____
	3. _____

Connect it! Observe the atmosphere outdoors today. Describe what you see and feel in your interactive notebook.

The Atmosphere

Use Vocabulary

1. The _____ is the atmospheric layer closest to Earth's surface.

2. The force exerted by air is called _____ .

Apply the Essential Questions

3. **Describe** how Earth's rotation affects global winds.

_____

_____

_____

_____

4. Which cloud is associated with thunderstorms?

   A. cirrus

   B. cumulonimbus

   C. easterlies

   D. westerlies

5. Local winds blow from

   A. an area of high pressure to an area of low pressure.

   B. an area of high pressure to another area of high pressure.

   C. an area of low pressure to an area of high pressure.

   D. an area of low pressure to another area of low pressure.

H.O.T. Questions (Higher Order Thinking)

6. **Analyze** where on Earth the convection cycle is the strongest.

_____

_____

_____

7. **Hypothesize** how an increase in air pollution might affect cloud formation.

_____

_____

_____

_____

8. **Predict** how global winds on Earth would be different if Earth did not rotate.

_____

_____

_____

_____

9. **Infer** where more clouds will form—over a desert or over the ocean. Why?

_____

_____

_____

_____

Do clouds have edges?

Air moving in the troposphere creates all types of weather, including storms such as this. Do you see how these storm clouds form a line behind the Dallas skyline? Why does this happen?

Write your response in your interactive notebook.

 LAB Manager

Go to your Lab Manual or visit connectED.mcgraw-hill.com to perform the labs for this lesson.

MiniLAB: *Can you measure what you cannot see?*
TEKS 7.1(A); 7.2(A), (C), (E); 7.3 (A); 7.4(A), (B)

Skill Practice: *How can you collect weather data and predict the weather?*
TEKS 7.1(A); 7.2(A), (C), (E); 7.3(A); 7.4(A), (B)

Explore Activity

TEKS 7.1(A); 7.2(A), (C), (E); 7.4(A), (B)

Will it drop, rise, or stay the same?

Weather changes when conditions of the atmosphere, including temperature and pressure, change. How are temperature and air pressure related?

Procedure

1. Read and complete a lab safety form.

2. Place a **thermometer strip** in an empty, dry **glass bottle.**

3. Wait about 30 s. Then read the temperature on the thermometer and record it in your Lab Manual or interactive notebook. Write a prediction about how the temperature will change if the pressure in the bottle changes.

4. Carefully read the directions on how to use an **air pump.**

5. Place the **plastic stopper** snugly into the opening of the bottle. Use the air pump to remove some of the air from the bottle.

6. Observe and record the temperature in the bottle.

Think About This

1. How does your prediction compare to your observations?

   _____

   _____

   _____

   _____

2. Describe how the pressure change affected the temperature.

   _____

   _____

   _____

3. Use your results to describe how you think weather changes when there is a decrease in air pressure or air temperature.

   _____

   _____

   _____

TEKS in this Lesson

This lesson provides background support for the following TEKS:

7.8(A) Predict and describe how different types of catastrophic events impact ecosystems such as floods, hurricanes, or tornadoes

7.8(B) Analyze the effects of weathering, erosion, and deposition on the environment in ecoregions of Texas

Also covers Process Standards: 7.1(A); 7.2(A), (C), (E); 7.3(A); 7.4(A), (B)

Essential Questions

- How is weather described?
- How does weather change?

Vocabulary

humidity
precipitation
air mass
pressure system
front

What is weather?

Do you check the forecast in the morning to know what the weather will be that day? Perhaps it will be scorching hot, and you will need light clothing. Or perhaps there will be storms and rain, as shown in **Figure 1,** and you will need a coat and an umbrella.

As the air in the troposphere moves around the world, all types of weather form. On any one day, some places are cool and rainy while others are hot and sunny. Weather is what is happening in the atmosphere at one time and in one place. Scientists describe weather using measurements of temperature, air pressure, humidity, wind speed and direction, and precipitation.

Air Temperature and Pressure

Weather reports usually start with temperature measurements. The temperature of the air is measured in degrees Fahrenheit or degrees Celsius using a thermometer. Air temperature depends on many factors, including the season, the amount of sunshine, the altitude, the wind, and the shape of the land.

Weather reports also include air-pressure measurements. Air pressure is measured using an instrument called a barometer. A barometer indicates whether air pressure is high or low. A change in air pressure is caused by the unequal heating of Earth's surface. Low air pressure indicates that stormy weather might be on the way. High air pressure usually indicates clear skies and calm weather.

Identify

1. What measurements are used to describe weather?

Weather Measurements

Figure 1 This dramatic photo shows the size and power of a thunderstorm over a city.

Humidity

The amount of water vapor in the air is the **humidity** (hyew MIH duh tee). Air with high humidity feels damp and muggy. Air that has low humidity feels drier. Warm air can hold more water vapor than cool air. This is why, in humid climates, air often feels muggy in summer but dry in winter.

Humidity levels often indicate the chance of precipitation. Higher humidity levels in an area of warm weather can increase the chance of thunderstorms and severe weather.

Wind Speed and Direction

Wind can be a light breeze or so strong it can knock down a person. Scientists usually describe wind using a combination of two measurements: the speed the wind is blowing and the direction from which the wind is blowing.

A wind sock is used to find wind direction. Wind speed can be measured with an instrument called an anemometer (a nuh MAH muh tur). Both are shown in **Figure 2.**

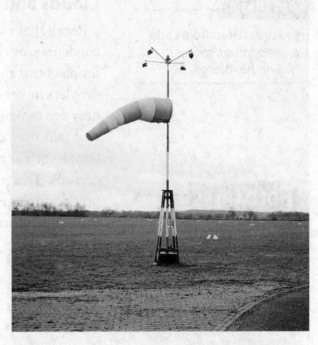

Figure 2 A wind sock shows the direction of wind, while an anemometer measures wind speed. This wind sock is pointing to the south, which means the wind is coming from the north.

LAB Manager

MiniLAB: *Can you measure what you cannot see?*
TEKS 7.1(A); 7.2(A), (C), (E); 7.3(A); 7.4(A), (B)
Skill Practice: *How can you collect weather data and predict the weather?*
TEKS 7.1(A); 7.2(A), (C), (E); 7.3(A); 7.4(A), (B)

Connect

2. What instruments are used to measure the weather variables below?

Air Temperature	Air Pressure
Wind Speed	Wind Direction

Word Origin

precipitation from Latin *praecipitatum*, means "falling headlong"

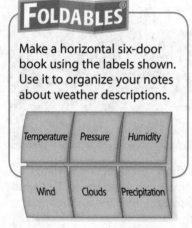
Clouds and Precipitation

Recall that clouds form as water vapor in the atmosphere condenses, or changes into a liquid. This forms the tiny water droplets that make clouds. When more water condenses, the droplets increase in size. They get heavier, and some become too heavy to remain in the sky. **Precipitation** *is liquid or solid water that falls from clouds to Earth's surface.* Sometimes the water is liquid, such as rain. Sometimes water vapor turns into solid ice crystals. This precipitation falls as snow. As shown in **Figure 3,** precipitation also can fall as sleet or freezing rain. It depends on the temperature of the air between a cloud and Earth's surface.

Changes in Weather

Have you ever stopped to wonder why the weather is different every day? It is because air is not all the same. Some air in the atmosphere is warm, and some is cold. Air pressure and humidity can differ, too. As air moves around the troposphere, it comes in contact with air that has different temperature, pressure, and humidity. This leads to weather changes.

Locate

3. Highlight what causes changes in weather.

Winter Precipitation

Figure 3 Snowflakes fall when the air temperature is below freezing both in the cloud and between the cloud and Earth's surface. Sleet forms when rain freezes on its way to Earth's surface. Freezing rain freezes after it reaches Earth and can form a layer of ice on everything.

Snow

28°
29°
30°
31°
31°
30°
30°

Sleet

34°
33°
32°
31°
30°
30°
30°
30°

Freezing rain

36°
36°
34°
33°
32°
31°
30°

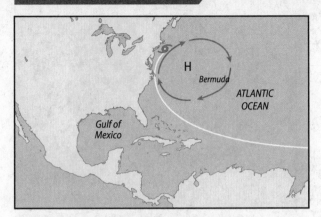

Normal High-Pressure System

When the high-pressure system around Bermuda is normal, a hurricane will move along the east coast of the United States, away from the high pressure.

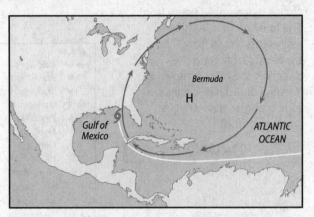

Larger High-Pressure System

When the high-pressure system around Bermuda is larger than usual, hurricanes move away from the high pressure into the Gulf of Mexico.

Air Masses

A large area of air that has uniform temperature, humidity, and pressure is called an **air mass.** An air mass can be several hundred kilometers across. Storms often occur where different air masses meet.

Pressure Systems

Because molecules always are moving in the troposphere, areas of high and low air pressure at Earth's surface change continually. *A moving air mass with a particular pressure is referred to as a* **pressure system.** Pressure systems can move over land and large bodies of water, such as the ocean. They also can move around one another, as shown in **Figure 4.**

High-Pressure Systems As you have read, high pressure results when molecules in the atmosphere are packed tightly together. Most high-pressure systems form when air high in the troposphere cools and sinks to Earth's surface. The sinking air pushes down the molecules below it. This creates high pressure. High-pressure systems are associated with clear skies.

Low-Pressure Systems Most low-pressure systems form when air heated at Earth's surface rises in the troposphere. As the air rises, fewer molecules remain at Earth's surface. This creates an area of low pressure where the warm air was. Low-pressure systems are associated with precipitation and storms.

Figure 4 A high-pressure system almost always exists near Bermuda. When it is larger than usual, it pushes hurricanes into the Gulf of Mexico. In 2004 and 2005, a larger-than-normal pressure system pushed hurricanes Katrina and Rita into the Gulf of Mexico and onto land.

Contrast

4. How do high-pressure and low-pressure systems differ?

_____

_____

_____

_____

_____

_____

_____

_____

_____

_____

_____

_____

Figure 5 The line of red half-circles represents a warm front. The line of blue triangles represents a cold front. The shapes point toward the direction the front is moving. The line of red half-circles and blue triangles represents a stationary front.

Go Online!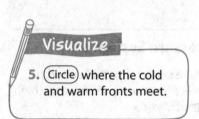

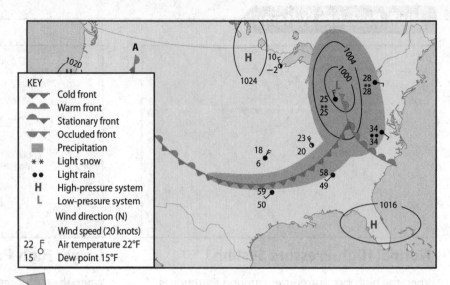

KEY

▼▼	Cold front
⌒⌒	Warm front
⌒▼	Stationary front
⌒▼	Occluded front
▨	Precipitation
✱ ✱	Light snow
• •	Light rain
H	High-pressure system
L	Low-pressure system
	Wind direction (N)
	Wind speed (20 knots)
22	Air temperature 22°F
15	Dew point 15°F

Visualize

5. Circle where the cold and warm fronts meet.

Word Origin

front from Latin *frontem,* means "forehead"

Fronts

If a weather map, such as the one in **Figure 5,** shows that a front will move through your area, you can expect a change in the weather. **Fronts** *are boundaries where two air masses meet.* Storms often form where fronts come together. If the two air masses are different, and if one front is moving fast, you sometimes can feel it pass. The temperature might change quickly, and the wind speed might increase. When a front moves in, there is often a change in the types of clouds in the sky. Fronts can move quickly over an area, or they can stay in place for days. A front that is not moving is called a stationary front.

Cold Fronts The area where a cold air mass replaces a warm air mass is called a cold front. As a cold front moves through an area, the temperature decreases. At the edge of the front where the cold and warm air masses meet, cumulus clouds, and sometimes thunderstorms, can form.

Warm Fronts Where a warm air mass replaces a cold air mass, a warm front forms. As a warm front moves through an area, the temperature and the humidity increase. Sometimes there will be thunderstorms at a warm front. Or, you might see stratus clouds as a warm front approaches and then cirrus clouds after it passes.

Discuss

6. How do fronts create changes in weather?

_____

_____

_____

5.2 Review

 Go Online! Check ✓

 Summarize it!

Use the chart below to show how cold fronts and warm fronts compare. Include as much information as you can.

Relationships

Cold Fronts		Warm Fronts
	↔	
	↔	
	↔	
	↔	
	↔	
	↔	

 Connect it! Explain why you might be interested in looking at weather measurements on a map showing places other than where you live. Write your response in your interactive notebook.

Weather

Use Vocabulary

1. A boundary where two different air masses meet is called a(n)

_____ .

2. The amount of water vapor in the air is called _____ .

Apply the Essential Questions

3. **Explain** two ways to measure wind.

_____

_____

_____

_____

_____

4. **Analyze** how a high-pressure system affects the path of storms.

_____

_____

_____

_____

🔥 H.O.T. Questions (Higher Order Thinking)

5. **Explain** why decreasing air pressure indicates an approaching storm.

_____

_____

_____

_____

6. **Interpret Graphics** What type of fronts are shown in the weather map? What weather is associated with these fronts? What type of front will reach the town, marked as a star, first?

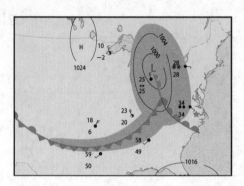

_____

_____

_____

_____

_____

7. **Evaluate** Imagine that it was warm and sunny a few hours ago, but now the weather has turned windy and cold. There are cumulonimbus clouds in the sky. Why is the weather changing?

_____

_____

_____

_____

_____

_____

_____

My Notes

INQUIRY

What makes a tornado?

The atmosphere can do some amazing things. This tornado, in Hodges, Texas, formed in a severe thunderstorm. It might last only a minute or two before its winds die down. Or it might last for hours! Most tornadoes occur in rural areas instead of in urban settings. Why do you think this is so?

Write your response in your interactive notebook.

LAB Manager

Go to your Lab Manual or visit connectED.mcgraw-hill.com to perform the lab for this lesson.

MiniLAB: *What is the "recipe" for a tornado?*

TEKS 7.2(E); 7.8(A)

Explore Activity

TEKS 7.1(A); 7.2(A); 7.4(B); 7.8(A)

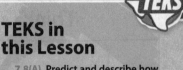

Can you produce lightning?

Have you experienced a severe thunderstorm? If so, you might know that lightning looks like a gigantic spark that lights up the sky. Lightning strikes when positive and negative particles move toward each other. How can you make your own lightning?

Procedure

1. Read and complete a lab safety form.

2. Inflate a round **balloon** until the balloon is nearly three-fourths full of air. Tie off the balloon. Use a **permanent marker** to write an X on one side of the balloon.

3. Darken the room. Let your eyes adjust to the darkness.

4. Rub the X back and forth on a **piece of wool** for 20 s.

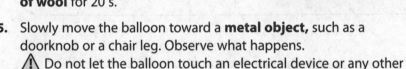

5. Slowly move the balloon toward a **metal object,** such as a doorknob or a chair leg. Observe what happens.
⚠ Do not let the balloon touch an electrical device or any other object while you are moving it toward the metal object.

Think About This

1. Describe what happened when the balloon touched the metal object.

_____

_____

_____

_____

2. Predict the impacts of lightning during a thunderstorm.

_____

_____

_____

TEKS in this Lesson

7.8(A) Predict and describe how different types of catastrophic events impact ecosystems such as floods, hurricanes, or tornadoes

Also covers Process Standards: 7.1(A); 7.2(A), (E); 7.4(A), (B)

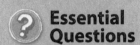

? Essential Questions

- What are the different types of catastrophic weather events?
- How do floods, hurricanes, and tornadoes impact ecosystems?

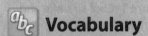

ᵃᵇᶜ Vocabulary

cumulonimbus cloud
thunderstorm
lightning
tornado
hurricane
storm surge
drought

1. Before you read this lesson, think about your experience with severe weather. Record your thoughts in the first column. Pair with a partner and discuss his or her thoughts. Write those thoughts in the second column. Then record in the third column what you both would like to share with the class.

Think	Pair	Share

Figure 1 Cool air sinks, and warm air rises, creating convection flow within clouds. This cumulonimbus cloud likely will form a thunderstorm.

Hot, moist air rises.

Water vapor cools, condenses, and falls as rain.

Thunderstorms TEKS 7.8(A)

If you have ever watched clouds, you know they constantly change. A cumulus cloud that becomes massive and tall is a towering, dark **cumulonimbus cloud**—*the type of cloud that can form thunderstorms. A* **thunderstorm** *is a weather event that includes rain, strong winds, thunder, and lightning.* The average thunderstorm is 25 km across and lasts only 30 minutes. However, some thunderstorms are huge and long-lasting, especially those that happen in the central part of the United States.

Thunderstorm Formation

When warm, moist air rises, it cools. Some of the cooled air sinks, starting the process of convection. Thunderstorms usually have many convection flows of air moving up and down. As the air cools, some of the water vapor in the air condenses, and clouds form. As shown in **Figure 1,** a huge cloud can grow as more warm, moist air rises and more water vapor condenses. When the water droplets become large enough, rain starts to fall. The largest thunderstorms form where a warm, moist air mass meets a cool, dry air mass.

Thunder and Lightning

You probably have heard thunder rumble and seen lightning flash across the sky. But do you know what causes them? **Lightning** *is electricity discharged within a cloud, between clouds, or between a cloud and the ground.* When a bolt of lightning rapidly heats air molecules, it produces a loud bang—thunder. Thunder happens at the same time as lightning. However, because light travels faster than sound, you often see a flash of light before you hear a rumble of thunder.

What causes lightning? Convection causes molecules to bump into each other, creating tiny electric charges. As illustrated in **Figure 2,** negative charges build up in some areas of a cloud and are attracted to positive charges. Lightning strikes when negatively and positively charged areas connect. Positive charges on Earth will flow to a high point and get close to negative charges in the sky. That is why lightning usually strikes mountaintops, tall trees, and buildings.

Thunderstorm Impacts

Although thunderstorms bring much-needed rain to many areas, they also can be dangerous. Lightning strikes can be deadly and sometimes start wildfires. Thunderstorms that drop rain quickly can cause flash flooding. Hail also is a danger to people, wildlife, and property. And the strong winds associated with thunderstorms can knock over trees and power lines.

Forecasting Weather forecasters monitor thunderstorms with weather satellites and use radar to track a storm's precipitation and winds, as shown in **Figure 3.** They use computer models to predict whether a thunderstorm is likely. A model combines recent weather data with hundreds of calculations.

Safety When weather models indicate a thunderstorm is likely, forecasters issue a thunderstorm watch. When there is a thunderstorm, they issue a thunderstorm warning. If a thunderstorm warning is issued for your area, go inside to stay safe.

Figure 2 Lightning strikes when negative charges within a cloud connect with positive charges on Earth's surface, in another area of the cloud, or in another cloud.

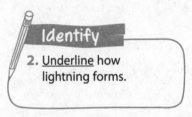

Identify

2. <u>Underline</u> how lightning forms.

Academic Vocabulary

monitor

(verb) to watch, to keep track of

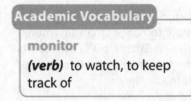

Figure 3 Weather forecasters use computer models to predict thunderstorms and other weather events.

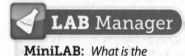
Tornadoes TEKS 7.8(A)

A violent, whirling column of air in contact with the ground is a **tornado,** *or sometimes called a twister.* Sometimes tornados are so powerful they can destroy everything in their paths. Tornadoes usually do not last long—sometimes just a few seconds—but some can last much longer.

Tornado Formation

Tornadoes can form during thunderstorms and hurricanes. Within a thunderstorm, air warmed at Earth's surface rises quickly. Sometimes rising air can rotate and form a funnel in the clouds. The spinning funnel grows downward and sometimes reaches Earth's surface.

More than 1,000 tornadoes occur each year in the United States. Tornadoes occur in all 50 states but are most common in the area called Tornado Alley, shown in **Figure 4.** The huge thunderstorms that happen in this area cause the tornadoes.

Tornado Impacts

When a tornado touches down, it pulls objects on Earth's surface up into the funnel. Strong, violent tornadoes can pick up houses, trees, and soil. The objects swirl around but eventually crash back to Earth. Tornadoes have even been known to pull up entire ponds and then rain fish from the sky! Because they can carry objects for several miles, tornadoes can move species to new locations.

LAB Manager

MiniLAB: *What is the "recipe" for a tornado?*
TEKS 7.2(E); 7.8(A)

Figure 4 The United States has more tornadoes than anywhere else on Earth. Most of them occur in the highlighted area called Tornado Alley.

Identify

3. Which states are a part of Tornado Alley?

Watch

Go Online!

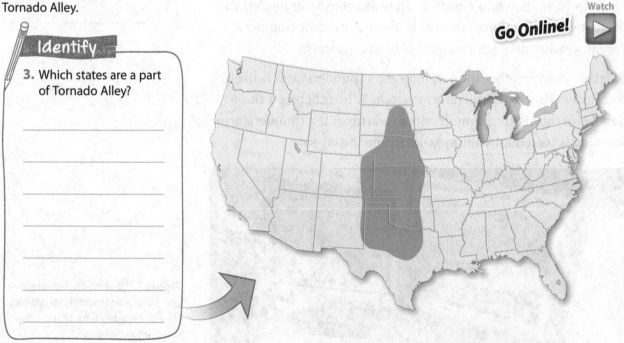

Table 1 Enhanced Fujita Damage Intensity Scale

Watch
Go Online!

Category	Wind Speed	Damage
EF-0	105–137 km/h (65–85 mi/h)	**Light Damage** Chimneys are damaged; tree branches are broken; shallow-rooted trees are toppled.
EF-1	138–177 km/h (86–110 mi/h)	**Moderate Damage** Roof surfaces are peeled off; windows are broken; tree trunks are snapped.
EF-2	178–218 km/h (111–135 mi/h)	**Considerable Damage** Roof structures are damaged; manufactured homes are destroyed.
EF-3	219–266 km/h (136–165 mi/h	**Severe Damage** Roofs and some walls are torn from structures; small buildings are destroyed; most trees in forests are uprooted.
EF-4	267–322 km/h (166–200 mi/h)	**Devastating Damage** Some structures are lifted from their foundations and blown some distance. Cars also are blown some distance. Large debris becomes airborne.
EF-5	>322 km/h (>200 mi/h)	**Incredible Damage** Strong frame houses are lifted from foundations; reinforced concrete structures are damaged. Automobile-sized debris becomes airborne. Trees are completely debarked.

Table 1 Tornadoes are described and categorized according to the damage they cause.

Tornado Strength

Using a scale called the Enhanced Fujita Damage Intensity Scale, shown in **Table 1,** meteorologists classify tornadoes by wind speed and the damage they cause. Most tornadoes are considered weak, with winds up to 177 km/h. Weak tornadoes cause damage but not destruction. Strong tornadoes have wind speeds of 178 km/h or higher. The most violent tornadoes have wind speeds over 322 km/h and cause total destruction where they touch down. These tornadoes are rare.

Tornado Safety

Tornadoes can be dangerous. To help keep people safe, forecasters issue a tornado watch when the correct conditions are present to form a tornado. If a tornado is spotted, forecasters issue a tornado warning. If a tornado warning is issued for your area, go inside a sturdy building. If possible, go to the basement. If an underground shelter is not available, move to an interior room or hallway on the lowest floor and get under a sturdy piece of furniture.

Describe

4. What are tornadoes?

Definition:

How they are described:

Where to seek shelter in case of a tornado:

Impact:

How they are related to other severe weather:

Figure 5 This satellite image shows a hurricane's bands of clouds rotating counterclockwise.

Figure 6 Hurricane winds can push ocean water onto land, causing storm-surge flooding. This photograph shows storm-surge flooding in Houston, Texas, caused by Hurricane Ike.

Hurricanes TEKS 7.8(A)

A **hurricane** *is an intense tropical storm with winds exceeding 119 km/h.* A hurricane can produce strong winds, heavy downpours, lightning, and even tornadoes. As **Figure 5** shows, hurricanes are huge, averaging 480 km across. In other parts of the world, these large storms are called typhoons or tropical cyclones. When they occur in the north Atlantic Ocean, they are called hurricanes. An average of six hurricanes form each year in the north Atlantic Ocean.

At the center of these storms is a small area called the eye. In the eye, skies are clear, and winds are light. Winds are strongest and the rain is most intense in the area around the eye.

A hurricane's winds can stir up huge waves. Also, *as a hurricane approaches land, its winds can push ocean water higher along the coast, creating* **storm surge.** As shown in **Figure 6,** storm surge can increase the sea level 6–10 m. This is high enough to cover buildings in low coastal areas. In 2008 during Hurricane Ike, the storm surge flooded downtown Galveston, Texas, including the Galveston County Courthouse, which had 2 m of water in it.

Hurricane Formation

In the Atlantic Ocean, hurricane season is from June 1 to November 30. Hurricanes usually start as thunderstorms near the west coast of northern Africa. Warm ocean water provides energy for thunderstorms to become tropical storms. Humid air adds water vapor to the growing clouds. If enough water and energy are added, tropical storms strengthen and become hurricanes. The storms move west across the Atlantic Ocean and then north along the eastern U.S. coast or into the Caribbean Sea or the Gulf of Mexico.

Forecasting Hurricanes Meteorologists monitor hurricanes with satellites, ships, and buoys at sea. Sometimes crews fly airplanes into hurricanes to collect data. Radar is used when a storm is close to land. Data about the storm are put into computer models to help scientists predict the storm's path and how strong it will become.

Hurricane Safety Meteorologists and weather forecasters warn people when a hurricane is on the way. They issue a hurricane warning for coastal areas that are in the predicted path of the storm. People living in those coastal areas evacuate to safer areas.

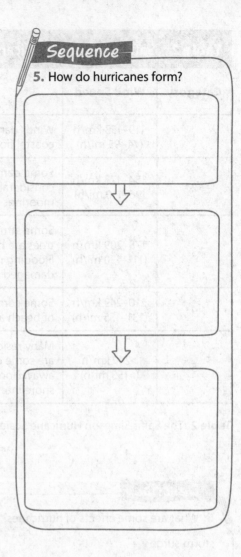

Sequence

5. How do hurricanes form?

Math Skills **Math** **TEKS** 7.1(A); 7.3(A), (B); 7.9(B)

Use Geometry

If you know the diameter of a hurricane, you can calculate other properties of the storm, such as the distance around the storm (circumference) and the area of the storm. Use the following equations:

Circumference = 2π × radius

$C = 2\pi r$ $\pi = 3.14$

Area = π × radius²

$A = \pi r^2$

What is the area of a hurricane with a radius of 240 km?

1. Select the correct equation $A = \pi r^2$

2. Substitute the values and calculate.

$A = 3.14 \times (240 \text{ km})^2$

$A = 181,000 \text{ km}^2$

Practice

What is the circumference of a hurricane with a radius of 240 km?

Check   Tutor

Table 2 Saffir-Simpson Hurricane Scale

Category	Wind Speed	Damage
1	119–153 km/h (74–95 mi/h)	Winds damage unanchored mobile homes and poorly constructed signs. Some coastal flooding and minor pier damage occur.
2	154–177 km/h (96–110 mi/h)	Some damage to building roofs, doors, and windows occurs. Mobile homes have considerable damage. Flooding damages piers, and small craft in unprotected moorings may break their moorings. Some trees are blown down.
3	178–209 km/h (111–130 mi/h)	Some structural damage occurs to small residences and utility buildings. Large trees are blown down. Mobile homes and poorly built signs are destroyed. Flooding near the coast destroys smaller structures. Larger structures are damaged by floating debris. Inland terrain may be flooded.
4	210–249 km/h (131–155 mi/h)	Some complete roof-structure failure occurs on small residences. Major erosion of beach areas occurs, and terrain may be flooded far inland.
5	>249 km/h (>155 mi/h)	Many residences and industrial buildings experience complete roof failure. There are some complete building failures with small utility buildings blown over or away. Flooding causes major damage to lower floors of all structures near the shoreline. Massive evacuation of residential areas may be required.

Table 2 The Saffir-Simpson Hurricane Scale is used to measure the strength of hurricanes.

Describe

6. What are some effects of hurricanes?

storm surge

_____

wind

_____

rain

_____

Hurricane Impacts

Wind, waves, rain, storm surge, and tornadoes caused by a hurricane impact coastal areas when a storm comes ashore. Waves and storm surge can move sand, flood coastal towns and ecosystems, and damage buildings. Winds destroy trees, topple power lines, and blow roofs off buildings. Farther inland, excessive rain can cause mudslides and landslides in hilly areas.

The extent of a hurricane's damage depends on the strength of the hurricane and the characteristics of the coastal area. The strength of hurricanes is rated on the Saffir-Simpson Hurricane Scale, shown in **Table 2.** The scale is based on wind strength and damage caused by hurricanes.

Hurricanes can sometimes cause more damage than their category suggests. Hurricane Sandy in 2012 was a category 1 storm, but the damage it caused was much more than a typical cateogory 1 storm would cause.

Cut out the Lesson 5.3 Foldables in the back of the book. Use it to compare and contrast the formation and impact of severe weather. Use illustrations to add to your understanding.

Severe Weather

Thunderstorms

Tornadoes

Hurricanes

Winter Storms

Flooding

Extreme Heat/Drought

Tape here

Other Natural Events TEKS 7.8(A)

Some dramatic atmospheric events, such as winter storms, happen in just one day. Others, such as droughts, can happen over weeks, months, or years.

Winter Storms

Snowstorms can be relatively mild, such as the one shown in **Figure 7,** or they can be extremely hazardous. Hazards can include slippery roads, reduced visibility, freezing rain, and strong winds causing blizzard conditions.

Floods

Floods are the most common weather-related natural disaster. Flooding can occur as a result of excessive rainfall, storm surge from hurricanes, or quickly melting snow.

Flash floods are the most dangerous floods. These floods rise quickly, without warning, and can cause major destruction.

Extreme Heat

Unusually hot weather that lasts for several days is called a heat wave. Heat waves are more common in large cities, where buildings and pavement, such as the roadway pictured in **Figure 7**, absorb and hold the Sun's thermal energy. Heat waves can lead to heat stroke and heat exhaustion for some people. Both conditions can be life-threatening.

Drought

A **drought** *is a period of below average precipitation in an area that can last for several months or years.* Changing atmospheric patterns can cause drought. For example, changing wind patterns can block fronts from reaching an area. This can prevent rain from falling. Less water changes rivers and other ecosystems. There might not be enough water for crops. As shown in **Figure 7,** if plants die for lack of water, winds can remove the top layer of fertile soil.

Explain

7. What are some effects of winter storms, extreme heat, and drought?

_____

_____

Figure 7 Some natural events, such as the winter storm in Denton, Texas (left), extreme heat in Washington County, Texas (center), and drought in West Texas farm fields (right) can affect people, property, and crops.

Summarize it!

Organize your understanding of this chapter's vocabulary words to complete the chart below.

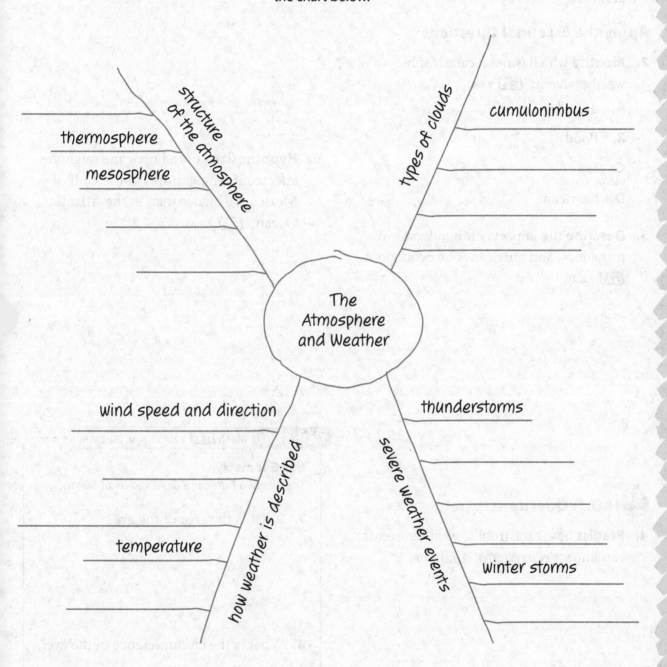

structure of the atmosphere

thermosphere

mesosphere

types of clouds

cumulonimbus

The Atmosphere and Weather

wind speed and direction

temperature

how weather is described

thunderstorms

severe weather events

winter storms

Connect it! Explain why weather-forecasting methods are important, based on what you have learned about severe weather. Write your response in your interactive notebook.

Severe Weather

Use Vocabulary

1. Sea level can be raised 6-10 m by
   _____ .

   TEKS 7.8(A)

Apply the Essential Questions

2. **Identify** which is not a catastrophic weather event. **TEKS** 7.8(A)

   A. drought

   B. flood

   C. fog

   D. hurricane

3. **Describe** the impacts of thunderstorms, tornadoes, and hurricanes on ecoregions. **TEKS** 7.8(A)

   _____

   _____

   _____

   _____

   _____

H.O.T. Questions (Higher Order Thinking)

4. **Predict** how catastrophic weather events can impact ecosystems. **TEKS** 7.8(A)

   _____

   _____

   _____

   _____

   _____

   _____

5. **Analyze** how drought is different from other weather events described in this lesson. **TEKS** 7.8(A)

   _____

   _____

   _____

   _____

   _____

6. **Hypothesize** how a hurricane might be affected if temperatures in the Gulf of Mexico are higher than in the Atlantic Ocean. **TEKS** 7.8(A)

   _____

   _____

   _____

   _____

Math Skills **Math** **TEKS** 7.1(A); 7.3(A), (B); 7.9(B)

Use Geometry

The eye of a hurricane has a radius of 50 km.

7. What is the area of the eye?

8. What is the circumference of the eye?

Check Tutor

Go Online!

In a Hurricane's Path

Protecting Cities from Powerful Storms

Millions of people live near the coastlines of the Atlantic Ocean and the Gulf of Mexico. Each year, some of these communities are in the direct paths of hurricanes. Powerful winds, huge waves, and heavy rain from these storms can destroy towns and natural habitats—even miles from the coast. Repairing the damage costs billions of dollars each season.

After a hurricane devastated the Texas barrier island of Galveston in 1900, Galveston constructed a protective 5-m seawall. In 1915, the seawall protected the barrier island from a hurricane as powerful as the 1900 storm.

When Hurricane Ike hit Galveston in September 2008, the storm surge rose on the gulf side of the island and on the Galveston Bay side. The bay side was unprotected from rising waters. The island flooded, and about 90 percent of the city's homes and businesses were damaged or destroyed.

Just months after the storm hit, Galveston launched an extensive project to repair and strengthen the seawall. The effort cost $10 million, but the city is confident that the rebuilt seawall can protect it from future hurricanes.

TEXAS

Galveston Bay

Galveston

Galveston Island

Gulf of Mexico

—— Seawall

After Hurricane Ike, about 382,000 m³ of sand were brought in to reinforce the seawall's base and create a beach 21 m wide and nearly 6.5 km long. ▶

▲ After the 1900 hurricane, Galveston's seawall was constructed, and the ground level of the island was raised about 5 m, sloping toward the bay side of the island to allow water to run off.

AMERICAN MUSEUM ᴏ̄ NATURAL HISTORY

It's Your Turn!

RESEARCH Use stereoscopes to view images of Galveston before and after hurricanes. Present your findings. Listen to other presentations and take notes.

Where is the water?

Does this look like a lake to you? This is E.V. Spence Reservoir near Robert Lee, Texas. It may not have water in it now, but it did before the drought of 2011. How do weather patterns affect the land surface and the plants and animals that live there?

Write your response in your interactive notebook.

LAB Manager

Go to your Lab Manual or visit connectED.mcgraw-hill.com to perform the labs for this lesson.

MiniLAB: *How can watersheds be cleaned up?*
TEKS 7.1(A); 7.2(A), (C), (E); 7.3(B); 7.4(A), (B); 7.8(C)

LAB: *Hurricanes and Their Effects*
TEKS 7.1(B); 7.2(A), (C), (E); 7.4(A); 7.8(A)

Explore Activity

TEKS 7.1(A); 7.2(A), (C), (E); 7.3(B); 7.4(A), (B); 7.8(A), (B)

Can storms be beneficial?

Severe weather can be destructive. However, some storms, including thunderstorms and even hurricanes, can be beneficial, too. How can a storm have a positive effect on an ecoregion?

Procedure

1. Read and complete a lab safety form.

2. Use **clay** to make a river and its floodplain in the bottom of a **container.** Your river should be about 1 cm deep and about 1 cm wide. The river should run the length of the container and have several tributaries.

3. Sprinkle some **sand** along the bottom of the riverbed.

4. Use a **beaker** to slowly pour water into the channel until the main river is half full.

5. Wait until the sand settles. Prop up the container at one end with a **pencil.**

6. Use the beaker to pour a slow, steady stream of water into the upper part of the river. Record what happens in your Lab Manual or interactive notebook.

Think About This

1. What happened when you poured the second portion of water into the river? Be specific.

_____

_____

_____

_____

2. Analyze what happened to the sand. How might this be beneficial?

_____

_____

3. Predict how severe weather could affect the rivers in an ecoregion.

_____

_____

_____

TEKS in this Lesson

7.8(A) Predict and describe how different types of catastrophic events impact ecosystems such as floods, hurricanes, or tornadoes

7.8(B) Analyze the effects of weathering, erosion, and deposition on the environment in ecoregions of Texas

7.8(C) Model the effects of human activity on groundwater and surface water in a watershed

Also covers Process Standards: 7.1(A), (B); 7.2(A), (C), (E); 7.3(B); 7.4(A), (B)

? Essential Questions

- How does weather affect ecoregions?
- How does human activity affect a watershed?

abc Vocabulary

ecoregion
climate
groundwater
surface water
watershed
erosion
deposition

1. Before reading this lesson on ecoregions, write down what you know. In the first column, write down what you know already about ecoregions. In the second column, write down what you want to learn. And after you have completed this lesson, you will write down what you learned in the third column.

What I Know	What I Want to Know	What I Learned

Figure 1 Ecoregions are defined by the species that live in them.

Ecoregions **TEKS** 7.8(A), (B), (C)

*An **ecoregion** is a large area of land that has a distinct group of plants, animals, and other species.* The species in an ecoregion have adaptations for the weather, elevation, soil, and amount of water available.

Examples of ecoregions are shown in **Figure 1.** The Arctic tundra of Canada is frigid and has a thin layer of soil. Only adapted plant species can survive there.

In many areas, human activities have disturbed ecoregions. For example, in Texas's Pineywoods ecoregion, only about 3 percent of the forests remain. Most of the original forests were cut down for timber and to make room for towns and cities.

The Great Plains is an ecoregion of central North America. It usually receives little rain. Grasses can grow there because they can survive periods with little moisture.

Weather, Climate, and Ecoregions

Some areas of Earth are hot and dry. Other areas are cool and rainy. Some places are cold all year long. Although there can be short-term variations in the wind, rain, and temperature in an area, each area has a typical overall weather pattern. *The long-term weather conditions in an area make up its* **climate.** Climates determine the distribution of ecoregions on Earth. Different species of plants, animals, and other organisms thrive in different climates.

Have you noticed that some areas of Texas are different from other areas? That is because different parts of the state have different weather patterns. That means the state has many different ecoregions. **Figure 2** shows some of the varied ecoregions in Texas and their characteristics.

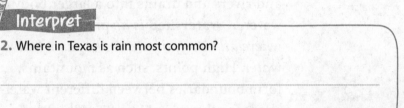

FOLDABLES®

Make a two-tab matchbook using the labels as shown. Use it to organize your notes about the impact of humans on ecoregions and watersheds.

... Ecoregions   ... Watersheds

Human Impact on...

Interpret

2. Where in Texas is rain most common?

_____

_____

Figure 2 Texas has 11 ecoregions. Each has its own climate.

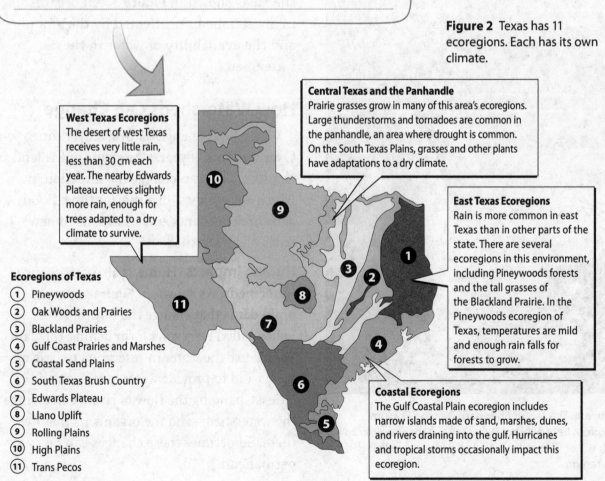

West Texas Ecoregions
The desert of west Texas receives very little rain, less than 30 cm each year. The nearby Edwards Plateau receives slightly more rain, enough for trees adapted to a dry climate to survive.

Central Texas and the Panhandle
Prairie grasses grow in many of this area's ecoregions. Large thunderstorms and tornadoes are common in the panhandle, an area where drought is common. On the South Texas Plains, grasses and other plants have adaptations to a dry climate.

East Texas Ecoregions
Rain is more common in east Texas than in other parts of the state. There are several ecoregions in this environment, including Pineywoods forests and the tall grasses of the Blackland Prairie. In the Pineywoods ecoregion of Texas, temperatures are mild and enough rain falls for forests to grow.

Coastal Ecoregions
The Gulf Coastal Plain ecoregion includes narrow islands made of sand, marshes, dunes, and rivers draining into the gulf. Hurricanes and tropical storms occasionally impact this ecoregion.

Ecoregions of Texas
1. Pineywoods
2. Oak Woods and Prairies
3. Blackland Prairies
4. Gulf Coast Prairies and Marshes
5. Coastal Sand Plains
6. South Texas Brush Country
7. Edwards Plateau
8. Llano Uplift
9. Rolling Plains
10. High Plains
11. Trans Pecos

Rocky Mountains Mississippi River Appalachian Mountains

Pacific Ocean

Atlantic Ocean

Gulf of Mexico

Figure 3 Water on the two sides of a boundary flows to different places. Water that flows to the same area is part of a particular watershed.

Figure 4 The Morris Sheppard Dam on Possum Kingdom Lake, west of Dallas, allows the reservoir to fill with water. The water is essential for people living in this region.

Surface Water and Groundwater

The amount of water available to an area is an important feature of an ecoregion. How much precipitation falls and where it drains are factors that determine which organisms can live in an area. *Precipitation that soaks into the cracks and pores beneath Earth's surface is* **groundwater. Surface water** *is the water that fills lakes and rivers.* Humans rely on groundwater and surface water for irrigating crops, for drinking water, for recreation, and for other uses.

Watersheds

Water that falls on land flows in streams and rivers and drains into a larger body of water. *A* **watershed** *is an area of the land where all runoff drains to the same body of water.* High points, such as mountains, form boundaries between different watersheds, as shown in **Figure 3.** All organisms in a watershed are affected by the amount and the availability of water in the watershed.

How Watersheds Can Change

Watersheds change naturally over time. Over millions of years, the shape of the land changes. This can change the direction in which water flows. In a shorter time, floods can carry nutrients and sediments to new parts of a watershed.

Human Impacts Humans also can change watersheds. As shown in **Figure 4,** people build dams that change the flow of rivers. Lakes called reservoirs form behind the dams. People use the water in reservoirs to irrigate farms and to provide water for towns and cities. Changing the flow of rivers can change the watershed—and the organisms that live there. Sometimes these changes can be permanent.

Changing the Flow of Rivers Built to make reservoirs or control flooding, dams on a river prevent water from flowing through the watershed. That means areas downstream do not have as much water as they once did. This can change ecoregions.

Water Pollution Rivers and lakes can be affected by pollution like the one in **Figure 5.** If the water in a watershed is polluted, it can harm organisms living in the watershed. Pollutants can come from factories that release harmful chemicals into a river. Or, water flowing through farms can pick up pesticides and carry it into lakes and rivers. These pollutants will pass through layers of soil and rocks, but some will still make it into the groundwater. This groundwater is what we depend on for our drinking water. If pollution is not controlled or stopped, then the groundwater and drinking supply will be polluted and will not be suitable for consumption.

Irrigation To provide crops with needed water, some farmers irrigate land with groundwater pumped from wells, as shown in **Figure 6.** Others use water from trenches that carry water to crops.

Figure 5 Water pollution happens everywhere, including the Trinity River in Dallas, Texas.

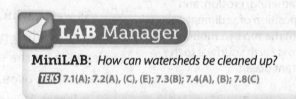

LAB Manager

MiniLAB: *How can watersheds be cleaned up?*
TEKS 7.1(A); 7.2(A), (C), (E); 7.3(B); 7.4(A), (B); 7.8(C)

Figure 6 This is an aerial veiw of irrigated farm fields in Texas.

Weathering is the breakdown of rock. Chemical weathering changes the mineral composition of rock. Physical weathering breaks rock into smaller pieces without changing its composition.

Go Online!
Tutor

Figure 7 The continual weathering, erosion, and deposition of sediment occurs from the top of a mountain and across Earth's surface to the distant ocean.

Weathering, Erosion, and Deposition

As water, wind, and ice move across Earth, they can break down rock in a process called weathering. The rate of weathering depends on the temperature and humidity in an area. Typically, weathering occurs more quickly in hot, humid areas, such as a rain forest. Weathering occurs more slowly in cold, dry areas. Look back at the map of Texas ecoregions in **Figure 2**. Where do you think weathering occurs quickly? Where do you think weathering occurs slowly? Refer to **Figure 7** to show locations of weathering, erosion, and deposition.

Weathering In Texas, weathering would likely occur rapidly along the southeastern coast, where temperatures and humidity are high. The coast is also subject to weathering from the Gulf of Mexico and severe weather events, such as hurricanes. The west Texas ecoregions contain mostly desert areas, where temperatures are high and humidity is low. Weathering would likely be slower there than in other areas of the state.

Predict

3. Based on your knowledge of weathering, where will high rates of weathering occur in the United States? Where would low rates of weathering occur?

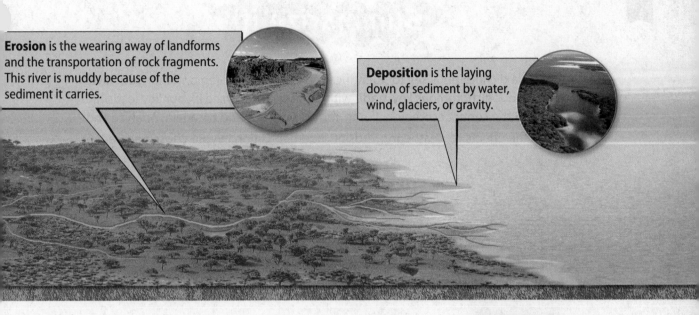

Erosion is the wearing away of landforms and the transportation of rock fragments. This river is muddy because of the sediment it carries.

Deposition is the laying down of sediment by water, wind, glaciers, or gravity.

Erosion After rock is broken down into smaller pieces, or sediment, water, wind, ice, and gravity can move sediment from place to place. *The process of moving weathered material from one location to another is called* **erosion.** Erosion can change ecoregions because it can change the landscape, change a river's course, or sweep beaches into the ocean.

Deposition *As water slows, eroded material is laid down and settles in a process called* **deposition.** The cycle of erosion and deposition can move fertile soil to new areas, build barrier islands, and build and move sand dunes. Erosion and deposition also can move pollutants or cover up areas where plants and animals once lived. Erosion and deposition are natural processes, but the way humans use land can increase or decrease the impact of these processes. For example, erosion increases when trees, grasses and other natural vegetation are cleared from the land.

Word Origin

erosion from Latin *erosionem,* means "gnaw away"

LAB Manager

LAB: *Hurricanes and Their Effects*

TEKS 7.1(B); 7.2(A), (C), (E); 7.4(A); 7.8(A)

Explain

4. How can erosion and deposition affect ecoregions?

Summarize it!

Create a dichotomous key for identification of a Texas ecoregion. After you have created your dichotomous key, trade with a classmate and see if your key leads him or her to the correct ecoregion. If not, correct your key and try again. Analyze and discuss the effects of weathering, erosion, and deposition in your chosen ecoregion.

TEKS 7.8(B)

Connect it! Hurricane Sandy devastated the northeast coast of the United States in October 2012. Rapid weathering, erosion, and flooding occurred. What precautions could have been taken to lessen the impact on the land?

_____

_____

_____

_____

Effects of Weather on the Land

Use Vocabulary

1. **Use** the terms *erosion* and *deposition* in a sentence. **TEKS** 7.8(B)

   _____

   _____

   _____

Apply the Essential Questions

2. **Identify** Which does NOT affect an ecoregion in Texas? **TEKS** 7.8(B)

   A. erosion

   B. deposition

   C. volcanism

   D. weathering

3. **Compare** the effects of human activity and natural processes on watersheds.
   TEKS 7.8(C) *supporting*

   _____

   _____

   _____

4. **Describe** what effect weather patterns can have on ecoregions. **TEKS** 7.8(B)

   _____

   _____

   _____

   _____

   _____

H.O.T. Questions (Higher Order Thinking)

5. **Hypothesize** two ways water pollution released from a factory into a small stream could travel through a watershed.
   TEKS 7.8(C) *supporting*

   _____

   _____

   _____

   _____

   _____

   _____

6. **Predict** the positive and negative effects heavy rainfall could have on a desert ecoregion. **TEKS** 7.8(A), (B)

   _____

   _____

   _____

   _____

   _____

7. **Analyze** some of the effects of soil erosion in a heavily populated area.
   TEKS 7.8(B)

   _____

   _____

   _____

   _____

   _____

Clues from the
Canyon

American Museum
ᵒ̇ Natural History

Rocks of the majestic Grand Canyon tell a story about Earth's past.

Visitors to the Grand Canyon in Arizona are often awestruck by its magnificent size and depth. However, to many scientists, the canyon's walls are even more impressive. The soaring walls hold about 40 layers of colorful rocks in shades of red, yellow, brown, and gray. Each layer is like a page in a history book about Earth's past—and the deeper the layer, the older it is. The different layers reflect the particular types of environments in which they formed.

Weathering The canyon walls continue to weather and erode today. Rockfalls and landslides are common. Harder rock such as sandstone weathers in big chunks that break off, forming steep cliffs. The softer rocks weather and erode more easily. This forms gentle slopes.

Deposition These rock layers formed 280 to 260 million years ago. During the early part of this period, the region was covered by sand dunes and wind-deposited layers of sand. Later, shallow seas covered this area and layers of shells settled on the seafloor. Gradually, the sediments were compacted and cemented together, and these multicolored layers of sedimentary rock were formed.

Erosion Several million years ago, the movement of tectonic plates pushed up the layers of rock. This formed what is called the Colorado Plateau. As the rocks rose higher, the slope of the Colorado River became steeper, and its waters flowed faster and with greater force. The Colorado River cut through the weathered rock and carried away sediment. Over millions of years, this erosion formed the canyon.

It's Your
Turn!

DIAGRAM With a partner, find a photo of a local natural land formation. Research and write short descriptions explaining how parts of the formation were created. Attach your descriptions to the appropriate places on the photo.

TEKS Review

Test-Taking Strategy

Eliminate Choices Some questions ask you to interpret information to find an answer. By using given information to eliminate choices, you have a better chance of selecting the best answer for the question.

Example

Use the chart below to answer question 3.

2 Next, eliminate possible choices. Since the tornado snapped tree trunks, you can eliminate EF-0. No homes were destroyed, so you can eliminate EF-2 and above. So the best answer is EF-1.

Enhanced Fujita Damage Intensity Scale		
Category	**Wind Speed**	**Damage**
EF-0	105—137 km/h	**Light Damage** Chimneys are damaged; tree branches are broken; shallow-rooted trees are toppled.
EF-1	138–177 km/h	**Moderate Damage** Roof surfaces are peeled off; windows are broken; tree trunks are snapped.
EF-2	178–218 km/h	**Considerable Damage** Roof structures are damaged; manufactured homes are destroyed.
EF-3	219–266 km/h	**Severe Damage** Roofs and some walls are torn from structures; small buildings are destroyed; most trees in forests are uprooted.
EF-4	267–322 km/h	**Devastating Damage** Some structures are lifted from their foundations and blown some distance. Cars also are blown some distance. Large debris becomes airborne.
EF-5	>322 km/h	**Incredible Damage** Strong frame houses are lifted from foundations; reinforced concrete structures are damaged. Automobile-sized debris becomes airborne. Trees are completely debarked.

3 A tornado occurs in a small town. Trees' trunks are snapped. No homes were destroyed, other than some minor roof damage and broken windows. Most likely, what category was the tornado? **TEKS** 7.8 (A)

1 Carefully read the question, and identify clues to help eliminate possible answers. In this case, you know tree trunks were snapped and there was roof damage, but NO homes were destroyed.

A EF-0

B EF-1

3 Find EF-1 in the possible answers. The correct answer is choice **B**.

C EF-2

D EF-3

TIP: Underlining clues provided in the question will help you focus on the important information to look for in a given chart, graph, or reading passage.

Multiple Choice

1 The map below shows some features of the Gulf Coast region of Texas.
TEKS 7.8(B); 7.2(E)

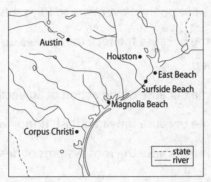

Which feature formed mainly through the process of deposition?

A the curving coastline

B the meandering river beds

C the narrow barrier islands

D the natural harbors

2

> Ryan designs and constructs a model to illustrate the effects of one type of catastrophic event. He begins by filling a 2-liter plastic bottle about three-quarters full of water. Next, he adds a small pebble. Finally, he moves the jar in a circle until the water begins to spin and form a column of water and air.

Which describes the event Ryan is modeling and its impact on ecosystems?
TEKS 7.8(A); 7.3(B)

A Flood; rapidly moving waters can carry away plants and animals.

B Thunderstorm; hail can damage crops, people, and wildlife.

C Tornado; high winds can pick up and carry away trees, soil, and plants.

D Tropical storm; heavy rain can erode soils and destroy habitat.

3 The rock formation called the Lighthouse is unusual because of its rock layers. It is located in Palo Duro Canyon in the panhandle of Texas near Amarillo. **TEKS** 7.8(B)

Which statement best explains what happened over time to form this rock formation?

A The Lighthouse formed over time because the rock that makes up the structure is harder than the surrounding rock that eroded.

B The Lighthouse formed over time because of the action of an ancient volcano.

C The Lighthouse formed over time because repeated flash floods washed looser rocks away.

D The Lighthouse formed over time because the root systems of desert plants protected the rock layers from erosion.

---

4 A rocky cliff in the high mountains has areas of rocks like the ones shown below. **TEKS** 7.8(B)

Which process is most likely to cause these rocks to break apart?

A chemical weathering

B deposition of sediments

C physical weathering

D wind erosion

5   Big Bend National Park, located in the Trans-Pecos region of west Texas, is popular with hikers. Many of the park's trails have warning signs about the danger of injury or death from flash floods. The graph shows the monthly average precipitation in the park. *TEKS* 7.8(A); 7.2(E)

Month	Monthly Average Precipitation (cm)
January	1.12
February	0.86
March	0.79
April	1.78
May	3.81
June	4.91
July	5.31
August	5.97
September	5.38
October	5.77
November	1.78
December	1.45

What is the average monthly precipitation of the month when flash floods are likely to occur most often? Record and bubble in your answer in the answer document.

CHAPTER 6

Impacts on Water Systems

The **BIG** Idea

Freshwater is water that occurs naturally on Earth's surface. Freshwater systems are impacted by human activity.

LESSON

6.1 Glaciers and Polar Ice Sheets

More than two-thirds of Earth's freshwater is frozen in ice.

TEKS 7.8(C); Also covers 7.1(A); 7.2(A), (C), (E); 7.3(B); 7.4(A), (B)

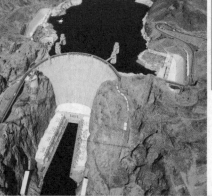

LESSON

6.2 Streams and Lakes

Water flowing over Earth's surface can form freshwater streams and lakes.

TEKS 7.8(C); Also covers 7.1(A); 7.2(A), (C), (E); 7.3(B); 7.4(A), (B)

LESSON

6.3 Groundwater and Wetlands

Groundwater accounts for one-third of Earth's freshwater.

TEKS 7.8(C); Also covers 7.1(A); 7.2(A), (C), (E); 7.3(B); 7.4(A), (B)

Groundwater

Jane was drinking a glass of water. She asked her father where the water came from. Her father said it was groundwater that was pumped up by their well. Jane wondered what the water looked like underground. This is what her family said:

Mom: I think it looks like a huge ocean underground.

Dad: I think it looks like a small lake underground.

Jack: I think it seeps into little holes or spaces between the soil and the rocks.

Annie: I think it looks like a long, underground tube filled with water.

Philip: I think it looks like an underground volcano with water spurting out of the top.

Which person do you agree with the most? _____
Explain your ideas about groundwater.

6.1 Glaciers and Polar Ice Sheets

Why is the ice melting? Notice the water streaming off the edge of the iceberg. Why is this ice melting so rapidly? Where does all of the water go? Ice melts as temperature increases. When ice melts, the meltwater eventually enters the oceans, where it can cause a rise in sea level. What might cause a rise in temperature? What happens if too much ice melts?

Write your responses in your interactive notebook.

 LAB Manager

Go to your Lab Manual or visit connectED.mcgraw-hill.com to perform the lab for this lesson.

MiniLAB: *Does the ground's color affect temperature?*

TEKS 7.1(A); 7.2(A), (C), (E); 7.3(B); 7.4(A); 7.8(C)

Explore Activity

TEKS 7.1(A); 7.3(B); 7.4(A), (B)

Where is all the water on Earth?

Earth is often called the "water planet." That is because about 70 percent of Earth's surface is covered with water stored in the oceans. Where is the rest of Earth's water?

Procedure

1. Read and complete a lab safety form.

2. Using a **globe**, locate areas on Earth where water is found. Record your findings in your Lab manual or interactive notebook.

3. Pour 970 mL of **water** into a **1-L container.** Then add a drop of **red food coloring.** This represents all of the salt water on Earth.

4. Add 20.7 mL of water to a **clear plastic cup** using a **graduated cylinder.** Then add a drop of **blue food coloring** to represent all freshwater stored in glaciers.

5. Add 9.0 mL of water to a **clear plastic cup,** and then add a drop of **green food coloring.** This represents all the freshwater stored as groundwater.

6. Finally, add one drop (about 0.3 mL) of **yellow food coloring** to a clear plastic cup. This represents all the freshwater in Earth's lakes, rivers, wetlands, atmosphere, and other sources.

Think About This

1. Where is Earth's water and in what forms does it exist?

_____

_____

_____

2. Can you think of any other places on Earth where you might find water?

_____

_____

? Essential Questions

- How does ice and snow cover affect climate?
- How do human activities affect glaciers?

abc Vocabulary

freshwater
alpine glacier
ice sheet
sea ice
ice core

Freshwater on Earth

Groundwater
30.1%

Glaciers
68.7%

Lakes, streams,
and other sources
1.2%

Figure 1 Most of Earth's freshwater is frozen in glaciers.

What is freshwater?

Satellite images of Earth show more water than dry land. Most of the water that covers Earth is salt water. Only about 3 percent is **freshwater**—*water that has less than 0.2 percent salt dissolved in it.* Life, as we know it, cannot continue without freshwater.

Water cycles on Earth. Water moves from Earth's surface into the atmosphere by evaporation. The water then condenses and falls back to the surface as precipitation—rain, snow, sleet, or hail. Only freshwater enters Earth's atmosphere and returns to Earth's surface.

More than two-thirds of Earth's freshwater is frozen, as illustrated in **Figure 1.** The rest is liquid water, and most is stored underground. Less than 1 percent of Earth's liquid freshwater is in streams and lakes.

Connect

1. Circle the active part(s) of the water cycle that represent freshwater.

Precipitation

Snow

Rain

Water vapor condenses

Lake

Evaporation

Surface runoff

Ocean

Explain your reasoning.

_____

_____

_____

Glaciers and Ice Sheets

Glaciers are large masses of moving ice that form on land. Glaciers cover about 10 percent of Earth's surface. They are near the North Pole and the South Pole and on mountaintops, as shown in **Figure 2**.

How do glaciers form? Imagine what happens when snow falls but does not melt. Year after year, layers of snow pile up. The weight and pressure of the snow above compresses the snow on the bottom into ice. Over time, the mass of ice and snow gets so heavy that gravity starts to slowly drag it downhill. For most glaciers this process takes more than 100 years.

Alpine Glaciers

A glacier that forms in the mountains is an **alpine glacier.** Alpine glaciers are on every continent except Australia. They flow downhill like slow-moving rivers of ice. As an alpine glacier flows downhill, it eventually reaches an elevation where temperatures are warm enough to melt the ice. The melted ice is called glacial meltwater.

Review Vocabulary

glacier a large, slow-moving mass of ice and snow

Word Origin

alpine from French *Alpes*, means "Alps"—mountain system of Europe

Define

2. Highlight the definition of an alpine glacier. Then underline where alpine glaciers are found.

Watch

Go Online!

Glaciers

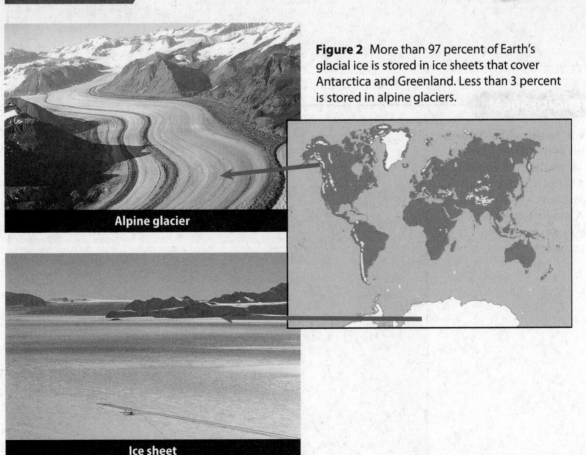

Alpine glacier

Ice sheet

Figure 2 More than 97 percent of Earth's glacial ice is stored in ice sheets that cover Antarctica and Greenland. Less than 3 percent is stored in alpine glaciers.

Ice Sheets

A glacier that spreads over land in all directions is called an **ice sheet.** Ice sheets are also called continental glaciers. They cover large areas of land (more than 50,000 km²) and store enormous amounts of freshwater. The only two ice sheets currently on Earth are in Antarctica and Greenland.

Parts of the Antarctic and Greenland Ice Sheets extend into the ocean. When a glacier flows into the ocean, an ice shelf forms. Ice shelves occur along the coastlines of Alaska, Canada, Greenland, and Antarctica. Icebergs are blocks of ice that break away from ice shelves and float in the ocean.

Antarctic Ice Sheet Earth's largest ice sheet is the Antarctic Ice Sheet. The ice sheet covers most of Antarctica and is larger in surface area than the continental United States. Scientists subdivide the ice sheet into two areas—the West and East Antarctic Ice Sheets—as illustrated in **Figure 3.** The average thickness of the Antarctic Ice Sheet is about 2.4 km. In some places, the ice can be as much as 5 km, or 3 miles, thick.

Greenland Ice Sheet Earth's second-largest ice sheet covers most of Greenland. Its average thickness is about 2.3 km. The total area of the ice sheet is about 1.8 million km².

Recognize

3. Fill in the boxes to show your understanding of ice sheets.

2 Largest ice sheets:	How they move:	Also called:

Antarctic Ice Sheet

Figure 3 Antarctica has an area of about 14 million km². That is much larger than the area of the United States, which is about 10 million km². Ice shelves extend into the ocean from several places along the Antarctic coast.

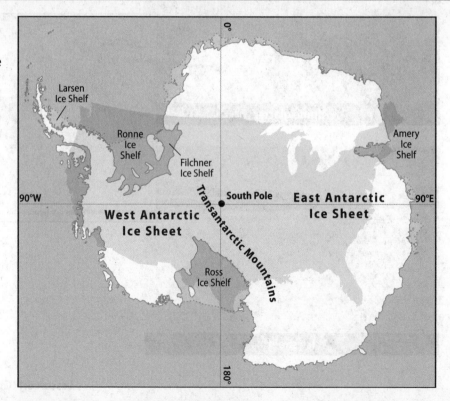

How much freshwater is in glaciers?

Glaciers can stay frozen for thousands of years. During some periods of Earth's history, the climate was colder than it is now. During those periods, many glaciers formed. The coldest periods are called ice ages—long periods of time when large areas of land were covered by glaciers and ice sheets. The last ice age ended about 10,000 years ago.

Past Changes in Sea Level Even if you have never traveled to either coast, you probably know that sea level is the average level of the surface of Earth's oceans. Changes in sea level have occurred throughout Earth's history. As climate changes cause the melting or forming of glaciers, sea level rises or falls.

As illustrated in the first image in **Figure 4,** sea level during the last ice age was much lower than it is today. That is because of the enormous amount of Earth's water frozen in vast ice sheets. When the ice sheets melted at the end of the ice age, the melt-water flowed into the ocean and raised sea level.

Melting Glaciers Scientists estimate that if all the glaciers on Earth melted, sea level would rise about 70 meters. Some low-lying areas, such as the Florida peninsula and a large portion of Louisiana, would be under water.

How much water is frozen in the Antarctic Ice Sheets? The middle image in **Figure 4** illustrates how sea level around the Florida peninsula could change if the West Antarctic Ice Sheet melted. The last image in **Figure 4** illustrates how sea level for Florida would change if the East Antarctic Ice Sheet melted.

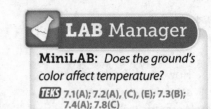
LAB Manager

MiniLAB: *Does the ground's color affect temperature?*

TEKS 7.1(A); 7.2(A), (C), (E); 7.3(B); 7.4(A); 7.8(C)

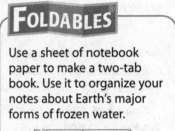
FOLDABLES

Use a sheet of notebook paper to make a two-tab book. Use it to organize your notes about Earth's major forms of frozen water.

Glaciers | Snow and Sea Ice

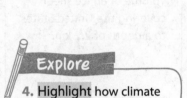
Explore

4. **Highlight** how climate change affects sea level and glaciers.

Changing Sea Level

Figure 4 These maps show the outline of Florida's coast today. The green area in the first illustration shows how much land was above sea level during the last ice age.

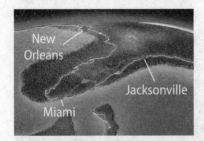

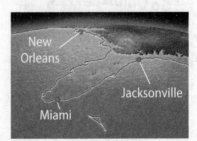

At the height of the last ice age, 20,000 years ago, sea level was about 120 meters lower than it is today.

If the West Antarctic ice sheet melted, sea level would rise about 5 meters above current sea level. The southern tip of Florida would be under water.

If the larger East Antarctic ice sheet melted, sea level could rise about 51.8 meters. This would put most of Florida under water.

Volume

How much freshwater is stored as ice in the Antarctic Ice Sheet?

The area (*A*) of the Antarctic Ice Sheet is **14 million km²**. Calculate the volume (*V*) of ice by multiplying the area by the thickness or height (*h*).

$$V = A \times h$$

For example, the average thickness of the Antarctic Ice Sheet is 2.4 km.

$V = $ **14,000,000 km²** $\times$ **2.4 km**, or 33,600,000 km³

Practice

The total area of the entire United States is approximately 10 million km². What would be the volume of an ice sheet covering the United States to a depth of 2.2 km?

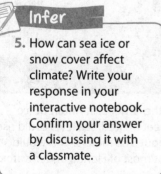

Check Tutor

Go Online!

Infer

5. How can sea ice or snow cover affect climate? Write your response in your interactive notebook. Confirm your answer by discussing it with a classmate.

Sea Ice and Snow Cover

Snow and sea ice are also frozen forms of freshwater. **Sea ice** *is ice that forms when seawater freezes.* As seawater freezes, salt is left behind in the ocean. Much of the Arctic Ocean is covered with sea ice.

Unlike glaciers, sea ice does not raise sea level by adding water to the ocean. Consider an ice cube floating in a glass. The amount of water frozen in the ice cube is equal to the amount of water that it displaces in the glass. When the ice cube melts, the water level in the glass stays the same. Likewise, when sea ice melts, sea level stays the same.

However, melting snow or sea ice can affect climate. Snow and ice reflect more solar energy than land and water do. When sunlight is reflected it does not warm Earth's surface as much as when it is absorbed. As illustrated in **Figure 5,** most of the sunlight that hits snow or ice is reflected back into space. Reflection helps keep surface temperatures and air temperatures low. When sea ice melts, the polar regions have less of a reflective surface. Therefore, more heat is absorbed, which causes more melting.

Scientists have recorded a decreasing trend in the amount of snow cover. When snow melts, Earth's surface absorbs more solar energy and heats the air above it. When large areas of Earth's surface are affected over long periods of time, climate changes. Scientists hypothesize that this decrease in snow cover is related to an increase in global temperature.

Figure 5 Up to 80 percent of the sunlight that strikes snow or sea ice is reflected into space.

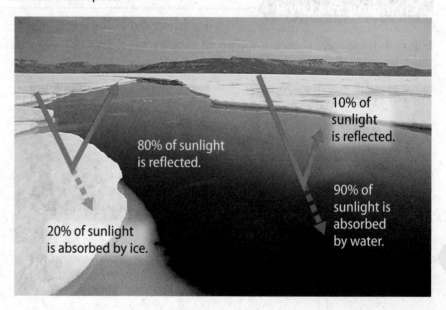

10% of sunlight is reflected.

80% of sunlight is reflected.

90% of sunlight is absorbed by water.

20% of sunlight is absorbed by ice.

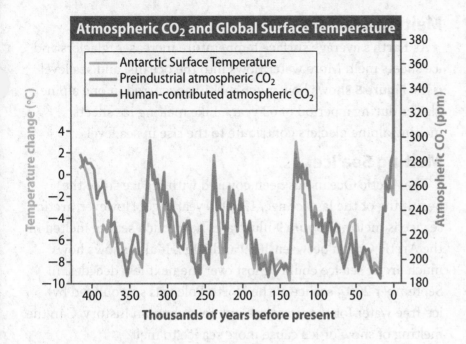

Atmospheric CO₂ and Global Surface Temperature

Legend:
— Antarctic Surface Temperature
— Preindustrial atmospheric CO_2
— Human-contributed atmospheric CO_2

Y-axis (left): Temperature change (°C): 4, 2, 0, −2, −4, −6, −8, −10

Y-axis (right): Atmospheric CO_2 (ppm): 380, 360, 340, 320, 300, 280, 260, 240, 220, 200, 180

X-axis: Thousands of years before present: 400, 350, 300, 250, 200, 150, 100, 50, 0

Figure 6 This graph shows changes in global temperature and atmospheric CO_2 over the past 400,000 years. The steepest rise in CO_2 levels, shown by the red line, began about 150 years ago, when people first began burning fossil fuels.

Figure 7 Bubbles of gas locked in Antarctic ice cores provide evidence of the CO_2 content of the atmosphere during different periods of Earth's history.

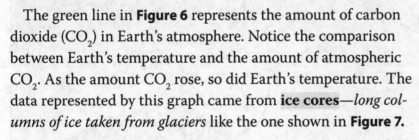

Human Impacts on Glaciers TEKS 7.8(C)

Scientific studies indicate that Earth's glaciers are melting. Sea ice that covers the Arctic Ocean is also melting. Why? Earth is getting warmer. Data collected by scientists who study Earth's climate show that Earth's average surface temperature has risen approximately 0.5°C since the start of the twentieth century.

Evidence of Climate Change

The orange line in the graph in **Figure 6** represents Earth's average surface temperature during the past 400,000 years. Notice that Earth's temperature fluctuated during that span of time. During cold periods, glaciers formed and sea level fell. During warm periods, glaciers melted and sea level rose.

The green line in **Figure 6** represents the amount of carbon dioxide (CO_2) in Earth's atmosphere. Notice the comparison between Earth's temperature and the amount of atmospheric CO_2. As the amount CO_2 rose, so did Earth's temperature. The data represented by this graph came from **ice cores**—*long columns of ice taken from glaciers* like the one shown in **Figure 7.**

Look again at **Figure 6** and notice the sharp rise in CO_2 shown by the red line. Human activities—especially the burning of fossil fuels—add CO_2 to the atmosphere. Atmospheric CO_2 has risen sharply since the 1800s. Scientists hypothesize that this rise in CO_2 has contributed to the recent rise in global temperature. Many scientists also hypothesize that this rise in temperature is causing many of Earth's glaciers to melt.

1941

2004

Figure 8 Much of the Muir Glacier in Alaska has melted since 1941.

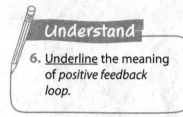
Understand

6. Underline the meaning of *positive feedback loop*.

Figure 9 The white portion of this computer-generated image shows the size of the Arctic Ocean ice cap in 2005. The yellow outline shows the edges of the ice cap in 1979. Red and purple outlines show where scientists predict the edges of the ice cap will be in future years.

Melting Glaciers

As Earth's average surface temperature increases, glaciers and ice sheets melt. More water flows into the oceans, and sea level rises. **Figure 8** shows how much melting occurred in one alpine glacier during a period of 63 years. Like melting ice sheets, melting alpine glaciers contribute to the rise in sea level.

Melting Sea Ice

The Arctic Ocean has been covered with sea ice since the beginning of the last ice age, 125,000 years ago. However, arctic sea ice is melting. **Figure 9** illustrates how much sea ice melted in the Arctic Ocean between 1979 and 2005. It also shows how much arctic sea ice could be lost over the next few decades. In September 2007, sea ice at the North Pole was surrounded by ice-free water for the first time in known human history. Can the melting of snow or ice cause more sea ice to melt?

Positive Feedback Loop

A back-and-forth relationship occurs between melting snow and rising temperature—an increase in one causes an increase in the other. For example, as snow or ice melts, the amount of energy absorbed from the Sun increases. As the amount of energy absorbed from the Sun increases, global temperature rises. As global temperature rises, more snow or ice melts. This repeating cycle is called a positive feedback loop—an increase in one variable causes a corresponding increase in another variable.

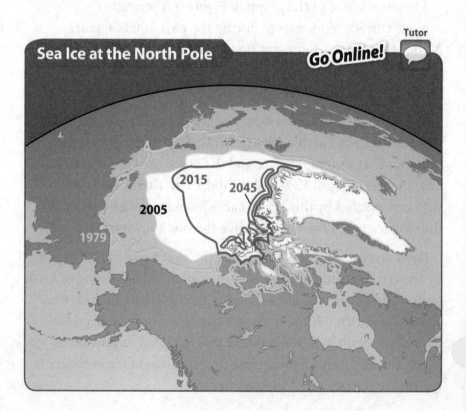

Sea Ice at the North Pole

Go Online!

Tutor

2015

2045

2005

1979

Summarize it!

Model how glaciers and ice sheets are affected by human activity. Design a comic strip that represents a human activity impacting glaciers and ice sheets. **TEKS** 7.8(C)

Generate a solution to the problem that you illustrated above. **TEKS** 7.8(C)

_____

_____

_____

_____

_____

Connect it! **Analyze** changes in sea level that have occurred in the past and might occur again in the future. How will these changes affect sea level? How have humans affected these changes? Write your response in your interactive notebook. **TEKS** 7.8(C)

Summarize it!

Glaciers and Polar Ice Sheets

Apply the Essential Questions

1. Interpret Graphics The graph below illustrates how the CO_2 content of Earth's atmosphere has changed since 1850. According to these data, how would glaciers and sea level be affected?

TEKS 7.8(C) *supporting*

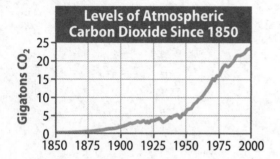

Levels of Atmospheric Carbon Dioxide Since 1850

_____

_____

_____

_____

_____

2. Explain how the reflection of sunlight on snow and ice can affect climate.

TEKS 7.8(C) *supporting*

_____

_____

_____

_____

_____

_____

_____

_____

3. Summarize how glaciers and sea ice are changing because of human activities.

TEKS 7.8(C) *supporting*

_____

_____

_____

_____

_____

_____

_____

_____

_____

_____

_____

 H.O.T. Question (Higher Order Thinking)

4. Predict how the melting of glaciers would affect humans. Write your response on a separate sheet of paper. **TEKS** 7.8(C) *supporting*

Math Skills | **Math** **TEKS** 7.1(A); 7.3(A), (B)

Volume

5. The Greenland Ice Sheet has an area of 1.8 million km^2 and an average thickness of 2.3 km. Solve for the volume of the Greenland Ice Sheet.

Check Tutor

Go Online!

Life at the Top of the World

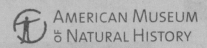

AMERICAN MUSEUM
OF NATURAL HISTORY

Average temperatures on Earth are increasing. Sea ice is melting and disrupting entire ecosystems, which could threaten the survival of polar bears.

Life is not easy when you are living at the top of the world in the vast, icy region known as the Arctic. It is so cold that ice covers parts of the Arctic Ocean all year long. However, a variety of species thrive in this polar climate. In fact, many ecosystems depend on the Arctic's ice for survival.

However, as Earth's average temperatures increase, ice in the Arctic is melting. This includes sea ice—the ice that forms in an ocean. Sea ice follows a natural cycle in the Arctic. It spreads across the Arctic Ocean in winter then decreases in area during summer. With rising temperatures, sea ice forms later and melts earlier each year. Over the last few decades, the amount of ice in the Arctic has decreased dramatically.

The disappearing ice is threatening the Arctic's top predator, the polar bear. Polar bears travel across sea ice to hunt for seals. As sea ice breaks up and melts, polar bears must swim longer distances to find prey. Also, late freezes and early thaws of sea ice mean shorter hunting seasons for them. Polar bears have been classified as a threatened species because their numbers are decreasing. If warming continues, they could become extinct.

The future of Arctic life is uncertain. Scientists continue to monitor climate data to understand the impact of increasing average temperatures on Arctic ecosystems. However, if Earth's climate continues to warm, life in the Arctic might never be the same.

Scientists use satellite images to monitor the amount of arctic sea ice. These 1979 (top) and 2007 (bottom) images show that the area covered by summer sea ice is about half of what it was more than 30 years ago. ▼

◄ Polar bears are strong swimmers and hunt from the ice out at sea as well as from land. During the winter, they build up a layer of fat that helps them survive the rest of the year.

It's Your Turn!

RESEARCH Learn how the dwindling population of polar bears would affect other Arctic species. Create a cause-and-effect diagram with an if-then statement describing the effects of polar-bear population decline on other wildlife in the Arctic.

INQUIRY

What is this structure?

The large concrete structure shown here is the Hoover Dam, in Nevada. The dam was built to control water flow along the Colorado River. Notice the large reservoir, Lake Mead, behind the dam. Freshwater from Lake Mead is used for recreational purposes, drinking water, irrigation, and hydroelectric power. Dams can also have negative effects on the environment and the ecosystem around a river. What do you think are the negative effects of a dam on the surrounding area?

Write your response in your interactive notebook.

LAB Manager

Go to your Lab Manual or visit connectED.mcgraw-hill.com to perform the labs for this lesson.

MiniLAB: *How does a thermocline affect pollution in a lake?*
TEKS 7.1(A); 7.2(A), (C), (E); 7.3(B); 7.4(A), (B); 7.8(C)

Skill Practice: *How does water flow into and out of streams?*
TEKS 7.1(A); 7.2.(A), (E); 7.3(B); 7.4(A), (B); 7.8(C)

Explore Activity

TEKS 7.1(A); 7.2(A), (E); 7.8(C)

How can you measure the health of a stream?

The quality of the water in a stream affects the organisms that live in the stream. Macroinvertebrates are tiny animals without backbones. Their presence can be used to determine the health of a stream. For example, the riffle beetle is only in streams where dissolved oxygen is high and the stream is healthy. Use the data below to measure the health of a stream near a new housing development.

Procedure

1. Read and complete a lab safety form.

2. Use **graph paper** and **colored pencils** to draw a graph using the data provided.

3. Plot the water temperature, dissolved-oxygen concentration, and population density for each year represented.

Year	Water Temp (°c)	Dissolved-Oxygen Concentration (ppm)	Riffle Beetle (adults/rock)
1998	10.4	11.5	9.8
2000	11	10.5	9.3
2002	12.7	8	7.9
2004	13.3	7.5	6.2
2006	14.1	6.5	4.4
2008	15.2	5.5	2.6

Think About This

1. According to the graph that you created, what is happening to the stream?

_____

_____

2. Make a prediction about the number of adult riffle beetles per rock in 2015.

_____

_____

TEKS in this Lesson

7.8(C) Model the effects of human activity on groundwater and surface water in a watershed

Also covers Process Standards: 7.1(A); 7.2(A), (C), (E); 7.3(B); 7.4(A), (B)

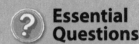

Essential Questions

- What is a watershed?
- How do human activities affect streams and lakes?

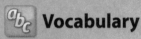

Vocabulary

runoff
stream
watershed
estuary
lake

1. Before reading this lesson on streams and lakes, write down what you know. In the first column, write down what you know already about streams and lakes. In the second column, write down what you want to learn. After you have completed this lesson, you will write down what you learned in the third column.

What I Know	What I Want to Learn	What I Learned

Runoff

If you've ever been outside during a heavy rain, you might have noticed sheets of water rushing downhill over pavement or soil. Water can follow many different paths during a rainstorm. Some water soaks into soil. Some water collects in puddles that evaporate. Water that cannot soak into the soil flows over the land as runoff.

Water that flows over Earth's surface is called **runoff**. It comes from rain, melting snow or ice, or any water that does not soak into the soil or evaporate. Runoff is part of the water cycle. Gravity causes runoff to flow downhill, from higher ground to lower ground. Runoff usually starts as a thin layer, or a sheet, of water flowing over the ground, such as the runoff shown in **Figure 1**.

Figure 1 Runoff often starts as sheets of water that flow downhill.

2. What causes runoff to flow downhill?

_____

Streams

A body of water that flows within a channel is a **stream**, as shown in **Figure 2.** Scientists use the term *stream* to refer to any naturally flowing channel of water. For example, a river is a large stream. A brook is a small stream. A creek is larger than a brook but smaller than a river.

All streams form from similar processes. As water flows downhill, it wears away rock and soil, forming tiny channels called rills. Every time it rains, more rock and soil is removed from a rill. Eventually a rill grows in size and forms a larger and more permanent stream channel. Small streams can combine and form a larger stream. Large streams can eventually become rivers that flow into a lake or an ocean.

Figure 2 Streams form when runoff erodes channels that carry water and sediment downhill.

Pools and Riffles

If you have ever watched a small stream, you might have noticed differences in the way the water flows. Sometimes the water appears smooth, and sometimes it is turbulent or rough, as shown in **Figure 3.** The water is slow, steady, and smooth in places where the stream channel is flat. Pools often form in depressions or low spots within a stream channel. Where the stream channel is rough or the slope is steep, the water tumbles and splashes. A riffle is a shallow part of a stream that flows over uneven ground. Riffles help mix water as it splashes and swirls over rough areas. This action increases the oxygen content of the water and makes the stream healthier.

Determine

3. Underline how a riffle can make a stream healthier.

Figure 3 Oxygen from the air mixes into water as it passes over riffles. Water from riffles helps supply oxygen to the pools downstream.

Turbulent flow in riffles

Smooth flow in pools

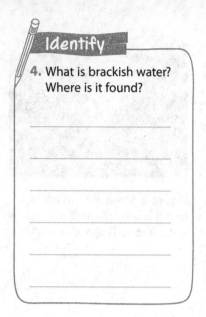

4. What is brackish water? Where is it found?

_____

_____

_____

_____

_____

Watershed

Go Online!

Figure 4 This watershed includes several streams. They flow into a river, which flows into the ocean.

Watersheds

Imagine a house with a roof that is higher in the middle than at its edges. Rain falls on both sides of the roof and runs downward. However, rain runs down the roof in opposite directions. The same thing happens when rain falls to Earth. The direction in which runoff flows depends on which side of a slope the rain falls. A **watershed** *is an area of land that drains runoff into a particular stream, lake, ocean, or other body of water.*

Like the example described, the boundaries of a watershed are the highest points of land that surround it. These high points are called divides. **Figure 4** shows examples of watersheds and divides.

estuary from Latin *aestuarium,* means "a tidal marsh"

From Headwaters to Estuaries

Small streams that form near divides are called headwaters. Streams begin at the headwaters. Streams end at the mouth of a river, where runoff drains into a lake, an ocean, or another large body of water.

Figure 5 Estuaries form in places where freshwater streams flow into an ocean, a sea, or a bay.

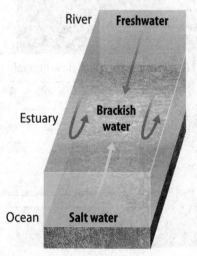

What happens when a river meets the sea? Freshwater mixes with salt water. Many large watersheds end in an **estuary**—*a coastal area where freshwater from rivers and streams mixes with salt water from seas or oceans.* Estuaries contain brackish water—a mixture of freshwater and salt water. As **Figure 5** shows, the water in an estuary gets saltier as it gets closer to the ocean. Estuaries are rich in minerals and nutrients and provide important habitats for many organisms.

Lakes

When runoff flows into a **basin**, or a depression in the landscape, a lake can form. A **lake** *is a large body of water that forms in a basin surrounded by land*. Most of Earth's lakes are in the northern hemisphere. More than 60 percent are in Canada. Lakes are reservoirs that store water, and most contain freshwater.

Science Use v. Common Use

basin

Science Use a shallow depression surrounded by higher ground

Common Use a tub or container used to hold liquids such as water

How Lakes Form

Erosion, landslides, movements of Earth's crust, and the collapse of volcanic cones can form lake basins. Water can enter a lake basin from precipitation, streams, or groundwater that rises to the surface. Most lakes have one or more streams that remove water when the lake overflows. Lakes also lose water by evaporation or when lake water soaks into the ground.

The water level in a lake is not constant. If the lake loses water to evaporation, the lake level will drop. Occasionally a lake will disappear entirely if precipitation does not replenish water lost from the lake. In contrast, if the lake receives too much rainfall, the water can spill over the lake banks and cause a flood.

LAB Manager

Skill Practice: *How does water flow into and out of streams?*

TEKS 7.1(A); 7.2(A), (E); 7.3(B); 7.4(A), (B); 7.8(C)

FOLDABLES

Cut out the Lesson 6.2 Foldable in the back of your book. Use it to compare information on the characteristics of streams and lakes.

Tape here

Lakes and Streams

Characteristics	Characteristics

Academic Vocabulary

distinct
(adjective) different or not the same

Recognize

5. Circle the items in runoff that can be harmful to organisms living in or near the water.

Figure 6 Pollutants that flow into freshwater can harm living organisms, including the people who use the water for drinking, washing, and irrigation.

Properties and Structure

Water changes temperature more slowly than land changes temperature. This can affect weather conditions near a lake. For example, on a hot summer day you might be refreshed by a cool breeze blowing across a lake.

Have you ever been swimming in a lake and noticed that the water changes temperature with depth? Sunlight heats the surface layer, making it warmer and less dense than the layers below. Less sunlight is absorbed the deeper you swim. Some deep northern lakes develop two distinct layers of water—a warm top layer and a cold bottom layer. The two layers are separated by a region of rapid temperature change called the thermocline. It acts as a barrier and prevents mixing between the layers.

Human Impact on Streams and Lakes   **TEKS** 7.8 (C)

People worldwide depend on streams and lakes for their water supplies. Streams are dammed to create reservoirs that store water. Because of dams, some rivers, such as the Colorado River shown in the lesson opener, are nearly dry before they reach the ocean.

As illustrated in **Figure 6,** people can affect the health of streams and lakes in many other ways. Runoff can carry fertilizers, pesticides, sewage, and other pollutants that are harmful to organisms living in or near the water. For example, excess nutrients from fertilizers or sewage can enter a stream and result in an increase in the population of algae. When the algae die, bacteria break down the algae and use oxygen in the decay process. If decay rates are too high, oxygen levels in the water can be so low that fish and other animals cannot survive.

Watershed unaltered by human activity

Forest

O_2 rich

Watershed altered by human activity

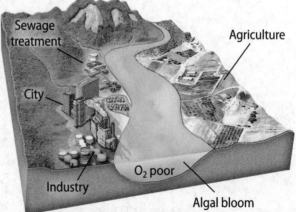

Sewage treatment

Agriculture

City

Industry

O_2 poor

Algal bloom

6.2 Review

Create a graphic organizer that describes how human activity can impact a lake or stream. **TEKS** 7.8(C)

Connect it! **Infer** how these two events might be related: A city dams a nearby river to create a reservoir that will store water and provide a recreational area for people in the community. The estuary at the end of the river has low water levels, and many organisms can no longer survive. **TEKS** 7.8(C)

_____

_____

_____

_____

_____

_____

_____

Summarize it!

Streams and Lakes

Use Vocabulary

1. **Distinguish** between a stream and a lake.
   TEKS 7.8(C) *supporting*

Apply the Essential Questions

2. **Explain** how pollution can affect a watershed. **TEKS** 7.8(C) *supporting*

3. **Assess** two human activities that can affect the health of a stream or lake.
   TEKS 7.8(C) *supporting*

🔥 H.O.T. Questions (Higher Order Thinking)

4. **Analyze** how the destruction of a forest to make room for a factory could affect organisms in a nearby stream.
   TEKS 7.8(C) *supporting*

5. **Research** a factory or organization in your area that might impact a lake or stream. What guidelines must they follow to protect lakes or streams from pollution or contamination? Write a paragraph about your findings on a separate sheet of paper. **TEKS** 7.8(C) *supporting*

Desalination

Taking the Salt out of Salt Water

AMERICAN MUSEUM
ö NATURAL HISTORY

Anyone who has been toppled by a big ocean wave knows that salt water does not taste like the water we drink. People cannot drink salt water. It is about 200 times more salty than freshwater. About 97 percent of Earth's water is salt water. Most freshwater is frozen in glaciers and ice caps, leaving less than 1 percent of the planet's water available for 6.7 billion people and countless other organisms that require freshwater to live.

The need for freshwater has scientists searching for efficient ways to take the salt out of salt water. One solution is a desalination plant, where dissolved salts are separated from seawater through a process called reverse osmosis. This is how it works:

▲ **Desalination plants are found all over the world, including the United States.**

❶ Salt water is pumped from the ocean.

❷ High pressure forces water through a semipermeable membrane.

❸ The semipermeable membrane acts as a filter, allowing the water, but not the salt, to pass through.

❺ Water containing the waste salts flows out of the tank.

❹ Clean freshwater is collected in a separate tank.

Because it takes a lot of energy to change salt water into freshwater, desalination plants are expensive to operate. However, desalination is used in places such as Saudi Arabia and Japan, where people have few freshwater resources.

It's Your
Turn!

RESEARCH What is the cost of desalinated water for households? How does it compare to the cost of water for households in your area? Present your findings to the class.

6.3 Groundwater and Wetlands

Where did this water come from?

Why is this water bubbling up out of the ground? Have you ever seen anything like it? Groundwater, which is stored in rocks below the surface, can flood the landscape after a severe storm when the ground is saturated. It can also surface in low-lying areas. In what other ways do you think groundwater can reach the surface?

Write your response in your interactive notebook.

LAB Manager

Go to your Lab Manual or visit connectED.mcgraw-hill.com to perform the labs for this lesson.

MiniLAB: *Can you model fresh-water environments?*

TEKS 7.1(A); 7.2(A), (C) (E); 7.3(B); 7.4(A), (B); 7.8(C)

LAB: *What can be done about pollution?*

TEKS 7.1(A); 7.2(A), (C), (E); 7.3(B); 7.4(A), (B); 7.8(C)

Explore Activity

TEKS 7.1(A); 7.2(A), (E); 7.4(A), (B); 7.8(C)

How do different water sources compare?

Nitrates are essential nutrients needed for plant growth, which makes them a main ingredient for most fertilizers. Nitrates can easily dissolve into groundwater and can eventually end up in wetland areas due to runoff. High levels of nitrates can decrease water quality and be harmful to organisms that live in these environments.

Procedure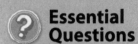

1. Read and complete a lab safety form

2. Obtain **water samples** from several local bodies of water.

3. Use a **water test kit** to analyze these samples, as well as a sample of **tap water,** for the presence of nitrates. Record your results in your Lab Manual or interactive notebook.

4. Use **graph paper** and **colored pencils** to draw a graph using the data you have collected.

5. Use the chart to help analyze the water quality of your samples.

Water Quality	Seawater Nitrate Levels (ppm)	Freshwater Nitrate Levels (ppm)
High	less than 0.6	less than 1.0
Fair	0.6–1.0	1.0–1.8
Fair to poor	1.0–1.8	1.8–2.8
Poor	greater than 1.8	greater than 2.8

* Water with nitrate levels over 10 ppm is unsafe for drinking

Think About This

1. What human activities could have impacted your results? Explain your reasoning.

_____

_____

2. How might a body of water that received a poor rating affect a wetland as a habitat for wildlife?

_____

_____

TEKS in this Lesson

7.8(C) Model the effects of human activity on groundwater and surface water in a watershed

Also covers Process Standards: 7.1(A); 7.2(A), (C), (E); 7.3(B); 7.4(A), (B)

? Essential Questions

- How do human activities affect groundwater and wetlands?
- Why are wetlands important?

abc Vocabulary

groundwater
water table
porosity
permeability
aquifer
wetland

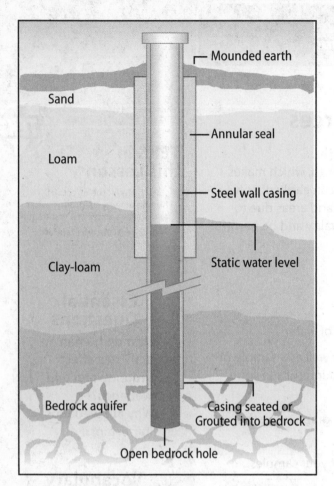

- Mounted earth
- Sand
- Annular seal
- Loam
- Steel wall casing
- Clay-loam
- Static water level
- Bedrock aquifer
- Casing seated or Grouted into bedrock
- Open bedrock hole

Figure 1 Groundwater wells are used to draw water up from the water table to the surface. People who live in areas where water is scarce, like deserts, rely on groundwater as their primary water source.

LAB Manager

MiniLAB: *Can you model freshwater environments?*

TEKS 7.1(A); 7.2(A), (C), (E); 7.3(B); 7.4(A), (B); 7.8(C)

FOLDABLES

Use a sheet of notebook paper to make a two-tab book. Use it to organize your notes on groundwater, wetlands, and how each relates to the other.

Groundwater Wetlands

Groundwater   **TEKS** 7.8 (C)

Some water that falls to Earth as precipitation soaks into the ground. *Generally, water that lies below ground is called* **groundwater.** Water seeps through soil and into tiny pores, or spaces, between sediment and rock. If you have ever been inside a cave and seen water dripping down the sides, you have seen groundwater seeping through rock.

In some areas, groundwater is very close to the surface and keeps the soil wet. In other areas, especially deserts and other dry climates, groundwater is hundreds of meters below the surface.

Groundwater can remain underground for long periods of time—thousands or millions of years. Eventually, it returns to the surface and reenters the water cycle. Humans interfere with this process when they drill wells, like the one shown in **Figure 1,** into the ground to remove water for everyday use.

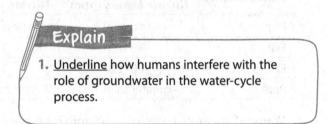

Explain

1. Underline how humans interfere with the role of groundwater in the water-cycle process.

Importance of Groundwater

The water beneath Earth's surface is much more plentiful than the freshwater in lakes and streams. Recall that groundwater is about one-third of Earth's freshwater. Groundwater is an important source of water for many streams, lakes, and wetlands. Some plant species absorb groundwater through long roots that grow deep underground.

People in many areas of the world rely on groundwater for their water supply. In the United States, about 20 percent of the water people use daily comes from groundwater.

Organize it!

Organize information on groundwater using the graphic organizer below.

Groundwater: _____

_____

Collects as water seeps through _____ and into

_____

Some groundwater lies _____	Some groundwater lies hundreds of meters _____

Groundwater can stay underground for long periods, but
eventually it returns to the surface and reenters the

_____

Identify four important facts about groundwater.

provides water to
_____ of plants

helps form _____
lakes, and _____,

Groundwater

more plentiful than
_____

used as a _____

_____

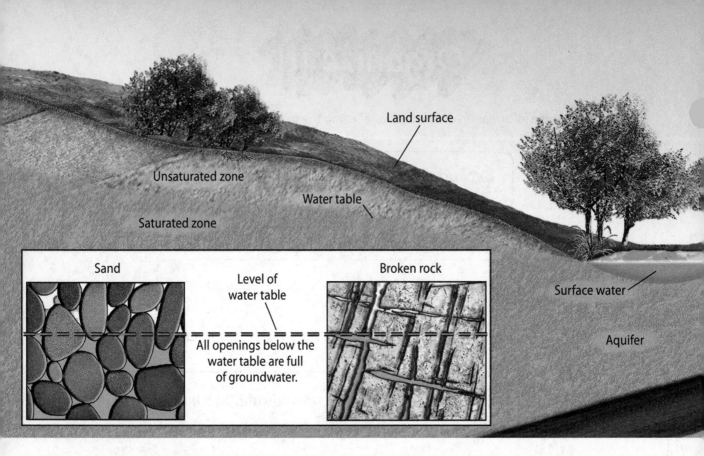

Land surface

Unsaturated zone

Water table

Saturated zone

Sand

Level of
water table

Broken rock

All openings below the
water table are full
of groundwater.

Surface water

Aquifer

The Water Table

As illustrated in **Figure 2,** groundwater seeps into tiny cracks and pores within rocks and sediment. Near Earth's surface, the pores contain a mixture of air and water. This region is called the unsaturated zone. It is called unsaturated because the pores are not completely filled with water. Farther beneath the surface, the pores are completely filled with water. This region is called the saturated zone. *The upper limit of the saturated zone is called the* **water table.**

Porosity Rocks vary in the amount of water they can hold and the speed with which water flows through the rock. Some rocks can hold a lot of water and some rocks cannot. The more open space a rock has, the more water it can hold. **Porosity** *is a measure of a rock's ability to hold water.* Porosity increases with the number of pores in the rock. Pore size can vary from microscopic to very large. The higher the porosity, the more water a rock can contain.

Permeability *The measure of water's ability to flow through rock and sediment is called* **permeability.** This ability to flow through rock and sediment depends on pore size and the connections between the pores. Even if pore space is abundant in a rock, the pores must form connected pathways for water to flow easily through the rock.

Groundwater Flow

Just as runoff flows downhill across Earth's surface, groundwater flows downhill beneath Earth's surface. Groundwater flows from higher elevations to lower elevations. In low-lying areas at Earth's surface, groundwater might eventually seep out of the ground and into a stream, a lake, or a wetland, as also shown in **Figure 2.** In this way, groundwater can become surface water. Likewise, surface water can seep into the ground and become groundwater. This is how groundwater is replenished.

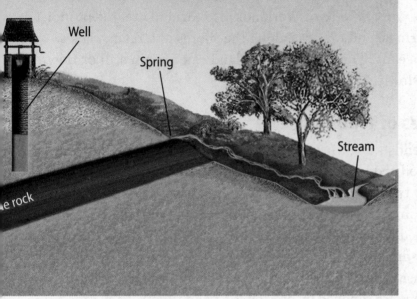

Figure 2 Aquifers store groundwater. Groundwater becomes surface water, including springs and streams, in places where the water table meets the surface of the land.

Well

Spring

Stream

...e rock

STEMonline

Debate the issue of water diversion in a mock town hall meeting. Visit ConnectED for the **STEM** activity **Freshwater Transportation Debate.** Resources

Go Online!

Describe

2. How do human activities affect groundwater? Write your response in your interactive notebook.

Wells People often bring groundwater to Earth's surface by drilling wells like the one shown in **Figure 2.** Wells are usually drilled into an **aquifer**—*an area of permeable sediment or rock that holds significant amounts of water.* Groundwater then flows into the well from the aquifer and is pumped to the surface where it can be collected for use by humans. Wells are very important for people who do not have access to freshwater.

Precipitation Rain, snow, sleet, and hail help to replace groundwater drawn out of wells. During a drought, less groundwater is replaced, so the water level in a well drops. The same thing happens if water is removed from a well faster than it is replaced. If the water level drops too low, a well runs dry.

Springs A spring forms where the water table rises to Earth's surface, as shown in the lesson opener. Some springs bubble to Earth's surface only after heavy rain or snowmelt. Many springs fed by large aquifers flow continuously onto Earth's surface.

Human Impact on Groundwater

Water is very important to human survival. As stated earlier, many people rely on groundwater for everyday use. If polluted surface water seeps into the ground, it can pollute the groundwater below it. Pollutants include pesticides, fertilizers, sewage, industrial waste, and salt used to melt ice on highways. Pollutants can travel through the ground and into aquifers that supply wells. People's health can be harmed if they drink contaminated water from a well.

The water in an aquifer helps to support the rocks and soil above it. In some parts of the world, water is being removed from aquifers faster than it can be replaced by natural processes in the water cycle. This creates empty space underground. The empty space underground cannot support the weight of the overlying rock and soil. Sinkholes form where the ground collapses due to lack of sufficient support from below.

Wetlands **TEKS** 7.8(C)

Water often collects in flat areas or depressions that are too shallow to form lakes. Conditions like these can create a **wetland**—*an area of land that is saturated with water for part or all of the year.* Wetlands also form in areas kept moist by springs, and in areas along the shores of streams, lakes, and oceans. The water in a wetland can remain still or flow very slowly.

Types of Wetlands

Scientists identify wetlands by the characteristics of the water and soil and by the kinds of plants that live there. There are three major types of wetlands, as shown in **Table 1.** Bogs form in cool, wet climates. They produce a thick layer of peat—the partially decayed remains of sphagnum moss. Peat holds water, so bogs rarely dry out. Unlike bogs, marshes and swamps form in warmer, drier climates and do not produce peat. Marshes and swamps are supplied by precipitation and runoff. They can temporarily dry out in hot, dry weather.

Word Origin

sphagnum from Greek *sphagnos*, means "a spiny shrub"

Table 1 Types of Wetlands	
Bogs—Big Thicket National Park • supplied by runoff, low oxygen content • soil acidic, nutrient-poor • dominant plants: *Sphagnum* moss, wildflowers, cranberries	
Marshes—Aransas National Wildlife Refuge • supplied by runoff and precipitation • soil slightly acidic, nutrient-rich • dominant plants: grasses and shrubs	
Swamps—Caddo Lake • supplied by runoff and precipitation • soil slightly acidic, nutrient-rich • dominant plants: trees and shrubs	

Figure 3 Wetlands, such as the Aransas National Wildlife Refuge shown above, are an important habitat for wildlife, providing water, food, and shelter.

Importance of Wetlands

Wetlands provide important habitat for plants and wildlife. They help control flooding and erosion and also help filter sediments and pollutants from water.

Habitat A wide variety of plants and animals live in wetlands. Wetlands provide plentiful food and shelter for young and newly hatched animals, including fish, amphibians, and birds. Wetlands are also important rest stops and food sources for migrating animals, especially birds. Every year, Texas wetlands provide wintering areas for millions of migrating birds, including the endangered whooping crane shown in **Figure 3.** Wetland environments provide a safe habitat for many species.

Flood Control Wetlands help reduce flooding because they store large quantities of water. They fill with water during the wet season and release the water slowly during times of drought.

Erosion Control Coastal wetlands help prevent beach erosion. Wetlands can reduce the energy of wave action and storm surges—water pushed onto the shore by strong winds produced by severe storms.

Filtration Wetlands help keep sediments and pollutants from reaching streams, lakes, groundwater, or the ocean. They are natural filtration systems. Runoff that enters a wetland often contains excess nitrogen from fertilizers or animal waste. Plants and the bacteria in wetland soils absorb excess nitrogen. Wetland plants and soils also trap sediments and help remove toxic metals and other pollutants from the water.

Human Impact on Wetlands

Many wetlands throughout the world have been drained and filled with soil for roads, buildings, airports, and other uses. The disappearance of wetlands has also been associated with rising sea level, coastal erosion, and the introduction of species that are not naturally found in wetlands. Scientists estimate that more than half of all wetlands in Texas have been destroyed over the past 200 years.

Pollution from fertilizers, landfills, and agricultural fields can also be very hazardous to wetland environments. These pollutants can be devastating to many plant and animal species. Wetlands are a valuable resource and need to be protected from destruction.

6.3 Review

Go Online!

Check   Virtual

Summarize it!

Compare information about bogs, swamps, and marshes. Include at least three facts about each.

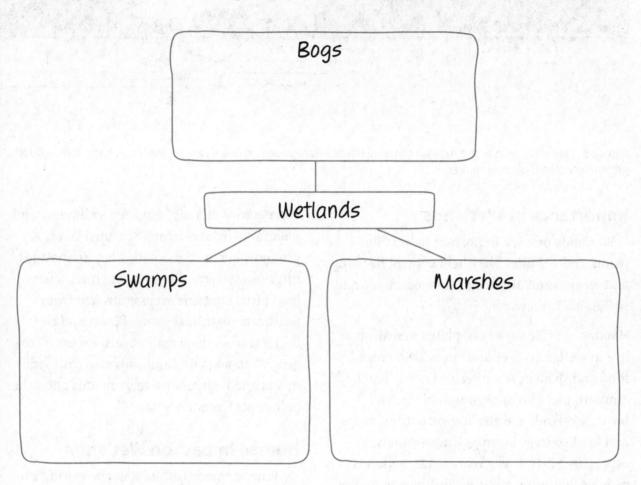

Bogs

Wetlands

Swamps

Marshes

Connect it! **Analyze** the following scenario. A developer wants to build houses near a lake. Much of the ground is currently covered with marsh. What would you tell the developer about filling in the marsh and building on it? Support your answer with information from this section. **TEKS** 7.8(C)

Groundwater and Wetlands

Apply the Essential Questions

1. **Explain** the importance of groundwater and how it is affected by humans.
   TEKS 7.8(C) *supporting*

   _____

   _____

   _____

   _____

   _____

   _____

   _____

   _____

   _____

   _____

   _____

2. **Generate** three reasons wetlands are important to people and the environment.
   TEKS 7.8(C) *supporting*

   _____

   _____

   _____

   _____

   _____

   _____

   _____

   _____

3. **Analyze** how the porosity and permeability of rocks can affect human impact on groundwater. **TEKS** 7.8(C) *supporting*

   _____

   _____

   _____

   _____

   _____

   _____

   _____

   _____

   _____

   _____

🔥 H.O.T. Questions (Higher Order Thinking)

4. **Identify** how wetland destruction can negatively impact humans.
   TEKS 7.8(C) *supporting*

   _____

   _____

   _____

   _____

   _____

   _____

5. **Extend** your knowledge of wetland protection. Design a model of an idea or tool that would keep pollution out of a protected wetland area. Write your response on a separate sheet of paper.
   TEKS 7.8(C) *supporting*

Texas Wetland
Restoration

The Birding Center, a wetland in South Padre Island, Texas

Yuck! That's what many people think of wetlands. They think wetlands are murky swamps, filled with algae and teeming with snakes, alligators, and mosquitos. They do not realize that wetlands are extremely important. Here are just a few of their benefits:

- They provide habitat for thousands of species, including fish, mollusks, birds, reptiles, amphibians, and insects.

- Wetlands filter natural and manufactured pollutants before they can enter rivers, lakes, or groundwater.

- Wetlands reduce storm and flood damage, prevent erosion, and restore groundwater and surface water.

As important as they are, more than half the wetlands in Texas have been destroyed and many more damaged. Humans have drained, filled in, contaminated, and used wetlands as dumps. This loss of wetlands has negatively affected watersheds by increasing erosion, increasing storm and flood damage, and harming groundwater and surface water quality. The commercial fishing industry in Texas has also been impacted by the loss of wetlands.

Now that the economic and environmental importance of wetlands is understood, steps are taken to avoid damaging or destroying wetlands. Government agencies, universities, and environmental organizations in Texas have joined forces to restore wetlands that have been damaged or destroyed. Their efforts have resulted in thousands of square kilometers of new and restored Texas wetlands.

Wetland restoration project at Bensten State Park in Mission, Texas

It's Your
Turn!

RESEARCH Investigate a local wetland and see how it has changed over time. Use the data you collected to design a poster to promote wetlands conservation.

My Notes

Test-Taking Strategy

Always, Not, Never Definitive words, such as *always, not,* and *never,* are used to help clarify what information is being asked in a question.

Example

Use the chart below to answer question 4.

Groundwater 30.1%

Glaciers 68.7%

Lakes, streams, and other sources 1.2%

1 Carefully read the question and identify signal words to understand what the question is asking. In this case, the words "not true" lead you to search for the one statement about freshwater that is false.

4 Which statement is not true of freshwater? **TEKS** 7.8(C) *supporting*

A 1.2% of Earth's freshwater is groundwater.

B 30.1% of Earth's freshwater is groundwater.

C 31.3% of Earth's freshwater is liquid.

D 68.7% of Earth's freshwater is frozen.

2 Next, use the diagram to determine which statement is false. Answers **B, C,** and **D** are all true statements about Earth's freshwater. Choice **A** is not true of Earth's freshwater. The correct answer is choice **A.**

TIP: *Always, not,* and *never* are signal words. These are important words that tell you what information you need to find in order to answer the question.

Multiple Choice

1

> Estuaries form where rivers containing freshwater flow into the salty waters of an ocean. The mixture of fresh and salt water stays balanced as long as both the river and ocean tides continue to mix at the river's mouth. Estuaries are usually calm and often contain many food sources. Because of this, many species of fish and other organisms breed and raise their offspring in estuaries. These organisms are adapted to life in brackish estuary waters.

A new recreation area is being built upstream from an estuary that is known for its abundance of fish and turtles. A dam will be built across the river and a large lake will form behind it. What effect will the dam have on the organisms living in the estuary? **TEKS** 7.8(C) *supporting;* 7.3(A)

A Organisms adapted to living only in brackish water will survive.

B Organisms adapted to living in brackish water will move to live in the open ocean.

C Some of the organisms will die because the water will be less salty.

D Some of the organisms will die because the water will be more salty.

2

> The part of our planet that is ice reflects the Sun's warming rays away from the surface. Liquid sea water and solid Earth absorb heat better than they reflect it. These two mechanisms need to be in balance. Human activities, such as the burning of fossil fuels and deforestation, cause more carbon dioxide—a greenhouse gas—to remain in the atmosphere. The buildup of excess greenhouse gases prevents reflected heat from escaping the atmosphere and causes the ice to melt.

Which is a model that best represents Earth when the warming and cooling mechanisms are in balance? **TEKS** 7.8(C) *supporting;* 7.3(B)

A Georgia inflates a small dark-blue balloon and paints a small circle at the top in silver paint. Then she paints a yellow line around the middle.

B Maria glues small mirrors all over the top and bottom of a tennis ball. Then she paints the middle part mostly blue with big brown patches.

C Paolo paints a foam ball blue all over. Then he paints three round brown shapes around the middle of the ball.

D Terry chooses a white plate. On it he glues black buttons in the shape of two small continents.

3 One way that humans have an impact on groundwater is by using it as a primary water source. It is important to try to conserve this resource. The table lists a family's average water usage per day for several activities. **TEKS** 7.8(C) *supporting;* 7.2(E)

Average Daily Water Use	
Daily Activity	**Water Used**
Flushing the toilet once	15 L
Taking a short shower	95 L
Taking a bath	150 L
Washing clothes	190 L
Automatic dishwasher	38 L
Brushing teeth while leaving the water running	7.5 L
Washing hands while leaving the water running, avg. washing time - 3 minutes	30 L/min
Watering the lawn or plants with a hose, avg. watering time - 30 minutes	30 L/min

The family wishes to reduce their weekly water usage as much as possible. Here are three proposals for how to do this.

Proposal 1: Five times a week substitute a short shower for a bath.

Proposal 2: Run the dishwasher five times a week instead of seven times a week.

Proposal 3: Water the plants three times a week instead of five times a week.

Determine which proposal will save the most water each week and then record the number of liters of water that will be saved each week. Record and bubble in your answer on the answer document.

				.		
⓪	⓪	⓪	⓪		⓪	⓪
①	①	①	①		①	①
②	②	②	②		②	②
③	③	③	③		③	③
④	④	④	④		④	④
⑤	⑤	⑤	⑤		⑤	⑤
⑥	⑥	⑥	⑥		⑥	⑥
⑦	⑦	⑦	⑦		⑦	⑦
⑧	⑧	⑧	⑧		⑧	⑧
⑨	⑨	⑨	⑨		⑨	⑨

4 Humans produce a lot of garbage that must be disposed of safely. Improper disposal of garbage can make the world unfit to live in and can make the whole environment sick. In a landfill, below the garbage layer, there are four layers that make it a safe place to dispose of garbage. The layers include a gravel or sand layer, a plastic liner, a layer of clay, and a layer of compacted soil. Each layer is designed to filter, collect, or block pollutants from entering the environment.
TEKS 7.8(C) *supporting*

If these four mechanisms are not in place, which part of the environment will be impacted first?

A crop production

B local water wells

C surrounding farmland

D wildlife habitats

---

5 The community shown in the figure uses river water for drinking and recreation. The river flows from the factory towards the community. Runoff and waste from the community buildings also wash into the river. A dam is going to be built on the river, and a lake will form behind the dam. This lake water will become the water source for the community. **TEKS** 7.8(C) *supporting*

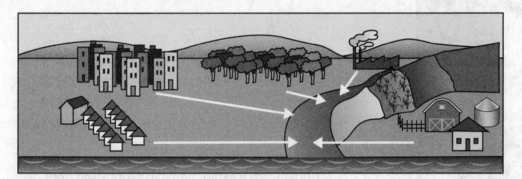

Where is the best location for the dam to be built?

A just before the factory

B just before the farmed hillside

C just before the forest of trees

D just before the housing development

7

Exploring the Solar System

The **BIG** Idea

Specific conditions are needed for exploration and travel to find new life in our solar system.

LESSON

7.1 Life in the Solar System

Life on Earth requires specific conditions, such as water, organic compounds, and energy from the Sun.

TEKS 7.9(A); Also covers 7.1(A); 7.2(A), (C), (E); 7.3(B); 7.4(A), (B)

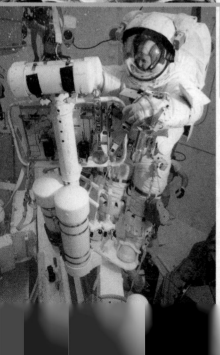

LESSON

7.2 Human Space Travel

Human space exploration has progressed from robotic, unmanned spaceflight to humans living and working in space.

TEKS 7.9(B); Also covers 7.1(A); 7.2(A), (C), (E); 7.3(B), (D); 7.4(A), (B)

Life Beyond Earth?

Three friends were talking about scientists' search for life beyond Earth.
They each had different ideas. This is what they said:

Helda: I think Earth is the only place in our solar system where there is evidence of life.

Jesse: There is life on Earth. Scientists haven't actually seen life on Mars yet, but they have evidence that life exists there.

Mia: There is life on Earth and probably on Mars. Scientists also have evidence that there is life on one of the moons of Jupiter.

Which friend do you agree with the most? _____
Explain why you agree.

INQUIRY

Extraterrestrial Life?

No, scientists have not yet found life beyond Earth. This is a methane ice worm that burrows deep into methane ice in the Gulf of Mexico. How do you think studying organisms that live in extreme environments on Earth helps scientists search for life beyond Earth?

 Write your response in your interactive notebook.

 LAB Manager

Go to your Lab Manual or visit connectED.mcgraw-hill.com to perform the labs for this lesson.

MiniLAB: *What is one factor that makes Earth "just right" for life?*

TEKS 7.1(A); 7.2(A), (C), (E); 7.3(B); 7.4(A), (B); 7.9(A)

Skill Practice: *What solar system objects beyond Earth might have conditions that support life?*

TEKS 7.1(A); 7.2(A), (C), (E); 7.9(A)

Explore Activity

TEKS 7.1(A), 7.2(A), (C), (E); 7.3(B); 7.4(A), (B); 7.9(A)

How are Earth's organisms protected from harmful solar energy?

The Sun's ultraviolet, or UV, radiation is useful to many organisms on Earth. However, too much UV radiation can be harmful.

Procedure

1. Read and complete a lab safety form.

2. Use **scissors** to cut out a **cardboard circle** about 5 cm wide.

3. Use **tape** to attach the circle to the piece of **special paper** provided by your teacher.

4. Place your paper, with the cardboard circle on top, on a sunny windowsill for 3 min.

5. Take the paper back to your work area. With the room darkened, remove the cardboard circle from the paper. Observe the paper and draw what you see in your Lab Manual or interactive notebook.

Think About This

1. The cardboard circle models the part of Earth that protects the planet's organisms from harmful UV energy. Which part of Earth do you think the circle models?

2. Analyze the conditions necessary for life to exist on Earth. What are they, and how are they important?

TEKS in this Lesson

7.9(A) Analyze the characteristics of objects in our solar system that allow life to exist such as the proximity of the Sun, presence of water, and composition of the atmosphere.

Also covers Process Standards: 7.1(A), 7.2(A), (C), (E); 7.3(B); 7.4(A), (B)

Essential Questions

- What conditions on Earth enable life to exist?
- What conditions on other bodies in the solar system might enable life to exist?

Vocabulary

astrobiology
organic
geyser

Conditions for Life on Earth **TEKS** 7.9(A)

Life exists in nearly every environment on Earth. Some environments have conditions so extreme that humans cannot live in them. These places might have extreme temperatures, high salt levels, total darkness, or little water. Even though humans cannot live in these places, other organisms can.

Despite the extreme conditions in which some organisms live, all Earth's life-forms need the same basic things to survive: a source of energy, liquid water, and nourishment. Scientists have not yet found life anywhere else in the solar system. However, by studying the conditions that support life on Earth, they are learning about conditions that might support life elsewhere. **Astrobiology** *is the study of the origin, development, distribution, and future of life in the universe.*

Extremophiles are organisms that have been found living in very extreme conditions. These conditions can include extreme temperatures, high acidity levels, absence of oxygen, or a high level of salt. Some examples are shown in **Figure 1** below. The water that those organisms live in is saturated with chemicals that could kill other organisms.

Energy from the Sun

The Sun is the source of almost all energy on Earth. Sunlight provides light and thermal energy. It also provides energy for plants, which are at the base of most food chains. However, a small percentage of organisms on Earth receive energy from chemicals or from Earth itself, such as the animals shown in **Figure 1.**

Figure 1 A variety of animals live in complete darkness near hot water vents in the ocean floor.

Protection by the Atmosphere

Earth's moon receives about the same amount of sunlight as Earth. Yet conditions on the surface of the Moon are more extreme than they are on Earth. The Moon's surface temperature can rise to 100°C during the day and drop to –150°C at night. Temperatures are extreme on the Moon because the Moon, unlike Earth, does not have an atmosphere.

Maintains Temperatures Earth's atmosphere is like a blanket around Earth. It absorbs sunlight during the day and keeps heat from escaping into space during the night. It maintains Earth's average surface temperature at a comfortable 14°C.

Absorbs Harmful Radiation Have you ever had a painful sunburn? Sunburns are caused by the Sun's ultraviolet light. Even though you cannot see ultraviolet light, you can feel its effects. Too much ultraviolet light can harm you. Fortunately, Earth's atmosphere absorbs most of the Sun's ultraviolet light, as well as X-rays and other potentially harmful energy from the Sun. The atmosphere also helps protect Earth from highly charged particles that erupt from the Sun in powerful storms.

Burns Up Meteoroids Earth's atmosphere also protects Earth's surface from meteoroids. Millions of meteoroids strike Earth's atmosphere every day. But most of them burn up in the atmosphere before they impact Earth's surface.

A *Closer* Look ⟩ at Extremophiles

The biologically classified domain Archaea is a diverse group of organisms. They often live in extreme environments, such as hot springs, oxygen-free environments, and salt lakes. They often are referred to as extremophiles because they not only survive, they thrive in environments that most other living things cannot tolerate.

One of these environments is the dark, hot, and high-pressure environment known as a hydrothermal vent. Hydrothermal vents are on the seafloor along mid-ocean ridges, volcanic arcs, and at hot spots, such as Hawaii. This environment, first discovered in 1977, is one of the most densely populated locations on the seafloor. Life-forms at hydrothermal vents include tubeworms, octopi, clams, mussels, bacteria, crabs, and scaleworms. All these species have adapted to this harsh environment.

- Tubeworms do not have mouths or stomachs. They obtain their nutrients from the bacteria that live symbiotically in their bodies.

Tubeworms can withstand pressures above 2,000 pounds per square inch.

- Mussels have a symbiotic relationship with bacteria that use hydrogen as their energy source.

- The scaly-foot gastropod (*Crysomallon squamiferum*), a snail, uses iron sulfides, such as pyrite, to create its shell. No other organism is known to use iron like this.

- A vent shrimp (*Rimicaris exoculata*) does not have eyes. It is hypothesized that these shrimp use visual pigments to detect thermal radiation produced by hydrothermal vents at a temperature around 350°C.

Because of these findings, many scientists now think that if life can survive in such harsh environments on Earth, then why couldn't it survive on planets and moons in our solar system and beyond?

Figure 2 Water changes from liquid into a gas or a solid as temperatures and pressures change.

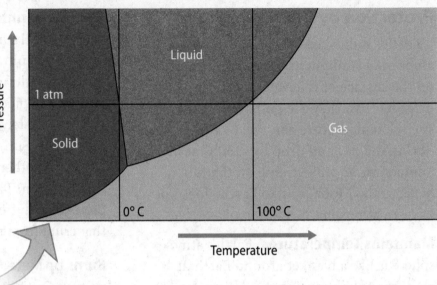

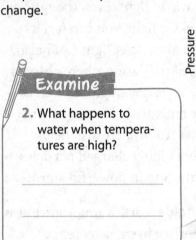

Examine

2. What happens to water when temperatures are high?

_____

_____

_____

Science Use v. Common Use

organic

Science Use relating to carbon compounds in living organisms

Common Use relating to food grown without fertilizers, pesticides, or antibiotics

FOLDABLES

Make a three-tab Venn book. Label it as shown. Use it to compare and contrast the ability of Earth and the Moon to sustain life.

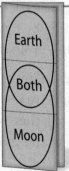

Liquid Water

Liquid water is necessary for all life on Earth. Water dissolves minerals and transports molecules in cells. Without liquid water, cells could not function and life would not exist. Earth's atmosphere keeps pressures and temperatures on Earth's surface within a range where water can exist as a liquid.

Depending on temperature and pressure on Earth, water is solid, liquid, or gas, as shown in **Figure 2**. At sea level on Earth, 1 atmosphere (atm) of pressure, water is liquid between 0°C and 100°C. Above 100°C, water boils and becomes water vapor. Below 0°C, it freezes into ice. However, at different altitudes on Earth, such as on the top of a mountain, the boiling and freezing temperatures of water change slightly because the pressure in the atmosphere changes. Without Earth's atmosphere, pressures on Earth's surface would be too low for water to be liquid. Water would exist only as water vapor or ice.

Nourishment

Living things are nourished by nutrients they take from the air, water, and land around them. They use the nutrients for energy, growth, and other processes, such as reproduction and cellular repair. All molecules that provide nourishment for life on Earth contain carbon. They are organic molecules. **Organic** _refers to a class of chemical compounds in living organisms that are based on carbon._ Though it is possible that inorganic life could exist elsewhere, astrobiologists are most interested in places beyond Earth where water is liquid and carbon is plentiful.

Looking for Life Elsewhere TEKS 7.9(A)

In 1835, a New York newspaper published articles claiming that herds of bison and furry, winged bat-men had been observed on Earth's moon. Many people were fooled. Today, people know that the Moon is airless, and scientists have yet to find life there. Because liquid water is essential for life on Earth, scientists look for places in our solar system where liquid water might exist or might have existed in the past. In 2009, scientists discovered water on the Moon. Although water might not exist on the surface of a planet or a moon, it might exist beneath the surface.

Mars

Other than Earth, Mars is the planet scientists think is most likely to have liquid water. On the surface of Mars, pressures probably are too low for water to be liquid; water would likely evaporate quickly in the thin, dry atmosphere. Temperatures are also low. They generally range from −87°C to −5°C, though they can reach a high of 20°C during the Martian summer.

Scientists have sent many uncrewed spacecrafts to Mars, but none has detected liquid water. However, there is abundant evidence for water vapor and water ice on the Martian surface. And photographs show surface features on Mars that appear to have been carved by moving water. The channels shown in **Figure 3** look like streambeds. It is possible that water from an underground ocean seeped to the surface and flowed as rivers or floods before evaporating. How much water was in these channels and how long ago it flowed are still unknown.

Figure 3 Scientists hypothesize that these Martian channels could be ancient streambeds.

LAB Manager

Skill Practice: *What solar system objects beyond Earth might have conditions that support life?*
TEKS 7.1(A); 7.2(A), (C), (E); 7.9(A)

Math Skills   TEKS 7.4(A) **Math** TEKS 7.1(A); 7.3(A), (B)

Finding the Mean
The mean of a set of data is the arithmetic average. To find the mean, add the numbers in the data set and then divide by the number of items in the set. For example, during one Martian day, surface temperatures were measured at −51.3°C, −31.9°C, −0.800°C, −0.200°C, and −17.6°C. What was the mean temperature during that day?

1. Find the sum of all the values. Use a calculator to find the answer.

2. Divide by the number of temperatures in the set.

Practice
The temperature at the Martian polar ice caps can drop to −143°C. The warmest spots on the planet can reach 20°C.

What is the mean of these extreme temperatures?

Check   Tutor

Go Online!

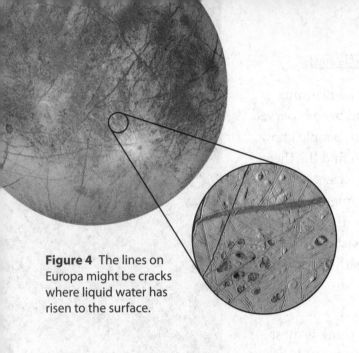

Figure 4 The lines on Europa might be cracks where liquid water has risen to the surface.

Identify

3. Highlight locations where life might exist beyond the inner planets. Underline the possible conditions that are present to support life.

Figure 5 Geysers on Enceladus are evidence that liquid water might exist beneath the moon's icy surface.

Other Planets

Mercury and Venus are too hot for water to be liquid on or near their surfaces. The four outer planets are too cold. The outer planets also are too gaseous. They have no solid surfaces on which liquid water could form. Though some liquid water might exist deep in the interiors of the outer planets, it is unlikely that the water could support life.

Natural Satellites

Scientists continue to look for further evidence of water on Earth's moon and on the moons of other planets. Even though temperatures in the outer solar system are extremely cold, scientists have found that as a satellite orbits a massive planet, the planet's gravity can cause the satellite's interior to heat. This might provide enough thermal energy to allow liquid water to exist near their icy surfaces.

Several moons have surface features that indicate the presence of liquid water not far below. For example, scientists suggest that the ridges on Europa (yuh ROH puh), one of Jupiter's moons, shown in **Figure 4,** could be cracks in the ice where liquid water has seeped to the surface and frozen solid. Callisto and Ganymede, two other moons of Jupiter, and Titan, a moon of Saturn, show similar surface features.

Several other moons in the solar system, including Enceladus (en SEL uh dus), a moon of Saturn, and Triton, a moon of Neptune, show evidence of geysers (GI zurz). *A* **geyser** *is a warm spring that sometimes ejects a jet of liquid water or water vapor into the air.* The massive geysers on Enceladus, shown in **Figure 5,** are hundreds of kilometers high. Two other moons of Saturn, Tethys (TEE thus) and Dione (di OH nee), also have geyserlike plumes.

Illustrate how Earth differs from other objects in the solar system in ways that allow it to support abundant life. Explain your illustration **TEKS** 7.9(A)

Connect it! **Propose** other technologies and items that would help support life on another planet or satellite. Why would you choose these items? Write your response in your interactive notebook.

Life in the Solar System

Apply the Essential Questions

1. Analyze why scientists look for water when searching for life in the solar system. **TEKS** 7.9(A)

_____

_____

2. Compare Which is NOT a good place to look for life? **TEKS** 7.9(A)

A. Enceladus

B. Europa

C. Mars

D. Venus

3. Summarize Which is critical for all life on Earth? **TEKS** 7.9(A)

A. average temperature above 0°C

B. energy from the Sun

C. liquid water

D. oxygen to breathe

H.O.T. Questions (Higher Order Thinking)

4. Evaluate why studying life on Earth helps scientists search for life in the rest of the solar system. **TEKS** 7.9(A)

_____

_____

_____

_____

5. Explain how scientists use their understanding of life on Earth in their search for evidence that life has existed or does exist on Mars or other objects. **TEKS** 7.9(A)

_____

_____

_____

_____

_____

_____

_____

_____

Math Skills | **TEKS** 7.4(A) **Math** **TEKS** 7.1(A); 7.3(A), (B)

Finding the Mean

6. What is the mean of the following temperatures taken at a single location on Mars's surface over four days: −25.4°C, −24.7°C, −28.1°C, and −28.7°C?

Check   Tutor

Go Online!

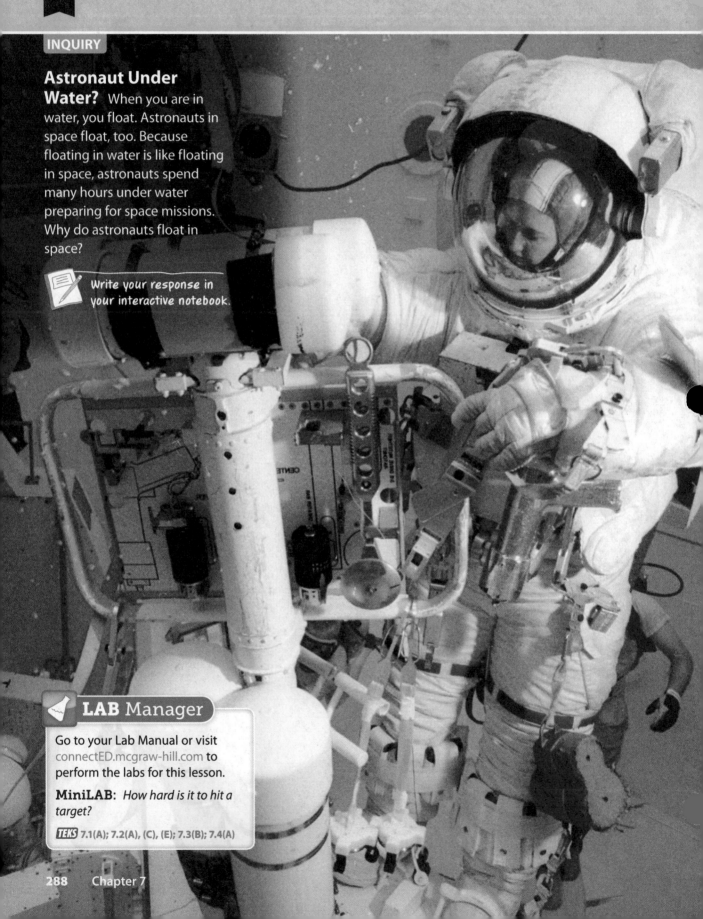

INQUIRY

Astronaut Under Water? When you are in water, you float. Astronauts in space float, too. Because floating in water is like floating in space, astronauts spend many hours under water preparing for space missions. Why do astronauts float in space?

Write your response in your interactive notebook.

LAB Manager

Go to your Lab Manual or visit connectED.mcgraw-hill.com to perform the labs for this lesson.

MiniLAB: *How hard is it to hit a target?*

TEKS 7.1(A); 7.2(A), (C), (E); 7.3(B); 7.4(A)

Explore Activity

TEKS 7.1(A); 7.2(A), (C), (E); 7.4(A), (B); 7.9(B)

How well can you work under pressure?

Technology has had to adapt to enable manned spaceflight. One of those accommodations is the space suit. Astronauts wear space suits when they work outside a spacecraft. The suits, which include gloves, are pressurized to protect the astronauts' bodies. What is it like to work in space wearing space suit gloves?

Procedure

1. Read and complete a lab safety form.

2. Have a partner use a **stopwatch** to see how long it takes you to build a rectangular object using **20 plastic building blocks.** Record the time in your interactive notebook. Then take it apart.

3. Put on a pair of **disposable gloves**. Blow a small amount of air into each glove using a **plastic straw**. Add just enough air to slightly inflate the fingers. Have your partner seal each inflated glove by wrapping **masking tape** around your wrist.

4. Repeat step 2. Then switch roles and repeat the activity.

Think About This

1. How did the construction time required differ in steps 2 and 4?

_____

_____

_____

_____

2. Why do you think all parts of a space suit are pressurized?

_____

_____

_____

3. Identify the factors humans must consider when traveling into space.

_____

_____

TEKS in this Lesson

7.9(B) Identify the accommodations, considering the characteristics of our solar system, that enabled manned space exploration.

Also covers Process Standards: 7.1(A); 7.2(A), (C), (E); 7.3(B), (D); 7.4(A), (B)

? Essential Questions

- What technology and accommodations have allowed humans to explore and travel into space?
- What factors must humans consider when traveling into space?

abc Vocabulary

artificial satellite
rocket
space probe

Technology and Early Space Travel

TEKS 7.9(B)

Figure 1 The exhaust from a rocket launch propels a rocket skyward.

You have lived your entire life in the space age. Most people consider the launch of *Sputnik I* in 1957 by the former Soviet Union to be the beginning of the space age. *Sputnik I* was the first artificial satellite sent into orbit around Earth. *An* **artificial satellite** *is any human-made object placed in orbit around a body in space.* Today, hundreds of artificial satellites operate in orbit around Earth. Some artificial satellites are communication satellites. Some observe Earth. A few observe stars and other objects in distant space.

Escaping Gravity

How do artificial satellites and other spacecrafts reach space? You know that when you jump up into the air, you land back on the ground because of Earth's gravity. But if you could jump fast enough and high enough, you would launch into space! Only a rocket can travel fast enough and far enough to escape Earth's gravity. *A* **rocket** *is a vehicle propelled by the exhaust made from burning fuel.* As its exhaust is forced out, the rocket accelerates forward as shown in **Figure 1.** Most rockets that travel long distances carry two or more tanks of fuel to be able to travel far enough to escape Earth's gravity.

Describe

1. Define the technologies associated with space travel.

Artificial Satellite	Rocket

Then explain what is used to launch artificial satellites into space and why.

Explanation: _____

_____

_____

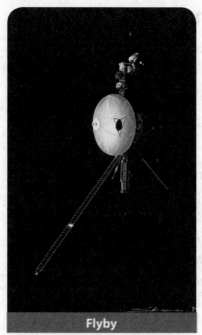

Flyby

Flybys travel to one or more distant space objects and fly by without orbiting or landing.

Orbiter

Orbiters travel to a distant space object and are placed into orbit around the object.

Lander

Landers travel to a distant space object and land on the surface.

Figure 2 Some space probes pass by an object. Others land on the surface.

Robotic Space Probes [TEKS] 7.9(B)

The Moon is the farthest object from Earth that humans have visited. However, scientists have sent robotic missions to every planet, as well as to some moons, asteroids, dwarf planets, and comets. *A* **space probe** *is an uncrewed vehicle that travels to and obtains information about objects in space.* Examples of the three main types of space probes are shown in **Figure 2.** Probes do not return to Earth. They are equipped with cameras and scientific instruments that transmit data to Earth.

There are many reasons to send probes instead of people into space. It costs less and is often safer to send probes. Also, objects in space are very far away. A visit to Mars and back would take more than a year. A round trip to Saturn could take 15 years. Robotic missions are dangerous, too. Only half of the missions sent to Mars have been successful. Space probes that do arrive at their destinations experience harsh conditions and often do not function long.

The National Aeronautics and Space Administration (NASA) is the U.S. government agency that is responsible for most space missions and space-flight technology. Other nations also have space programs. Astronauts from more than 30 countries have traveled to space, and several countries have sent robotic missions to the Moon and beyond.

Identify

2. Which probe would transport a rover, a craft that moves on the surface of an object?

_____

Academic Vocabulary

transmit
(verb) to send something from one person, place, or thing to another

LAB Manager

MiniLAB: *How hard is it to hit a target?*

TEKS 7.1(A); 7.2(A), (C), (E); 7.3(B); 7.4(A)

Word Origin

astronaut from Greek *astron*, means "star"; and Greek *nautes*, means "sailor"

Figure 3 An EMU suit enables an astronaut to spend up to eight hours outside a spacecraft.

Challenges for Humans in Space **TEKS** 7.9(B)

When astronauts travel into space, they must bring their environments and life-support systems with them. Otherwise, they could not withstand the temperatures, the pressures, and the other extreme conditions that exist in space.

Solar Radiation

One threat to astronauts is harmful radiation from the Sun. You read that Earth's atmosphere protects life on Earth from most of the Sun's dangerous radiation. However, as astronauts travel in space, they move far beyond Earth's atmosphere. They must rely on their spacecraft and space suits to shield them from dangerous solar radiation and solar particles. Even with this protection, astronauts have a much higher rate of skin cancers.

Oxygen

Humans need oxygen. Outside Earth's atmosphere, there is not enough oxygen for humans to survive. Air circulation systems inside spacecraft supply oxygen and keep carbon dioxide, which people breathe out, from accumulating. The air humans breathe on Earth is a mixture of nitrogen and oxygen. For short trips into space, spacecrafts carry tanks of oxygen and nitrogen, which are mixed into the proper proportions onboard. For long trips, oxygen is supplied by passing an electric current through water. This separates water's hydrogen and oxygen atoms.

Temperature and Pressure Extremes

Most places in the solar system are extremely cold or extremely hot. Pressures in space are also extreme. In most places, pressure is much lower than the pressure humans experience on Earth. Environmental control systems in a spacecraft protects astronauts from temperature and pressure extremes. Outside the spacecraft, astronauts wear Extravehicular Mobility Unit (EMU) suits, as shown in **Figure 3.** EMU suits provide oxygen, protect astronauts from radiation and meteoroids, and enable astronauts to talk to each other.

Identify

3. Underline the purposes of an EMU suit.

Microgravity

You might think astronauts are weightless in space. But astronauts in orbit around Earth are subjected to almost the same gravity as they are on Earth's surface. Then why is the astronaut shown in **Figure 4** floating? As their spacecraft orbits Earth, the astronauts inside it are continually falling toward Earth. But because their spacecraft is moving, they do not fall. They float. If their spacecraft suddenly stopped moving, they would plunge downward.

The space environment that astronauts experience is often called microgravity. In microgravity, objects seem to be weightless. This can be an advantage. Despite how much something weighs on Earth, it can be moved with ease in space. Microgravity also makes tasks such as turning a screwdriver more difficult. If an astronaut is not careful, instead of the screw turning, he or she might turn instead.

On Earth, working against gravity helps keep your muscles, bones, and heart strong and healthy. But in microgravity, astronauts' bones and muscles don't need to work as hard, and they begin to lose mass and strength. Astronauts in space must exercise several hours each day to keep their bodies healthy.

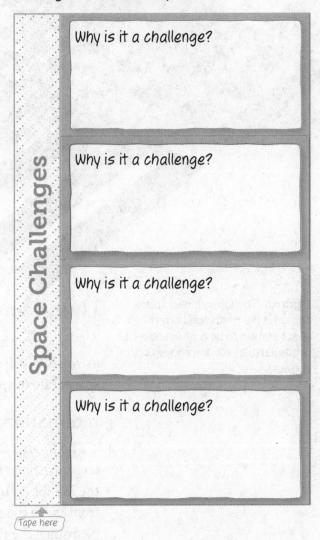

FOLDABLES

Cut out the Lesson 7.2 Foldable in the back of the book. Use it to identify the accommodations and challenges for humans in space.

Space Challenges

Why is it a challenge?

Why is it a challenge?

Why is it a challenge?

Why is it a challenge?

Tape here

Figure 4 Astronaut Eileen Collins floats because she is constantly falling toward Earth as her spacecraft orbits Earth.

Tutor

Go Online!

Eight pairs of solar panels provide power for the *International Space Station.* Each panel measures 34 m x 12 m.

Up to seven astronauts live and work in 14 pressurized modules. Together, the modules are about the same size as two jumbo jets.

Figure 5 The *International Space Station* is the ninth and largest space station to be built in space. It orbits Earth at 400 km above Earth's surface.

Figure 6 European astronaut Paolo Nespoli sleeps strapped into a sleeping bag.

Living and Working in Space   **TEKS** 7.3(D); 7.9(B)

Even when they are protected from the extremes of space, astronauts still face many challenges when living and working in space. Life in space is dramatically different from life on Earth.

International Space Station

The *International Space Station (ISS),* shown in **Figure 5,** is a large, artificial satellite that orbits Earth. People work and live on the *ISS* for up to six months at a time. Constructed by astronauts from more than 15 nations, the *ISS* has been continuously occupied since the first crew arrived in 2000.

The *ISS* crew conducts scientific and medical experiments. These include experiments to learn how microgravity affects people's health and how it affects plants. People living in space for long periods might need to grow plants for food and oxygen. In the future, in addition to being an orbiting research laboratory, the *ISS* eventually might serve as a testing and repair station for missions to the Moon and beyond.

Living in space is not easy. For example, astronauts must place a clip on a book to hold it open to the right page. They eat packaged food using magnetized trays and tableware. Toilets flush with air instead of water. And astronauts must be strapped down while they sleep, as shown in **Figure 6.** Otherwise, they would drift and bump into things.

Transportation Systems

Space transportation systems are the rockets, the shuttles, and the other spacecrafts that deliver cargo and humans to space. **Figure 7** shows the progression of NASA's space transportation systems. Early rockets and spacecrafts, such as those used to transport astronauts to the Moon, were used only once. The early rockets and spacecrafts included three programs. The Mercury program obtained the goal of putting a human into orbit. The Gemini program goals were to test each spacecraft and the crews' thresholds before beginning the Apollo program. The Apollo program achieved the goal of placing the first human on the Moon.

The Space Shuttle was NASA's first reusable transportation system. First launched in 1981, there were five shuttles designed to hold a maximum of seven crew members in each shuttle. The shuttles were designed to transport astronauts to the *International Space Station* to conduct experiments and to service uncrewed satellites, such as the *Hubble Space Telescope*.

Future Space Exploration

Space engineers are continuously working on new technologies and ideas that could advance human space flight and exploration. The last image in **Figure 7** shows what future space transportation systems might look like.

Conclude

4. How has the human space flight program changed?

_____

_____

_____

_____

_____

_____

_____

_____

Figure 7 NASA has launched many different types of spacecrafts carrying humans into space. This timeline shows the variety of the spacecrafts.

◄ **Mercury Mission**
1961–1963

▲ **Gemini Missions**
1965–1966

► **Skylab**
1973–1979

▲ *International*
Space Station
1998–present

◄ **Apollo Missions**
1968–1972

Future Missions ►

Summarize it!

Describe the *International Space Station* and the accommodations
needed and used for exploration. **TEKS** 7.9(B)

Use:

Power source:

Possible future use:

ISS

Interior size:

Crew size:

Location:

Connect it! **Differentiate** the challenges of uncrewed versus crewed space flight.

Human Space Travel

Use Vocabulary

1. **Distinguish** between a *rocket* and a *space probe*. **TEKS** 7.9(B)

_____

_____

_____

Apply the Essential Questions

2. **Identify** which of the following is NOT a type of space probe. **TEKS** 7.9(B)

   A. flyby   **C.** orbiter

   B. lander   **D.** shuttle

3. **Compare** how a microgravity environment is an advantage and a disadvantage for space travelers. **TEKS** 7.9(B)

_____

_____

_____

_____

4. **Explain** how the *International Space Station* is used now and how it might be used in the future. **TEKS** 7.9(B)

_____

_____

_____

_____

_____

 H.O.T. Questions (Higher Order Thinking)

5. **Interpret Graphics** The photo below shows the *International Space Station*. What purpose does the part labeled X serve? **TEKS** 7.9(B)

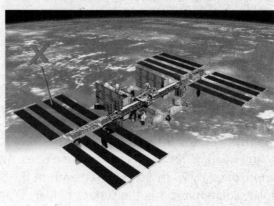

_____

_____

_____

6. **Evaluate** the following statement: *Astronauts in orbit are weightless because they are so far from Earth's surface.* **TEKS** 7.9(B)

_____

_____

_____

7. **Infer** why the *International Space Station* is being assembled in space and not on Earth. **TEKS** 7.9(B)

_____

_____

_____

Science and
SOCIETY

Salads on Mars

Have you eaten a salad today?

The plants that make up a salad have vitamins and nutrients that humans need to survive. Salads are hard to find on Mars, but scientists are working to fix that.

You may recall that as the Sun's energy passes through Earth's atmosphere, some of that energy is absorbed by gases and particles and some is reflected back into space. Scientists call this interaction the greenhouse effect.

Unfortunately, the greenhouse effect barely occurs in the Martian atmosphere. The thin atmosphere is not able to absorb and reflect solar radiation like Earth's atmosphere does. Although Mars is approximately 79 million km farther from the Sun than Earth is, more solar radiation reaches the surface of Mars than the surface of Earth. This means that more radiation also escapes the atmosphere instead of being trapped and warming the surface. The greenhouse effect that exists on Earth to help regulate its temperature and grow crops will need to be duplicated by astronauts on Mars for them to survive. Being able to live and work with solar radiation on Mars is an important problem facing scientists and astronauts at the National Aeronautics and Space Administration (NASA).

At NASA's Kennedy Space Center in Florida, scientists have already started experiments to address these problems. They are developing small, pressurized greenhouses for the Martian landscape.

These greenhouses will be able to maintain an atmospheric pressure like that of Earth. They also will regulate the temperature inside the greenhouse so the plants will feel like they are right at home. If the pressure and temperature are not right, the plants will use too much water, wither, and die.

By mimicking Earth's atmosphere, Martian greenhouses will play a very important role in allowing astronauts to live successfully on Mars. The food and oxygen they provide will be essential to allowing astronauts to survive on Mars for long time periods. Hopefully, astronauts will be able to grow enough plants for a good salad.

It's Your Turn!

RESEARCH What kinds of plants should astronauts take with them to Mars? Research the nutritional values of various edible plants. Create a menu of what the astronauts should take. Compare your menu with those of your classmates.

TEKS Review

Test-Taking Strategy

Eliminate Possible Answers If you are unsure about a question, an easy way to increase your odds of getting the correct answer is by eliminating possible answers. If you know that one or two of the possible answers are not correct, you should eliminate them from your options. Then you can focus on determining which of the final two possible answers is correct.

Example

Use the graph below in order to answer question 3.

2 Next, interpret the information provided by the graph. You can see that both pressure and temperature affect when water will experience a change in state. So choices **A** and **B** can be eliminated. You will also see that in order to change from a solid to a liquid, both pressure and temperature need to increase, so choice **C** can be eliminated.

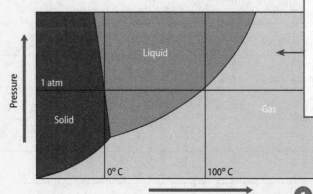

1 Carefully read the question and identify signal words to understand what the question is asking. With this question, we know we're trying to find out which description most accurately describes when solid water will become liquid.

3 Which best describes when water changes from a solid to a liquid?

TEKS 7.9(A)

A Water changes from a solid to a liquid as only pressure decreases.

B Water changes from a solid to a liquid as only pressure increases.

C Water changes from a solid to a liquid as both pressure and temperature decrease.

3 The correct answer is choice **D**.

D Water changes from a solid to a liquid as both pressure and temperature increase.

TIP: When working with graphs and charts, track your pencil from the axis to the point you are reading to ensure you have the correct data value.

Multiple Choice

1 A scientist is analyzing images of an object in the solar system. Which features in the images would cause the scientist to hypothesize that the object might be able to support life?
TEKS 7.9(A); 7.3(A)

A channels that indicate flowing water

B craters that indicate collisions with meteoroids

C poles that indicate a magnetic field

D ridges that indicate tectonic activity

---

2 The diagram shows the parts of a space suit. **TEKS** 7.9(B)

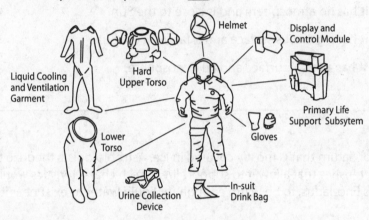

Which correctly explains the function of a space suit part?

A The helmet and solar visors are needed because noise is loud in space.

B The gloves are needed to prevent injury while operating equipment on the spacecraft.

C The liquid cooling and ventilation garment is needed because temperatures can be high when facing the Sun.

D The primary life support subsystem is needed because there are pockets of oxygen-deficient air in space.

3 The table below shows characteristics of objects in the solar system. **TEKS** 7.9(A); 7.2(E)

	Atmosphere	Surface conditions	Signs of tectonic activity	Distance from Sun	Organic compounds
Characteristics of Objects in the Solar System					
Object A	yes	icy	active geysers	8 AU	yes
Object B	no	rocky	extinct volcanoes	0.2 AU	yes
Object C	yes	gaseous	no	30 AU	no
Object D	yes	rocky	no	1.5 AU	no

Which object would interest a scientist most in terms of characteristics necessary to support life?

A Object A because it has geysers and organic compounds.

B Object B because it has no atmosphere and is close to the Sun.

C Object C because it has a gaseous surface and is far from the Sun.

D Object D because it has a rocky surface and an atmosphere.

---

4 Enceladus is a moon of Saturn that is mostly covered in ice. Astrobiologists theorize that Enceladus may have characteristics that allow it to support life. Which characteristics would allow a distant object, such as Enceladus, to be warm enough for liquid water to exist near its surface? **TEKS** 7.9(A)

A An atmosphere made of oxygen, which traps energy from the Sun.

B A thin crust, so solar energy can easily penetrate the ice.

C An interior that experiences tidal heating because the object orbits a massive planet and has an eccentric orbit.

D An orbit that is eccentric, causing the object to approach the Sun during part of the year.

5

Go Online!

Spacecrafts and space stations are enclosed areas with microgravity environments. Recent studies show that microorganisms that can cause disease can multiply very fast in these environments. Astronauts in space must therefore take extra precautions to avoid spreading infectious diseases, such as colds. For example, sleeping and dining areas are cleaned on a routine basis.

Identify which additional action would best prevent the spread of infectious diseases among astronauts in a spacecraft. **TEKS** 7.9(B); 7.2(E)

A sealing trash and used clothes in plastic bags

B taking cold medicine on a daily basis

C exercising regularly

D wearing spacesuits while in the spacecraft

My Notes

TEKS Strand 5
Organisms and Environments

✓ **7.10** The student knows that there is a relationship between organisms and the environment.

✓ **7.11** The student knows that populations and species demonstrate variation and inherit many of their unique traits through gradual processes over many generations.

✓ **7.12** The student knows that living systems at all levels of organization demonstrate the complementary nature of structure and function.

✓ **7.13** The student knows that a living organism must be able to maintain balance in stable internal conditions in response to external and internal stimuli.

✓ **7.14** The student knows that reproduction is a characteristic of living organisms and that the instructions for traits are governed in the genetic material.

Texas Fun Fact

Did You Know? The largest bat colony in North America roosts under the Congress Avenue Bridge in Austin, Texas. About 1.5 million Mexican free-tailed bats nest in the crevices under the bridge. They eat between 4,500 and 9,000 kg of insects each night.

Relationships Between Organisms and Environments

💡 ## The **BIG** Idea

Each of Earth's land biomes and aquatic ecosystems is characterized by distinct environments and organisms. Biomes and ecosystems change by natural processes and by human activities.

LESSON

8.1 Land Biomes

Each of Earth's seven land biomes has a distinct climate and contains animals and plants that are well adapted to their environment.

TEKS 7.10(A), (B); Also covers 7.1(A); 7.2(A), (C), (E); 7.3(B); 7.4(A), (B)

LESSON

8.2 Aquatic Ecosystems

Earth's aquatic ecosystems include saltwater and freshwater ecosystems.

TEKS 7.10(A), (B); Also covers 7.1(A); 7.2(A), (C), (E); 7.3(A), (B), (D); 7.4(A), (B)

LESSON

8.3 How Ecosystems Change

Land and aquatic ecosystems change over time in predictable processes.

TEKS 7.10(C); Also covers 7.2(A), (E)

Watch   Resources   Vocab   Tutor   IWB   Check   Lab

Desert Descriptions

Deserts are one of the seven major land biomes. Put an X next to any of the characteristics that can describe a desert.

☐ **A.** Earth's driest ecosystem

☐ **B.** Can be hot during the day and cold at night

☐ **C.** Can be very cold all the time

☐ **D.** Has soil that holds water

☐ **E.** Has plants that can store water

☐ **F.** Has plants with large leaves

☐ **G.** Can be near an ocean

☐ **H.** Only found in subtropical areas

☐ **I.** Are always sand-covered

☐ **J.** Lizards, bats, birds, and snakes live there.

Explain your thinking. Describe what makes a desert different from other biomes.

INQUIRY

Plant or Animal? Believe it or not, this is a flower. One of the largest flowers in the world, *Rafflesia* (ruh FLEE zhuh), grows naturally in the tropical rain forests of southeast Asia. What do you think would happen if you planted a seed from this plant in a desert? Would it survive?

Write your response in your interactive notebook.

LAB Manager

Go to your Lab Manual or visit connectED.mcgraw-hill.com to perform the labs for this lesson.

MiniLAB: *How hot is sand?*
TEKS 7.1(A); 7.2(A), (C), (E); 7.3(B); 7.4(A), (B); 7.10(A)

Skill Practice: *Which biome is it?*
TEKS 7.2(C), (E); 7.4(A); 7.10(A)

Explore Activity

TEKS 7.1(A); 7.2(A), (C), (E); 7.4(A), (B); 7.10(A)

What lives in a microhabitat?

An ecosystem can be a large area, such as the Chihuahuan Desert, or a small area, such as a flower bed. Very small ecosystems, such as a rotting log or a clump of grass, are often called microhabitats. What organisms live in microhabitats around your schoolyard?

Procedure

1. With a partner, find a microhabitat in your schoolyard.

2. Examine the area of your microhabitat closely. Use an **insect trap** or a **collecting net** to obtain smaller organisms. Use a **magnifying lens** to observe them.

3. In your Lab Manual or your interactive notebook, list and describe the abiotic and biotic factors you observe.

4. Compare your findings with those of another group.

Think About This

1. Compare and contrast the abiotic factors in the two microhabitats.

_____

_____

_____

_____

2. Describe how the organisms in the two microhabitats compare. How do they differ?

_____

_____

_____

_____

3. Describe how the environment of each microhabitat supports the organisms that live there.

_____

_____

_____

TEKS in this Lesson

7.10(A) Observe and describe how different environments, including microhabitats in schoolyards and biomes, support different varieties of organisms.

7.10(B) Describe how biodiversity contributes to the sustainability of an ecosystem.

Also covers Process Standards: 7.1(A); 7.2(A), (C), (E); 7.3(B); 7.4(A), (B)

? Essential Questions

- How do Earth's land biomes differ?
- How does biodiversity impact the sustainability of an ecosystem?

Vocabulary

biome
desert
grassland
temperate
taiga
tundra

Land Ecosystems and Biomes **TEKS** 7.10(A), (B)

When you go outside, you might notice people, grass, flowers, birds, and insects. You also are probably aware of nonliving things, such as air, sunlight, and water. The living or once-living parts of an environment are the biotic parts. The nonliving parts that the living parts need to survive are the abiotic parts. The biotic and abiotic parts of an environment together make up an ecosystem.

Earth's continents have many different ecosystems, from deserts to rain forests. Scientists classify similar ecosystems in large geographic areas as biomes. *A* **biome** *is a geographic area on Earth that contains ecosystems with similar biotic and abiotic features.* As shown in **Figure 1,** Earth has seven major land biomes. Areas classified as the same biome have similar climates and organisms.

Identify

1. (Circle) the names of the two biomes that contain most of Texas.

Watch

Go Online!

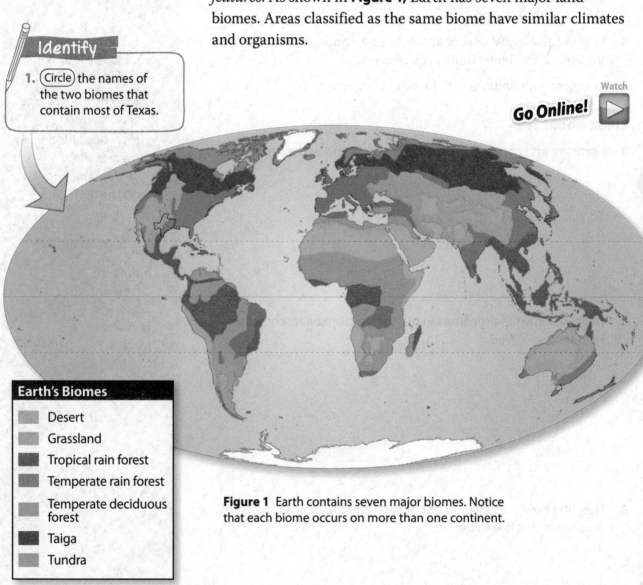

Earth's Biomes

- Desert
- Grassland
- Tropical rain forest
- Temperate rain forest
- Temperate deciduous forest
- Taiga
- Tundra

Figure 1 Earth contains seven major biomes. Notice that each biome occurs on more than one continent.

Biodiversity in Ecosystems and Biomes

The abiotic factors in each major land biome determine which organisms can live in those ecosystems. The organisms that live in deserts might not survive in tropical rain forests. However, each biome supports a variety of species. The number of different species in an area is its biodiversity. The greater the biodiversity in an ecosystem, the more likely that ecosystem will be sustainable, maintaining diversity and staying healthy.

How does biodiversity contribute to the sustainability of an ecosystem? High biodiversity means that there are a large number of different plant and animal species in an ecosystem. And this means that the animals in that ecosystem have many sources of food. For example, the zebras and wildebeests in **Figure 2** are prey for lions in that ecosystem. If the population of zebras is decreased due to a disease, the lions can feed on the wildebeests until the zebra population increases.

Figure 2 Wildebeests and zebras live in the same ecosystem. Both are prey for lions.

FOLDABLES

Cut out the Lesson 8.1 Foldable in the back of the book. Record what you learn about desert and temperate rain forest biomes under the tabs, and use the information to compare and contrast these biomes.

Two Biomes

Biodiversity:

Human Impact:

Biodiversity:

Human Impact:

U.S. Desert

Temperature (°C): 38, 32, 27, 21, 16, 10, 5, -1, -6, -12, -18, -23, -29, -34

Precipitation (cm): 65, 60, 55, 50, 45, 40, 35, 30, 25, 20, 15, 10, 5, 0

Month: J F M A M J J A S O N D

Guadalupe Mountains
National Park, Texas

Gila woodpecker nesting in a giant saguaro cactus

Desert Biome   **TEKS** 7.10(A)

Deserts *are biomes that receive very little rain.* They are on nearly every continent and are Earth's driest ecosystems.

- Most deserts are hot during the day and cold at night. Others, like those in Antarctica, remain cold all of the time.
- Rainwater drains away quickly because of thin, porous soil. Large patches of ground are bare.

Biodiversity

- Animals include lizards, bats, woodpeckers, and snakes. Most animals avoid activity during the hottest parts of the day.
- Plants include spiny cactus and thorny shrubs. Shallow roots absorb water quickly. Some plants have accordion-like stems that expand and store water. Small leaves or spines reduce the loss of water.

Human Impact

- Cities, farms, and recreational areas in deserts use valuable water.
- Desert plants grow slowly. When they are damaged by people or livestock, recovery takes many years.

Describe

2. <u>Underline</u> text evidence that describes how organisms survive in a desert biome.

Grassland Biome   **TEKS** 7.10(A)

Grassland *biomes are areas where grasses are the dominant plants.* Also called prairies, savannas, and meadows, grasslands are the world's "breadbaskets." Wheat, corn, oats, rye, barley, and other important cereal crops are grasses. They grow well in these areas.

- Grasslands have a wet and a dry season.
- Deep, fertile soil supports plant growth.
- Grass roots form a thick mass, called sod, which helps soil absorb and hold water during periods of drought.

Biodiversity

- Trees grow along moist banks of streams and rivers. Wildflowers bloom during the wet season.
- In North America, large herbivores, such as bison and elk, graze here. Insects, birds, rabbits, prairie dogs, and snakes find shelter in the grasses.

- Predators in North American grasslands include hawks, ferrets, coyotes, and wolves.
- African savannas are grasslands that contain giraffes, zebras, and lions. Australian grasslands are home to kangaroos, wallabies, and wild dogs.

Human Impact

- People plow large areas of grassland to raise cereal crops. This reduces habitat for wild species.
- Because of hunting and loss of habitat, large herbivores, such as bison, are now uncommon in many grasslands.

Infer

3. **Highlight** reasons why cereal crops grow well in grasslands.

U.S. Grassland

Burrowing owls in burrow on tallgrass prairie

Bison grazing on grassland, Montana

Organize it!

Organize information about desert and grassland biomes.

Deserts

High Temperature (°C)	Low Temperature (°C)	Rainfall (cm)
January: _____	January: _____	January: _____
June: _____	June: _____	June: _____

Grasslands

High Temperature (°C)	Low Temperature (°C)	Rainfall (cm)
January: _____	January: _____	January: _____
June: _____	June: _____	June: _____

Connect it! **Analyze** the data you recorded above, and **predict** which biome has the greatest biodiversity. Explain your reasoning. **TEKS** 7.10(A)

_____

_____

_____

_____

Tropical Rain Forest Biome

TEKS 7.10(A)

The forests that grow near the equator are called tropical rain forests. These forests receive large amounts of rain and have dense growths of tall, leafy trees.

- Weather is warm and wet year-round.
- The soil is shallow and easily washed away by rain.
- Less than 1 percent of the sunlight that reaches the top of forest trees also reaches the forest floor.
- Half of Earth's species live in tropical rain forests. Most live in the canopy—the uppermost part of the forest.

Biodiversity

- Few plants live on the dark forest floor.
- Vines climb the trunks of tall trees.
- Mosses, ferns, and orchids live on branches in the canopy.
- Insects make up the largest group of tropical animals. They include beetles, termites, ants, bees, and butterflies.
- Larger animals include parrots, toucans, snakes, frogs, flying squirrels, fruit bats, monkeys, jaguars, and ocelots.

Human Impact

- People have cleared more than half of Earth's tropical rain forests for lumber, farms, and ranches. Poor soil does not support rapid growth of new trees in cleared areas.
- Cutting down forests allows insect pests to reproduce rapidly in cleared areas.
- Some organizations are working to encourage people to use less wood harvested from rain forests.

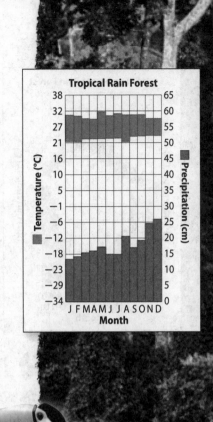

Tropical Rain Forest

Temperature (°C) / Precipitation (cm)

Month — J F M A M J J A S O N D

Toucan

Lowland rain forest, Borneo, Malaysia

Infer

4. How do human actions affect biodiversity in rain forests? Write your response in your interactive notebook.

Temperate Rain Forest Biome **TEKS** 7.10(A)

Regions of Earth between the tropics and the polar circles are **temperate** *regions.* Temperate regions have relatively mild climates with distinct seasons.

Several biomes are in temperate regions, including rain forests. Temperate rain forests are moist ecosystems mostly in coastal areas. They are not as warm as tropical rain forests.

- Winters are mild and rainy.
- Summers are cool and foggy.
- Soil is rich and moist.

U.S. Temperate Rain Forest

Temperature (°C) / Precipitation (cm)

32 — 65
27 — 60
21 — 55
16 — 50
10 — 45
5 — 40
−1 — 35
−6 — 30
−12 — 25
−18 — 20
−23 — 15
−29 — 10
−34 — 5
−39 — 0

J F M A M J J A S O N D
Month

Determine

5. On the graph at left, (circle) the hottest and driest months. What is the relationship between precipitation and temperature on the graph? Write your response in your interactive notebook.

Biodiversity

- Forests are dominated by spruce, hemlock, cedar, fir, and redwood trees, which can grow very large and tall.
- Fungi, ferns, mosses, vines, and small flowering plants grow on the moist forest floor.
- Animals include mosquitoes, butterflies, frogs, salamanders, woodpeckers, owls, eagles, chipmunks, raccoons, deer, elk, bears, foxes, and cougars.

Human Impact

- Temperate rain forest trees are a source of lumber. Logging can destroy the habitat of forest species.
- Rich soil enables cut forests to grow back. Tree farms help provide lumber without destroying habitat.

Hoh Rain Forest, Olympic National Park, Washington

Evaluate

6. After logging, which rain forest would be more likely to recover—tropical or temperate? Explain your reasoning. Write your response in your interactive notebook.

Review the information on the biodiversity of plants in the *Tropical Rain Forest Biome* section. In the space below, draw the different types of plants and where they grow in a tropical rain forest.

TEKS 7.10(A)

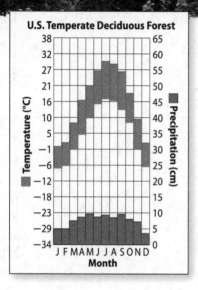

Great Smoky Mountains National Park, Newfound Gap, North Carolina

Red fox

U.S. Temperate Deciduous Forest

Temperature (°C): 38, 32, 27, 21, 16, 10, 5, −1, −6, −12, −18, −23, −29, −34

Precipitation (cm): 65, 60, 55, 50, 45, 40, 35, 30, 25, 20, 15, 10, 5, 0

Month: J F M A M J J A S O N D

Temperate Deciduous Forest Biome TEKS 7.10(A)

Temperate deciduous forests grow in temperate regions where winter and summer climates have more variation than those in temperate rain forests. These forests are the most common forest ecosystems in the United States. They contain mostly deciduous trees, which lose their leaves in the fall.

- Winter temperatures are often below freezing. Snow is common.
- Summers are hot and humid.
- Soil is rich in nutrients and supports a large amount of diverse plant growth.

Biodiversity

- Most plants, such as maples, oaks, birches, and other deciduous trees, stop growing during the winter and begin growing again in the spring.
- Animals include snakes, ants, butterflies, birds, raccoons, opossums, and foxes.
- Some animals, including chipmunks and bats, spend the winter in hibernation.
- Many birds and some butterflies, such as the monarch, migrate to warmer climates for the winter.

Human Impact

Over the past several hundred years, humans have cleared thousands of acres of Earth's deciduous forests for farms and cities. Today, much of the clearing has stopped, and some forests have regrown.

STEMonline

Build a scale model of a floral shop featuring plants from the different biomes. Visit ConnectED for the **STEM** activity **Floral Shop**. Resources

Go Online!

Recall

7. Highlight the characteristics that enable different varieties of organisms to live in a temperate deciduous forest.

Taiga Biome **TEKS** 7.10(A)

A **taiga** (TI guh) *is a forest biome consisting mostly of cone-bearing evergreen trees*. The taiga biome exists only in the northern hemisphere. It occupies more space on Earth's continents than any other biome.

Brown bear

- Winters are long, cold, and snowy. Summers are short, warm, and moist.

- Soil is thin and acidic.

Biodiversity

- Evergreen trees, such as spruce, pine, and fir, are thin and shed snow easily.

- Animals include owls, mice, moose, bears, and other cold-adapted species.

- Abundant insects in summer attract many birds, which migrate south in winter.

Human Impact

- Tree harvesting reduces taiga habitat.

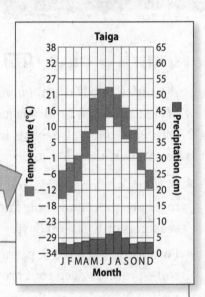

Observe

8. In which month does the taiga biome receive the most precipitation?

The least precipitation? _____

What do you notice about the amount of monthly precipitation in the taiga biome?

Denali National Park, Alaska

Tundra, Ilulissat, Greenland

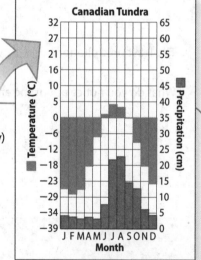

Lemming

Tundra Biome TEKS 7.10(A)

*A **tundra** (TUN druh) biome is cold, dry, and treeless.* Most tundra is just south of the North Pole, but it also exists in mountainous areas at high altitudes.

- Winters are long, dark, and freezing. Summers are short and cool. The growing season is only 50–60 days.

- Permafrost—a layer of permanently frozen soil—prevents deep root growth.

Biodiversity

- Plants include shallow-rooted mosses and grasses. Lichens are also common.

- Many animals hibernate or migrate south during winter. A few animals, including lemmings, live in tundras year-round.

Human Impact

- Drilling for oil and gas can interrupt migration patterns.

Calculate

9. Use the space below to calculate the average monthly temperature in the Canadian tundra during the coldest months (October through May) and during the warmest months (June through September). Infer how the differences in temperature affect biodiversity in the tundra.

Canadian Tundra

Temperature (°C) axis: 32, 27, 21, 16, 10, 5, 0, −6, −12, −18, −23, −29, −34, −39

Precipitation (cm) axis: 65, 60, 55, 50, 45, 40, 35, 30, 25, 20, 15, 10, 5, 0

Month: J F M A M J J A S O N D

Organize it!

Evaluate the human impact on the temperate deciduous forest biome, the taiga biome, and the tundra biome.

Temperate Deciduous Forest

Cause	Effect

Taiga

Cause	Effect

Tundra

Cause	Effect

 Connect it! Select a biome, and describe to your class what might happen to the biodiversity of the biome as a result of human impact. In your interactive notebook, summarize what your classmates say about the other biomes. **TEKS** 7.10(B)

Summarize it!

Identify Earth's seven major land biomes, and describe the biodiversity of plants and animals for each. **TEKS** 7.10(A)

Biome: _____

Plants and animals: _____

_____

_____

Biome: _____

Plants and animals: _____

_____

_____

Biome: _____

Plants and animals: _____

_____

_____

Biome: _____

Plants and animals: _____

_____

_____

Biome: _____

Plants and animals: _____

_____

_____

Biome: _____

Plants and animals: _____

_____

_____

Biome: _____

Plants and animals: _____

_____

_____

Connect it! **Predict** which biome would have the most sustainable biodiversity if the environment in each biome suddenly changed. Which biome would be least sustainable? Write your response in your interactive notebook. **TEKS** 7.10(B)

Use Vocabulary

1. **Distinguish** between tropical rain forests and temperate rain forests.
   TEKS 7.10(A)

   _____

   _____

   _____

2. A cold, treeless biome is a(n)

   _____ .

   TEKS 7.10(A)

Apply the Essential Questions

3. Which biomes have rich, fertile soil?
   TEKS 7.10(A)

   A. grassland and taiga

   B. grassland and tundra

   C. grassland and tropical rain forest

   D. grassland and temperate deciduous forest

4. **Describe** how biodiversity impacts the sustainability of an ecosystem.
   TEKS 7.10(B) _supporting_

   _____

   _____

   _____

   _____

   _____

   _____

H.O.T. Questions (Higher Order Thinking)

5. **Compare** mammals that live in tundra biomes with those that live in desert biomes. What adaptations does each group have that help them survive?
   TEKS 7.10(A)

   _____

   _____

   _____

   _____

   _____

   _____

   _____

6. **Analyze** the sustainability of a tropical rain forest if a drought affects the area.
   TEKS 7.10(B) _supporting_

   _____

   _____

   _____

   _____

   _____

Writing in Science

7. **Observe** your schoolyard and one other microhabitat. On a separate sheet of paper, explain how the different environments of these microhabitats support different varieties of organisms.
   TEKS 7.10(A)

Texas Land Ecosystems

A Diverse State Many people think Texas is a flat, dry state, but it actually has many diverse ecosystems and terrains. You might remember reading that an ecosystem is all the living things and nonliving things in a given area. In order for scientists to better protect and manage the resources in an ecosystem, they group similar ecosystems together and call them an ecoregion. Texas is divided into 11 different ecoregions—Pineywoods, Oak Woods and Prairies, Blackland Prairies, Gulf Coast Prairies and Marshes, Coastal Sand Plains, South Texas Brush Country, the Edwards Plateau, the Llano Uplift, Rolling Plains, High Plains, and the Trans Pecos.

Texas Land Ecosystems

Ecoregion	Soil	Vegetation	Annual Rainfall
1. Pineywoods	gray sands or sandy loam	pines, oaks, hardwood trees (such as elm, ash, tupelo)	91–127 cm
2. Oak Woods and Prairies	sand and sandy loam to clays	oaks, grasses	71–102 cm
3. Blackland Prairies	dark clays and sandy loam	tall-growing grasses	71–102 cm
4. Gulf Coast Prairies and Marshes	sands and sandy loam	tall–growing grasses and oak woodlands	76–127 cm
5. Coastal Sand Plains	windblown sands	tall–growing grasses and oak woodlands	61–71 cm
6. South Texas Brush Country	clays and clay loam	thorny brush, grasses	51–81 cm
7. Edwards Plateau	varied shallow soils over limestone	grasses, juniper, oak woodlands	38–86 cm
8. Llano Uplift	varied shallow soils; large granite domes	oaks, hickory, juniper, short-growing grasses	61–81 cm
9. Rolling Plains	vary from coarse sands to clay and shale	short-growing grasses, mesquite, hardwood trees	51–71 cm
10. High Plains	sand to clay	short-growing grasses	38–56 cm
11. Trans Pecos	varied	varies greatly	<31 cm

RESEARCH Determine which ecoregion your school is in. Research the most abundant types of plants, wildlife, and minerals in your ecoregion. Create a poster describing your findings.

INQUIRY

Floating Trees? These plants, called mangroves, are one of the few types of plants that grow in salt water. They live along ocean coastlines in tropical and subtropical ecosystems, including along the coast of Texas. What other organisms do you think live near mangroves?

Write your response in your interactive notebook.

LAB Manager

Go to your Lab Manual or visit connectED.mcgraw-hill.com to perform the labs for this lesson.

MiniLAB: *How do ocean ecosystems differ?*
TEKS 7.1(A); 7.2(A), (C), (E); 7.3(B); 7.4(A), (B); 7.10(A), (B)

LAB: *A Biome for Radishes*
TEKS 7.1(A); 7.2(A), (C), (E); 7.3(A), (B); 7.4(A), (B); 7.10(A)

Explore Activity

TEKS 7.1(A); 7.2(A), (C), (E); 7.3(A); 7.4(B); 7.10(A)

What happens when rivers and oceans mix?

Freshwater and saltwater ecosystems have different characteristics. What happens in areas where freshwater rivers and streams flow into oceans?

Procedure

1. Read and complete a lab safety form.

2. In a **plastic tub,** add 100 g of **salt** to 2 L of **water.** Stir with a **long-handled spoon** until the salt dissolves.

3. In another **container,** add 5 drops of **blue food coloring** to 1 L of water. Gently pour the colored water into one corner of the plastic tub. Observe how the color of the water changes in the tub.

4. Observe the tub again in 5 min.

Think About This

1. What bodies of water do the containers represent?

_____

_____

2. What happened to the water in the tub after 5 min? What do you think happens to the salt content of the water?

_____

_____

3. Describe how you think the biodiversity of rivers and oceans differs. What organisms do you think might live at the place where the two meet?

_____

_____

_____

_____

_____

TEKS in this Lesson

7.10(A) Observe and describe how different environments, including microhabitats in schoolyards and biomes, support different varieties of organisms

7.10(B) Describe how biodiversity contributes to the sustainability of an ecosystem

Also covers Process Standards: 7.1(A); 7.2(A), (C), (E); 7.3(A), (B), (D); 7.4(A), (B)

? Essential Questions

- How do Earth's aquatic ecosystems differ?

- How does biodiversity impact the sustainability of an aquatic ecosystem?

abc Vocabulary

salinity
wetland
estuary
intertidal zone
coral reef

Aquatic Ecosystems

If you have ever spent time near an ocean, a river, or another body of water, you might know that water is full of life. There are four major types of water, or aquatic, ecosystems: freshwater, wetland, estuary, and ocean. Each type of ecosystem contains a unique variety of organisms. Whales, dolphins, and corals live only in ocean ecosystems. Catfish and trout live only in freshwater ecosystems. Many other organisms that do not live under water, such as seals and the birds in **Figure 1,** also depend on aquatic ecosystems for food and shelter.

A healthy aquatic ecosystem has great biodiversity in the variety of plants and animals living there. This biodiversity sustains the ecosystem by providing numerous organisms that can produce food or be eaten as food.

Important abiotic factors in aquatic ecosystems include temperature, sunlight, and dissolved oxygen gas. Aquatic species have adaptations that enable them to use the oxygen in water. The gills of a fish separate oxygen from water and move it into the fish's bloodstream. Mangrove plants take in oxygen through small pores in their leaves and roots.

Salinity (say LIH nuh tee) is another important abiotic factor in aquatic ecosystems. **Salinity** *is the amount of salt dissolved in water.* Water in saltwater ecosystems has high salinity compared to water in freshwater ecosystems, which contains little salt.

Figure 1 These pelicans depend upon the organisms that live in the waters along the Texas coast for food.

Math Skills Math TEKS 7.1(A); 7.3(A); 7.4(D)

Use Proportions

Salinity is measured in parts per thousand (PPT). Water with a salinity of 1 PPT contains 1 g salt and 1,000 g water. Use proportions to calculate salinity. What is the salinity of 100 g of water with 3.5 g of salt?

$$\frac{3.5 \text{ g salt}}{100 \text{ g seawater}} = \frac{x \text{ g salt}}{1,000 \text{ g seawater}}$$
$$100x = 3,500$$
$$x = \frac{3,500}{100}$$
$$x = 35 \text{ PPT}$$

Practice

A sample of seawater contains 0.1895 g of salt per 50 g of water. What is its salinity?

Check   Tutor

Go Online!

Freshwater: Streams and Rivers TEKS 7.10(A)

Freshwater ecosystems include streams, rivers, ponds, and lakes. Streams are usually narrow, shallow, and fast-flowing. Rivers are larger, deeper, and flow more slowly.

- Streams form from underground sources of water, such as springs, or from runoff from rain and melting snow.
- Stream water is often clear. Soil particles are quickly washed downstream.
- Oxygen levels in streams are high because air mixes into the water as it splashes over rocks.
- Rivers form when streams flow together.
- Soil that washes into a river from streams or nearby land can make river water muddy. Soil also introduces nutrients, such as nitrogen, into rivers.
- Slow-moving river water has higher levels of nutrients and lower levels of dissolved oxygen than fast-moving water.

Salmon

Biodiversity

- Willows, cottonwoods, and other water-loving plants grow along streams and on riverbanks.
- Species adapted to fast-moving water include trout, salmon, crayfish, and many insects.
- Species adapted to slow-moving water include snails and catfish.

Human Impact

- People take water from streams and rivers for drinking, laundry, bathing, crop irrigation, and industrial purposes.
- Hydroelectric plants use the energy in flowing water to generate electricity. Dams stop the water's flow.
- Runoff from cities, industries, and farms is a source of pollution.

Describe

1. What is one major difference between a stream and a river?

_____

_____

_____

_____

_____

_____

River near Lake Tahoe, California

329

Compare and contrast streams and rivers.

	Streams	Rivers
Water movement		
How formed		
Clarity of water		
Oxygen level		
Nutrient level		
Animals		
Plants		
Human impact		

 Connect it! Predict how the biodiversity of a river might be affected if its water movement suddenly changed to be like that of a stream. Write your response in your interactive notebook. **TEKS** 7.10(B)

Dix Lake, Superior National Forest, Minnesota

Freshwater: Ponds and Lakes TEKS 7.10(A)

Ponds and lakes contain freshwater that is not flowing downhill. These bodies of water form in low areas on land.

- Ponds are shallow and warm.
- Sunlight reaches the bottom of most ponds.
- Pond water is often high in nutrients.
- Lakes are larger and deeper than ponds.
- Sunlight penetrates the top few feet of lake water. Deeper water is dark and cold.

LAB Manager

LAB: *A Biome for Radishes*

TEKS 7.1(A); 7.2(A), (C), (E); 7.3(A), (B); 7.4(A), (B); 7.10(A)

Biodiversity

- Plants surround ponds and lake shores.
- Surface water in ponds and lakes contains plants, algae, and microscopic organisms that use sunlight for photosynthesis.
- Organisms living in shallow water near shorelines include cattails, reeds, insects, crayfish, frogs, fish, and turtles.
- Fewer organisms live in the deeper, colder water of lakes, where there is little sunlight.
- Lake fish include perch, trout, bass, and walleye.

Smallmouth bass

Identify

2. **Highlight** reasons why few organisms live in the deep water of lakes.

Human Impact

- Humans fill in ponds and lakes with sediment to create land for houses and other structures.
- Runoff from farms, gardens, and roads washes pollutants into ponds and lakes, disrupting food webs.

Wetlands TEKS 7.10(A)

Some types of aquatic ecosystems have mostly shallow water. **Wetlands** *are aquatic ecosystems that have a thin layer of water covering soil that is wet most of the time.* Wetlands contain freshwater, salt water, or both. They are among Earth's most fertile ecosystems.

- Freshwater wetlands form at the edges of lakes and ponds and in low areas on land. Saltwater wetlands form along ocean coasts.
- Nutrient levels and biodiversity are high.
- Wetlands trap sediments and purify water. Plants and microscopic organisms filter out pollution and waste materials.

Describe

3. How do the different environments of lakes and wetlands support different varieties of organisms? Write your response in your interactive notebook.

Biodiversity

- Water-tolerant plants include grasses and cattails. Few trees live in saltwater wetlands. Trees in freshwater wetlands include cottonwoods, willows, and swamp oaks.
- Insects are abundant and include flies, mosquitoes, dragonflies, and butterflies.
- More than one-third of North American bird species, including ducks, geese, herons, loons, warblers, and egrets, use wetlands for nesting and feeding.
- Other animals that depend on wetlands for food and breeding grounds include alligators, turtles, frogs, snakes, salamanders, muskrats, and beavers.

Human Impact

- In the past, many people considered wetlands to be unimportant environments. Water was drained away to build homes and roads and to raise crops.
- Today, many wetlands are being preserved, and drained wetlands are being restored.

Common loon

Camas Prairie Centennial Marsh, near Fairfield, Idaho

Estuaries TEKS 7.10(A)

Estuaries (ES chuh wer eez) *are regions along coastlines where streams or rivers flow into a body of salt water.* Most estuaries form along coastlines, where freshwater in rivers meets salt water in oceans. Estuary ecosystems have varying degrees of salinity.

- Salinity depends on rainfall, the amount of freshwater flowing from land, and the amount of salt water pushed in by tides.
- Estuaries help protect coastal land from flooding and erosion. Like wetlands, estuaries purify water and filter out pollution.
- Nutrient levels and biodiversity are high.

Biodiversity

- Plants that grow in salt water include mangroves, pickleweeds, and seagrasses.
- Animals include worms, snails, and many species that people use for food, including oysters, shrimp, crabs, and clams.
- Striped bass, salmon, flounder, and many other ocean fish lay their eggs in estuaries.
- Many species of birds depend on estuaries for breeding, nesting, and feeding.

Human Impact

- Large portions of estuaries have been filled with soil to make land for roads and buildings.
- Destruction of estuaries reduces habitat for estuary species and exposes the coastline to flooding and storm damage.

Word Origin

estuary from Latin *aestuarium,* means "a tidal marsh or opening"

Harvest mouse in pickleweed

FOLDABLES

Make a horizontal two-tab book and label it as shown. Use it to compare how biodiversity and human impact differ in wetlands and estuaries.

Wetlands Estuaries

Estuary along Texas coastline

Describe features of a wetland.

Definition: _____

_____

Physical description: _____

_____

Benefit to living things: _____

_____

_____

Human impact: _____

_____

Complete the chart below with information about estuaries.

Definition	
Benefit to humans	
Human impact	

Open Oceans TEKS 7.10(A)

Most of Earth's surface is covered by ocean water with high salinity. The oceans contain different types of ecosystems. If you took a boat trip several kilometers out to sea, you would be in the open ocean—one type of ocean ecosystem. The open ocean extends from the steep edges of continental shelves to the deepest parts of the ocean. The amount of light in the water depends on depth.

- Photosynthesis can occur only in the upper-most, or sunlit, zone. Very little sunlight reaches the twilight zone. None reaches the deepest water, known as the dark zone.

- Decaying matter and nutrients float down from the sunlit zone, through the twilight and dark zones, to the seafloor.

Biodiversity

- Microscopic algae and other producers in the sunlit zone form the base of most ocean food chains. Other organisms living in the sunlit zone are jellyfish, tuna, mackerel, and dolphins.

- Many species of fish stay in the twilight zone during the day and swim to the sunlit zone at night to feed.

- Sea cucumbers, brittle stars, and other bottom-dwelling organisms feed on decaying matter that drifts down from above.

- Many organisms in the dark zone live near cracks in the seafloor where lava erupts and new seafloor forms.

Human Impact

- Overfishing threatens many ocean fish.

- Trash discarded from ocean vessels or washed into oceans from land is a source of pollution. Animals such as seals become tangled in plastic or mistake it for food.

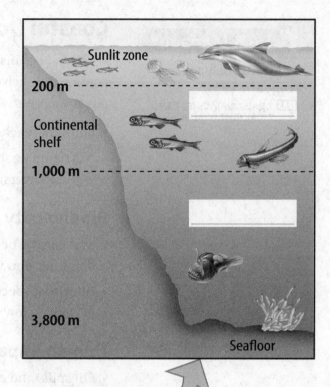

Sunlit zone
200 m
Continental shelf
1,000 m
3,800 m
Seafloor

Identify

4. Fill in the remaining ocean-zone labels. How do the varieties of organisms differ in each ocean zone? Write your response in your interactive notebook.

Jellyfish

Recall

5. Underline which organisms are at the base of ocean food chains.

Coastal Oceans   **TEKS** 7.10(A)

Coastal oceans include several types of ecosystems, including continental shelves and intertidal zones. *The **intertidal zone** is the ocean shore between the lowest low tide and the highest high tide.*

- Sunlight reaches the bottom of shallow coastal ecosystems.
- Nutrients washed in from rivers and streams contribute to high biodiversity.

Biodiversity

- The coastal ocean is home to mussels, fish, crabs, sea stars, dolphins, and whales.
- Intertidal species have adaptations for surviving exposure to air during low tides and to heavy waves during high tides.

Human Impact

- Oil spills and other pollution harm coastal organisms.

A *Closer* Look   at Texas Coastlines

The Texas coastline stretches for 591 km along the Gulf of Mexico. Animals and humans living along the coast use it for habitat and a variety of resources, including oil. The Gulf of Mexico supplies about 25 percent of the oil produced in the United States. On April 20, 2010, an explosion occurred on the *Deepwater Horizon* oil-drilling platform in the Gulf of Mexico. Pollution from the oil spill had a negative impact on the coastal ecosystems of Texas.

Oil pollution can stick to the fur or feathers of many marine mammals and birds. When this happens, they are unable to maintain buoyancy and homeostasis—leaving them vulnerable to predators, over-heating, and hyperthermia. Oil pollution can even cause problems in non-coastal species as the pollution accumulates in top-level predators. Scientists use many different methods to try to contain oil spills. Floating barriers are used to corral oil pollution that floats on the top of ocean water. Chemicals are also used to disperse the oil molecules.

Research Conduct research on the *Deepwater Horizon* oil spill to learn how the spill was contained and cleaned up. Compare the positive and negative aspects of each method and record the results in your interactive notebook.

Black grouper with sea fans and sponges, Caribbean

Spiny lobster

Coral Reefs TEKS 7.10(A)

Another ocean ecosystem with high biodiversity is the coral reef. *A* **coral reef** *is an underwater structure made from outside skeletons of tiny, soft-bodied animals called coral.*

- Most coral reefs form in shallow tropical oceans.
- Coral reefs protect coastlines from storm damage and erosion.

Biodiversity

- Coral reefs provide food and shelter for many animals, including parrotfish, groupers, angelfish, eels, shrimp, crabs, lobsters, scallops, clams, worms, snails, sea fans, and sponges.

Human Impact

- Pollution, overfishing, and harvesting of coral threaten coral reefs.

Describe

6. Write the similarities and differences between coastal oceans and coral reefs in the diagram below.

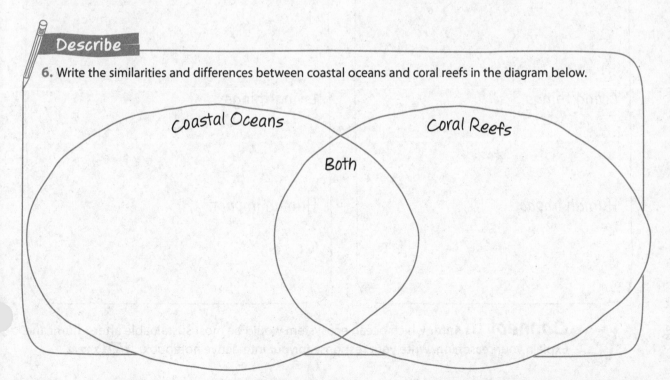

Coastal Oceans   Both   Coral Reefs

Organize it!

Summarize information about ocean ecosystems. **TEKS** 7.10(A)

Open Ocean

Description:

Living things:

Human impact:

Ocean Ecosystems

Coastal Oceans

Description:

Living things:

Human impact:

Coral Reefs

Description:

Living things:

Human impact:

Connect it! **Infer** which ocean ecosystem would be most sustainable after a hurricane. Explain your reasoning. Write your response in your interactive notebook. **TEKS** 7.10(B)

Summarize it!

Use vocabulary terms and other terms from the lesson to complete the concept map. **TEKS** 7.10(A)

```
                    ( Aquatic Ecosystems )

  ┌──────────────┐  ┌──────────┐  ┌──────────┐  ┌──────────────┐
  │  freshwater  │  │          │  │          │  │    oceans    │
  └──────────────┘  └──────────┘  └──────────┘  └──────────────┘

      ┌────────────────────────────┐   ┌────────────────────────────┐
      │ lakes and _____  │   │        open ocean          │
      └────────────────────────────┘   └────────────────────────────┘

      ┌────────────────────────────┐   ┌────────────────────────────┐
      │    streams and rivers      │   │                            │
      └────────────────────────────┘   └────────────────────────────┘

                                       ┌────────────────────────────┐
                                       │                            │
                                       └────────────────────────────┘
```

Connect it! Think about the path of water from a stream to an estuary. **Describe** how prevention of pollution in streams is important to the health and biodiversity of estuaries. **TEKS** 7.10(B)

_____

_____

_____

_____

_____

_____

_____

Aquatic Ecosystems

Use Vocabulary

1. **Distinguish** between a wetland and an estuary. **TEKS** 7.10(A)

Apply the Essential Questions

2. Which ecosystem contains both salt water and freshwater? **TEKS** 7.10(A)

    A. estuary

    B. lake

    C. pond

    D. stream

3. **Describe** what might happen to a coastal area if its estuary were filled in to build houses. **TEKS** 7.10(B) *supporting*

H.O.T. Questions (Higher Order Thinking)

4. **Assess** How can the biodiversity of organisms contribute to the sustainability of a wetlands area? **TEKS** 7.10(B) *supporting*

5. **Contrast** How are ecosystems in the deep water of lakes and oceans different? **TEKS** 7.10(A)

Math Skills | **Math TEKS** 7.1(A); 7.3(A); 7.4(D)

Use Proportions

6. The salinity of the Gulf waters off the Texas coast is about 35 PPT. What weight of salt is present in 2,500 g of seawater?

Check Tutor

Go Online!

Saving an Underwater Wilderness

AMERICAN MUSEUM
ᵒᶠ NATURAL HISTORY

▼ A researcher takes a water sample from a marine reserve.

How do scientists help protect coral reefs?

Pollution and human activities, such as mining and tourism, have damaged many ecosystems, including coral reefs. Scientists and conservation groups are working together to help protect and restore coral reefs and areas that surround them. One way is to create marine reserves where no fishing or collection of organisms is allowed.

A team of scientists, including marine ecologists Dr. Dan Brumbaugh and Kate Holmes from the American Museum of Natural History, are investigating how well reserves are working. These scientists compare how many fish of one species live both inside and outside reserves. Their results indicate that more species of fish and greater numbers of each species live inside reserves than outside—one sign that reefs in the area are improving.

Reef ecosystems do not have to be part of a reserve in order to improve, however. Scientists can work with local governments to find ways to limit damage to reef ecosystems. One way is to prevent overfishing by limiting the number of fish caught. Other ways include eliminating the use of destructive fishing practices that can harm reefs and reducing runoff from farms and factories.

By creating marine reserves, regulating fishing practices, and reducing runoff, humans can help reefs that were once in danger become healthy again.

Kate Holmes examines a coral reef. ▶

It's Your Turn!

COMPOSE Write a letter to a town near a marine reserve describing why it is important to maintain a protected area.

INQUIRY

How did this happen?
This object was once part of a mining system used to move copper and iron ore. Today, so many forest plants have grown around it that it is barely recognizable. How do you think this happened? What do you think this object will look like after 500 more years?

Write your response in your interactive notebook.

Explore Activity

TEKS 7.2(A), (E); 7.10(C)

How do communities change?

An ecosystem can change over time. Change usually happens so gradually that you might not notice differences from day to day.

Procedure

1. Below are two pictures of ecosystem communities. One is labeled A, and the other is labeled B.

2. Imagine community A changed and became like community B. In your Lab Manual or interactive notebook, draw what you think community A might look like midway in its change to becoming like community B.

Think About This

1. Describe the changes you imagined. How long do you think it would take for community A to become like community B?

_____

_____

_____

2. Summarize the changes you think would happen as the community changed from A to B.

_____

_____

_____

TEKS in this Lesson

7.10(C) observe, record, and describe the role of ecological succession such as in a microhabitat of a garden with weeds

Also covers Process Standards: 7.2(A), (E)

? Essential Questions

- How do land ecosystems change over time?
- How do aquatic ecosystems change over time?

$^{a}b_{c}$ Vocabulary

ecological succession
climax community
pioneer species
eutrophication

How Land Ecosystems Change **TEKS** 7.10(C)

Have you ever seen weeds growing up through cracks in a concrete sidewalk? If they were not removed, the weeds would keep growing. The crack would widen, making room for more weeds. Over time, the sidewalk would break apart. Shrubs and vines would move in. Their leaves and branches would grow large enough to cover the concrete. Eventually, trees could start growing there.

This process is an example of **ecological succession**—*the process of one ecological community gradually changing into another.* Ecological succession occurs in a series of steps. These steps can usually be predicted. For example, small plants usually grow first. Larger plants, such as trees, usually grow last.

The final stage of ecological succession in a land ecosystem is a **climax community**—*a stable community that no longer goes through major ecological changes.* Climax communities differ depending on the type of biome in which they are located. In a tropical forest biome, a climax community would be a mature tropical forest. In a grassland biome, a climax community would be a mature grassland. Climax communities are usually stable over hundreds of years. As plants in a climax community die, new plants of the same species grow and take their places. The community will continue to contain the same kinds of plants as long as the climate remains the same.

FOLDABLES

Fold a sheet of paper into fourths. Use two sections on one side of the paper to describe and illustrate what land might look like before secondary succession and the other side to describe and illustrate the land after secondary succession is complete.

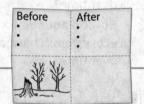

Before	After
•	•
•	•
•	•

Create

1. Draw a comic strip that illustrates the first paragraph in *How Land Ecosystems Change*.

Primary Succession

What do you think happens to a lava-filled landscape when a volcanic eruption is over? As shown in **Figure 1,** volcanic lava eventually becomes new soil that supports plant growth. Ecological succession in new areas of land with little or no soil, such as on a lava flow, a sand dune, or exposed rock, is primary succession. *The first species that colonizes new or undisturbed land is a* **pioneer species.** The lichens and mosses in **Figure 1** are pioneer species.

Figure 1 Following a volcanic eruption, a landscape undergoes primary succession.

① Molten lava flows during a volcanic eruption. As the lava cools, it hardens into bare rock.

② Airborne lichen spores settle on the rock. Lichens release acid that helps break down the rock and create soil. Lichens add nutrients to the soil as they die and decay.

③ Airborne spores from mosses and ferns settle onto the thin soil and add to the soil when they die. The soil gradually becomes thick enough to hold water. Insects and other small organisms move into the area.

④ After many years, the soil is deep and has enough nutrients for grasses, wildflowers, shrubs, and trees. The new ecosystem provides habitats for many animals. Eventually, a climax community develops.

Define

2. (Circle) the description of where secondary succession occurs.

Secondary Succession

In areas where existing ecosystems have been disturbed or destroyed, secondary succession can occur. One example is forestland in New England that early colonists cleared hundreds of years ago. Some of the cleared land was not planted with crops. This land gradually grew back to a climax forest community of beech and maple trees, as illustrated in **Figure 2**.

Figure 2 When disturbed land grows back, secondary succession occurs.

Go Online! Watch

1 Settlers in New England cleared many acres of forests to create cropland. In places where people stopped planting crops, the forest began to grow back.

2 Seeds of grasses, wildflowers, and other plants quickly began to sprout and grow. Young shrubs and trees also started growing. These plants provided habitats for insects and other small animals, such as mice.

3 White pines and poplars were the first trees in the area to grow to their full height. They provided shade and protection to slower growing trees, such as beech and maple.

4 Eventually, a climax community of beech and maple trees developed. As older trees die, new beech and maple seedlings grow and replace them.

Ecological succession can happen in any habitat, including very small, specialized habitats called microhabitats. **Illustrate and describe** the role of ecological succession in a microhabitat of a garden with weeds. **TEKS** 7.10(C)

1.

What is happening:

2.

What is happening:

3.

What is happening:

4.

What is happening:

Aquatic succession begins with a body of water such as a pond.

Over time, sediments and decaying organisms build up and create soil. This soil fills the bottom of the pond or lake.

Eventually, the pond or lake fills completely with soil, and a land ecosystem develops.

Figure 3 The water in a pond is slowly replaced by soil. Eventually, land plants take over, and the pond disappears.

Word Origin

eutrophication from Greek *eutrophos,* means "nourishing"

Describe

3. Summarize how eutrophication speeds up aquatic succession.

How Freshwater Ecosystems Change TEKS 7.10(C)

Like land ecosystems, freshwater ecosystems change over time in a natural, predictable process. This process is called aquatic succession.

Aquatic Succession

Aquatic succession is illustrated in **Figure 3.** Sediments carried by rainwater and streams accumulate on the bottoms of ponds, lakes, and wetlands. The decomposed remains of dead organisms add to the buildup of soil. As time passes, more and more soil accumulates. Eventually, so much soil has collected that the water disappears, and the area becomes land.

Eutrophication

As decaying organisms fall to the bottom of a pond, lake, or wetland, they add nutrients to the water. **Eutrophication** (yoo troh fuh KAY shun) *is the process of a body of water becoming nutrient-rich.*

Eutrophication is a natural part of aquatic succession. However, humans also contribute to eutrophication. The fertilizers that farmers use on crops and the waste from farm animals can be very high in nutrients. So can other forms of pollution. When fertilizers and pollution run off into a pond or lake, nutrient concentrations increase. High nutrient levels support large populations of algae and other microscopic organisms. These organisms use most of the dissolved oxygen in the water, and less oxygen is available for fish and other pond or lake organisms. As a result, many of these organisms die. Their bodies decay and add to the buildup of soil, speeding up succession.

8.3 Review

Go Online! Check ✓

List the main ideas about primary succession, secondary succession, and aquatic succession in the boxes below. Then describe specific details related to each main idea. **TEKS** 7.10(C)

Main Ideas

> Primary Succession

> Secondary Succession

> Aquatic Succession

Specific Details

1.

2.

3.

1.

2.

3.

1.

2.

3.

How Ecosystems Change

Use Vocabulary

1. **Compare and contrast** succession and eutrophication in freshwater ecosystems.

   TEKS 7.10(C) *supporting*

Apply the Essential Questions

2. What is eutrophication?

   TEKS 7.10(C) *supporting*

   A. decreasing nutrients

   B. decreasing salinity

   C. increasing nutrients

   D. increasing salinity

3. **Draw** a picture of what your school might look like in 500 years if it were abandoned. **TEKS** 7.10(C) *supporting*

🔥 H.O.T. Questions (Higher Order Thinking)

4. **Assess** Why are the first plants that appear in primary succession small?

   TEKS 7.10(C) *supporting*

5. **Evaluate** Is aquatic succession more like primary succession or secondary succession on land? Explain your reasoning. **TEKS** 7.10(C) *supporting*

Writing in Science

6. On a separate sheet of paper, write a paragraph explaining why the micro-habitat of a small pond in a farmer's field might be gone in 50 years. Include a main idea, supporting details, and concluding sentence. **TEKS** 7.10(C) *supporting*

Succession

You just learned about succession. So what? What does it mean to you?
How does it affect your life? Why should you care about succession?

Did you know fire can be good for people and the land? It can also benefit wildlife and livestock. Really? How can fire benefit wildlife and livestock?

Think about secondary succession. Some parts of South Texas have large areas of grasslands used for livestock grazing. In times of little rainfall or drought, the grass becomes dry, preventing new grass growth and increasing the risk for wildfires.

To fix this problem, officials, such as members of the National Forestry Service, use controlled burns to remove the dry grass. After the burn, the resulting black ash helps fertilize the soil and raises the temperature of the soil to help new grass grow. The controlled burn is the first step in secondary succession—clearing the land to help new crops grow.

So how can controlled burns prevent wildfires? If you have ever had a campfire, you probably used kindling to start the fire. Think back to the large area of dry grass. If a spark or lightning strike were to happen, a fire would spread rapidly and quickly get out of control. Using controlled burns eliminates the dry "kindling," reducing the risk of wildfires.

Starting a controlled burn is a little more involved than lighting a match. Fire specialists create burn plans. These plans consider factors, such as temperature, humidity, wind, and moisture of vegetation, to determine the best conditions for when a burn should be started. In Texas, winter is the preferred season.

So WHAT?!

Succession does have an impact on your life. It's happening all the time, all around you, and all around the country.

THAT'S what!!

361

Test-Taking Strategy

Analyze a Graph A graph is a representation that shows the relationship between two variables. Some questions will require that you analyze a graph in order to correctly answer the question.

Example

Use the graph below to answer question 9.

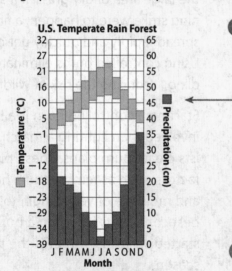

U.S. Temperate Rain Forest

② Next, analyze the graph. Notice that in January, the temperature is coldest and precipitation amount is high. As the temperature rises through July, the precipitation amount decreases. Then the temperature begins to decrease through December and the precipitation amount increases again. You can generalize that "as the temperature increases, precipitation decreases."

① Carefully read the question to understand what the question is asking. This question wants you to find the relationship between temperature and precipitation amounts throughout the year.

9 Which is true about the relationship between temperature and precipitation in the temperate rain forest biome? **TEKS** 7.10A

A As the temperature rises, precipitation increases.

B As the temperature rises, precipitation decreases.

③ The correct answer is choice **B**.

C Precipitation is constant as temperature changes.

D Temperature is constant as precipitation changes.

TIP: Use your pencil to track along the lines when analyzing a graph. This will help to ensure you are reading the correct values for each variable.

Multiple Choice

1

> Biodiversity refers to the different kinds of living things in a given area. An area that shows biodiversity can include a garden. It can include the biosphere. Humans affect biodiversity through our actions. We hunt and fish, sometimes to the extinction of a species. We cut down trees to build our homes. We allow pollutants to enter the air. When species die out or become rare, biodiversity is lost. Places that have lost biodiversity are often badly affected by disease and climate changes. Humans need to save biodiversity for its beauty, economic, and recreational value.

Which statement describes how biodiversity contributes to the health of an ecosystem?
TEKS 7.10(B) *supporting*; 7.3(A)

A A variety of species allows for more survivors in an environmental disturbance.

B Having more species in nature allows for the human population to increase.

C Many varieties of species provide economic goods for human use.

D Selective extinction opens up new habitats for other species to live and reproduce.

---

2 The illustration is of a pond ecosystem. This ecosystem has a small trickling stream feeding into it, and it is mostly reduced by evaporation. The wind is constant and the soil around the banks has become eroded. Dead plant matter and silt are slowly filling the pond. The pond is undergoing succession. **TEKS** 7.10(C) *supporting*; 7.3(A)

Suppose you can observe this area 100 years from now. What does it look like, and how has the environment changed?

A It looks the same because there is still a little water flowing into the pond.

B It is deeper and has a rocky bottom because of the wind and climate change.

C It is a dry land ecosystem and supports trees and land animals and birds.

D It is a lake with many aquatic plants and algae growing over the surface.

3   Disturbances in an environment, such as fires, floods, storms, and farming, cause changes in the species that make up a community. The drawing is one of a newly-plowed field and another crop growing next to it. Suppose these fields were abandoned for more than 50 years.
   TEKS 7.10(C) *supporting*; 7.3(A)

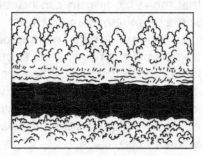

If there are no more disturbances, which scenario accurately describes what this newly-plowed field will look like in 50 years?

A The field will appear abandoned of farming activity and will have weeds and shrubs.

B The field will be growing the crop last cultivated on the field because of seeds in the ground.

C The field will change through several types of growth and will look like a growing forest.

D The field will look like it does now because there is nothing growing there.

---

4   Every ecosystem has characteristics that enable a variety of organisms to thrive there. Different organisms can be found in the various parts of the habitat, such as the desert ecosystem illustrated in the figure. This desert ecosystem has very high summer temperatures and very little water available to plants and animals.   **TEKS** 7.10(A)

Which organisms are more likely to be found in a desert area like the one in the illustration?

A eagles, lizards, squirrels, and frogs

B hares, prickly pear cacti, scorpions, and owls

C oak trees, songbirds, coyotes, and chipmunks

D wolves, mosses, pine trees, and roses

5 In a tundra biome, even the cold dry weather supports plant and animal life. The graph shown below has average temperature per month plotted on the same graph as precipitation per month. **TEKS** 7.10(A); 7.2(E)

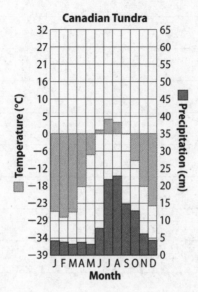

In this biome, what would the precipitation be in the coldest month in centimeters? Round your answer to the nearest whole number. Record and bubble in your answer on the answer grid below.

Inheritance and Adaptations

The **BIG** Idea

Organisms can be classified by their traits. Many of the unique traits that help a species survive are inherited through gradual changes over time.

LESSON 9.1 Classifying Organisms

Living things are classified into different groups based on physical or molecular similarities. Scientific tools, such as dichotomous keys, can be used to identify unknown living organisms.

TEKS 7.11(A); Also covers 7.1(A); 7.2(A), (C), (E); 7.3(A), (D); 7.4(A)

LESSON 9.2 Natural Selection and Adaptation

Organisms with traits best suited to their environment are most likely to survive and reproduce. Over time, variations in populations can result in adaptations.

TEKS 7.11(B), (C); 7.12(A); Also covers 7.1(A), 7.2(A), (C), (E); 7.3(B); 7.4(A), (B)

Peter and Rosemary Grant

Observing Natural Selection

▲ Peter and Rosemary Grant make observations and collect data in the field.

Charles Darwin was a naturalist during the mid-1800s. Based on his observations of nature, he developed the theory of evolution by natural selection. Do scientists still work this way—drawing conclusions from observations? Is there information still to be learned about natural selection? The answer to both questions is yes.

Peter and Rosemary Grant are naturalists who have observed finches in the Galápagos Islands for more than 30 years. They have found that variations in the finches' food supply determine which birds will survive and reproduce. They have observed natural selection in action.

The Grants live on Daphne Major, an island in the Galápagos, for part of each year. They observe and take measurements to compare the size and shape of finches' beaks from year to year. They also examine the kinds of seeds and nuts that are available for the birds to eat. They use this information to relate changes in the birds' food supply to changes in the finch species' beaks.

The island's ecosystem is fragile, so the Grants take great care not to change the environment of Daphne Major as they observe the finches. They carefully plan their diet to avoid introducing new plant species to the island. They bring all the freshwater they need to drink, and they wash in the ocean. For the Grants, it's just part of the job. As naturalists, they try to observe without interfering with the habitat in which they are living.

▲ This large ground finch is one of the kinds of birds studied by the Grants.

It's Your Turn!

RESEARCH AND REPORT With a group, find out more about careers in evolution, ecology, or population biology. What kind of work is done in the laboratory? What kind of work is done in the field? Write a report to explain your findings.

TEKS Review

Test-Taking Strategy

Reading Passage Some questions will be in reference to a reading passage. The information needed to answer the questions can be found in or inferred from the passage.

Example

Use the reading passage below to answer question 7.

Darwin's Theory

After years of studying Galápagos finches, Darwin proposed that the different finch species developed over a long period of time from one group of finches. He proposed that this group had arrived on one of the islands a long time ago. Perhaps a storm carried it from the mainland.

> **2** Next, read the passage. Pay close attention to sections or phrases that relate to the information in the question. Then, relate the important information back to the question and respond.

Over time, as the finch population grew, the finches moved to the other islands. Soon, the food and other resources on each island began to run out. The finches had to compete with each other to survive. The finches with traits that made them better competitors for resources in their environments lived longer. The better competitors had more offspring than those that did not have those traits. This concept is the core of Darwin's theory of evolution by natural selection.

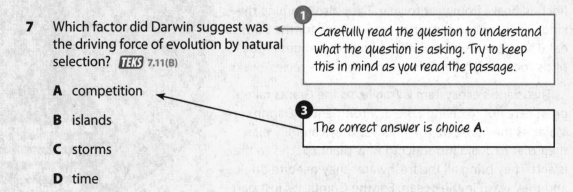

7 Which factor did Darwin suggest was the driving force of evolution by natural selection? **TEKS** 7.11(B)

> **1** Carefully read the question to understand what the question is asking. Try to keep this in mind as you read the passage.

  A competition

> **3** The correct answer is choice **A**.

  B islands

  C storms

  D time

TIP: Underline any parts that you feel may be important information in regards to the question.

Multiple Choice

1

Charles Darwin, at age 22, set sail aboard the HMS *Beagle* in 1831. He was the naturalist onboard. Darwin collected samples of animals and fossils during his five year voyage. His travels took him to many places, including the Galápagos Islands. It was there that Darwin noticed that each island had its own form of finch. The finches were closely related, but had some structural differences and eating habits that adapted them to the different food sources on each island. This observation was an important part of Darwin's thinking as he developed his theory of natural selection. Charles Darwin's explanation of natural selection is now the foundation for modern biology. Darwin developed the idea of inherited traits and change over time without ever knowing about modern genetics. Two of the finches Darwin studied are shown below.

Which structural genetic change in the finches can be identified as the one most influenced by feeding habits, as proposed by Charles Darwin? **TEKS** 7.3(D); 7.11(C) *supporting*

A ability to fly from island to island to find the food they prefer

B beak size and shape to take advantage of the food they had

C claw shapes for perching on limbs while catching insects in their beaks

D cooperative behavior so they could share limited seeds and nectar

2 A student wants to create a dichotomous key to identify Fish A from Fish B, which are shown below. **TEKS** 7.11(A)

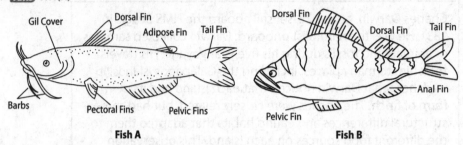

Fish A   Fish B

Which characteristics could the student use to create the steps for a dichotomous key?

A no whiskerlike barbs, forked tail fin, one dorsal fin

B no whiskerlike barbs, rounded tail fin, two dorsal fins

C whiskerlike barbs, forked tail fin, one dorsal fin

D whiskerlike barbs, rounded tail fin, two dorsal fins

---

3 Use the dichotomous key to classify this leaf. **TEKS** 7.2(A); 7.11(A) *supporting*

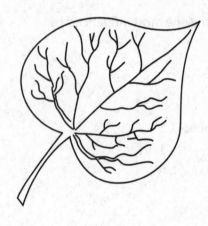

1.a.	Leaf has several leaflets	Go to Step 2
1.b.	Leaf is a single, simple leaf	Go to Step 3
2.a.	Leaflets attached at several points	black walnut
2.b.	Leaflets attached at one point	white clover
3.a.	Veins branch out	Go to Step 4
3.b.	One vein through the center	Go to Step 5
4.a.	Leaf is heart-shaped	redbud
4.b.	Leaf is star-shaped	sugar maple
5.a.	Leaf has a smooth edge	magnolia
5.b.	Leaf has a jagged edge	birch

A birch leaf

B black walnut leaf

C magnolia leaf

D redbud leaf

4 Birds often migrate great distances to breed, raise offspring, and find food in a warmer climate during winter. Some birds migrate farther than others. The chart below shows the average daily migration distances for three bird species. **TEKS** 7.3(A); 7.11(B) *supporting*

Species	km/Day
barn swallow	150
Swainson's hawk	170
broadwing hawk	480

As they migrate, how many more kilometers do Swainson's hawks fly in 30 days than barn swallows? Record and bubble in your answer on the answer grid below.

5 A student prepared this chart comparing examples of natural selection with selective breeding. **TEKS** 7.11(C)

Natural Selection Traits that Benefit the Species	Selective Breeding Traits that Benefit Humans
• ability to escape predators • ability to resist droughts	• _____ • _____

Which can the student add in the column under Selective Breeding to complete the chart?

1. ability to grow large kernels of corn

2. ability to find and rescue people

3. ability to attract pollinators

4. ability to produce milk for offspring

   A 1 and 3

   B 1 and 2

   C 2 and 3

   D 3 and 4

My Notes

10 Structure and Function of Organisms

The **BIG** Idea

All living things are made up of structures that perform specific functions in order to survive.

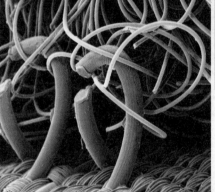

The Basic Unit of Life

The cell is called the basic unit of life. What do you think that means? (Circle) the answer that best matches your thinking.

    A. I think it means the cell is the smallest part of matter.

    B. I think it means the cell is the smallest part of mass.

    C. I think it means the cell is the smallest part of volume.

    D. I think it means the cell is the smallest part of mass and volume.

    E. I think it means the cell is the smallest part of energy.

    F. I think it means the cell is the smallest part of structure.

    G. I think it means the cell is the smallest part of structure and function.

    H. I think it means the cell is the smallest part of matter, structure, and function.

    I. I think it means the cell is the smallest part of matter, energy, and structure.

Explain your answer. Describe your thinking about the cell as a basic unit of life.

Two of a Kind? At first glance, the plant and animal in the photo might seem like they have nothing in common. The plant is rooted in the ground, and the rabbit can move quickly. Are they more alike than they appear? How can you find out?

Write your responses in your interactive notebook.

LAB Manager

Go to your Lab Manual or visit connectED.mcgraw-hill.com to perform the labs for this lesson.

MiniLAB: *How can you observe DNA?*

TEKS 7.1(A); 7.2(A), (C), (D), (E); 7.4(A), (B); 7.12(F)

Explore Activity

TEKS 7.1(A); 7.2(A), (C), (E); 7.4(A), (B); 7.12(F)

What's in a cell?

Most plants grow from seeds. A seed began as one cell, but a mature plant can be made up of millions of cells. How does a seed change and grow into a mature plant?

Procedure 🥽 🧤 ✂️ 🧤

1. Read and complete a lab safety form.

2. Use a **toothpick** to gently remove the thin outer covering of a **bean seed** that has soaked overnight.

3. Open the seed with a **plastic knife,** and observe its inside with a **magnifying lens.** Draw the insides of the seed in your Lab Manual or your interactive notebook.

4. Gently remove the small, plantlike embryo, and weigh it on a **balance.** Record its mass in your Lab Manual or your interactive notebook.

5. Gently pull a **bean seedling** from the soil. Rinse the soil from the roots. Weigh the seedling and record the mass.

Think About This

1. How did the mass of the embryo and the bean seedling differ?

_____

_____

_____

_____

2. If a plant begins as one cell, where do all the cells come from?

_____

_____

_____

_____

_____

TEKS in this Lesson

7.3(D) Relate the impact of research on scientific thought and society, including the history of science and contributions of scientists as related to the content.

7.12(F) Recognize that according to cell theory all organisms are composed of cells and cells carry on similar functions such as extracting energy from food to sustain life.

Also covers Process Standards: 7.1(A); 7.2(A), (C), (D), (E); 7.4(A), (B)

❓ Essential Questions

- How did scientists' understanding of cells develop?
- What are the basic principles of the cell theory?

🔤 Vocabulary

cell theory
macromolecule
lipid
nucleic acid
protein
carbohydrate

393

Understanding Cells TEKS 7.3(D); 7.12(F)

Have you ever looked up at the night sky and tried to find other planets in our solar system? It is hard to see them without using a telescope. This is because the other planets are millions of kilometers away. Just like we can use telescopes to see other planets, we can use microscopes to see the basic units of all living things—cells. But people didn't always know about cells. Because cells are so small, early scientists had no tools to study them. It took hundreds of years for scientists to learn about cells.

More than 300 years ago, an English scientist named Robert Hooke built a microscope. He used the microscope to look at cork, which is part of a cork oak tree's bark. What he saw looked like the openings in a honeycomb, as shown in **Figure 1.** The openings reminded him of the small rooms called cells where monks lived. He called the structures cells, from the Latin word *cellula* (SEL yuh luh), which means "small rooms."

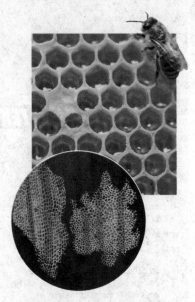

Figure 1 To Robert Hooke, the cells of cork looked like the openings in a honeycomb.

A *Closer* Look at Microscopes

Have you ever used a magnifying lens to see details of an object? If so, then you have used a tool similar to the first microscope.

One characteristic of all microscopes is that they magnify objects. Magnification makes an object appear larger than it really is. Another characteristic of microscopes is resolution—how clearly the magnified object can be seen. The two main types of microscopes—light microscopes and electron microscopes—differ in magnification and resolution.

If you have used a microscope at school, then you have probably used a light microscope. Light microscopes use light and lenses to enlarge an image of an object. They can enlarge images up to 1,500 times their original size. The resolution of a light microscope is about 0.2 micrometers, or two-millionths of a meter.

You might know that electrons are tiny particles inside atoms. Electron microscopes use a magnetic field to focus a beam of electrons through an object or onto an object's surface. An electron microscope can magnify an image 100,000 times or more. The resolution of an electron microscope can be as small as 0.2 nano-meters, or two-billionths of a meter.

Research Conduct research on the different types of light and electron microscopes. Describe your findings in your interactive notebook.

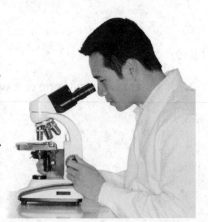

The Cell Theory

After Hooke's discovery, other scientists began making better microscopes and looking for cells in many other places, such as pond water and blood. The newer microscopes enabled scientists to see different structures inside cells. Matthias Schleiden (SHLI dun), a German scientist, used one of the new microscopes to look at plant cells. Around the same time, another German scientist, Theodor Schwann, used a microscope to study animal cells. Schleiden and Schwann realized that plant and animal cells have similar features and carry on similar functions, such as extracting energy from food and eliminating wastes. From this evidence, Schleiden and Schwann concluded that cells are the basic unit of life.

Almost two decades later, Rudolf Virchow (VUR koh), a German doctor, proposed that all cells come from preexisting cells, or cells that already exist. The observations made by Schleiden, Schwann, and Virchow were combined into one theory. As illustrated in **Table 1,** *the* **cell theory** *states that all living things are made of one or more cells, the cell is the smallest unit of life, and all new cells come from preexisting cells.* After the development of the cell theory, scientists raised more questions about cells. If all living things are made of cells, what are cells made of?

Review Vocabulary

theory
explanation of things or events based on scientific knowledge resulting from many observations and experiments

Table 1 Scientists developed the cell theory after studying cells with microscopes.

Table 1	The Cell Theory
Principle	**Example**
All living things are made of one or more cells.	Leaf cells
The cell is the smallest unit of life.	This unicellular amoeba is surrounding an algal cell to get food and energy. Amoeba Algal cell
All new cells come from preexisting cells.	Existing cell Cell dividing New cells

Apply it!

Cell Theory Time Line As a class, create a time line of the important discoveries that led to the development of the cell theory. Draw a time line on the board or chart paper. Add entries at the appropriate time points. For each entry on the time line, note the scientist and any relevant facts about the discovery. When the time line is complete, copy the diagram in the space below to help you understand the key principles of the cell theory. **TEKS** 7.12(F)

Basic Cell Substances

Have you ever noticed how a train locomotive pulls train cars that are hooked together? Like a train, many of the substances in cells are made of smaller parts that are joined together. *These substances, called* **macromolecules,** *form by joining many small molecules together.* Macromolecules have many important roles in cells. But they cannot function without one of the most important substances in cells—water.

The Main Ingredient—Water

The main ingredient in any cell is water. It makes up more than 70 percent of a cell's volume and is essential for life. Why is water such an important molecule? In addition to making up a large part of the inside of cells, water also surrounds cells. The water surrounding your cells helps insulate your body, which maintains homeostasis, or a stable internal environment.

Substances must be in a liquid to move into and out of cells. The structure of a water molecule makes it ideal for dissolving many other substances. A water molecule has two areas. An area that is more negative (–), called the negative end, can attract the positive part of another substance. An area that is more positive (+), called the positive end, can attract the negative part of another substance. Examine **Figure 2** to see how the positive and negative ends of water molecules dissolve salt crystals.

Infer

1. Which part of the salt crystal is attracted to the oxygen in the water molecule?

_____

_____

Figure 2 The positive and negative ends of a water molecule attract the positive and negative parts of another substance, similar to the way magnets are attracted to each other.

Salt
(sodium chloride)

Salt dissolved
in water

| Chloride | — | Oxygen | — |
| Hydrogen | + | Sodium | + |

Macromolecules

Although water is essential for life, all cells contain other substances that enable them to function. Recall that macromolecules are large molecules that form when smaller molecules join together. As shown in **Figure 3** on the next page, there are four types of macromolecules in cells: lipids, nucleic acids, proteins, and carbohydrates. Each type of macromolecule has unique functions in a cell. These functions range from growth and communication to movement and storage.

Lipids One group of macromolecules found in cells is lipids. *A* **lipid** *is a large macromolecule that does not dissolve in water.* Because lipids do not mix with water, they play an important role as protective barriers in cells. They are also the major part of cell membranes. Lipids play roles in energy storage and in cell communication. Examples of lipids are cholesterol (kuh LES tuh rawl), phospholipids (fahs foh LIH pids), and vitamin A.

FOLDABLES®

Cut out the Lesson 10.1 Foldable in the back of the book. Use it to organize your notes on the macromolecules and their uses in a cell.

Tape here

Tab 1	Macromolecules	
Uses:		Uses:
Uses:		Uses:
Tab 2		

Tape here

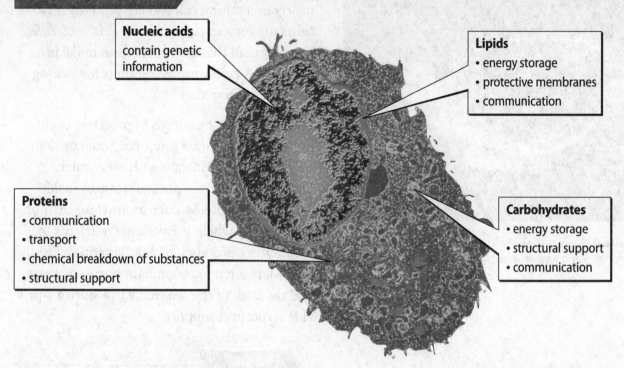

Nucleic acids
contain genetic information

Lipids
• energy storage
• protective membranes
• communication

Proteins
• communication
• transport
• chemical breakdown of substances
• structural support

Carbohydrates
• energy storage
• structural support
• communication

Nucleic Acids Deoxyribonucleic (dee AHK sih ri boh noo klee ihk) acid (DNA) and ribonucleic (ri boh noo KLEE ihk) acid (RNA) are nucleic acids. **Nucleic acids** *are macromolecules that form when long chains of molecules called nucleotides* (NEW klee uh tidz) *join together.* The order of nucleotides in DNA and RNA is important. If you change the order of words in a sentence, you can change the meaning of the sentence. In a similar way, changing the order of nucleotides in DNA and RNA can change the genetic information in a cell.

Nucleic acids are important in cells because they contain genetic information. This information can pass from parents to offspring. DNA includes instructions for cell growth, cell reproduction, and cell processes that enable a cell to respond to its environment. DNA makes RNA. RNA makes proteins.

Figure 3 Each type of macromolecule has a special function in a cell.

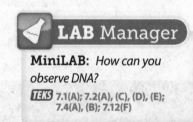

LAB Manager

MiniLAB: *How can you observe DNA?*
TEKS 7.1(A); 7.2(A), (C), (D), (E); 7.4(A), (B); 7.12(F)

Contrast

2. List the two types of nucleic acids, and indicate what cells make with each type.

1. _____ is used to make _____.

2. _____ is used to make _____.

Figure 4 A sea turtle's shell is made up of an outer layer of keratin and an inner layer of fused bones.

Proteins The macromolecules necessary for nearly everything cells do are proteins. **Proteins** *are long chains of amino acid molecules.* You just read that RNA is used to make proteins. RNA contains instructions for joining amino acids together.

Cells contain hundreds of proteins. Each protein has a unique function. Some proteins help cells communicate with each other. Other proteins transport substances inside cells. Some proteins, such as amylase (AM uh lays) in saliva, help break down nutrients in food. Other proteins, such as keratin (KER uh tun)—a protein found in hair, horns, feathers, and the shell of the sea turtle in **Figure 4**—provide structural support.

Predict

3. What might happen to a cell if it were unable to make proteins?

_____

_____

_____

_____

_____

Figure 5 The long chain of sugar molecules that make up cellulose provides support. It also attracts water. This enables cotton to absorb about 25 times its weight in water.

Carbohydrates *One sugar molecule, two sugar molecules, or a long chain of sugar molecules make up* **carbohydrates** (kar boh HI drayts). Carbohydrates store energy, provide structural support, and are needed for communication between cells. Sugars and starches are carbohydrates that store energy. Fruits contain sugars. Breads and pastas are mostly starch. The energy in sugars and starches can be released quickly through chemical reactions in cells. Cellulose is a carbohydrate in the cell walls of plants, such as the cotton plant in **Figure 5**. It provides structural support.

Summarize it!

Identify the types of macromolecules inside cells, and list two functions for each.

Type: _____

Functions:

Type: _____

Functions:

Macromolecules

Type: _____

Functions:

Type: _____

Functions:

 Connect it! Schleiden and Schwann recognized that all cells carry on similar functions, including extracting energy from food to sustain life. **Infer** which macromolecule(s) in a cell would be most likely to perform this function. Write your response in your interactive notebook. **TEKS** 7.12(F)

Cells and Life

Use Vocabulary

1. What states that the cell is the basic unit of all living things? **TEKS** 7.12(F) *supporting*

_____

2. **Distinguish** between a carbohydrate and a lipid.

_____

_____

_____

Apply the Essential Question

3. Which scientist's discovery enabled other scientists to develop a better understanding of cells? **TEKS** 7.3(D)

   A. Hooke

   B. Schleiden

   C. Schwann

   D. Virchow

4. **Summarize** the main principles of the cell theory. **TEKS** 7.12(F) *supporting*

_____

_____

_____

_____

_____

_____

H.O.T. Questions (Higher Order Thinking)

5. **Evaluate** the importance of the microscope to the development of the cell theory. **TEKS** 7.12(F) *supporting*

_____

_____

_____

_____

_____

_____

_____

6. **Assess** According to the cell theory, the cell is the smallest unit of life. How does this concept relate to the function of cells? **TEKS** 7.12(F) *supporting*

_____

_____

_____

_____

_____

_____

Writing in Science

7. **Explain** on a separate sheet of paper how the development of the cell theory shows that scientific ideas can change over time. Use specific examples. **TEKS** 7.3(D)

A Very Powerful Microscope

Using technology to look inside cells

If Robert Hooke had used an atomic force microscope (AFM), he would have observed more than just cells. He would have seen the macromolecules inside them! An AFM can scan objects that are only nanometers in size. A nanometer is one-billionth of a meter. That's 100,000 times smaller than the width of a human hair. AFM technology has enabled scientists to better understand how cells function. It also has given them a three-dimensional look at the macromolecules that make life possible. This is how it works.

Photodiode

2 The cantilever can bend up and down, similar to the way a diving board can bend, in response to pushing and pulling forces between the atoms in the tip and the atoms in the sample.

3 A laser beam senses the cantilever's up-and-down movements. A computer converts these movements into an image of the sample's surface.

1 A probe moves across a sample's surface to identify the sample's features. The probe consists of a cantilever with a tiny, sharp tip. The tip is about 20 nm in diameter at its base.

It's Your Turn!

RESEARCH NASA's *Phoenix Mars Lander* included an atomic force microscope. As a group, find out what scientists discovered on Mars with this instrument.

INQUIRY

Hooked Together?

What do you think happens when one of the hooks in the photo goes through one of the loops? The two sides fasten together. The shapes of the hooks and loops in the hook-and-loop tape are suited to their function—to hold the two pieces together. Do you think the shape of a cell relates to its function? Why or why not?

Write your responses in your interactive notebook.

LAB Manager

Go to your Lab Manual or visit connectED.mcgraw-hill.com to perform the labs for this lesson.

MiniLAB: *What can you see in a cell?*

TEKS 7.1(A); 7.2(A), (C), (E); 7.4(A), (B); 7.12(D)

Skill Practice: *How are plant cells and animal cells similar and how are they different?*

TEKS 7.1(A), (B); 7.2(A), (C), (E); 7.4(A), (B); 7.12(D)

Explore Activity

Why do eggs have shells?

Bird eggs have different structures, such as a shell, a membrane, and a yolk. Each structure has a different function that helps keep the egg safe and assists in development of the baby bird inside of it.

Procedure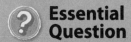

1. Read and complete a lab safety form.

2. Place an **uncooked egg** in a **bowl.**

3. Feel the shell, and record your observations in your Lab Manual or your interactive notebook.

4. Crack open the egg. Pour the contents into the bowl.

5. Observe the inside of the shell and the contents of the bowl. Record your observations.

Think About This

1. What do you think the role of the eggshell is?

_____

_____

2. What does the structure of the eggshell tell you about its function?

_____

_____

_____

3. Do you think an organism's cell might have a structure that performs the same function as the eggshell? Explain.

_____

_____

_____

TEKS in this Lesson

7.12(D) Differentiate between structure and function in plant and animal cell organelles, including cell membrane, cell wall, nucleus, cytoplasm, mitochondrion, chloroplast, and vacuole.

Also covers Process Standards: 7.1(A), (B); 7.2(A), (C), (E); 7.4(A), (B)

? Essential Question

- What do the structures in a cell do?

abc Vocabulary

cell membrane
cell wall
cytoplasm
cytoskeleton
organelle
nucleus
chloroplast

Cell Shape and Movement

TEKS 7.12(D)

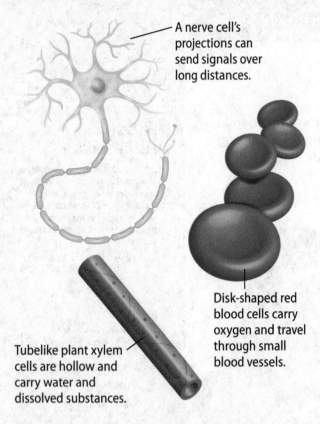

A nerve cell's projections can send signals over long distances.

Disk-shaped red blood cells carry oxygen and travel through small blood vessels.

Tubelike plant xylem cells are hollow and carry water and dissolved substances.

Figure 1 The shape of a cell relates to the function it performs.

You might recall that all living things are made up of one or more cells. As illustrated in **Figure 1,** cells come in many shapes and sizes. The size and shape of a cell relates to its job or function. For example, a human red blood cell cannot be seen without a microscope. Its small size and disk shape enable it to pass easily through the smallest blood vessels. The shape of a nerve cell enables it to send signals over long distances. Some plant cells are hollow and make up tubelike structures that carry materials throughout a plant.

The structures that make up a cell also have unique functions. Think about how the players on a football team perform different tasks to move the ball down the field. In a similar way, a cell is made of different structures that perform different functions that keep a cell alive. You will read about some of these structures in this lesson.

Infer

1. Like the cells in **Figure 1,** other cells also have shapes that are related to their functions. Some skin cells are flat and square-shaped. This allows them to fit tightly together. In the space below, illustrate how skin cells fit together.

Based on your drawing and what you know about skin, what do you think one function of skin cells might be?

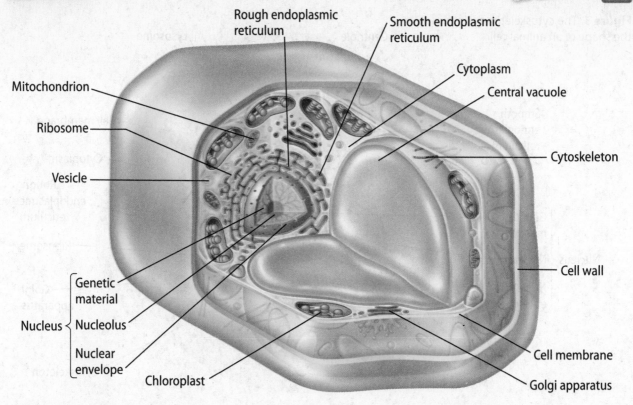

Rough endoplasmic reticulum

Smooth endoplasmic reticulum

Cytoplasm

Central vacuole

Mitochondrion

Cytoskeleton

Ribosome

Vesicle

Cell wall

Genetic material

Nucleus { Nucleolus

Nuclear envelope

Chloroplast

Cell membrane

Golgi apparatus

Cell Membrane

Although different types of cells perform different functions, all cells have some structures in common. As shown in **Figure 2** above and in **Figure 3** on the next page, every cell is surrounded by a protective covering called a membrane. *The* **cell membrane** *is a flexible covering that protects the inside of a cell from the environment outside a cell.* Cell membranes are mostly made of two different macromolecules—proteins and a type of lipid called phospholipids. Think again about a football team. The defensive line tries to stop the other team from moving forward with the football. In a similar way, a cell membrane protects the cell from the outside environment.

Cell Wall

Every cell has a cell membrane, but some cells are also surrounded by a structure called the cell wall. Plant cells such as the one in **Figure 2,** fungal cells, bacteria, and some types of protists have cell walls. *A* **cell wall** *is a stiff structure outside the cell membrane.* It is composed mainly of carbohydrates, such as cellulose. A cell wall protects a cell from attack by viruses and other harmful organisms. In some plant and fungal cells, a cell wall helps maintain the cell's shape and gives structural support.

Figure 2 The cell wall maintains the shape of a plant cell.

Academic Vocabulary

function *(noun)* the purpose for which something is used

Contrast

2. How does the composition of cell membranes and cell walls differ? Write your response in your interactive notebook.

Figure 3 The cytoskeleton maintains the shape of an animal cell.

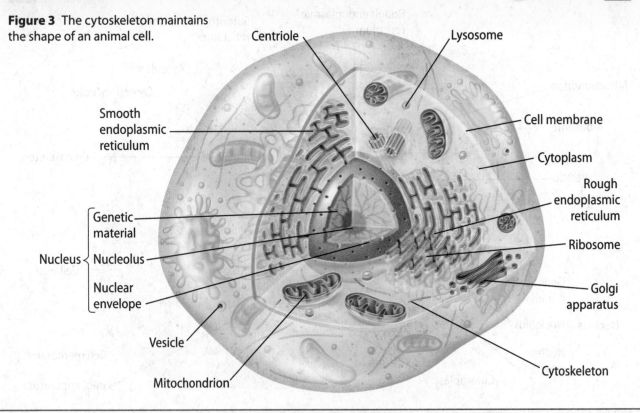

Centriole
Lysosome
Smooth endoplasmic reticulum
Cell membrane
Cytoplasm
Rough endoplasmic reticulum
Genetic material
Ribosome
Nucleus { Nucleolus
Nuclear envelope
Golgi apparatus
Vesicle
Cytoskeleton
Mitochondrion

Word Origin

cytoplasm from Greek *kytos*, means "hollow vessel"; and *plasma*, means "something molded"

Cytoplasm and the Cytoskeleton

You might recall that water is the main ingredient in a cell. Most of this water is in the **cytoplasm,** *a fluid inside a cell that contains salts and other molecules.* The cytoplasm also contains a cell's cytoskeleton, as shown in **Figure 3.** *The* **cytoskeleton** *is a network of threadlike proteins that are joined together.* The proteins form a framework inside a cell. This framework gives a cell its shape and helps it move. Cilia and flagella are made from the same proteins that make up the cytoskeleton.

Cell Appendages

Arms, legs, claws, and antennae are types of appendages. Cells can have appendages too. Cell appendages are often used for movement. Flagella (fluh JEH luh; singular, flagellum) are long, tail-like appendages that whip back and forth and move a cell. A cell can also have cilia (SIH lee uh; singular, cilium) like the ones shown in **Figure 4.** Cilia are short, hairlike structures. They can move a cell or move molecules away from a cell. A microscopic organism called a paramecium (per uh MEE see um) moves around its watery environment using its cilia. The cilia in your windpipe move harmful substances away from your lungs.

Figure 4 Lung cells have cilia that help move fluids and foreign materials.

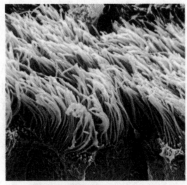

Color-enhanced SEM Magnification: Unavailable

Cell Types

Recall that the use of microscopes enabled scientists to discover cells. With more advanced microscopes, scientists discovered that all cells can be grouped into two types—prokaryotic (proh kayr ee AH tihk) cells and eukaryotic (yew kayr ee AH tihk) cells.

Prokaryotic Cells

The genetic material in a prokaryotic cell is not surrounded by a membrane, as shown in **Figure 5.** This is the most important feature of a prokaryotic cell. Prokaryotic cells also do not have many of the other cell parts that you will read about later in this lesson. Most prokaryotic cells are unicellular organisms and are called prokaryotes.

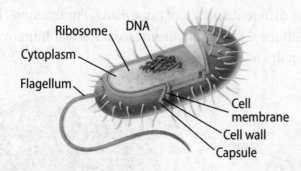

Ribosome DNA
Cytoplasm
Flagellum
Cell membrane
Cell wall
Capsule

Figure 5 In prokaryotic cells, the genetic material floats freely in the cytoplasm.

Eukaryotic Cells

Plants, animals, fungi, and protists are made of eukaryotic cells, such as the ones shown in **Figure 2** and **Figure 3,** and are called eukaryotes. With few exceptions, each eukaryotic cell has genetic material that is surrounded by a membrane. Every eukaryotic cell also has *other structures, called* **organelles,** *which have specialized functions. Most organelles are surrounded by membranes.* Eukaryotic cells are usually larger than prokaryotic cells. About ten prokaryotic cells would fit inside one eukaryotic cell.

Classify

3. In the table at right, classify cells as eukaryotic or prokaryotic by writing "E" or "P" in the right-hand column.

Characteristic	Cell Type
Cell's genetic material is surrounded by a membrane.	
Cell is usually a unicellular organism.	
It is usually the smaller of the two types of cell.	
Cells contain organelles.	

Cell Organelles TEKS 7.12(D)

As you have just read, organelles are eukaryotic cell structures with specific functions. Organelles enable cells to carry out different functions at the same time. For example, cells can obtain energy from food, store information, make macromolecules, and get rid of waste materials at the same time because different organelles perform the different tasks.

The Nucleus

The largest organelle inside most eukaryotic cells is the nucleus, shown in **Figure 6.** *The **nucleus** is the part of a eukaryotic cell that directs cell activities and contains genetic information stored in DNA.* DNA is organized into structures called chromosomes. The number of chromosomes in a nucleus is different for different species of organisms. For example, kangaroo cells contain six pairs of chromosomes. Most human cells contain 23 pairs of chromosomes.

Figure 6 The nucleus directs cell activity and is surrounded by a membrane.

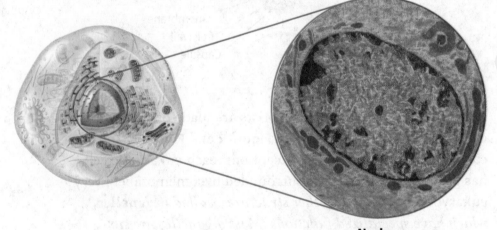

Nucleus
Color-enhanced TEM Magnification: 15,500×

In addition to chromosomes, the nucleus contains proteins and an organelle called the nucleolus (new KLEE uh lus). The nucleolus is often seen as a large dark spot in the nucleus of a cell. The nucleolus makes ribosomes, which are organelles that are involved in the production of proteins. You will read about ribosomes later in this lesson.

Surrounding the nucleus are two membranes that form a structure called the nuclear envelope. The nuclear envelope contains many pores. Certain molecules, such as proteins and RNA, move into and out of the nucleus through these pores.

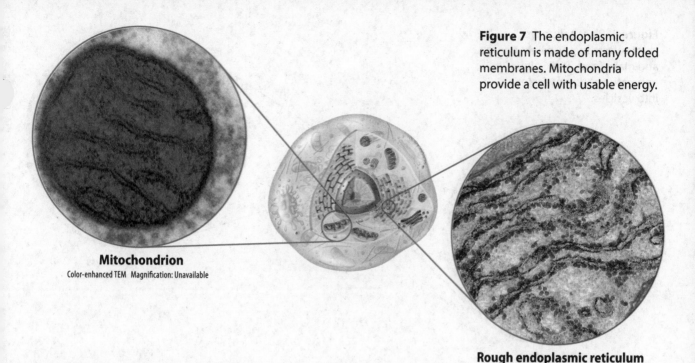

Figure 7 The endoplasmic reticulum is made of many folded membranes. Mitochondria provide a cell with usable energy.

Mitochondrion
Color-enhanced TEM Magnification: Unavailable

Rough endoplasmic reticulum
Color-enhanced EM Magnification: 19,030×

Manufacturing Molecules

You might recall that proteins are important molecules in cells. Proteins are made on ribosomes. Unlike other cell organelles, a ribosome is not surrounded by a membrane. Ribosomes are located in a cell's cytoplasm. They also can be attached to a weblike organelle called the endoplasmic reticulum (en duh PLAZ mihk • rih TIHK yuh lum), or ER. As shown in **Figure 7,** the ER spreads from the nucleus throughout most of the cytoplasm. ER with ribosomes on its surface is called rough ER. Rough ER is the site of protein production. ER without ribosomes is called smooth ER. It makes lipids such as cholesterol. Smooth ER is important because it helps remove harmful substances from a cell.

Processing Energy

All living things require energy to survive. Cells process some energy in specialized organelles. Most eukaryotic cells contain hundreds of organelles called mitochondria (mi tuh KAHN dree uh; singular, mitochondrion), shown in **Figure 7.** Some cells in a human heart can contain a thousand mitochondria.

Like the nucleus, a mitochondrion is surrounded by two membranes. Energy is released during chemical reactions that occur in the mitochondria. This energy is stored in high-energy molecules called ATP—adenosine triphosphate (uh DEN uh seen • tri FAHS fayt). ATP is the fuel for cellular processes such as growth, cell division, and material transport.

> **Differentiate**
>
> 4. How do the differences between rough ER and smooth ER affect their functions?

Figure 8 Plant cells have chloroplasts that use light energy and make food. The Golgi apparatus packages materials into vesicles.

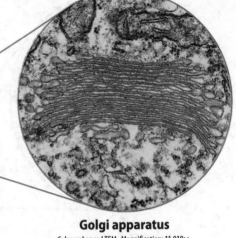

Golgi apparatus
Color-enhanced TEM Magnification: 11,010×

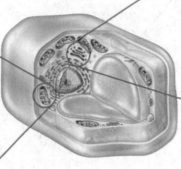

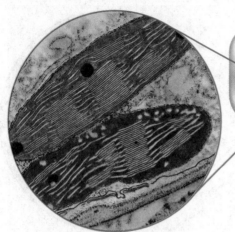

Chloroplasts
Color-enhanced TEM Magnification: 16,000×

Plant cells and some protists, such as algae, also contain organelles called chloroplasts (KLOR uh plasts), shown in **Figure 8.** **Chloroplasts** *are membrane-bound organelles that use light energy and make food—a sugar called glucose—from water and carbon dioxide in a process known as photosynthesis* (foh toh SIHN thuh sus). The sugar contains stored chemical energy that can be released when a cell needs it.

Processing, Transporting, and Storing Molecules

Near the ER is an organelle that looks like a stack of pancakes. This is the Golgi (GAWL jee) apparatus, shown in **Figure 8.** It prepares proteins for their specific jobs or functions. Then it packages the proteins into tiny, membrane-bound, ball-like structures called vesicles. Vesicles are organelles that transport substances from one area of a cell to another. Some vesicles in an animal cell are called lysosomes. Lysosomes contain substances that help break down and recycle cellular components.

Some cells also have saclike structures called vacuoles (VAK yuh wohlz). Vacuoles are organelles that store food, water, and waste material. A typical plant cell usually has one large vacuole that stores water and other substances. Some animal cells have many small vacuoles.

Contrast

5. Highlight the difference between vacuoles in plant cells and animal cells.

10.2 Review

Summarize it!

Classify information about organelles. In the right-hand column, indicate whether the organelle is in a plant cell, an animal cell, or both. **TEKS** 7.12(D)

Organelle	Function	Plant, Animal, or Both?
Cell membrane		
Cell wall		
Chloroplast		
Cytoplasm		
Golgi apparatus		
Mitochondrion		
Nucleus		
Ribosome		
Rough endoplasmic reticulum		
Smooth endoplasmic reticulum		
Vacuole		

 Connect it! Some cells contain chloroplasts that use light energy and produce food. Do cells without chloroplasts also depend on sunlight for their food? **Explain.** Write your response in your interactive notebook. **TEKS** 7.12(D)

The Cell

Use Vocabulary

1. **Distinguish** between the cell wall and the cell membrane in a plant cell.

   TEKS 7.12(D) *supporting*

   _____

   _____

   _____

   _____

Apply the Essential Question

2. **Describe** the structure and function of a eukaryotic cell's nucleus.

   TEKS 7.12(D) *supporting*

   _____

   _____

   _____

   _____

3. **Compare** the roles of mitochondria and chloroplasts in plant and animal cells.

   TEKS 7.12(D) *supporting*

   _____

   _____

   _____

   _____

   _____

   _____

H.O.T. Questions (Higher Order Thinking)

4. **Evaluate** Name the kinds of organisms that have cells with cell walls. Name the kinds of organisms that have cells without cell walls. Briefly describe the benefits of cell walls for organisms. **TEKS** 7.12(D) *supporting*

   _____

   _____

   _____

   _____

   _____

   _____

5. **Analyze** Why are most organelles surrounded by membranes?

   TEKS 7.12(D) *supporting*

   _____

   _____

   _____

   _____

6. **Infer** Why does a plant cell have one large vacuole while an animal cell has many small vacuoles? **TEKS** 7.12(D) *supporting*

   _____

   _____

   _____

   _____

   _____

My Notes

10.3 Levels of Organization

Scales on Wings? This butterfly has a distinctive pattern of colors on its wings. The pattern is formed by clusters of tiny scales. In a similar way, multicellular organisms are made of many small parts working together. How do you think this happens?

 Write your response in your interactive notebook.

 LAB Manager

Go to your Lab Manual or visit connectED.mcgraw-hill.com to perform the labs for this lesson.

MiniLAB: *How do cells work together to make an organism?*
TEKS 7.1(A); 7.2(E); 7.3(B); 7.4(A), (B); 7.12(C)

LAB: *Cell Differentiation*
TEKS 7.1(A), (B); 7.2(A), (C), (E); 7.4(A), (B); 7.12(C)

Explore Activity

TEKS 7.1(A); 7.2(A); 7.3(B); 7.4(A); 7.12(C)

How is a system organized?

The places where people live are organized in a system. Do you live in or near a city? Cities contain things such as schools and stores that enable them to function on their own. Many cities together make up another level of organization.

Procedure

1. Read and complete a lab safety form.

2. Using a **metric ruler** and **scissors,** measure and cut squares of **construction paper** that are 4 cm, 8 cm, 12 cm, 16 cm, and 20 cm on each side. Use a different color for each square.

3. Stack the squares from largest to smallest and glue them together.

4. Cut apart the *City, Continent, Country, County,* and *State* labels your teacher gives you.

5. Use a **glue stick** to attach the *City* label to the smallest square. Sort the remaining labels from smallest to largest, and glue them to the corresponding square.

Think About This

1. What is the largest level of organization a city belongs to?

   _____

2. Can any part of the system function without the others? Explain.

   _____

   _____

   _____

3. How do you think the system used to organize where people live is similar to how your body is organized?

   _____

   _____

   _____

TEKS in this Lesson

7.12(C) Recognize levels of organization in plants and animals, including cells, tissues, organs, organ systems, and organisms.

7.12(E) Compare the functions of a cell to the functions of organisms such as waste removal.

Also covers Process Standards: 7.1(A), (B); 7.2(A), (C), (E); 7.3(B); 7.4(A), (B)

? Essential Questions

- How do unicellular and multicellular organisms differ?
- How does cell differentiation lead to the organization within a multicellular organism?

abc Vocabulary

cell differentiation
stem cell
tissue
organ
organ system

Color-enhanced SEM Magnification: 12×

Figure 1 Skin cells are only one of the many kinds of cells that make up a Komodo dragon.

Life's Organization TEKS 7.12(C), (E)

You might recall that all matter is made of atoms and that atoms combine and form molecules. Molecules make up cells. A large animal, such as a Komodo dragon, is not made of one cell. Instead, it is composed of trillions of cells working together. Its skin, shown in **Figure 1,** is made of many cells that are specialized for protection. The Komodo dragon has other types of cells, such as blood cells and nerve cells, that perform other functions. Cells work together in the Komodo dragon and enable it to function. In the same way, cells work together in you and in other multicellular organisms.

Recall that some organisms are made of only one cell. These unicellular organisms carry out all the activities necessary to survive, such as absorbing nutrients and getting rid of wastes. But no matter their sizes, all organisms are made of cells.

Recognize

1. Think back to the **Explore Activity,** and recall the levels of organization that make up a continent. What levels of organization do you think make up a tomato plant? Draw and label your ideas below.

Unicellular Organisms

TEKS 7.12(E)

You previously read that some organisms have only one cell. Unicellular organisms do all the things needed for their survival within that one cell. For example, the amoeba in **Figure 2** is ingesting another unicellular organism, called a paramecium, for food. Unicellular organisms also respond to their environment, get rid of waste, grow, and even reproduce on their own. Unicellular organisms can be prokaryotes or eukaryotes.

Prokaryotes

You might recall that a cell without a membrane-bound nucleus is a prokaryotic cell. In general, prokaryotic cells are smaller than eukaryotic cells and have fewer cell structures. A unicellular organism made of one prokaryotic cell is called a prokaryote. Some prokaryotes live in groups called colonies. Some can also live in extreme environments, as shown in **Figure 2.**

Eukaryotes

You might recall that a eukaryotic cell has a nucleus surrounded by a membrane and many other specialized organelles. For example, the amoeba shown in **Figure 2** has an organelle called a contractile vacuole. It functions like a bucket that is used to bail water out of a boat. A contractile vacuole collects excess water from the amoeba's cytoplasm. Then it pumps the excess water out of the amoeba. This prevents the amoeba from swelling and bursting.

A unicellular organism that is made of one eukaryotic cell is called a eukaryote. There are thousands of different unicellular eukaryotes, such as algae that grow on the inside of an aquarium and the fungus that causes the infection known as athlete's foot.

Figure 2 Unicellular organisms carry out life processes within one cell.

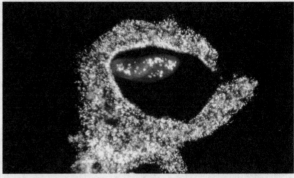

This unicellular amoeba captures a paramecium for food.

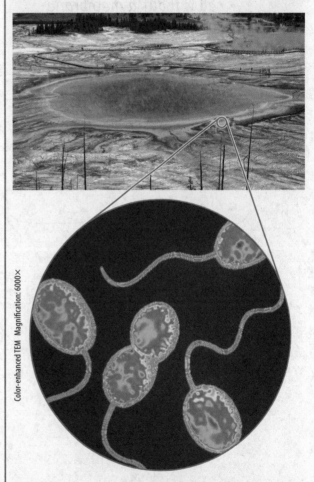

Color-enhanced TEM   Magnification: 6000×

These heat-loving bacteria are often found in hot springs as shown here. They get their energy to produce food from sulfur instead of from light like plants.

Organize it!

Organize information about unicellular organisms by completing the graphic organizer below.

Unicellular Organisms

_____

Description:
- cell without a membrane-
  bound _____

- smaller than _____ ;
  some live in _____

_____

_____

_____

Description:
- cell has a _____
  surrounded by a

  _____

- many specialized

_____

_____

_____

- obtain _____

- respond _____

- grow

- _____

_____

_____

_____

Multicellular Organisms TEKS 7.12(C), (E)

Multicellular organisms are made of many eukaryotic cells working together, like the crew on an airplane. Each member of the crew, from the pilot to the mechanic, has a specific job that is important for the plane's operation. Similarly, each type of cell in a multicellular organism has a specific job that is important to the survival of the organism.

Cell Differentiation

Recall that all cells in a multicellular organism come from one cell—a fertilized egg. Cell division starts quickly after fertilization. The first cells made can become any type of cell, such as a muscle cell, a nerve cell, or a blood cell. *The process by which cells become different types of cells is called* **cell differentiation** (dih fuh ren chee AY shun).

You might recall that a cell's instructions are contained in its chromosomes. Also, nearly all the cells of an organism have identical sets of chromosomes. If an organism's cells have identical sets of instructions, how can cells be different? Different cell types use different parts of the instructions on the chromosomes. A few of the many different types of cells that can result from human cell differentiation are shown in **Figure 3.**

FOLDABLES

Make a layered book from three sheets of notebook paper. Label it as shown. Use your book to describe the levels of organization that make up organisms. Discuss it with a partner.

Levels of Organization

Cell
Tissue
Organ
Organ System
Organism

Figure 3 A fertilized egg produces cells that can differentiate into a variety of cell types.

Go Online! Tutor

Cell Differentiation in Eukaryotes

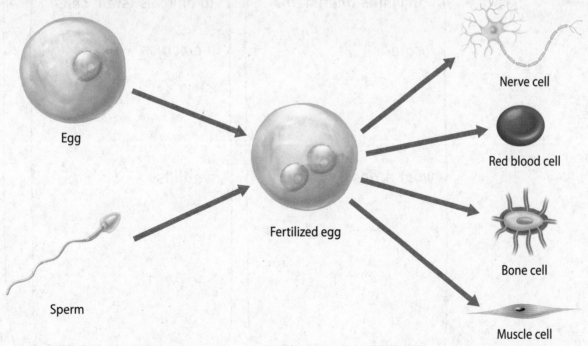

Egg

Sperm

Fertilized egg

Nerve cell

Red blood cell

Bone cell

Muscle cell

Animal Stem Cells Not all cells in a developing animal differentiate. **Stem cells** *are unspecialized cells that are able to develop into many different cell types.* There are many stem cells in embryos but fewer in adult organisms. Adult stem cells are important for cell repair and replacement. For example, stem cells in your bone marrow can produce more than a dozen different types of blood cells. These replace ones that are damaged or worn out. Stem cells have also been discovered in skeletal muscles. These stem cells can produce new muscle cells when the fibers that make up the muscle are torn.

Plant Cells Plants also have unspecialized cells similar to animal stem cells. These cells are grouped in areas of a plant called meristems (MER uh stemz). Meristems are in different areas of a plant, including the tips of roots and stems. Cell division in meristems produces different types of plant cells with specialized structures and functions, such as transporting materials, making food, storing food, or protecting the plant. These cells might become parts of stems, leaves, flowers, or roots.

Science Use v. Common Use

fiber

Science Use a long muscle cell

Common Use a thread

Organize

2. Use the chart at right to organize information about cell differentiation.

Cell Differentiation

Definition: _____

_____

In plants (meristems)

located:

what it does:

In animals (stem cells)

in embryos:

in adults:

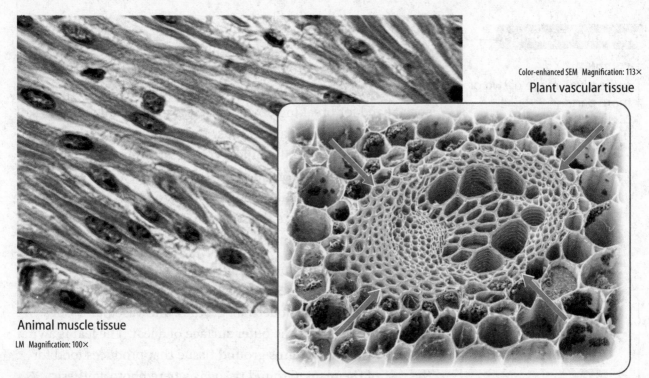

Color-enhanced SEM Magnification: 113×
Plant vascular tissue

Animal muscle tissue
LM Magnification: 100×

Tissues

In multicellular organisms, similar types of cells are organized into groups. **Tissues** *are groups of similar types of cells that work together to carry out specific tasks.* Humans, like most other animals, have four main types of tissue—muscle, connective, nervous, and epithelial (eh puh THEE lee ul). For example, the animal tissue shown in **Figure 4** is smooth muscle tissue that is part of the stomach. Muscle tissue causes movement. Connective tissue provides structure and support and often connects other types of tissue together. Nervous tissue carries messages to and from the brain. Epithelial tissue forms the protective outer layer of the skin and the lining of major organs and internal body cavities.

Plants also have different types of tissues. The three main types of plant tissue are dermal, vascular (VAS kyuh lur), and ground tissue. Dermal tissue provides protection and helps reduce water loss. Vascular tissue, shown in **Figure 4,** transports water and nutrients from one part of a plant to another. Ground tissue provides storage and support and is where photosynthesis occurs.

Figure 4 This animal muscle tissue contracts the stomach to help digestion. Plant vascular tissue, indicated by red arrows, moves water and nutrients throughout a plant.

Identify

3. What are the three main types of plant tissue? Tell the function of each.

Type	Function
1. Dermal	
2.	
3. Ground	

Organs

Complex jobs in organisms require more than one type of
tissue. **Organs** *are groups of different tissues working together to
perform a particular job.* For example, your stomach is an organ
specialized for breaking down food. It is made of all four types of
tissue: muscle, epithelial, nervous, and connective. Each type of
tissue performs a specific function necessary for the stomach to
work properly. Layers of muscle tissue contract and break up
pieces of food, epithelial tissue lines the stomach, nervous tissue
sends signals to indicate the stomach is full, and connective
tissue supports the stomach wall.

Plants also have organs, including roots, stems, and leaves. The
leaves shown in **Figure 5** are organs specialized for photosynthesis. Each leaf is made of dermal, ground, and vascular tissues.
Dermal tissue covers the outer surface of a leaf. The leaf is a vital
organ because it contains ground tissue that produces food for
the rest of the plant. Ground tissue is where photosynthesis
occurs. The ground tissue is tightly packed on the top half of a
leaf. The vascular tissue moves water and the food produced by
photosynthesis throughout the leaf and the rest of the plant.

Infer

4. Which plant tissue
   makes up the thinnest
   layer?

   _____

   _____

Figure 5 A plant leaf is an
organ made of several
different tissues.

LM Magnification: 50×

Dermal tissue

Ground tissue

Vascular tissue

Organ Systems

Usually organs do not function alone. Instead, **organ systems** *are groups of different organs that work together to complete a series of tasks.* Human organ systems can be made of many different organs working together. For example, the human digestive system is made of many organs, including the stomach, the small intestine, the liver, and the large intestine. These organs and others work together to break down food and take it into the body. Blood absorbs and transports nutrients from broken-down food to cells throughout the body.

Plants have two major organ systems—the shoot system and the root system. The shoot system includes leaves, stems, and flowers. Food and water are transported throughout the plant by the shoot system. The root system anchors the plant and takes in water and nutrients.

LAB Manager

MiniLAB: *How do cells work together to make an organism?*

TEKS 7.1(A); 7.2(E); 7.3(B); 7.4(A), (B); 7.12(C)

LAB: *Cell Differentiation*

TEKS 7.1(A), (B); 7.2(A), (C), (E); 7.4(A), (B); 7.12(C)

Sequence

5. How can the organization of cells, tissues, organs, and organ systems in a multicellular organism be sequenced?

Cells are organized in _____ .

Different _____ working together to perform a particular job are called _____ .

Groups of _____ that work together to complete a series of tasks are called _____ .

Many _____ working together make up an _____ .

Organisms

Multicellular organisms usually have many organ systems. These systems work together to carry out all the jobs needed for the survival of the organisms. For example, the cells in the leaves and the stems of a plant need water to live. They cannot absorb water directly. Water diffuses into the roots and is transported through the stem to the leaves by the transport system.

In the human body, there are many major organ systems. Each organ system depends on the others and cannot work alone. For example, the cells in the muscle tissue of the stomach cannot survive without oxygen. The stomach cannot get oxygen without working together with the respiratory and circulatory systems. **Figure 6** will help you review how organisms are organized.

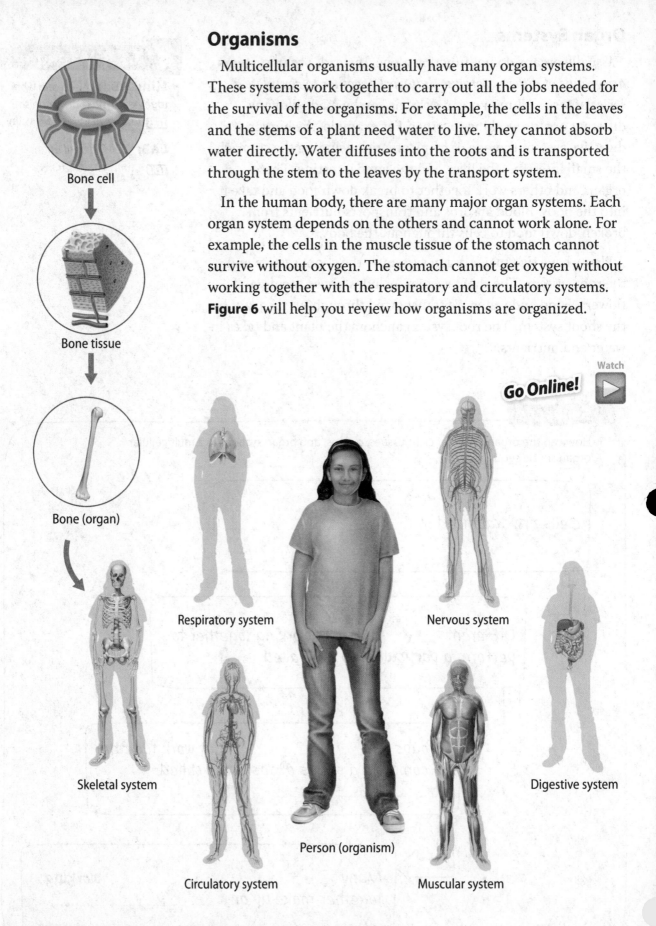

Bone cell

Bone tissue

Bone (organ)

Skeletal system

Respiratory system

Circulatory system

Person (organism)

Muscular system

Nervous system

Digestive system

Go Online! Watch

Figure 6 An organism is made of organ systems, organs, tissues, and cells that function together and enable the organism's survival.

10.3 Review

Summarize it!

Recognize levels of organization in plants. In the space below, draw and label the levels of organization in a tree. **TEKS** 7.12(C)

Connect it! The cells of all your organs have the same DNA in their nuclei, yet all perform different jobs in your body. **Explain** how this can be so. Use the term *cellular differentiation* in your explanation. Write your response in your interactive notebook. **TEKS** 7.12(C)

Levels of Organization

Use Vocabulary

1. Distinguish between an organ and an organ system. **TEKS** 7.12(C)

_____

_____

_____

_____

Apply the Essential Question

2. Which is the correct sequence of the levels of organization for plants and animals? **TEKS** 7.12(C)

A. cell, organ, tissue, organ system, organism

B. organism, organ, organ system, tissue, cell

C. cell, tissue, organ, organ system, organism

D. tissue, organ, organism, organ system, cell

3. Compare the functions of a cell to the functions of an organism, such as getting rid of wastes. **TEKS** 7.12(E)

_____

_____

_____

_____

_____

_____

H.O.T. Questions (Higher Order Thinking)

4. Classify a leaf as a tissue or an organ. Explain your choice. **TEKS** 7.12(C)

_____

_____

_____

_____

_____

_____

5. Analyze A chicken egg begins as one cell. How can one cell become a chick? **TEKS** 7.12(C)

_____

_____

_____

_____

_____

_____

_____

_____

_____

_____

Writing in Science

6. Characterize On a separate sheet of paper, write a five-sentence paragraph characterizing the levels of organization in a human organ system. Include a main idea, supporting details, and a concluding statement. **TEKS** 7.12(C)

10 TEKS Review

Test-Taking Strategy

Compare and Contrast Certain questions will have you compare and contrast certain parts of objects or processes. In these questions, you will need to carefully examine and be able to identify similarities and differences between the two items.

Example

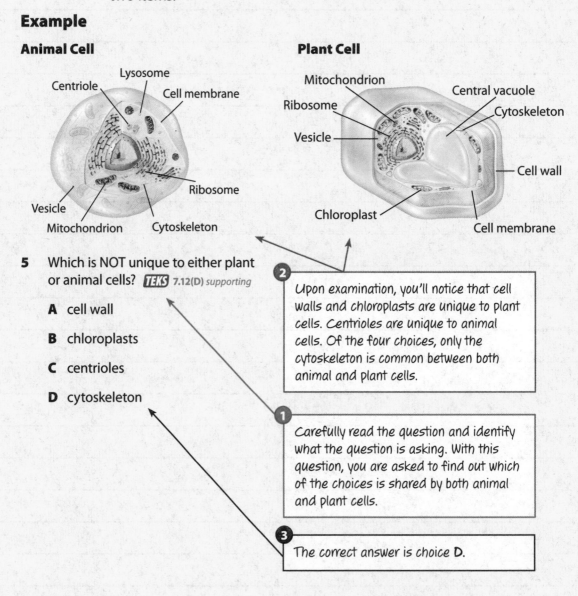

Animal Cell

Centriole
Lysosome
Cell membrane
Vesicle
Mitochondrion
Cytoskeleton
Ribosome

Plant Cell

Mitochondrion
Ribosome
Vesicle
Chloroplast
Central vacuole
Cytoskeleton
Cell wall
Cell membrane

5 Which is NOT unique to either plant or animal cells? **TEKS** 7.12(D) *supporting*

A cell wall

B chloroplasts

C centrioles

D cytoskeleton

2 Upon examination, you'll notice that cell walls and chloroplasts are unique to plant cells. Centrioles are unique to animal cells. Of the four choices, only the cytoskeleton is common between both animal and plant cells.

1 Carefully read the question and identify what the question is asking. With this question, you are asked to find out which of the choices is shared by both animal and plant cells.

3 The correct answer is choice **D**.

TIP: Even though many other parts of the cells are labeled on the diagrams above, you only need to be concerned with the four connected to the question. Don't waste time comparing and contrasting parts that have nothing to do with the question at hand.

Multiple Choice

1 Kaden is making a presentation on the levels of organization in plants and animals for his science class. He prepares this flowchart to illustrate his presentation. **TEKS** 7.12(C)

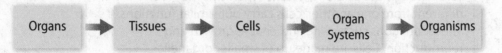

After further study, Kaden realizes his flowchart is incorrect. Which change should he make to correct the flowchart?

A add the phrase *Cell Membranes*

B move *Organ Systems* to the beginning

C remove *Tissues* and *Cells*

D swap *Organs* and *Cells*

---

2 Claudia made this diagram of a cell she observed during science class. Her teacher asked her to identify the cell as plant or animal, and to explain the reasoning for her conclusion.
TEKS 7.12(D) *supporting;* 7.4(A)

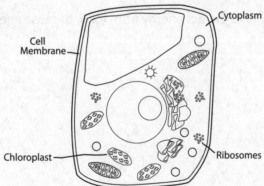

What should Claudia's correct response be, and what tool would she use to make her observations?

A The cell is an animal cell because it has ribosomes, which are required for protein synthesis in animals; a microscope.

B The cell is a plant cell because it has cytoplasm, which helps plants make their own food from sunlight; a hand lens.

C The cell is an animal cell because it has a cell membrane, and cell membranes are unique to animal cells; a hand lens.

D The cell is a plant cell because it has chloroplasts, which are structures found in plant cells; a microscope.

3

From the simplest unicellular organisms to the largest and most complex of Earth's animals, all living things are made of cells. Though the cells of different organisms may look different from one another, cells carry out similar functions. These functions sustain life and enable growth and reproduction. Cells are made up of smaller organelles. Organelles are specialized to perform specific vital functions. Organelles that are found in the cells of many organisms include mitochondria, endoplasmic reticulum, vesicles, and vacuoles.

Which describes a similar function that would likely be carried out in most cells?

TEKS 7.12(F) *supporting;* 7.3(A)

A Most cells can produce their own food, because food is essential for growth and development.

B Most cells have organelles that aid in the decomposition of minerals, because minerals must be broken down into a usable form and are necessary for survival.

C Most cells have structures that enable them to move around, because movement is important for the safety of a cell.

D Most cells have the capability to extract energy from food, because energy is required for all life processes.

4 The diagram shows the structures involved in respiration for a grasshopper. **TEKS** 7.12(C)

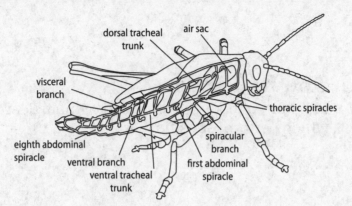

These structures are an example of which level of organization within an organism?

A The structures make up an organelle.

B The structures make up an organ system.

C The structures make up a specialized cell.

D The structures make up a tissue.

---

5 Like organisms, cells have structures that carry out vital functions. The diagram shows the function of a mitochondrion, which is a cellular structure. **TEKS** 7.12(E); 7.2(E)

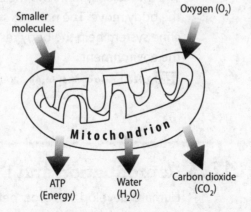

Which function carried out by an organism is most similar to the function carried out by a mitochondrion?

A circulation, because fluid and molecules are moved around

B digestion, because food is broken down into a usable form

C excretion, because waste is collected and removed

D respiration, because oxygen is taken in and moved throughout

The BIG Idea

The human body is composed of multiple, complex systems, which perform specific tasks.

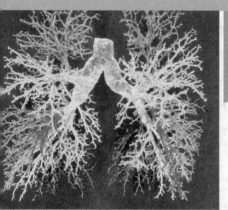

LESSON

11.1 Transport and Defense

The digestive, respiratory, circulatory, and excretory systems help transport nutrients, gases, and wastes. The lymphatic and integumentary systems defend the body against harmful invaders.

TEKS 7.6(B); 7.12(B); Also covers: 7.1(A); 7.2(A), (C), (E); 7.3(B); 7.4(A), (B)

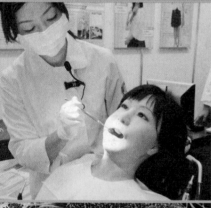

LESSON

11.2 Structure, Movement, and Control

The muscular system and the skeletal system help the body move. The nervous system and the endocrine system help the body respond to changes in the environment.

TEKS 7.12(B); Also covers: 7.1(A); 7.2(A), (C), (E), 7.3(B); 7.4(A), (B)

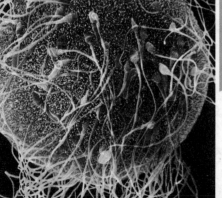

LESSON

11.3 Reproduction and Development

Humans develop and grow before and after birth.

TEKS 7.12(B); Also covers: 7.1(A); 7.2(A), (C), (E); 7.3(B), (C), (D); 7.4(A)

Is Bone Alive?

Five friends were arguing about bones. They each had different ideas about whether bones were living. This is what they said:

Mona: I think bones are living because they are inside our body.

Al: I think bones are living because they are made up of cells.

Bea: I think bones are non-living because they are made up of cells that become hard bone after they die.

Mia: I think bones are non-living because they are made up of minerals like calcium.

Tess: I think bones are non-living because they exist even after a person dies.

Who do you agree with the most? _____ Explain your thinking about bone as living or non-living material.

11.1 Transport and Defense

Unusual Web? This branching structure might look like a strange spider web, but it is actually a resin cast of human lungs. The yellowish tubes are large air passages, the white parts are small airways, and the blue parts are blood vessels. Why do the lungs need all these parts?

Write your response in your interactive notebook.

LAB Manager

Go to your Lab Manual or visit connectED.mcgraw-hill.com to perform the labs for this lesson.

MiniLAB: *How can you model digestion?*

TEKS 7.1(A); 7.2(A), (C), (E); 7.3(B); 7.4(A), (B); 7.6(B)

Skill Practice: *How can you model the function of blood cells?*

TEKS 7.1(A); 7.2(A); 7.3(B); 7.4(A), (B); 7.12(B)

Which tool can transport water quickly?

You need to transport materials throughout your body. Each cell must receive nutrients and oxygen and get rid of wastes. What kinds of tools do you think would be most effective in moving fluids such as water quickly?

Procedure

1. Read and complete a lab safety form.

2. Choose one of the **tools** for moving water.

3. Have another student use a **stopwatch** to keep time for 30 s. Use your tool to transport as much water as you can in 30 s from the main **bowl** into a **beaker.**

4. Use a **graduated cylinder** to measure the amount of water you moved from the bowl to the beaker. Record the measurement in your Lab Manual or interactive notebook.

5. Trade roles with your partner. Repeat steps 2 through 4.

6. Repeat step 5 until you have used all the tools.

Think About This

1. Which tool was most effective for moving water quickly? Which tool was least effective?

_____

_____

2. Why do you think moving small items in fluid might be more effective than moving them individually?

_____

_____

3. Which method do you think best models the function of the heart and circulatory system? Why?

_____

_____

TEKS in this Lesson

7.6(B) Distinguish between physical and chemical changes in matter in the digestive system.

7.12(B) Identify the main functions of the systems of the human organism, including the circulatory, respiratory, skeletal, muscular, digestive, excretory, reproductive, integumentary, nervous, and endocrine systems.

Also covers Process Standards: 7.1(A); 7.2(A), (C), (E); 7.3(B); 7.4(A), (B)

? Essential Questions

- How does food get broken down to be used by the body?
- How do nutrients travel through the body?
- How does the body defend itself from harmful invaders?

abc Vocabulary

organ system
homeostasis
nutrient
Calorie
lymphocyte
immunity

The Body's Organization

Have you ever tried to find a book in a library? Libraries have thousands of books grouped together by subject. Grouping books by subject in a library helps keep them organized and easier to find. Your body's organization helps it function.

All organisms have different parts with special functions. Recall that cells are the basic unit of all living organisms. Organized groups of cells that work together are tissues. Groups of tissues that perform a specific function are organs. *Groups of organs that work together and perform a specific task are* **organ systems.** Organ systems provide movement, transport substances, and perform many other functions that you will read about in this lesson.

Organ systems work together and maintain **homeostasis** (hoh mee oh STAY sus), *or steady internal conditions when external conditions change.* Have you ever jogged, jumped rope, or snowshoed, as shown in **Figure 1,** and started to sweat? When exercising, your body uses stored energy. Your body releases excess energy as thermal energy. Sweat, also called perspiration (pur spuh RAY shun), helps the body release thermal energy and maintain homeostasis.

Figure 1 Sweating helps the body maintain homeostasis by releasing excess thermal energy.

Identify

1. **Relate** the parts of an organism to each other by filling in the missing words.

Groups of cells that function together form _____.

Groups of _____ that function together form _____.

Groups of _____ that function together form _____.

Organ systems _____ and maintain _____.

Digestion and Excretion

TEKS 7.6(B); 7.12(B)

Humans need food, water, and oxygen to survive. Food contains energy that is processed by the body. The process by which food is broken down is called digestion. After digestion, substances that are not used by the body are removed through elimination.

The Digestive System

As shown in **Figure 2,** the digestive system is made up of several organs. Food and water enter the digestive system through the mouth.

Digestion Before your body can absorb nutrients from food, the food must be broken down into small molecules by digestion. There are two types of digestion—mechanical and chemical. In mechanical digestion, food is physically broken into smaller pieces. Mechanical digestion occurs when you chew, mash, and grind food with your teeth and tongue. Smaller pieces of food are easier to swallow and have more surface area, which helps with chemical digestion.

In chemical digestion, chemical reactions through enzymes break down pieces of food into small molecules. Enzymes are proteins that help break down larger molecules into smaller molecules.

Enzymes also speed up, or catalyze, the rate of chemical reactions. Without enzymes, some chemical reactions would be too slow or would not occur at all.

When you swallow, food, water, and other liquids move into a hollow tube called the esophagus (ih SAH fuh gus). The esophagus connects the mouth to the stomach. Digestion continues as food leaves the esophagus and enters the stomach. The stomach is a flexible, baglike organ that contains other enzymes that break down food into smaller parts so the food can be used by the body. An enzyme helps break down food molecules into smaller pieces. Even though the food molecule breaks apart, the enzyme itself does not change. Therefore, the enzyme can immediately be used to break down another food molecule.

Figure 2 Food enters the digestive system through the mouth, and nutrients are absorbed by the small intestine.

Watch

Go Online!

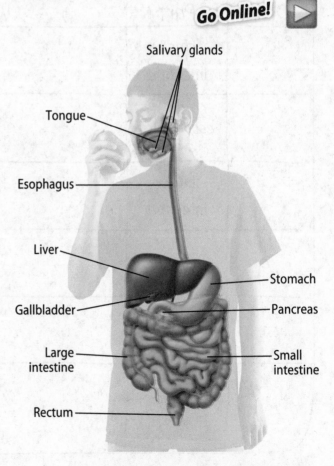

Salivary glands

Tongue

Esophagus

Liver

Gallbladder

Large intestine

Rectum

Stomach

Pancreas

Small intestine

FOLDABLES

Make three horizontal two-tab books. Label them with the body systems in this lesson and glue them side by side to form a booklet that has six tabs. Use your book to organize information about each body system in this lesson.

Absorption Next, food moves into the small intestine. By the time food gets to the small intestine, it is a soupy mixture. The small intestine is a tube that has two functions—digestion and absorption. The liver makes a substance called bile. The pancreas makes enzymes. Bile and enzymes are used in the small intestine to break down food further. Because the small intestine is very long, it takes food hours to move through it. During that time, particles of food and water are absorbed into the blood.

Elimination The large intestine, or colon (KOH lun), receives digested food that the small intestine did not absorb. The large intestine also absorbs water from the remaining waste material. Most foods are completely digested into smaller parts that can be easily absorbed by the small intestine. However, some foods travel through the entire digestive system without being digested or absorbed. For example, some types of fiber, called insoluble fiber, in vegetables and whole grains are not digested and leave the body through the rectum.

Identify

2. **Order** and identify the main functions of the digestive system. Explain what happens at each location.

Order	Part	What happens there?
	small intestine	
	esophagus	
	large intestine	
6	rectum	
1	mouth	
	pancreas	

Nutrition

As you have read, one of the functions of the small intestine is absorption. **Nutrients** *are the parts of food used by the body to grow and survive.* There are several types of nutrients. Proteins, fats, carbohydrates, vitamins, and minerals are nutrients. Nutrition labels on food, as shown in **Figure 3,** show the amount of each nutrient in that food. By looking at the labels on packaged foods, you can make sure you get the nutrients you need. Different people need different amounts of nutrients. For example, football players, swimmers, and other athletes need a lot of nutrients for energy. Pregnant women also need lots of nutrients to provide for their developing babies.

Digestion helps release energy from food. A **Calorie** *is the amount of energy it takes to raise the temperature of 1 kg of water by 1°C.* The body uses Calories from proteins, fats, and carbohydrates, which each contain a different amount of energy.

Figure 3 The information on a nutrition label can help you decide whether a food is healthful to eat.

✏️ *Characterize*

3. Explain how proper nutrition is connected to the main function of the digestive system.

_____

_____

_____

Math Skills | **Math TEKS** 7.1(A); 7.3(A); 7.4(D)

Use Proportions A proportion is an equation of two equal ratios. You can solve a proportion for an unknown value. For example, a 50-g egg provides 70 Calories (C) of energy. How many Calories would you get from 125 g of scrambled eggs?

Write a proportion.

$$\frac{50 \text{ g}}{70 \text{ C}} = \frac{125 \text{ g}}{x}$$

Find the cross products.

50 g (x) = 70 C × 125 g

50 g (x) = 8,750 C g

Divide both sides by 50.

$$\frac{50 \text{ g } (x)}{50 \text{ g}} = \frac{8,750 \text{ C g}}{50 \text{ g}}$$

Simplify the equation.

x = 175 C

Practice

The serving size of a large fast-food hamburger with cheese is 316 g. It contains 790 C of energy. How many Calories would you consume if you ate 100 g of the burger?

Check Tutor

Go Online! ✓ 💬

MiniLAB: *How can you model digestion?*

TEKS 7.1(A); 7.2(A), (C), (E); 7.3(B); 7.4(A), (B); 7.6(B)

Infer

4. List the missing parts and functions of the excretory system and match the parts to their roles.

Parts	Role
lungs	stores feces until it moves out of the body
liver	
	remove urea by producing urine
bladder	removes salt and water when you sweat

The Excretory System

The excretory system removes solid, liquid, and gas waste materials from the body. The lungs, skin, liver, kidneys, bladder, and rectum are parts of the excretory system.

The lungs remove carbon dioxide (CO_2) and excess water as water vapor when you breathe out, or exhale. The skin removes water and salt when you sweat.

The liver removes wastes from the blood. As you have read, the liver also is a part of the digestive system. The digestive and excretory systems work together to break down, absorb, and remove food.

When the liver breaks down proteins, urea forms. Urea is toxic if it stays in the body. The kidneys, shown in **Figure 4,** remove urea from the body by making urine. Urine contains water, urea, and other waste chemicals. Urine leaves each kidney through a tube called the ureter (YOO ruh tur), and it is stored in a flexible sac, called the bladder. Urine is removed from the body through a tube called the urethra (yoo REE thruh).

Like the liver, the rectum is part of the excretory system and the digestive system. Food substances that are not absorbed by the small intestine are mixed with other wastes and form feces. The rectum stores feces until it moves out of the body.

Figure 4 The kidneys remove waste material from the body.

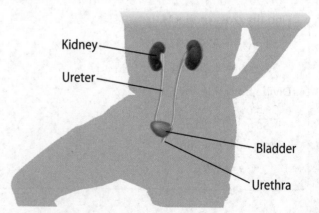

Kidney

Ureter

Bladder

Urethra

Draw each of the organs necessary to complete the digestive system in the human body outline below. Make sure the organs are drawn proportionally, connect in the right places, and connect in the right order.

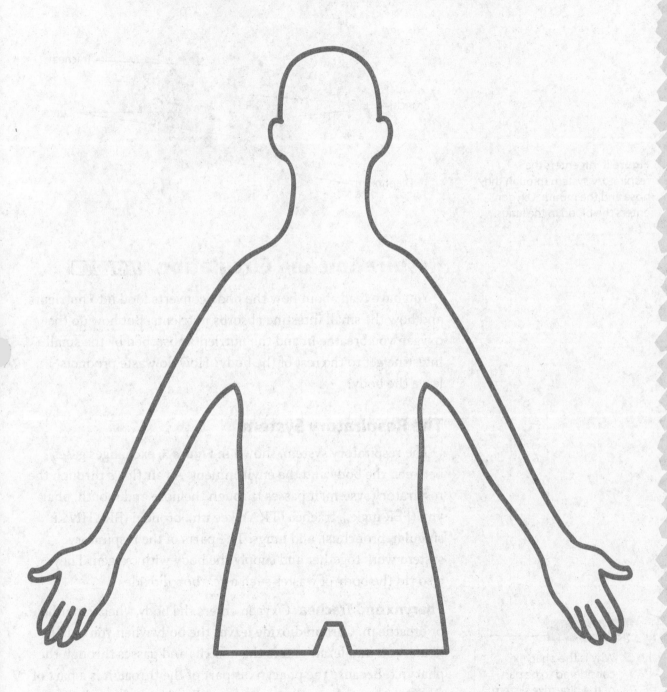

Connect it! Football players, swimmers, and other athletes need a lot of nutrients for energy. In your interactive notebook, explain why athletes need more nutrients than someone who does not exercise as much.

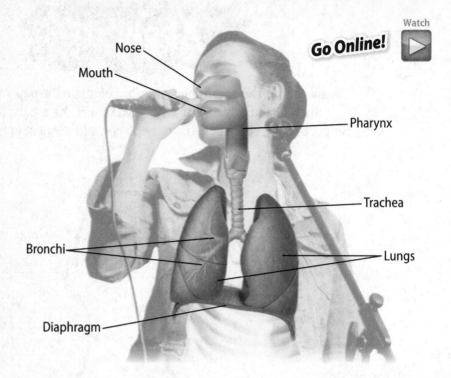

Nose

Mouth

Pharynx

Trachea

Bronchi

Lungs

Diaphragm

Figure 5 Air enters the respiratory system through the nose and the mouth. Oxygen enters the blood in the lungs.

Watch

Go Online!

Respiration and Circulation TEKS 7.12(B)

You have read about how the body converts food into nutrients and how the small intestine absorbs nutrients. But how do the oxygen you breathe in and the nutrients absorbed by the small intestine get to the rest of the body? How do waste products leave the body?

The Respiratory System

The respiratory system, shown in **Figure 5,** exchanges gases between the body and the environment. As air flows through the respiratory system, it passes through the nose and mouth, pharynx (FER ingks), trachea (TRAY kee uh), bronchi (BRAHN ki; singular, bronchus), and lungs. The parts of the respiratory system work together and supply the body with oxygen. They also rid the body of wastes such as carbon dioxide.

Pharynx and Trachea Oxygen enters the body when you inhale, or breathe in. Carbon dioxide leaves the body when you exhale. When you inhale, air enters the nostrils and passes through the pharynx. Because the pharynx is part of the throat, it is a part of the digestive and respiratory systems. Food goes through the pharynx to the esophagus. Air travels through the pharynx to the trachea. The trachea is also called the windpipe because it is a long, tubelike organ that connects the pharynx to the bronchi.

Infer

5. Why is the pharynx considered to be part of the digestive system and the respiratory system? Write your answer in your interactive notebook.

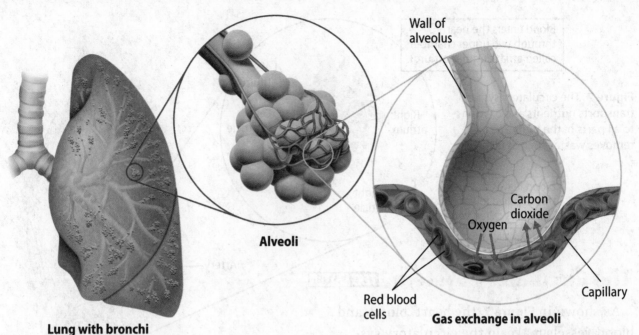

Wall of alveolus

Carbon dioxide

Oxygen

Red blood cells

Capillary

Alveoli

Gas exchange in alveoli

Lung with bronchi

Figure 6 Bronchi divide into smaller tubes that end in clusters of alveoli that are surrounded by capillaries.

Bronchi and Alveoli There are two bronchi; one enters the left lung, and one enters the right lung. As shown in **Figure 6,** the bronchi divide into smaller tubes that end in tiny groups of cells. These groups of cells are called alveoli (al VEE uh li). Inside each lung, there are more than 100 million alveoli. The alveoli are surrounded by blood vessels called capillaries. Oxygen in the alveoli enters the capillaries. The blood inside capillaries transports oxygen to the rest of the body.

Inhaling and exhaling require the movement of a muscle under the lungs called the diaphragm (DI uh fram). As the diaphragm contracts and moves down, air enters the lungs and you inhale. When the diaphragm relaxes and moves up, you exhale.

Show

6. **Sequence** the route that gases follow during respiration. Use the following terms: *lungs, pharynx, alveoli, bronchi,* and *trachea.*

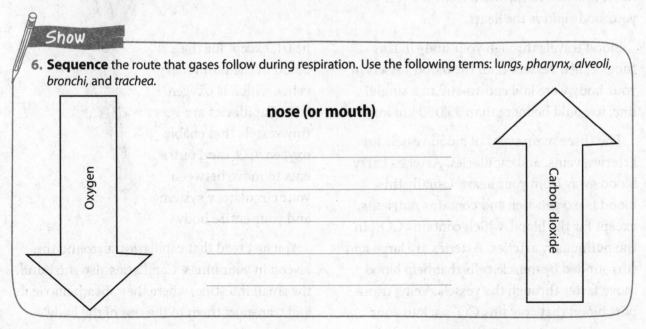

nose (or mouth)

Oxygen

Carbon dioxide

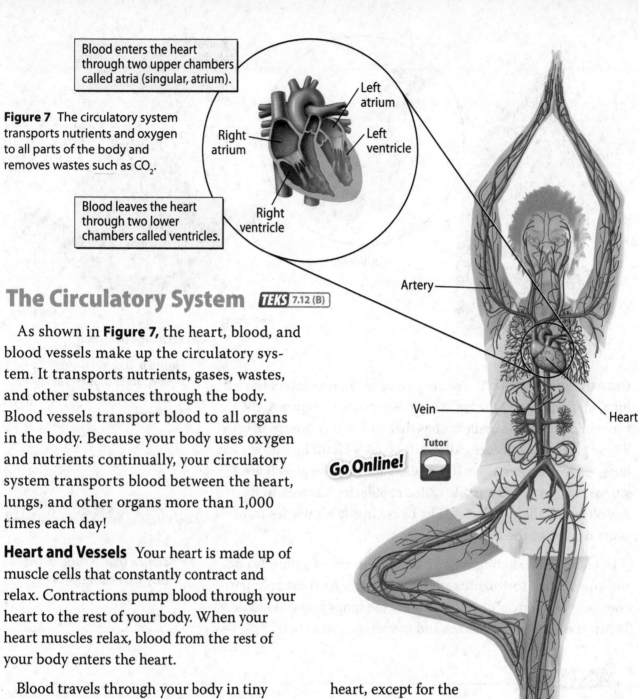

Blood enters the heart through two upper chambers called atria (singular, atrium).

Figure 7 The circulatory system transports nutrients and oxygen to all parts of the body and removes wastes such as CO$_2$.

Blood leaves the heart through two lower chambers called ventricles.

Left atrium

Left ventricle

Right atrium

Right ventricle

Artery

Vein

Heart

Go Online!

Tutor

The Circulatory System TEKS 7.12 (B)

As shown in **Figure 7,** the heart, blood, and blood vessels make up the circulatory system. It transports nutrients, gases, wastes, and other substances through the body. Blood vessels transport blood to all organs in the body. Because your body uses oxygen and nutrients continually, your circulatory system transports blood between the heart, lungs, and other organs more than 1,000 times each day!

Heart and Vessels Your heart is made up of muscle cells that constantly contract and relax. Contractions pump blood through your heart to the rest of your body. When your heart muscles relax, blood from the rest of your body enters the heart.

Blood travels through your body in tiny tubes called vessels. If all the blood vessels in your body were laid end-to-end in a single line, it would be more than 95,000 km long.

The three main types of blood vessels are arteries, veins, and capillaries. Arteries carry blood away from your heart. Usually this blood is oxygen-rich and contains nutrients, except for the blood, which contains CO$_2$, in the pulmonary arteries. Arteries are large and surrounded by muscle cells that help blood move faster through the vessels. Veins transport blood that contains CO$_2$ back to your heart, except for the blood in the pulmonary veins, which is oxygen-rich. Capillaries are very tiny vessels that enable oxygen, CO$_2$, and nutrients to move between your circulatory system and your entire body.

You just read that capillaries surround the alveoli in your lungs. Capillaries also surround the small intestine, where they absorb nutrients and transport them to the rest of the body.

Table 1 Human Blood Types

Go Online!

Blood Type	Type A	Type B	Type AB	Type O
Antigens on red blood cells	(A antigens)	(B antigens)	(A and B antigens)	(no antigens)
Percentage of U.S. population with this blood type	42	10	4	44
Clumping proteins in plasma	anti-B	anti-A	none	anti-A and anti-B
Blood type(s) that can be RECEIVED in a transfusion	A or O	B or O	A, B, AB. or O	O only
This blood type can DONATE TO these blood types	A or AB	B or AB	AB only	A, B, AB, O

Table 1 The red blood cells of each blood type have different proteins on their surfaces.

Blood The blood that circulates through vessels has several parts. The liquid part of blood is called plasma, and it contains nutrients, water, and CO_2. Blood also contains red blood cells, platelets, and white blood cells. Red blood cells carry oxygen. Platelets help the body heal when you get a cut. White blood cells help the body defend itself from toxins and diseases.

Everyone has red blood cells. However, different people have different proteins on the surfaces of their red blood cells, as shown in **Table 1.** Scientists classify these different red-blood cell proteins into groups called blood types.

People with A proteins on their red blood cells have type A blood. People with B proteins on their red blood cells have type B blood. Some people have A and B proteins on their red blood cells. They have type AB blood. People with type O blood have neither A nor B proteins on the surfaces of their red blood cells.

Medical professionals use blood types to determine which type of blood a person can receive from a blood donor. For example, because people with type O blood have no proteins on the surfaces of their red blood cells, they can receive blood only from a donor who also has type O blood.

Explain

7. Which blood types can be received by type B patients in a blood transfusion? Why?

_____

_____

_____

_____

_____

_____

_____

_____

_____

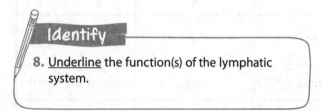

Word Origin

lymphocyte
from Latin *lympha,* means "water"; and Greek
kytos, means "hollow, as a cell or container"

Identify

8. Underline the function(s) of the lymphatic
system.

Figure 8 Lymph vessels are throughout your body.

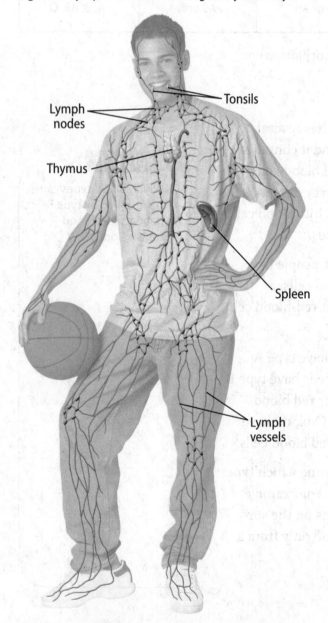

Lymph nodes

Thymus

Tonsils

Spleen

Lymph vessels

The Lymphatic System

Have you ever had a cold and found it painful to swallow? This can occur if your tonsils swell. Tonsils are small organs on both sides of your throat. They are part of the lymphatic (lihm FA tihk) system.

The spleen, the thymus, bone marrow, and lymph nodes also are parts of the lymphatic system. The spleen stores blood for use in an emergency. The thymus, the spleen, and bone marrow make white blood cells.

Your lymphatic system has three main functions: removing excess fluid around organs, producing white blood cells, and absorbing and transporting fats. The lymphatic system helps your body maintain fluid homeostasis. About 65 percent of the human body is water. Most of this water is inside cells. Sometimes, when water, wastes, and nutrients move between capillaries and organs, not all the fluid is taken up by the organs. When fluid builds up around organs, swelling can occur. To prevent swelling, the lymphatic system removes the fluid.

Lymph vessels are located throughout your body, as shown in **Figure 8.** Fluid that travels through the lymph vessels flows into organs called lymph nodes. Humans have more than 500 lymph nodes. The lymph nodes work together and protect the body by removing toxins, wastes, and other harmful substances.

The lymphatic system makes white blood cells. They help the body defend against infection. There are many different types of white blood cells. *A* **lymphocyte** (LIHM fuh sites) *is a type of white blood cell that is made in the thymus, the spleen, or the bone marrow.* Lymphocytes protect the body by traveling through the circulatory system and defending against infection.

9. Identify the parts and functions of the lymphatic system.

Six Parts	Three Functions
•	1.
•	
•	2.
•	
•	3.
• lymphocytes	

Immunity

The lymphatic system protects your body from harmful substances and infection. *The resistance to specific pathogens, or disease-causing agents, is called* **immunity.** The skeletal system produces immune cells, and the circulatory system transports them throughout the body. Immune cells include lymphocytes and other white blood cells. These cells detect and destroy viruses, bacteria, and other substances that are not normally made in the body, as shown in **Figure 9.**

If the body is exposed to the same bacteria, virus, or substance later, some immune cells remember and make proteins called antibodies. These antibodies recognize specific proteins on the harmful agent and help the body fight infection faster. Because there are many different types of bacteria and viruses, humans make billions of different types of antibodies. Each type of antibody responds to a different harmful agent.

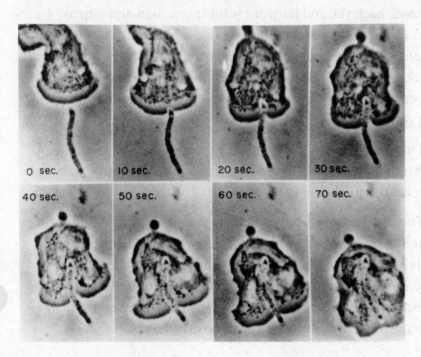

0 sec. 10 sec. 20 sec. 30 sec.

40 sec. 50 sec. 60 sec. 70 sec.

Figure 9 Lymphocytes surround bacteria and destroy or remove them from the body.

Table 2 Examples of Diseases

| Infectious Disease | | Noninfectious Disease |
Disease	Pathogen	
colds	virus	cancer
AIDS	virus	diabetes
strep throat	bacteria	heart disease
chicken pox	virus	allergy

LAB Manager

Skill Practice: *How can you model the function of blood cells?* **TEKS** 7.1(A); 7.2(A); 7.3(B); 7.4(A), (B); 7.12(B)

Summarize

10. Describe the body's lines of defense.

First

Second

Third

Types of Diseases

There are two main groups of diseases—infectious and non-infectious—as shown in **Table 2.** Infectious diseases are caused by pathogens, such as bacteria and viruses. Infectious diseases are usually contagious, which means they can be spread from one person to another. The flu is an example of an infectious disease. Viruses that invade organ systems of the body, such as the respiratory system, cause infectious diseases.

A noninfectious disease is caused by the environment or a genetic disorder, not a pathogen. Skin cancer, diabetes, and allergies are examples of noninfectious diseases. Noninfectious diseases are not contagious and cannot be spread from one person to another.

Lines of Defense

The human body has many ways of protecting itself from viruses, bacteria, and harmful substances. Skin and mucus (MYEW kus) are parts of the first line of defense. They prevent toxins and other substances from entering the body. Mucus is a thick, gel-like substance in the nostrils, trachea, and lungs. Mucus traps harmful substances and prevents them from entering your body.

The second line of defense is the immune response. In the immune response, white blood cells attack and destroy harmful substances, as shown in **Figure 9.**

The third line of defense protects your body against substances that have infected the body before. As you have read, immune cells make antibodies that destroy the harmful substances. Vaccines are used to help the body develop antibodies against infectious diseases. For example, many people get an influenza vaccine annually to protect them against the flu.

Explain how the digestive, excretory, respiratory, and lymphatic systems rely on the circulatory system. **TEKS** 7.12(B)

Digestive System	Excretory System

Circulatory System

Respiratory System	Lymphatic System

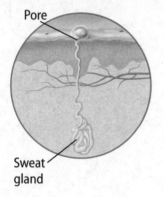

Pore

Sweat
gland

Figure 10 During exercise, sweat evaporates and blood vessels enlarge. This releases thermal energy.

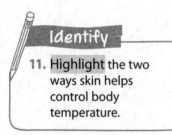

Identify

11. **Highlight** the two ways skin helps control body temperature.

The Integumentary System TEKS 7.12(B)

Touch your fingertips, your arm, and your face. The soft tissue you feel is the outermost layer of your skin. Skin is the largest organ of your body. It is part of the integumentary (ihn teh gyuh MEN tuh ree) system, which includes all the external coverings of the body, including the skin, nails, and hair.

Functions of the Integumentary System

Recall that skin is part of your body's first line of defense. It helps protect your body from harmful substances in the external environment. It keeps your body from drying out in sunlight and wind. Skin also protects the cells and tissues under the skin from damage. Too much exposure to the Sun can damage skin. The damage can result in sun burns or skin cancer. Skin can be protected by using sun block and regulating the amount of time it is exposed to the Sun.

Close your eyes and feel the surface of your desk and the objects on top of it. Even with your eyes closed, you can tell the difference between the desk, a book, paper, and pencils. You can feel these differences because your skin has special cells called sensory receptors that detect texture. Sensory receptors also detect temperature and sense pain. The more sensory receptors there are in an area of skin, the more sensitive it is.

Skin helps control body temperature. When you exercise, sweat comes from tiny holes, or pores, on the skin's surface. Sweating is one way skin lowers your body temperature, as shown in **Figure 10.** As sweat evaporates, excess thermal energy leaves the body and the skin cools. Another way that skin lowers body temperature is by releasing thermal energy from blood vessels. Has your face ever turned red while exercising? This happens because blood vessels near the skin's surface dilate, or enlarge.

If your skin is exposed to sunlight, it can make vitamin D. Your body needs vitamin D to help it absorb calcium and phosphorus, which are needed for healthy bones. Your skin is not the only source of vitamin D. Vitamin D is usually added to milk, and it is found naturally in certain types of fish.

Normal cellular processes produce waste products. The skin helps eliminate these wastes. Water, salts, and other waste products are removed through the pores. This removal occurs all the time, but you might only notice it when you sweat during exercise.

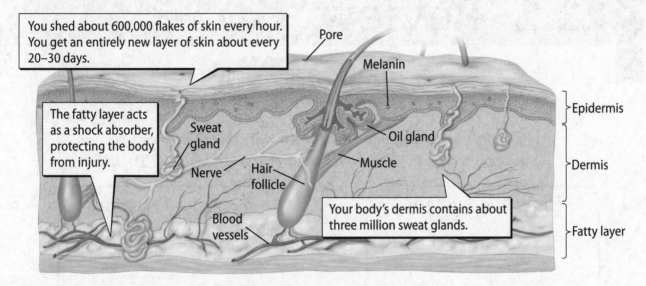

Figure 11 Skin has three layers, each with different functions.

Structures of the Skin

The skin that you see and feel on your body is the outermost layer of skin. Below it are two other layers of skin. These layers, shown in **Figure 11,** differ in structure and function.

Epidermis

The epidermis (eh puh DUR mus) is the outermost layer of skin and the only layer that comes into direct contact with the outside environment. The epidermis is tough but thin. The epidermis on your eyelids is thinner than a sheet of paper. Cells of the epidermis are constantly shed and replaced by new cells. One important function of the epidermis is the production of melanin (MEH luh nun). Melanin is a pigment that protects the body by absorbing some of the Sun's damaging ultraviolet rays.

Dermis

Below the epidermis is the dermis. The dermis is a thick layer of skin that gives skin strength, nourishment, and flexibility. The dermis contains sweat glands, blood vessels, nerves, hair follicles, and muscles, as shown in **Figure 11.** When the muscles in the dermis contract, you get goose bumps.

Fatty Layer

The innermost layer of skin insulates the body, acts as a protective padding, and stores energy. This layer is sometimes called the fatty layer. It can be very thin or very thick, depending on its location on the body.

Infer

12. Why is flexibility of the skin important?

Identify whether the human body systems listed below are involved in transport or defense. Then summarize how the system works. **TEKS** 7.12(B)

Digestive System

Excretory System

Integumentary System

Human Body Systems

Respiratory System

Lymphatic System

Circulatory System

Connect it! Suppose that you are on a school bus that broke down on a cold winter day. In your interactive notebook, explain what each person could do to stay warm.

Summarize it!

Transport and Defense

Apply the Essential Questions

1. Which body system removes carbon dioxide and waste? **TEKS** 7.12(B) *supporting*

   A. circulatory

   B. digestive

   C. excretory

   D. lymphatic

2. **Differentiate** the role of the liver in the digestive system from its role in the excretory system. **TEKS** 7.12(B) *supporting*

   _____

   _____

   _____

   _____

   _____

3. **Compare** and contrast mechanical and chemical digestion. **TEKS** 7.6(B) *supporting*

   _____

   _____

   _____

4. **Examine** how the circulatory and respiratory systems work together to move oxygen through the body.

   TEKS 7.12(B) *supporting*

   _____

   _____

   _____

   _____

H.O.T. Questions (Higher Order Thinking)

5. **Evaluate** how the skin's ability to continually produce new skin cells helps protect your body. **TEKS** 7.12(B) *supporting*

   _____

   _____

   _____

   _____

   _____

6. **Explain** what would happen to the digestion process if enzymes were not present. **TEKS** 7.6(B) *supporting*

   _____

   _____

   _____

   _____

Math Skills Math **TEKS** 7.1(A); 7.3(A); 7.4(D)

Use Proportions

7. If 30.5 g of milk contains 18 C, how many Calories will you consume by drinking a glass of milk (244 g)?

Check Tutor

Go Online! ✓ 💬

Bone Marrow Transplants

Why might you need new bone marrow?

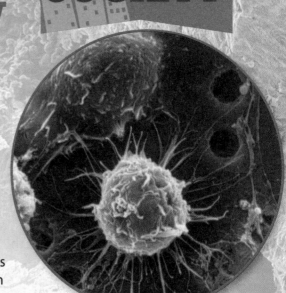

▲ In healthy bone marrow, a stem cell can develop into different types of blood cells.

Healthy blood cells are essential to overall health. Red blood cells carry oxygen throughout the body. Some white blood cells fight infections. Platelets help stop bleeding. A bone marrow transplant is sometimes necessary when a disease interferes with the body's ability to produce healthy blood cells.

Bone marrow is a tissue found inside some of the bones in your body. Healthy bone marrow contains cells that can develop into white blood cells, red blood cells, or platelets. Some diseases, such as leukemia and sickle cell disease, affect bone marrow. Replacing malfunctioning bone marrow with healthy bone marrow can help treat these diseases.

Bone marrow is harvested from the pelvic bone. An anesthetic is used to keep the donor from feeling pain during the procedure. ▼

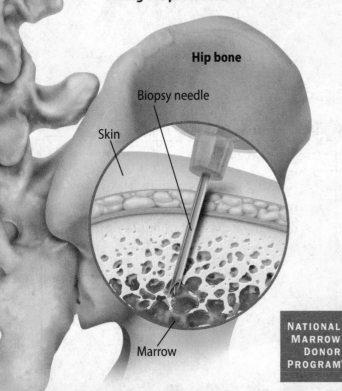

Hip bone

Biopsy needle

Skin

Marrow

NATIONAL MARROW DONOR PROGRAM®

A bone marrow transplant involves several steps. The patient receiving the bone marrow must have treatments to destroy his or her unhealthy bone marrow. Healthy bone marrow must be obtained for the transplant. Sometimes, the patient's own bone marrow can be treated and used for transplant. This transplant has the greatest chance of success. Other transplants involve healthy bone marrow donated by another person. The bone marrow must be tested to ensure that it is a good match for the patient.

The bone marrow donor undergoes a procedure called harvesting. Bone marrow is taken from the donor's pelvic bone. The donor's body replaces the harvested bone marrow, so there are no long-term effects for the donor.

The donated bone marrow is introduced into the patient's bloodstream. If the transplant is successful, the new bone marrow moves into the bone cavities and begins producing healthy blood cells.

It's Your Turn!

RESEARCH AND REPORT Find out more about bone marrow transplants. What other diseases can be treated using a bone marrow transplant? What is the National Marrow Donor Program? Present your findings to your class.

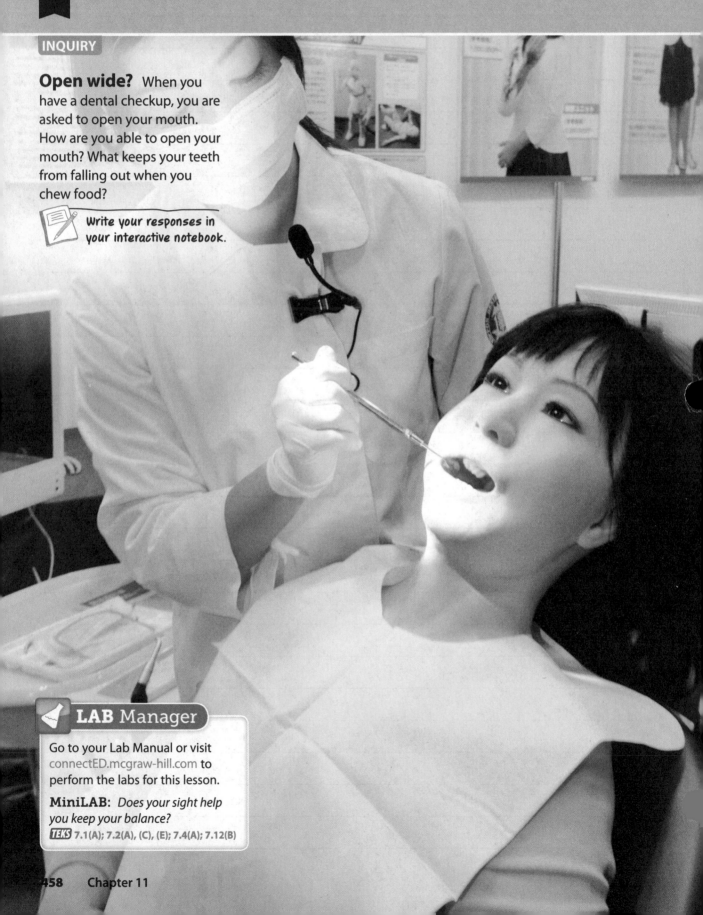

INQUIRY

Open wide? When you have a dental checkup, you are asked to open your mouth. How are you able to open your mouth? What keeps your teeth from falling out when you chew food?

Write your responses in your interactive notebook.

LAB Manager

Go to your Lab Manual or visit connectED.mcgraw-hill.com to perform the labs for this lesson.

MiniLAB: *Does your sight help you keep your balance?*
TEKS 7.1(A); 7.2(A), (C), (E); 7.4(A); 7.12(B)

Explore Activity

TEKS 7.1(A); 7.2(A), (E); 7.3(B); 7.4(A), (B); 7.12(B)

Why is the skeletal system so important?

Your skeletal system protects your body's organs, provides support, helps you move, and stores necessary minerals.

Procedure

1. Read and complete a lab safety form.

2. Obtain one of the **disassembled human figures** and a **kit of materials.**

3. Use the materials to build a backbone for your figure. Using your backbone, connect the head and the arms to the legs of the figure.

Think About This

1. Which materials did you find helpful in creating a backbone and skeletal structure for your figure? Which ones were not helpful?

_____

_____

_____

_____

2. Which characteristics of the "skeleton" were important as you built it? What problems would be caused by not having a skeleton?

_____

_____

_____

_____

3. Can you make your figure move? How does having a good support structure help it move?

_____

_____

_____

TEKS in this Lesson

7.12(B) Identify the main functions of the systems of the human organism, including the circulatory, respiratory, skeletal, muscular, digestive, excretory, reproductive, integumentary, nervous, and endocrine systems.

Also covers Process Standards: 7.1(A); 7.2(A), (C), (E); 7.3(B); 7.4(A), (B)

? Essential Questions

- How does the body move?
- How does the body respond to changes in its environment?

abc Vocabulary

compact bone
spongy bone
neuron
reflex
hormone

Structure and Movement **TEKS** 7.12(B)

Have you ever had to open your mouth for a dental checkup as shown in the photo at the beginning of the lesson? The human body can move in many different directions and perform a wide variety of tasks. It is able to do things that require many parts of the body to move, such as shooting a basketball into a hoop or swimming in a pool. The human body also can remain very still—posing for a picture or balancing on one leg.

In this lesson, you will read more about two organ systems—the skeletal system and the muscular system—that give the body structure, help the body move, and protect other organ systems.

The Skeletal System

The skeletal system has four major jobs. It protects internal organs, provides support, helps the body move, and stores minerals. The skeletal system is mostly bones. Adults have 206 bones. Ligaments, tendons, and cartilage are also parts of the skeletal system.

FOLDABLES

Cut out the Lesson 11.2 Foldable in the back of the book. Use it to organize information about the body systems in this lesson.

Tape here

Tab 1	**Human Body Systems**
Body Parts:	Body Parts:
Body Parts:	Body Parts:
Tab 2	**Human Body Systems**

Tape here

Storage The skeletal system is also an important storage site for minerals such as calcium. Calcium is essential for life. It has many functions in the body. Muscles require calcium for contractions. The nervous system requires calcium for communication. Most of the calcium in the body is stored in bone. Calcium helps build stronger compact bone. Cheese and milk are good sources of calcium.

Support Without a skeleton, your body would look like a beanbag. Your skeleton gives your body structure and support, as shown in **Figure 1.** Your bones help you stand, sit up, and raise your arms to play an instrument such as a trumpet.

Protection Many of the bones in the body protect organs that are made of softer tissue. For example, the skull protects the soft tissue of the brain, and the rib cage protects the soft tissue of the lungs and heart.

Movement The skeletal system helps the body move by working with the muscular system. Bones can move because they are attached to muscles. You will read more about the interaction of the skeletal system and the muscular system later in this lesson.

Bone Types Bones are organs that contain two types of tissue. **Compact bone** *is the hard outer layer of bone.* **Spongy bone** *is the interior region of bone that contains many tiny holes.* As shown in **Figure 1,** spongy bone is inside compact bone. Some bones also contain bone marrow. Recall that bone marrow is a part of the lymphatic system, and it makes white blood cells.

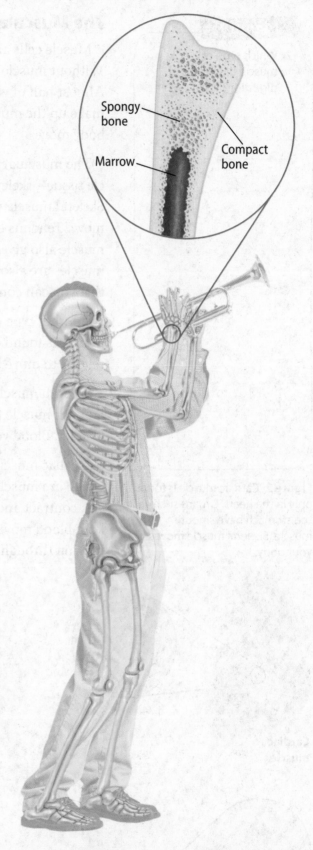

Figure 1 Bone is made up of a dense, hard exterior and a spongy interior.

Describe

1. **Explain** what the body uses calcium for. Write your answer in your interactive notebook.

The Muscular System

Muscle cells are everywhere in the body, as shown in **Figure 2**. Without muscle cells you would not be able to talk, write, or run. Almost half of your body mass is muscle cells. These muscle cells make up the muscular system. By working together, they help the body move.

The muscular system is made of three different types of muscle tissue—skeletal muscle, cardiac muscle, and smooth muscle. Skeletal muscle works with the skeletal system and helps you move. Tendons connect skeletal muscles to bones. Skeletal muscle also gives you the strength to lift heavy objects. Skeletal muscles are also called voluntary muscles, which are muscles that you can consciously control.

Another type of muscle tissue is cardiac muscle. Cardiac muscle is found only in the heart. It continually contracts and relaxes to move blood throughout your body.

Smooth muscle tissue moves materials through your body. Smooth muscle tissue is in organs such as the stomach and the bladder. Blood vessels also have smooth muscle tissue.

Cardiac muscle and smooth muscle are involuntary muscles, which are muscles you cannot consciously control. These muscles contract and retract without concious thought. This helps keep blood moving through your circulatory system and food moving through your digestive system.

Figure 2 Cardiac muscle is found only in the heart. Organs such as the stomach have smooth muscle. Skeletal muscle moves your body.

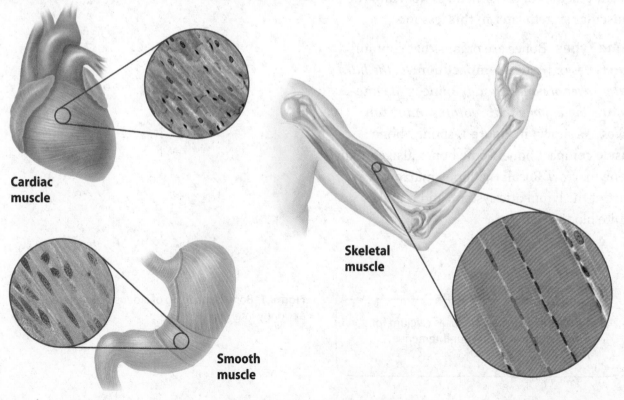

Cardiac muscle

Smooth muscle

Skeletal muscle

Classify details about the skeletal system and **differentiate** the types of muscle. **TEKS** 7.12 (B)

Four Jobs	Parts	Bone Types
•	•	•
	•	•
•	•	
•		
•		

Skeletal	Cardiac	Smooth

 Connect it! Using what you know about the function of the skeletal system, describe in your interactive notebook what your body would be like without bones. **TEKS** 7.12(B)

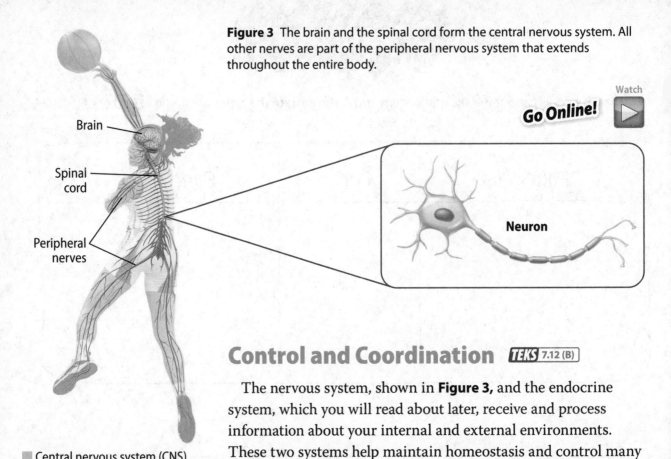

Figure 3 The brain and the spinal cord form the central nervous system. All other nerves are part of the peripheral nervous system that extends throughout the entire body.

Brain

Spinal cord

Peripheral nerves

Neuron

Watch

Go Online!

■ Central nervous system (CNS)
■ Peripheral nervous system (PNS)

Identify

3. What are the three parts of the nervous system?

Word Origin

neuron from Greek *neuron*, means "a nerve cell with appendages"

Control and Coordination *TEKS* 7.12 (B)

The nervous system, shown in **Figure 3,** and the endocrine system, which you will read about later, receive and process information about your internal and external environments. These two systems help maintain homeostasis and control many functions, including movement, communication, and growth, by working with other systems in the body.

The Nervous System

The nervous system is a group of organs and specialized cells that detect, process, and respond to information. The nervous system constantly receives information from your external environment and from internal parts of your body. It can receive information, process it, and produce a response in less than a second. A quick response from the nervous system helps enable the body to respond to dangerous situations.

Nerve cells, or **neurons**, *are the basic units of the nervous system.* Neurons can be many different lengths. In adults, some neurons are more than 1 m long. This is about as long as the distance between a toe and the spinal cord.

The nervous system includes the brain, the spinal cord, and nerves. The brain and the spinal cord form the central nervous system. Nerves outside the brain and the spinal cord make up the peripheral nervous system. The peripheral nervous system has sensory neurons and motor neurons that transmit information between the central nervous system and the rest of the body.

Processing Information The central nervous system is protected by the skeletal system. Muscles and other organs surround the peripheral nervous system. Information enters the nervous system through neurons in the peripheral nervous system. Most of the information then is sent to the central nervous system for processing. After the central nervous system processes information, it signals the peripheral nervous system to respond.

Voluntary and Involuntary Control The body carries out many functions that depend on the nervous system. Some of these functions such as breathing and digestion are automatic, or involuntary. They do not require you to think about them to make them happen. The nervous system automatically controls these functions and maintains homeostasis.

Most of the other functions of the nervous system are not automatic. They require you to think about them to make them happen. Tasks such as reading, talking, and walking are voluntary. These tasks require input, processing, and a response.

Reflexes Have you ever touched a hot pan with your hand? Touching a hot object sends a rapid signal that your hand is in pain. The signal is so fast that you do not think about moving your hand; it just happens automatically. *Automatic movements in response to a signal are called* **reflexes.** The spinal cord receives and processes reflex signals, as shown in **Figure 4.** Processing the information in the spinal cord instead of the brain helps the body respond more quickly.

Infer

4. **Categorize** parts of the nervous system.

Central Nervous System:

Peripheral Nervous System:

Go Online!   **Tutor**

Figure 4 Reflexes happen automatically.

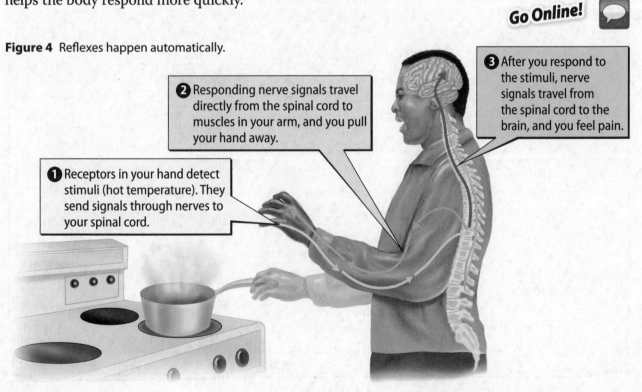

❷ Responding nerve signals travel directly from the spinal cord to muscles in your arm, and you pull your hand away.

❸ After you respond to the stimuli, nerve signals travel from the spinal cord to the brain, and you feel pain.

❶ Receptors in your hand detect stimuli (hot temperature). They send signals through nerves to your spinal cord.

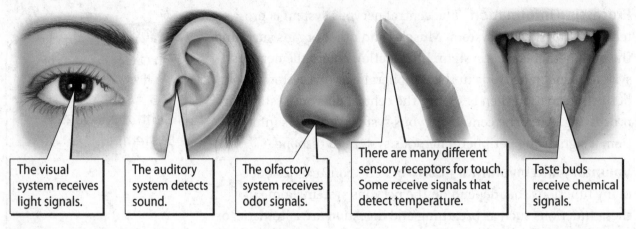

The visual system receives light signals.

The auditory system detects sound.

The olfactory system receives odor signals.

There are many different sensory receptors for touch. Some receive signals that detect temperature.

Taste buds receive chemical signals.

Figure 5 Each sense receives a different type of signal.

The Senses Humans detect their external environment with five senses—vision, hearing, smell, touch, and taste—as shown in **Figure 5.** Each of the five senses has specific neurons that receive signals from the environment. Information detected by the senses is sent to the spinal cord and then to the brain for processing and a response. Responses depend on the specific signal detected. Some responses cause muscles to contract and move, such as when you touch a hot surface. The aroma of baking cookies might cause your mouth to produce saliva. The five senses collect information about the environment and send it to your nervous system. Your brain is then able to respond and activate your body to maintain homeostasis.

Explain

5. **Describe** how any of the five senses are being used to pick up a cup of hot tea from a counter and to drink it. Are there any senses that were not used? If there weren't, why not?

_____

_____

_____

_____

_____

_____

_____

_____

_____

_____

The Endocrine System

TEKS 7.12 (B)

How tall were you in first grade? How tall are you now? From the time you were born until now, your body has changed. These changes are controlled by the endocrine system, shown in **Figure 6.** Like the nervous system, the endocrine system sends signals to the body. *Chemical signals released by the organs of the endocrine system are called* **hormones.** Hormones cause organ systems to carry out specific functions.

Why does your body need two organ systems to process information? The signals sent by the nervous system travel quickly through neurons. Hormones travel in blood through blood vessels in the circulatory system. These messages travel more slowly than nerve messages. A signal sent by the nervous system can travel from your head to your toes in less than 1 s, but a hormone will take about 20 s to make the trip. Although hormones take longer to reach their target organ system, their effects usually last longer.

Many of the hormones made by the endocrine system work with other organ systems to maintain homeostasis. For example, parathyroid hormone works with the skeletal system to control calcium storage. Insulin is a hormone that is released from the pancreas and signals the digestive system to control nutrient homeostasis. Other hormones, such as growth hormone, work with many organ systems to help you grow.

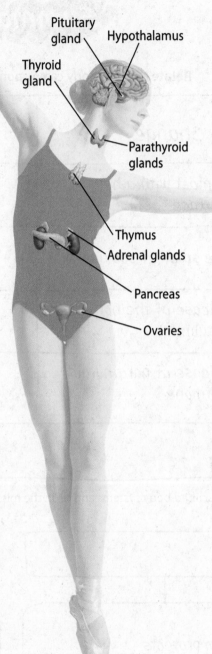

Pituitary gland
Hypothalamus
Thyroid gland
Parathyroid glands
Thymus
Adrenal glands
Pancreas
Ovaries

Figure 6 The endocrine system uses hormones to communicate with other organ systems.

11.2 Review

Go Online!  Check Virtual

Relate how the body can respond to changes in its environment.

	Change	Response
External	contact with a hot surface	
	the smell of cookies	
Internal	release of the hormone insulin	
	release of parathyroid hormone	

Identify

Name the described body systems and fill in the missing information. **TEKS** 7.12(B)

This system protects _____ and provides _____ to help the body keep its shape. It also stores _____ such as _____ to give it strength.

This system is made of _____ different types of muscle tissue. _____ muscle helps you _____. _____ muscle continually contracts and relaxes to move _____. _____ muscle works inside organs such as the _____ to help digestion.

Connect it! Compare and contrast the nervous system with the endocrine system. In your interactive notebook, describe their similarities and differences. **TEKS** 7.12(B)

Summarize it!

Structure, Movement, and Control

Using Vocabulary

1. Define the function of the endocrine system. **TEKS** 7.12(B) *supporting*

_____

_____

_____

_____

Apply the Essential Questions

2. Which is NOT a type of muscle tissue?
TEKS 7.12(B) *supporting*

A. cardiac

B. lymphatic

C. skeletal

D. smooth

3. Which is NOT a function of the skeletal system? **TEKS** 7.12(B) *supporting*

A. defense

B. movement

C. protection

D. storage

4. Name two hormones produced by the endocrine system and describe how they work with other organ systems to maintain homeostasis. **TEKS** 7.12(B) *supporting*

_____

_____

_____

_____

_____

H.O.T. Questions (Higher Order Thinking)

5. Assess the role of the skeletal system in the storage of nutrients. **TEKS** 7.12(B) *supporting*

_____

_____

_____

_____

_____

_____

6. Explain how the nervous system helps the muscular system control heart rate, digestion, and respiration.
TEKS 7.12(B) *supporting*

_____

_____

_____

_____

7. Hypothesize What would be the effect of losing one's sight on the ability to digest food? Explain your answer.
TEKS 7.12(B) *supporting*

_____

_____

_____

_____

A Bionic Arm

How brains control mechanical arms

Imagine what your arms would be like without muscles. They would simply swing from your shoulders like pendulums. You would not be able to control them. For many years, prosthetic, or artificial, arms looked real, but they didn't work like real arms. Recently, scientists have developed a bionic, or mechanical, arm. Signals from the patient's brain control it.

When the patient's brain sends signals to move the arm or the hand, the signals travel from the brain to the chest muscles.

Electronic sensors in the bionic arm's harness detect the chest muscle moving. The sensors send corresponding signals down the bionic arm.

Doctors perform surgery and attach nerves that were once part of the damaged arm to chest muscles. These nerves sent signals to the patient's arm muscles. ▶

Electrodes

Nerves

Chest muscles

Computer

▲ A computer processes the signals from the harness and moves the arm and hand. These movements are similar to those of a biological arm and hand.

It's Your Turn!

RESEARCH AND REPORT In science-fiction films, some characters have bionic body parts such as ears and eyes. Are any other bionic body parts in development? Summarize your findings in a paragraph.

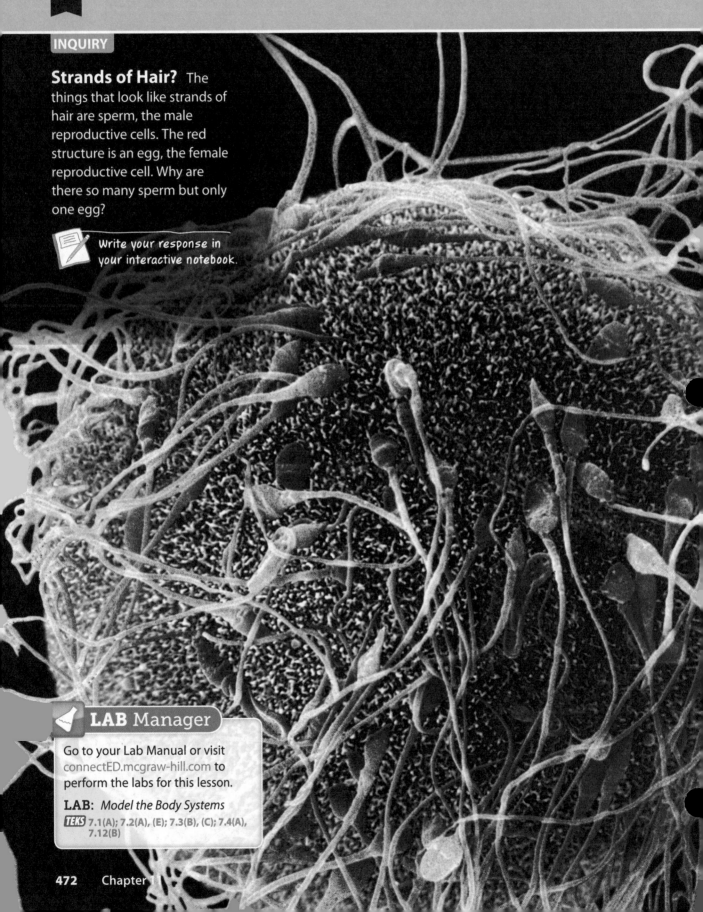

INQUIRY

Strands of Hair? The things that look like strands of hair are sperm, the male reproductive cells. The red structure is an egg, the female reproductive cell. Why are there so many sperm but only one egg?

Write your response in your interactive notebook.

LAB Manager

Go to your Lab Manual or visit connectED.mcgraw-hill.com to perform the labs for this lesson.

LAB: *Model the Body Systems*

TEKS 7.1(A); 7.2(A), (E); 7.3(B), (C); 7.4(A), 7.12(B)

Explore Activity

TEKS 7.1(A); 7.2(A), (C), (E); 7.3(B); 7.4(A); 7.12(B)

How do the sizes of egg and sperm cells compare?

A sperm cell combines with an egg cell to create a zygote that will eventually become a fetus and then a baby. The sperm and egg cells each contribute half the genetic material to the zygote.

Procedure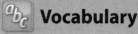

1. Read and complete a lab safety form.

2. Select one of the **spheres** to use as a model of an egg cell. With a **metric ruler,** measure the diameter of the sphere. Record the measurement in your Lab Manual.

3. If an average sperm cell is 3–6 microns in diameter, and an average egg cell is 120–150 microns in diameter, determine the diameter of a suitable model for a sperm cell.

4. Find another sphere that is approximately the size needed to create an accurate model to represent a sperm cell. Label both models.

Think About This

1. What were the sizes of the spheres you chose to model the sizes of the sperm and egg cells?

_____

_____

_____

_____

2. How do the egg cell and sperm cells interact in reproduction? How do you think size plays a role in this interaction?

_____

_____

_____

_____

TEKS in this Lesson

7.12(B) Identify the main functions of the systems of the human organism, including the circulatory, respiratory, skeletal, muscular, digestive, excretory, reproductive, integumentary, nervous, and endocrine systems.

Also covers Process Standards: 7.1(A); 7.2(A), (C), (E); 7.3(B), (C) (D); 7.4(A)

? Essential Questions

- What do the male and female reproductive systems do?
- How do humans grow and change?

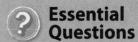 Vocabulary

reproduction
gamete
sperm
ovum
fertilization
zygote

473

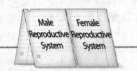

FOLDABLES

Make a horizontal two-tab book. Label it as shown. Use the book to organize information about the male and female reproductive systems.

| Male Reproductive System | Female Reproductive System |

LAB Manager

LAB: *Model the Body Systems*

TEKS 7.1(A); 7.2(A), (E); 7.3(B), (C); 7.4(A); 7.12(B)

Identify

1. **Organize** information about reproduction in the chart below.

Reproduction and Hormones **TEKS** 7.12 (B)

You have read how the endocrine system works with other organ systems to help the body grow and maintain homeostasis. The endocrine system has another very important function—to ensure that humans can reproduce. Some of the organs of the endocrine system produce hormones that help humans reproduce. **Reproduction** *is the process by which new organisms are produced.* Reproduction is essential to the continuation of life on Earth.

Males and females have special organs for reproduction. Organs in the male reproductive system are different from those in the female reproductive system. *Human reproductive cells, called* **gametes** (GA meets), *are made by the male and female reproductive systems. Male gametes are called* **sperm**. *Female gametes are called* **ova** (OH vah; singular ovum), *or eggs.*

As shown in the photo at the beginning of the lesson, *a sperm joins with an egg in a reproductive process called* **fertilization**. *The cell that forms when a sperm cell fertilizes an egg cell is called a* **zygote** (ZI goht). A zygote is the first cell of a new human. It contains genetic information from the sperm and the ovum. The zygote will grow and develop in the female's reproductive system.

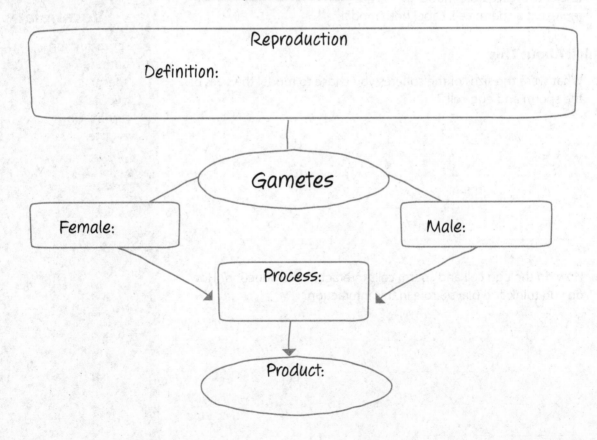

Reproduction

Definition:

Gametes

Female: Male:

Process:

Product:

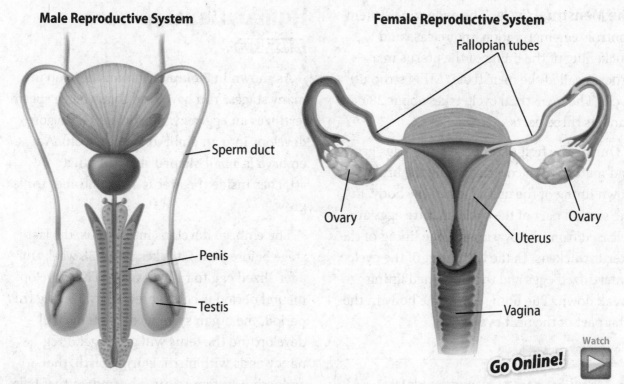

Male Reproductive System

- Sperm duct
- Penis
- Testis

Female Reproductive System

- Fallopian tubes
- Ovary
- Ovary
- Uterus
- Vagina

Go Online! Watch

Figure 1 Males and females have specialized organs for reproduction.

The Male Reproductive System

The male reproductive system, shown in **Figure 1,** produces sperm and delivers it to the female reproductive system. Sperm are produced in the testes (TES teez; singular, testis). Sperm develop inside each testis and then are stored in tubes called sperm ducts. Sperm matures in the sperm ducts.

The testes also produce a hormone called testosterone. Testosterone helps sperm change from round cells to long, slender cells that can swim. After sperm have fully developed, they can travel to the penis. The penis is a tubelike structure that delivers sperm to the female reproductive system. Sperm are transported in a fluid called semen (SEE mun). Semen contains millions of sperm and nutrients that provide the sperm with energy.

Identify

2. Highlight the purpose of testosterone.

The Female Reproductive System

The female reproductive system contains two ovaries, as shown in **Figure 1.** Eggs grow and mature in the ovaries. Two hormones made by the ovaries, estrogen (ES truh jun) and progesterone (proh JES tuh rohn), help eggs mature. Upon maturity, eggs are released from the ovaries and enter the fallopian tubes. As shown in **Figure 1,** the fallopian tubes connect the ovaries to the uterus.

If sperm are also present in the fallopian tube, fertilization can occur as the egg enters the fallopian tube. Sperm enter the female reproductive system through the vagina, a tube-shaped organ that leads to the uterus. A fertilized egg, or zygote, can move through the fallopian tube and attach inside the uterus.

If there are no sperm in the fallopian tube, the egg will not be fertilized. However, it will still travel through the fallopian tube and uterus and then break down.

The Menstrual Cycle The endocrine system controls egg maturation and release and thickening of the lining of the uterus in a process called the menstrual (MEN stroo ul) cycle. The menstrual cycle takes about 28 days and has three parts.

During the first part of the cycle, eggs grow and mature in the ovaries, while the broken down lining of the uterus leaves the body. In the second part of the cycle, mature eggs are released from the ovaries and the lining of the uterus thickens. In the third part of the cycle, unfertilized eggs and the thickened lining break down. The lining leaves the body in the first part of the next cycle.

Infer

3. How long does the menstrual cycle take?

_____

Human Development

TEKS 7.12 (B)

As shown in **Figure 2,** humans develop in many stages. You have read that when a sperm fertilizes an egg, a zygote forms. The zygote develops into an embryo (EM bree oh). An embryo is a ball-shaped structure that attaches inside the uterus and continues to grow.

The embryo develops into a fetus, the last stage before birth. It takes about 38 weeks for a fertilized egg to fully develop. This developmental period is called pregnancy. During this period, the organ systems of the fetus will develop and the fetus will get larger. Pregnancy ends with birth. During birth, the endocrine system releases hormones that help the uterus push the fetus through the vagina and out of the body.

Figure 2 During pregnancy, a unicellular zygote develops into a fetus.

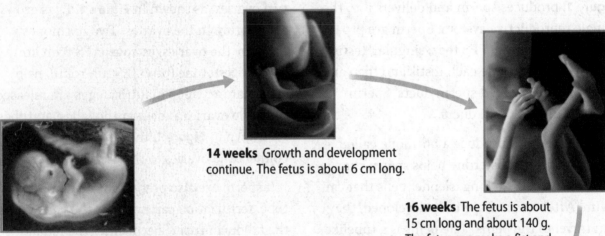

14 weeks Growth and development continue. The fetus is about 6 cm long.

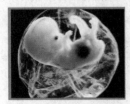

8 weeks The embryo is about 2.5 cm long. The heart is fully formed and beating, bones are beginning to harden, and nearly all muscles have appeared.

16 weeks The fetus is about 15 cm long and about 140 g. The fetus can make a fist and has a range of facial expressions.

5 weeks The embryo is about 7 mm long. The heart and other organs have started to develop. The arms and legs are beginning to bud.

22 weeks The fetus is about 27 cm long and about 430 g. Footprints and fingerprints are forming.

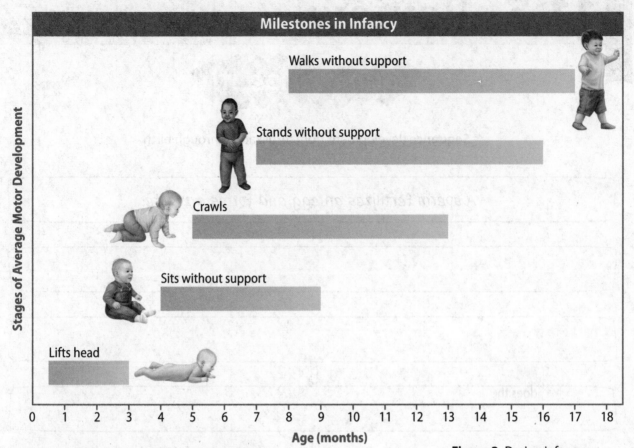

Milestones in Infancy

Stages of Average Motor Development (y-axis)

- Walks without support
- Stands without support
- Crawls
- Sits without support
- Lifts head

Age (months): 0 1 2 3 4 5 6 7 8 9 10 11 12 13 14 15 16 17 18

Figure 3 During infancy, a human learns to crawl and walk.

From Birth Through Childhood

The first life stage after birth is infancy, the first 2 years of life. During infancy, the muscular and nervous systems develop and an infant begins walking, as shown in **Figure 3.** Growth and development continue in childhood, which is from about 2 years to about 12 years of age. Bones in the skeletal system grow longer and stronger, and the lymphatic system matures.

Adolescence Through Adulthood

Adolescence follows childhood. During adolescence, growth of the skeletal and muscular systems continues. Organs such as the lungs and kidneys get larger. As the endocrine system develops, the male and female reproductive systems mature. The period of time during which the reproductive system matures is called puberty.

After adolescence is adulthood, as shown in **Figure 4.** During adulthood, humans continue to change. Although adults will not grow taller, physical changes in body mass can still occur. In later adulthood, hair turns gray, wrinkles might form in the skin, and bones become weaker in a process called aging. Vision and hearing decline, and the digestive system slows down. Aging is a slow process that can last for decades.

Figure 4 Humans continue to change during adolescence and adulthood.

11.3 Review

Sequence development from fertilization through birth.

A sperm fertilizes an egg and forms a zygote.

⇓

⇓

⇓

⇓

The fetus is pushed from the body through the vagina during birth.

Compare the stages of human development from birth through adulthood.

Stage	When?	Major Characteristics
	birth–2 years	
	about 2–12 years	
	during puberty	
	after puberty	Change continues.
Aging	later adulthood	

Summarize it!

Reproduction and Development

Use Vocabulary

1. Define the word *zygote*.

_____

_____

_____

Apply the Essential Questions

2. Which system works with the reproductive system? **TEKS** 7.12(B) *supporting*

A. endocrine

B. excretory

C. respiratory

D. skeletal

3. Which is NOT a function of the male reproductive system? **TEKS** 7.12(B) *supporting*

A. producing sperm

B. delivering sperm to the vagina

C. producing testosterone

D. producing progesterone

4. What is the period of time during which the reproductive system matures?
TEKS 7.12(B) *supporting*

A. adulthood

B. birth

C. infancy

D. puberty

H.O.T. Questions (Higher Order Thinking)

5. Summarize the role of puberty in the transition from adolescence to adulthood.
TEKS 7.12(B) *supporting*

_____

_____

_____

_____

_____

_____

6. Compare the functions of the male and female reproductive systems.
TEKS 7.12(B) *supporting*

_____

_____

_____

_____

_____

_____

7. Describe how the endocrine and reproductive systems are related.
TEKS 7.12(B) *supporting*

_____

_____

_____

_____

_____

_____

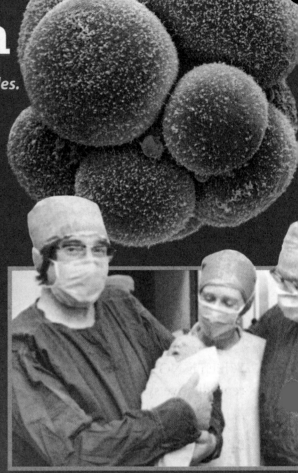

Science and SOCIETY

A Medical Breakthrough

Scientific research provides help for infertile couples.

Have you heard the term "test-tube baby"? Can a baby really come from a test tube? Three decades ago, two British scientists answered that question. Patrick Steptoe, an obstetrician and gynecologist, and Robert Edwards, a biologist and physiologist, developed a procedure that helped a British woman overcome infertility, or the inability to become pregnant. As a result of this procedure, the world's first test-tube baby, Louise Joy Brown, was born on July 25, 1978.

Prior to meeting, Steptoe and Edwards worked separately on human infertility. Steptoe developed a process called laparoscopy. Laparoscopy uses a narrow, tubelike instrument fitted with a fiber-optic light and a lens. This enables a doctor to examine a woman's ovaries, fallopian tubes, and uterus through a small incision in her abdomen. Edwards researched the fertilization of human eggs outside the body under laboratory conditions. As a team, Steptoe and Edwards developed a procedure now known as in vitro fertilization (IVF). In IVF, a doctor uses laparoscopy to remove mature eggs from a woman's ovaries. The eggs are fertilized in a Petri dish (the test tube) and grow into zygotes. A doctor transfers the zygotes into a woman's uterus, where they can continue to develop.

▲ **Dr. Steptoe (right) looks on as Dr. Edwards holds the world's first test-tube baby.**

Steptoe and Edwards worked for ten years to perfect their procedure. The successful implantation and pregnancy achieved through IVF opened new doors for infertile couples. By 2006, it was estimated that as many as 3 million babies had been born using IVF since the birth of Louise Joy Brown in 1978.

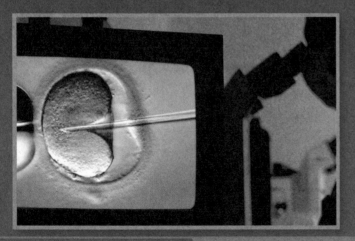

◀ **A doctor performs IVF by injecting a sperm cell into an egg cell.**

It's Your Turn!

REPORT How long has in vitro fertilization been practiced in the United States? What is its success rate? Research these questions and write a short report.

Test-Taking Strategy

Study Skills If you want to achieve your full potential, you'll need to practice proper study skills. Cramming the night before or minutes before an exam will not lead to actual learning or academic success. You might pass a test, but you will not retain important information. With subjects that build upon themselves, such as science and math, you have to fully understand the basic information in order to comprehend the upper level information. So instead of cramming, try to learn proper study skills early and make them part of your everyday academic routine.

At School:

- Attend class! It is fine to miss if you are truly ill, but missed class time is too difficult to recover. When you are absent, you may miss out on demonstrations that might end up being very important.

- Before class, review the material covered in the previous class session and read the material that will be covered in the upcoming class.

- During class, sit near the front of the room whenever possible. This will help you hear your teacher and see any demonstrations or work on the board.

- Take quality notes in your own words.

- Keep alert for sections on which your teacher places a high importance.

- Be an active learner. Participate in discussions. Ask questions.

At Home:

- Review each day's notes that evening in a place that is free from distractions.

- Refine your notes. Make sure to emphasize the most important sections.

- Recite your notes. Be able to talk about the subject material in your own words without having to look at the book.

- Make flashcards whenever applicable.

- Participate in group study sessions where you can reinforce your understanding of the concepts.

TIP: Studying is not a one-time occurrence; it is a process! Take time each day to find the answers to any questions you have about the material covered, reinforce what you've learned that day, and prepare for new topics.

Multiple Choice

1 The human body is covered by skin that has three layers, as shown in the diagram. Which description best summarizes the functions of each layer? **TEKS** 7.3(B) ; 7.12(B) *supporting*

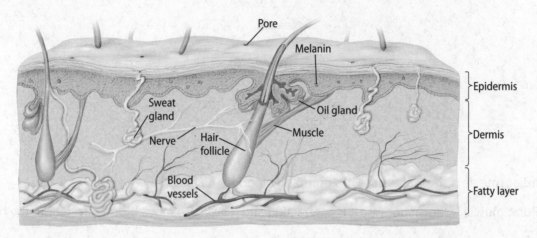

	Epidermis	**Dermis**	**Fatty Layer**
A	sensitive, thick skin that reflects ultraviolet rays	thick layer of skin containing blood vessels, nerves, sweat glands, and hair follicles	layer of cells that produces sweat
B	tough, thin skin that absorbs ultraviolet rays	thick layer of skin containing blood vessels, nerves, sweat glands, and hair follicles	layer of fat that insulates the body and stores energy
C	sensitive, thick skin that reflects ultraviolet rays	thick layer of skin containing fat	layer of cells that produces sweat
D	tough, thin skin that absorbs ultraviolet rays	thick layer of skin containing fat	layer of fat that insulates the body and stores energy

2 What type of muscle is shown in the image? Why? **TEKS** 7.12(B) *supporting;*

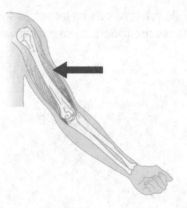

A Cardiac muscle is shown because it is pumping blood to the heart.

B Cardiac muscle is shown because it is contracting and relaxing to move blood throughout the body.

C Skeletal muscle is shown because it is voluntarily controlling muscles to move the body.

D Smooth muscle is shown because it is moving food through the digestive system.

---

3 The arrow in the diagram below shows where blood enters the heart through the atrium after coming from the lungs. Which best describes the blood entering the heart?

TEKS 7.3(B); 7.12(B) *supporting*

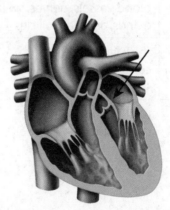

A The blood is carrying oxygen that it absorbed as it passed through the lungs.

B The blood is carrying carbon dioxide that it absorbed as it passed through the lungs.

C The blood is carrying nutrients that it absorbed as it passed through the small intestine.

D The blood is carrying capillaries that it absorbed as it passed through the stomach.

4

> When you breathe in, air moves into the lungs through the bronchial tubes. These tubes divide into smaller tubes and eventually end in tiny air sacs called alveoli. The lungs of an adult human contain more than 100 million alveoli. These tiny sacs have thin walls and are surrounded by blood vessels that also have thin walls.

Which best explains the role of the alveoli in the respiratory system? **TEKS** 7.12(B) *supporting*

A The alveoli help to keep the lungs healthy by providing a way for all the cells in the lungs to obtain nutrients from the bloodstream.

B The alveoli help to keep the lungs inflated when you breathe out and make it possible to absorb oxygen when you breathe in.

C The alveoli provide a large surface area for absorbing oxygen from the air and releasing carbon dioxide wastes from the bloodstream.

D The alveoli provide a large surface area for absorbing oxygen from the air when you breathe in and also keep out harmful microorganisms.

---

5 The endocrine system and the nervous system both send messages that control processes in other parts of the body. Which is an example of a process caused mainly by the endocrine system?

TEKS 7.12(B) *supporting*

A developing allergies to pollen, pet hair, or specific foods

B regulating growth and functions of certain body organs

C improving your skills at a sport or other physical activity

D pulling your hand away when you touch a hot stove

12 Plant and Animal Responses

🔦 The **BIG** Idea

Organisms respond to changes in their internal and external environments in order to maintain stable internal conditions.

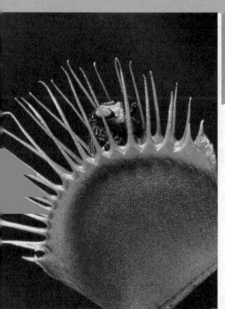

Is it an animal behavior?

Animals exhibit a variety of behaviors. Put an X next to the things that are examples of an animal behavior.

_____	dog growling	_____ dog catching a ball
_____	horse swishing its tail	_____ geese migrating south
_____	spider spinning a web	_____ cat purring when touched
_____	baby sea turtle's instinct to hatch at night	_____ mother bird feeding her young
_____	circus elephant doing tricks	_____ bear going into hibernation
_____	bird building a nest	_____ lion hunting prey
_____	bird startling at loud sound	_____ bull charging a farmer
_____	honeybee making honey	_____ bats sleeping during the day
_____	horse obeying commands from its rider	_____ baby chick recognizing its mother

Explain your thinking. How did you decide if something is an animal behavior?

12.1 Plant Responses

INQUIRY

A Meat-Eating Plant?
Venus flytraps have leaves that look like jaws. The leaves close only when a stimulus, such as a fly, brushes against tiny, sensitive hairs on the surface of the leaves. To what other stimuli do you think plants might respond?

Write your response in your interactive notebook.

LAB Manager

Go to your Lab Manual or visit connectED.mcgraw-hill.com to perform the labs for this lesson.

MiniLAB: *When will plants flower?*
TEKS 7.2(A), (C), (E); 7.13(A)

Skill Practice: *What happens to seeds if you change the intensity of light?*
TEKS 7.1(A), (B); 7.2(A), (C), (E); 7.3(A); 7.4(A), (B); 7.13(A)

LAB: *Design a Stimulating Environment for Plants*
TEKS 7.1(A), (B); 7.2(B), (C), (E); 7.3(A); 7.4(A), (B); 7.13(A)

Explore Activity

TEKS 7.1(A), (B); 7.2(A), (C), (E); 7.4(A), (B); 7.13(A)

How do plants respond to stimuli?

Plants use light energy and make their own food during photosynthesis. How else do plants respond to light in their environment?

Procedure

1. Read and complete a lab safety form.

2. Choose a **pot of young radish seedlings.**

3. Place **toothpicks** parallel to a few of the seedlings in the pot in the direction of growth.

4. Place the pot near a **light source,** such as a gooseneck lamp or next to a window. The light source should be to one side of the pot, not directly above the plants.

5. Check the position of the seedlings in relation to the toothpicks after 30 min. Record your observations in your Lab Manual.

6. Observe the seedlings when you come to class the next day. Record your observations.

7. Return or dispose of your materials as directed by your teacher.

Think About This

1. What happened to the position of the seedlings after the first 30 min? What is your evidence of change?

_____

_____

_____

_____

2. What happened to the position of the seedlings after a day?

_____

_____

3. Why do you think the position of the seedlings changed?

_____

_____

_____

TEKS in this Lesson

7.13(A) Investigate how organisms respond to external stimuli found in the environment such as phototropism and fight or flight

7.13(B) Describe and relate responses in organisms that may result from internal stimuli such as wilting in plants and fever or vomiting in animals that allow them to maintain balance

Also covers Process Standards: 7.1(A), (B); 7.2(A), (B), (C), (E); 7.3(A); 7.4(A), (B)

? Essential Questions

- How do plants respond to environmental stimuli?
- How do plants respond to chemical stimuli?

abc Vocabulary

stimulus
tropism
photoperiodism
plant hormone

Figure 1 The light is the stimulus, and the seedlings have responded by growing toward the light.

Stimuli and Plant Responses $\boxed{\text{TEKS}}$ 7.13(A)

Have you ever been in a dark room when someone suddenly turned on the light? You might have reacted by quickly shutting or covering your eyes. **Stimuli** (STIHM yuh li; singular, stimulus) *are any changes in an organism's environment that cause a response.*

Often a plant's response to stimuli might be so slow that it is hard to see it happen. The response might occur gradually over a period of hours or days. Light is a stimulus. A plant responds to light by growing toward it, as shown in **Figure 1.** This response occurs over several hours.

In some cases, the response to a stimulus is quick, such as the Venus flytrap's response to touch. When stimulated by an insect's touch, the two sides of the trap snap shut immediately, trapping the insect inside.

Identify

1. Highlight why it is sometimes hard to see a plant's response to a stimulus.

FOLDABLES

Cut out the Lesson 12.1 Foldable in the back of the book. Use it to record what you learn about the two types of stimuli that affect plant growth.

Tape here

Two Types of Stimuli

Flowering Responses
Long-Day Plants:

Short-Day Plants:

Day-Neutral Plants:

Hormone:
Description:

Hormone:
Description:

Environmental Stimuli

When it is cold outside, you probably wear a sweatshirt or a coat. Plants cannot put on warm clothes, but they do respond to their environments in a variety of ways. You might have seen trees flower in the spring or drop their leaves in the fall. Both are plant responses to environmental stimuli.

Growth Responses

Plants respond to a number of different environmental stimuli. These include light, touch, and gravity. *A* **tropism** (TROH pih zum) *is a response that results in plant growth toward or away from a stimulus.* When the growth is toward a stimulus, the tropism is called positive. A plant bending toward light is a positive tropism. Growth away from a stimulus is considered negative. A plant's stem growing upward against gravity is a negative tropism.

Light The growth of a plant toward or away from light is a tropism called phototropism. A plant has a light-sensing chemical that helps it detect light. Leaves and stems tend to grow in the direction of light, as shown in **Figure 2.** This response maximizes the amount of light the plant's leaves receive. Roots generally grow away from light. This usually means that the roots grow down into the soil and help anchor the plant.

> *Recognize*
>
> 2. <u>Underline</u> text evidence that describes why phototropism is beneficial to a plant.

LAB Manager

Skill Practice: *What happens to seeds if you change the intensity of light?*
TEKS 7.1(A), (B); 7.2(A), (C), (E); 7.3(A); 7.4(A), (B); 7.13(A)

LAB: *Design a Stimulating Environment for Plants*
TEKS 7.1(A), (B); 7.2(B), (C), (E); 7.3(A); 7.4(A), (B); 7.13(A)

Figure 2 As a plant's leaves turn toward the light, the amount of light that the leaves can absorb increases.

Figure 3 The tendrils of the vine respond to touch and coil around a wire fence.

Touch The response of a plant to touch is called a thigmotropism (thihg MAH truh pih zum). You might have seen vines growing up the side of a building or a fence. This happens because the plant has special structures that respond to touch. These structures, called tendrils, can wrap around or cling to objects, as shown in **Figure 3.** A tendril wrapping around an object is an example of positive thigmotropism. Roots display negative thigmotropism. They grow away from objects in soil, enabling them to follow the easiest path through the soil.

Gravity The response of a plant to gravity is called geotropism. Stems grow away from gravity, while roots grow toward gravity. The seedlings in **Figure 4** are exhibiting both responses. No matter how a seed lands on soil, when it starts to grow, its roots grow down into the soil. The stem grows up. This happens even when a seed is grown in a dark chamber, indicating that these responses can occur independently of light.

Interpret

3. How is the plant on the left responding to the pot being placed on its side? Write your response in your interactive notebook.

Figure 4 Both of these plant stems are growing away from gravity. The upward growth of a plant's stem is negative geotropism, and the downward growth of its roots is positive geotropism.

Apply it!

Name each tropism, and state whether it is positive or negative. **TEKS** 7.13(A)

A. Stem grows up.

_____

_____

B. Roots grow down.

_____

_____

C. Plant grows toward light.

_____

_____

D. Roots grow away from light.

_____

_____

E. Vine grows around a pole.

_____

_____

 Connect it! Gravity is a stimulus that affects how plants grow. Can plants grow without gravity? In space, the force of gravity is low. **Write** a paragraph in your interactive notebook that describes your idea for an experiment aboard the _International Space Station_ to test how low gravity affects plant growth. **TEKS** 7.13(A)

Apply it!

493

Flowering Responses

You might think all plants respond to light, but in some plants, flowering is actually a response to darkness! **Photoperiodism** *is a plant's response to the number of hours of darkness in its environment.* Scientists once hypothesized that photoperiodism was a response to light. Therefore, these flowering responses are called long-day, short-day, and day-neutral and relate to the number of hours of daylight in a plant's environment.

Long-Day Plants Plants that flower when exposed to fewer than 10–12 hours of darkness are called long-day plants. The carnations shown in **Figure 5** are examples of long-day plants. This plant usually produces flowers in summer, when the number of hours of daylight is greater than the number of hours of darkness.

Short-Day Plants Short-day plants require 12 or more hours of darkness for flowering to begin. An example of a short-day plant is the poinsettia, shown in **Figure 5.** Poinsettias tend to flower in late summer or early fall when the number of hours of daylight is decreasing and the number of hours of darkness is increasing.

Day-Neutral Plants The flowering of some plants seems not to be affected by the number of hours of darkness. Day-neutral plants flower when they reach maturity and the environmental conditions are right. Plants such as the roses in **Figure 5** are day-neutral plants.

Apply

4. Based on **Figure 5,** what time of year receives more darkness? What type of plant produces flowers during that season? Write your responses in your interactive notebook.

Figure 5 The number of hours of darkness controls flowering in many plants. Long-day plants flower when there are more hours of daylight than darkness, and short-day plants flower when there are more hours of darkness than daylight.

Chemical Stimuli TEKS 7.13(B)

Plants respond to internal chemical stimuli as well as environmental stimuli. **Plant hormones** *are substances that act as chemical messengers within plants.* These chemicals are produced in tiny amounts. They are called messengers because they usually are produced in one part of a plant and affect another part of that plant.

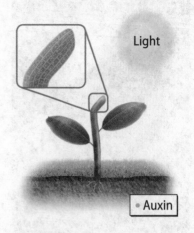

Light

• Auxin

Figure 6 Auxin on the left side of the seedling causes more growth and makes the seedling bend to the right.

Auxins

One of the first plant hormones discovered was auxin (AWK sun). There are many different kinds of auxins. Auxins generally cause increased plant growth. They are responsible for phototropism, the growth of a plant toward light. Auxins concentrate on the dark side of a plant's stem, and these cells grow longer. This causes the stem of the plant to grow toward the light, as shown in **Figure 6**.

Ethylene

The plant hormone ethylene helps stimulate the ripening of fruit. Ethylene is a gas that can be produced by fruits, seeds, flowers, and leaves. You might have heard someone say that one rotten apple spoils the whole barrel. This is based on the fact that rotting fruits release ethylene. This can cause other fruits nearby to ripen and possibly rot. Ethylene also can cause plants to drop their leaves.

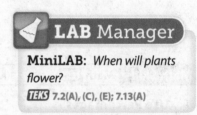

LAB Manager

MiniLAB: *When will plants flower?*
TEKS 7.2(A), (C), (E); 7.13(A)

Diagram

5. In the space below, illustrate how plants respond to the chemical stimuli, or hormones, auxin and ethylene.

Figure 7 The use of cytokinins helps scientists and horticulturists grow hundreds of identical plants.

Gibberellins and Cytokinins

Rapidly growing areas of a plant, such as roots and stems, produce gibberellins (jih buh REL unz). These hormones increase the rate of cell division and cell elongation. This results in increased growth of stems and leaves. Gibberellins also can be applied to the outside of plants. Applying gibberellins to plants can have a dramatic effect on the growth of the plants.

Root tips produce most of the cytokinins (si tuh KI nunz), another type of hormone. Xylem carries cytokinins to other parts of a plant. Cytokinins increase the rate of cell division and can be used in tissue culture, as shown in **Figure 7.** In some plants, cytokinins slow the aging process of flowers and fruits.

Summary of Plant Hormones

Plants produce many different hormones. The hormones you have just read about are groups of similar compounds. Often, two or more hormones interact and produce a plant response. Scientists are still discovering new information about plant hormones.

Math Skills Math **TEKS** 7.1(A); 7.3(A); 7.4(C), (D)

Use Percentages

A percentage is a ratio that compares a number to 100. For example, if a tree grows 2 cm per day with no chemical stimulus and 3 cm per day with a chemical stimulus, what is the percentage increase in growth?

Subtract the original value from the final value.

$$3 \text{ cm} - 2 \text{ cm} = 1 \text{ cm}$$

Set up a ratio between the difference and the original value. Find the decimal equivalent.

$$\frac{1 \text{ cm}}{2 \text{ cm}} = 0.5 \text{ cm}$$

Multiply by 100 and add a percent sign.

$$0.5 \times 100 = 50\%$$

Practice

Without gibberellins, pea seedlings grew to 2 cm in 3 days. With gibberellins, the seedlings grew to 4 cm in 3 days. What was the percentage increase in growth?

Check   Tutor

Go Online!

12.1 Review

Characterize tropisms. Tell whether each response is positive or negative. **TEKS** 7.13(A)

Tropism	Stimulus	Response (positive or negative)	
	light	stems:	roots:
	touch	drooping:	tendrils:
Gravitropism		stems:	roots:

Relate the effects of plant hormones. **TEKS** 7.13(B)

Plant Hormone	Chemical Message(s)
Auxins	
Ethylene	
Gibberellins	
Cytokinins	

 Connect it! Think about a plant that is familiar to you. **Write** a paragraph describing how the plant might respond to external and internal stimuli. **TEKS** 7.13(A), (B)

Plant Responses

Use Vocabulary

1. A plant's response to the number of hours of darkness in its environment is

   _____.

   TEKS 7.13(A)

2. **Distinguish** between *stimulus* and *tropism.* **TEKS** 7.13(A)

   _____

   _____

   _____

Apply the Essential Questions

3. **Describe** an example of a plant responding to external environmental stimuli. **TEKS** 7.13(A)

   _____

   _____

   _____

   _____

4. **Compare** the effects of auxins and gibberellins on plant cells. **TEKS** 7.13(B)

   _____

   _____

   _____

   _____

   _____

   _____

   _____

🔥 H.O.T. Questions (Higher Order Thinking)

5. **Assess** the need for plants to respond to stimuli in their internal and external environments. **TEKS** 7.13(A), (B)

   _____

   _____

   _____

   _____

   _____

   _____

Writing in Science

6. **Critique** the saying "One rotten apple spoils the whole barrel." Write your response on a separate sheet of paper. **TEKS** 7.13(B)

Math Skills	Math **TEKS** 7.1(A); 7.3(A); 7.4(C), (D)

Use Percentages

7. Without treatment with gibberellins, 500 out of 1,000 grass seeds germinated. When sprayed with gibberellins, 875 of the seeds germinated. What was the percentage increase?

Go Online!

Check Tutor

The Sundew Plant
Nature's Sticky Flypaper

▲ Dwarf sundew

Big Thicket National Preserve, in Southeast Texas, is a treasure of biological diversity. Its forests, meadows, wetlands, and rivers are home to hundreds of bird species, nearly 100 fish species, more than 50 species of mammals, and numerous species of reptiles and amphibians.

Big Thicket also contains nearly 900 species of plants, including a few plants that eat meat. These carnivorous plants live in nutrient-poor marshes and bogs and feed mostly on insects.

The dwarf sundew (*Drosera brevifolia*) and the pink sundew (*Drosera capillaris*) are two of the carnivorous plants found in Big Thicket. These sundews are small plants with some unusual leaves. The upper side of each leaf is covered with numerous glandular hairs. A gland at the tip of each hair secretes a sticky substance that glistens like morning dew, attracting insects. When an insect lands on the leaf, it gets stuck on the hairs.

As the insect struggles to free itself, the movement triggers a response. The hairs begin to bend around the insect, carrying it toward the center of the leaf. The hairs then begin to secrete a fluid that digests the insect so its nutrients can be absorbed by the plant.

▲ Pink sundew

It's Your Turn!

RESEARCH There are three other types of carnivorous plants in Big Thicket National Preserve. Identify the three types and how they capture and digest their prey.

INQUIRY

Sleeping? This dormouse appears to be sleeping, but it is actually in a state of inactivity called hibernation. A dormouse hibernates during cold weather to conserve energy while food is scarce. Do you think the dormouse learned or was born knowing to hibernate during cold weather? What other behaviors might a dormouse exhibit?

Write your responses in your interactive notebook.

LAB Manager

Go to your Lab Manual or visit connectED.mcgraw-hill.com to perform the labs for this lesson.

MiniLAB: *How do young birds recognize predators?*
TEKS 7.2(A), (C), (E); 7.4(A); 7.13(A)

Skill Practice: *Can the color or surface of an area determine how a mealworm will move?*
TEKS 7.1(A), (B); 7.2(A), (C), (D), (E); 7.4(A), (B); 7.13(A)

LAB: *What changes an earthworm's behavior?*
TEKS 7.1(A), (B); 7.2(B), (C), (E); 7.4(A), (B); 7.13(A)

What happens when you touch a pill bug?

Pill bugs are arthropods that live under leaf litter and rocks. They have a special behavior that helps them defend themselves against other animals that might eat them.

Procedure

1. Read and complete a lab safety form.

2. Obtain a **pill bug** and gently place it in a **petri dish** for observation. Study the pill bug without touching it, and draw it in your Lab Manual.

3. Use a **cotton swab** to gently touch the pill bug, and observe it again. Draw the pill bug's reaction.

Think About This

1. How did the pill bug react when you touched its back?

_____

_____

_____

2. What stimulus did you provide that was different from the pill bug's natural environment?

_____

_____

_____

3. What other stimuli do you think might affect the pill bug?

_____

_____

_____

_____

TEKS in this Lesson

7.13(A) Investigate how organisms respond to external stimuli found in the environment such as phototropism and fight or flight

7.13(B) Describe and relate responses in organisms that may result from internal stimuli such as wilting in plants and fever or vomiting in animals that allow them to maintain balance

Also covers Process Standards: 7.1(A), (B); 7.2(A), (B), (C), (D), (E); 7.4(A), (B)

? Essential Questions

- How do behaviors help animals maintain homeostasis?
- How are animal behaviors classified?

abc Vocabulary

behavior
innate behavior
instinct
migration
hibernation
imprinting
conditioning

Figure 1 A dog's sniffing behavior helps it get information about its surroundings.

Review Vocabulary

homeostasis an organism's ability to maintain steady internal conditions when outside conditions change

What is a behavior?

Have you ever watched a dog sniff the ground while it was out for a walk? Or have you seen a dog, such as the one in **Figure 1,** working with law enforcement and sniffing luggage at an airport? Why does a dog do this? Dogs receive information about their surroundings by sniffing. Dogs have a much more developed sense of smell than humans do. A dog's nose has about 220 million scent receptors, but a human's nose has only about 5 million.

The act of sniffing is a common dog behavior. *A **behavior** is the way an organism reacts to other organisms or to its environment.* Behaviors might be carried out by individual animals, such as a dog sniffing, or by groups of animals of the same species, such as a flock of birds flying together. You might recall that organisms' bodies work to maintain a steady internal state called homeostasis. Behaviors are a way to maintain homeostasis when the environment changes.

Characterize

1. What is animal behavior?

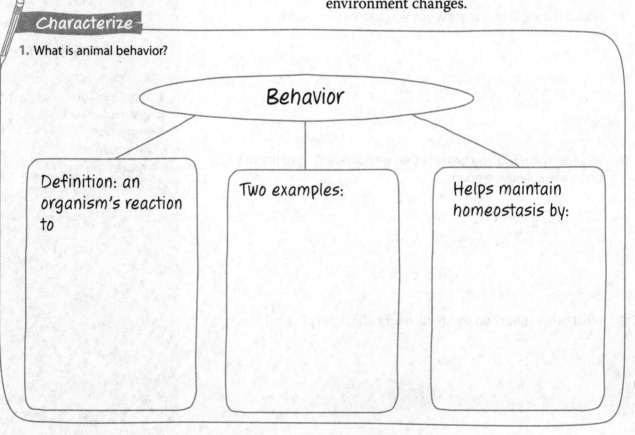

Behavior

Definition: an organism's reaction to

Two examples:

Helps maintain homeostasis by:

Stimuli and Responses TEKS 7.13(A), (B)

When an animal carries out a behavior, it is reacting to a
stimulus (STIHM yuh lus; plural, stimuli), or change. A stimulus
can be external, such as the weather getting warmer, or internal,
such as hunger. Scents coming from the pavement or a tree are
external stimuli for a dog. The dog's response to the stimuli is
sniffing.

Stimuli

Stimuli can come in many forms and result in different behaviors. Changes in the external environment, such as a temperature
change or a rainstorm, can affect an animal's behavior. Hunger,
thirst, illness, and other changes in an animal's internal environment are stimuli, too.

Responses to Change

Animals respond to changes and maintain homeostasis in
different ways. For example, when the weather gets cooler, an
organism might respond with a specific behavior. Birds, which
must keep their bodies at the same temperature year-round, fluff
their feathers and retain more thermal energy, as shown in
Figure 2. The cooler weather is the stimulus, and the bird's
feather fluffing is a response.

Animals also respond to internal stimuli, such as illnesses. If
an animal is sick, its body might respond with a fever. The fever
increases body temperature and might help the animal fight a
disease. Vomiting is another response to an internal stimulus. A
dog that ate something from the garbage might vomit to get the
material out of its body. This behavior helps the dog maintain
homeostasis by removing something that could cause an illness.

FOLDABLES

Make a small, horizontal
four-door shutterfold book.
Leave a 2-cm space between
the tabs so the inside shows.
Draw arrows, and label the
tabs as shown. Use your book
to compare and contrast
animal behaviors.

Figure 2 During warm weather,
a bird's feathers are close to its
body. When a bird fluffs its
feathers during cold weather, it
traps a layer of air around its
body. The air helps keep the bird
warm.

Figure 3 Some animals, such as gazelles, respond to threatening situations by running away.

Stress

Have you ever seen an animal run away when a human got too close? The human caused the animal to become stressed, and the animal reacted by running away. Some animals, such as the Thomson's gazelle shown in **Figure 3,** will almost always run away if they feel threatened. When an animal identifies a danger, its body prepares to either fight or run away from the perceived threat. This behavior is called the fight-or-flight response.

Not all animals have the same reaction and run away from dangerous situations. A wild male horse might attack another male in the same area to protect its herd. Some animals, such as rats, will run from danger but will fight if cornered.

Innate Behaviors TEKS 7.13(A), (B)

As you have read, behaviors are responses to some type of stimulus. An animal's behaviors are a combination of those that are learned and those that are inherited and not linked to past experiences. *A behavior that is inherited rather than learned is called an* **innate behavior.**

An innate behavior happens automatically the first time an animal responds to a certain stimulus. For example, when tadpoles hatch, they already know how to swim. They do not learn how to do so by watching other tadpoles. Tadpoles can swim away from danger and find food as soon as they hatch.

Animals with short life spans have mostly innate behaviors. Animals such as insects rely on behaviors that they do not have to learn. They are able to find food and mates and avoid danger early in their lives. Insect innate behaviors include a cricket's ability to chirp and a moth's attraction to light. These types of behaviors enable animals to survive without learning from another animal.

Identify

2. What are three characteristics of innate behaviors?

_____

_____

_____

_____

_____

_____

_____

Reflexes

Have you ever noticed what happens to the pupils in your eyes when you go into a dimly lit room? After a short period of time, they get larger. This happens without you thinking about it. This is an example of the simplest type of innate behavior, called a reflex. A reflex is an automatic response that does not involve a message from the brain.

Animals have reflexes, too. For example, an armadillo will jump straight upward about 1 m when startled, as shown in **Figure 4.** By jumping, the armadillo might be able to startle predators and escape.

Instincts

Reflexes happen quickly and involve one behavior. Some innate behaviors involve a number of steps performed in a specific order. *A complex pattern of innate behaviors is called an* **instinct** (IHN stingt). Finding food, running away from danger, and grooming are some behaviors that are instincts in many animals.

Instincts, such as web spinning in spiders, might take hours or days to complete and are usually made up of many behaviors. The feeding behavior of an egg-eating snake is shown in **Figure 5.** The snake's pattern of behavior is an instinct.

Go Online!

Tutor

Figure 4 This armadillo has a reflex that causes it to jump when startled.

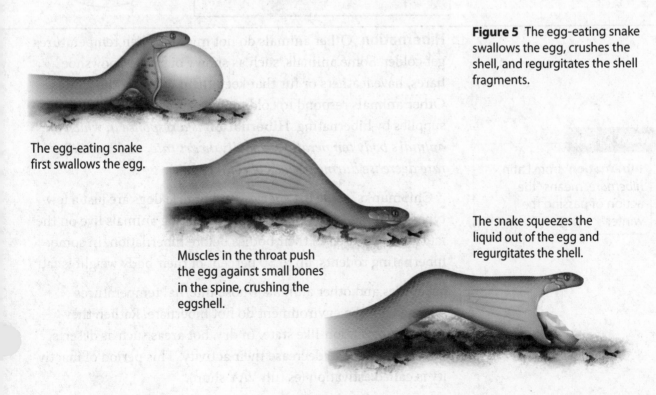

Figure 5 The egg-eating snake swallows the egg, crushes the shell, and regurgitates the shell fragments.

The egg-eating snake first swallows the egg.

Muscles in the throat push the egg against small bones in the spine, crushing the eggshell.

The snake squeezes the liquid out of the egg and regurgitates the shell.

Behavior Patterns

Many animal behaviors change in response to the change of seasons. In warm weather, there is plenty of food and water, and animals have no difficulty keeping warm. As the weather becomes cooler, food and water supplies might decrease, and animals might have difficulty surviving.

Migration Some animals move to warmer places during cooler weather. *This instinctive, seasonal movement of animals from one place to another is called* **migration.** Animals migrate to find food and water when the weather becomes too hot or too cold, or to return to specific breeding locations. Many birds, such as the ruby-throated hummingbird shown in **Figure 6,** fly many kilometers to warmer climates where they can find food.

Figure 6 Ruby-throated hummingbirds fly from New England to Louisiana. They then fly nonstop for about 805 km to the Yucatan Peninsula and Central and South America.

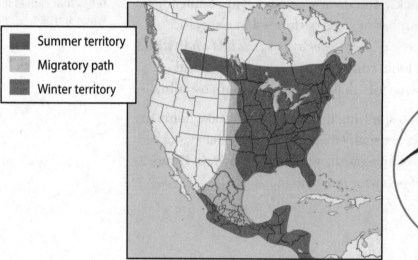

- Summer territory
- Migratory path
- Winter territory

Hibernation Other animals do not migrate when temperatures get colder. Some animals, such as snowy owls and snowshoe hares, have feathers or fur that keep them warm in the winter. Other animals respond to cold temperatures and limited food supplies by hibernating. **Hibernation** *is a response in which an animal's body temperature, activity, heart rate, and breathing rate decrease during periods of cold weather.*

Chipmunks, some bat species, and prairie dogs are just a few types of animals that hibernate. Hibernating animals live on the fat that was stored in their bodies before hibernation. In some hibernating rodents, up to 50 percent of their body weight is fat.

Reptiles and other animals whose internal temperatures change with the environment do not hibernate. Rather, they enter a hibernation-like state. In dry, hot areas such as deserts, many animals also decrease their activity. This period of inactivity is called estivation (es tuh VAY shun).

Word Origin

hibernation from Latin *hibernare,* means "the action of passing the winter"

Organize it!

Organize the concepts of stimulus and response.

	Stimulus	Response
External	Example:	Example:
Internal	Example:	Example:

Connect it! **Draw** a cartoon to illustrate how an animal responds to the change of seasons. Research and take notes on one of the following animals— Texas salamander, thirteen-lined ground squirrel, or whooping crane—to create your cartoon about migration, hibernation, or estivation. **TEKS** 7.13(A)

Figure 7 These baby sea turtles will return to this beach after they mature and are ready to lay eggs.

Learned Behaviors   **TEKS** 7.13(A)

You have probably heard about service dogs that help humans by opening doors or turning on light switches. How are these dogs able to do such amazing things? Dogs and all other mammals, birds, reptiles, amphibians, and fish learn. This means that these animals develop new behaviors through experience or practice. Other animals, such as mollusks and arthropods, also can learn, but most of their behaviors are innate, or inherited.

Imprinting

Young birds and mammals usually follow their mothers around. This helps them find food and protects them from danger. How do they learn to do this? **Imprinting** *occurs when an animal forms an attachment to an organism or place within a specific time period after birth or hatching.* Once a young animal has imprinted itself on an organism, it will usually not attach itself to another.

Not all imprinting occurs on organisms. Turtles, such as the ones in **Figure 7,** do not imprint on other turtles. Female sea turtles return to the beach where they were born to lay their eggs. These turtles have imprinted on the beach.

Trial and Error

Some behaviors, such as a child learning to tie a shoe or button a shirt, take many tries before they are performed correctly. The child might try several techniques before finding one that works. This type of learning, called trial and error, happens in animals as well. For example, a monkey presented with food in a box might try to open the box many ways before succeeding. The next time it encounters a similar box, it will remember how to open the box without retrying the techniques that did not work.

Conditioning

Another way that animals might learn new behaviors is through conditioning. *In* **conditioning,** *behavior is modified so that a response to one stimulus becomes associated with a different stimulus.* As shown in **Figure 8,** some fish learn to come to the surface of the water when a hand is held over the water. They have learned that the hand often holds food. Through conditioning, some birds learn to avoid stinging wasps and monarch butterflies, which have a bad taste.

Figure 8 Some fish learn through conditioning to come to the surface of the water when they are hungry.

Infer

3. Use what you know about conditioning to explain how the term *mouthwatering food* might have come about. Write your response in your interactive notebook. Then confirm your answer by discussing it with a classmate.

Cognitive Behavior

Thinking, reasoning, and solving problems are cognitive behaviors. Humans use cognitive behavior to solve problems and plan for the future. Scientists have done experiments with animals such as primates, dolphins, elephants, and ravens that suggest they also might use cognitive behaviors. For example, studies done with ravens showed the birds could figure out how to get meat by pulling a string attached to the food. Other animals appear to show cognitive behaviors such as using tools to get food. For example, woodpecker finches use cactus spines to pry grubs out of trees, as shown in **Figure 9.**

Figure 9 Scientists have observed finches using what appears to be cognitive behavior.

12.2 Review

Go Online! Check Virtual

Summarize it!

Contrast innate behaviors. **TEKS** 7.13(A)

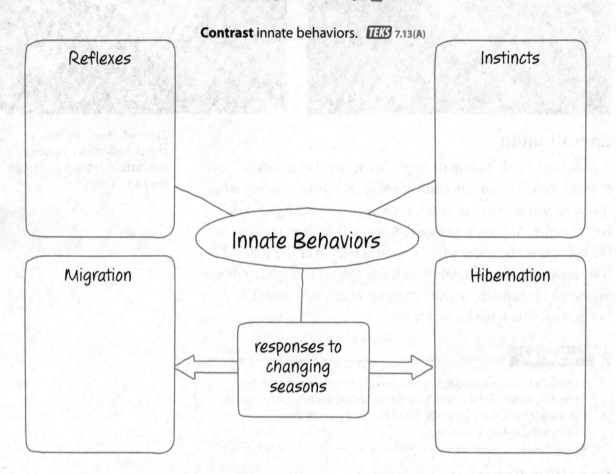

Reflexes

Instincts

Innate Behaviors

Migration

Hibernation

responses to changing seasons

Differentiate learned behaviors. **TEKS** 7.13(B)

Imprinting	Trial and Error	Conditioning

Connect it! **Relate** a mockingbird getting a drink of water from a bird bath to an external stimulus and an internal stimulus. How does the mockingbird's response to these stimuli help the bird? Write your responses in your interactive notebook. **TEKS** 7.13(A), (B)

Summarize it!

Types of Animal Behavior

Use Vocabulary

1. Use the term *migration* in a sentence.
TEKS 7.13(A)

_____

_____

_____

Apply the Essential Questions

2. Which is a reflex? *TEKS* 7.13(A)

   A. a bird building a nest

   B. pulling a string to get food

   C. pupils getting smaller in dim light

   D. tying your shoelaces

3. Describe how an animal's response to illness, such as fever or vomiting, helps the animal maintain homeostasis.
TEKS 7.13(B)

_____

_____

_____

🔥 **H.O.T. Questions** (Higher Order Thinking)

4. Summarize how animals respond to change. *TEKS* 7.13(A), (B)

_____

_____

_____

5. Assess What type of behavior is illustrated in the photo below? How does this behavior relate to maintaining balance? *TEKS* 7.13(B)

_____

_____

_____

_____

6. Evaluate the different ways an animal can respond to stress. *TEKS* 7.13(A)

_____

_____

_____

_____

_____

_____

_____

_____

Courtship Displays

A "Superb" Way to Find a Mate

What kind of animal do you think this is? Although it might look like a cartoon character, these are pictures of a male superb bird of paradise during a courtship display.

A courtship display is a series of specialized behaviors that help an animal attract a mate. It can include movements, sounds, and/or chemical communication. In its courtship display, the male superb bird of paradise transforms itself, as shown in the following sequence.

1 This pose is the beginning of the courtship display. At this stage, the bird sometimes moves its wings to make a clicking sound.

2 In this part of the courtship display, the feathers on the top of the bird's head are displayed, and the blue feathers on the bird's chest are extended outward.

3 The bird then extends the feathers on its head outward and around the head to form a rounded shape. Body feathers are extended as well. The bird appears as a black oval with a bright blue shape in the middle. The small blue spots are not the bird's eyes; they are spots on its feathers. In this stage of the display, the male bird hops around the female.

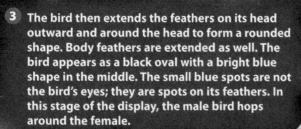

◄ Male superb bird of paradise

It's Your Turn!

REPORT Research another animal's courtship display. Draw diagrams to show the different appearances and behaviors that are part of the display. Share your research with your class.

12 TEKS Review

Test-Taking Strategy

Analyze a Diagram Sometimes a question will ask you to analyze a diagram. You will need to first assess what the question is asking, and then you must analyze the diagram to determine the answer.

Example

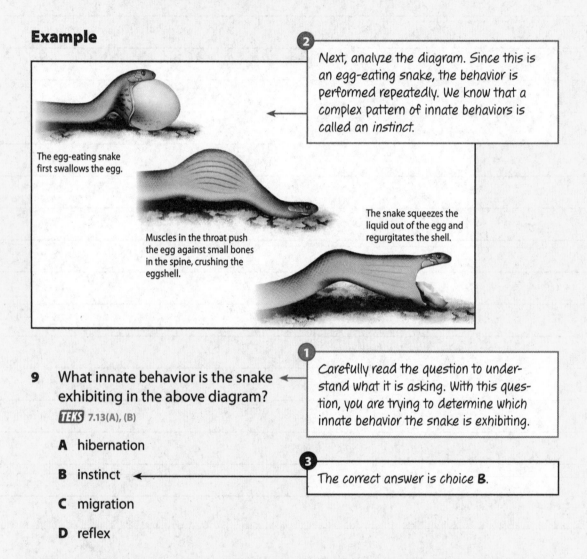

The egg-eating snake first swallows the egg.

Muscles in the throat push the egg against small bones in the spine, crushing the eggshell.

The snake squeezes the liquid out of the egg and regurgitates the shell.

2 Next, analyze the diagram. Since this is an egg-eating snake, the behavior is performed repeatedly. We know that a complex pattern of innate behaviors is called an *instinct*.

9 What innate behavior is the snake exhibiting in the above diagram?

TEKS 7.13(A), (B)

A hibernation

B instinct

C migration

D reflex

1 Carefully read the question to understand what it is asking. With this question, you are trying to determine which innate behavior the snake is exhibiting.

3 The correct answer is choice **B**.

TIP: Look for signal words in the question to help identify what to look for in the diagram. This might help you save time by avoiding unnecessary material.

Multiple Choice

1 The data table below shows the internal temperature of a person who has the flu. At 11 A.M., the person breaks out into a sweat. **TEKS** 7.13(B); 7.2(E)

Time	10 A.M.	11 A.M.	12 P.M.	1 P.M.	2 P.M.
Temperature	38.9°C	39.6°C	38.7°C	38.1°C	37.7°C

How do the data in the table show homeostasis in humans?

A The sweat cools the person, allowing the body temperature to return to normal.

B The sweat heats the person, allowing the body temperature to return to normal.

C The sweat cools the person, causing the body temperature to rise.

D The sweat heats the person, causing the body temperature to rise.

---

2 The illustration shows a plant after 1 week without water. **TEKS** 7.13(B)

Which statement describes the plant's response as a result of internal stimuli?

A Lack of water causes the plant cells to expand.

B Lack of water causes the plant cells to shrink.

C Photosynthesis causes the plant leaves to wilt.

D Photosynthesis causes the plant to absorb water.

3 A student performed an investigation in which she grew a bean seed in a petri dish. She placed the bean on a moist paper towel. She put the petri dish on its side on a well-lit windowsill. Then she observed the bean seed's growth. The student's bean seed is shown in the illustration below. **TEKS** 7.13(A); 7.2(C)

Which explains the direction of the growth of roots?

A negative phototropism

B negative geotropism

C positive phototropism

D positive geotropism

4

> Fight or flight is a response that involves adrenaline, a chemical in a person's bloodstream. Adrenaline causes the body to react in a certain way after experiencing stress. The effects of adrenaline occur after only a few seconds. This gives the body a burst of energy that enables it to act quickly. The effects of adrenaline are called fight or flight because they allow the body to fight off what is causing the stress or take flight and escape. A hissing cat with its tail puffed up and back hunched is an example of fight or flight.

Which are examples of how the body might change during a rush of adrenaline? **TEKS** 7.13(A)

A sweating decreases, less blood goes to the brain, muscles tense

B sweating increases, more blood goes to the brain, muscles relax

C heart rate decreases, less blood goes to the brain, muscles relax

D heart rate increases, more blood goes to the brain, muscles tense

5 The chart shows the average number of daylight hours in New York City. A poinsettia plant responds to changes in the length of daylight hours. It has a short-day plant cycle and will bloom only if it has more than 12 hours of darkness. Imagine that a poinsettia plant is not exposed to any artificial light. According to the data in the graph, how many months would the poinsettia plant be able to bloom? Record and bubble in your answer on the answer grid below.

TEKS 7.13(A); 7.2(D)

Average Number of Daylight Hours											
Jan	Feb	Mar	Apr	May	Jun	Jul	Aug	Sept	Oct	Nov	Dec
9	10	12	14	16	17	17	16	14	12	10	8

13 Inheritance and Reproduction

The **BIG** Idea

Reproduction ensures the survival of species. The instructions for traits are carried in the genetic material that is passed from one generation to the next generation through reproduction.

LESSON

13.1 Traits and Their Changes

Traits are determined by genes, which are inherited. The expression of traits can be influenced by physical and environmental factors.

TEKS 7.14(A), (C); Also covers 7.1(A); 7.2(A), (C); 7.3(B); 7.4(A), (B)

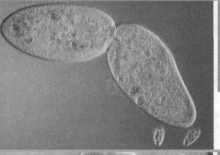

LESSON

13.2 The Cell Cycle and Cell Division

During the cell cycle, the cell's nucleus and its contents divide to create two identical daughter cells.

TEKS 7.14(C); Also covers 7.1(A); 7.2(A), (E); 7.3(B)

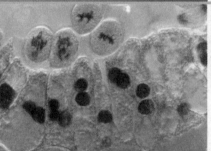

LESSON

13.3 Sexual Reproduction and Meiosis

Sexual reproduction helps maintain genetic variation in populations.

TEKS 7.14(B), (C); Also covers 7.1(A); 7.2(A), (C), (E); 7.3(B); 7.4(A)

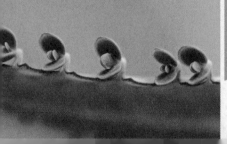

LESSON

13.4 Asexual Reproduction

Asexual reproduction is the production of offspring by one parent, which results in offspring that are genetically identical to the parent.

TEKS 7.14(B); Also covers 7.1(A); 7.2(A), (C), (E); 7.3(A), (B); 7.4(A), (B)

Baby Birds

Baby birds grow up to be similar to their parents. Which best explains why their traits are similar to their parents' traits? (Circle) the answer that best matches your thinking.

A. They inherited their traits from their parents.

B. Their traits are acquired, not inherited.

C. Their traits are both inherited and acquired.

D. Their traits are neither inherited nor acquired; they come from nature.

Explain your thinking. Describe your ideas about how offspring get their traits.

INQUIRY

A White Flamingo? Did you know that a flamingo is pink only because of the food it eats? If a flamingo is missing a certain type of algae in its diet, its feathers will be white. What do you think might cause a flamingo to be both pink and white?

Write your response in your interactive notebook.

 LAB Manager

Go to your Lab Manual or visit connectED.mcgraw-hill.com to perform the labs for this lesson.

MiniLAB: *Can you mutate a word?*

TEKS 7.4(A); 7.14(C)

Explore Activity

TEKS 7.1(A); 7.2(A), (C); 7.3(B); 7.4(B); 7.14(A)

Why does your dog look different from mine?

How would you describe a dog? Is a dog small, black, and brown-eyed? Or is a dog large, spotted, and blue-eyed? Animals come in a variety of sizes and colors and have many different characteristics. These characteristics are passed to offspring from the parents through heredity. Heredity is the passage of genetic instructions from one generation to the next generation.

Procedure

1. Read and complete a lab safety form.

2. Using **clay,** create a model of a dog. Decide which characteristics it will have, such as size, color, and coat type.

3. Compare your clay dog to the clay models your classmates have made.

Think About This

1. How are the model dogs alike? How are they different?

_____

_____

_____

2. How many different characteristics can you observe among the clay dogs?

_____

_____

3. What do you think determines the characteristics of a dog?

_____

_____

_____

TEKS in this Lesson

7.14(A) Define heredity as the passage of genetic instructions from one generation to the next generation.

7.14(C) Recognize that inherited traits of individuals are governed in the genetic material found in the genes within chromosomes in the nucleus.

Also covers Process Standards: 7.1(A); 7.2(A), (C); 7.3(B); 7.4(A), (B)

? Essential Questions

- What is heredity?
- What are traits, and how are they inherited?

𝒶𝒷𝒸 Vocabulary

trait
gene
phenotype
genotype
mutation

521

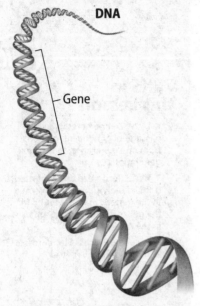

DNA

Gene

Figure 1 Genes are segments of molecules called DNA. Each gene determines a trait or part of a trait.

What are traits? **TEKS** 7.14(A), (C)

How would you describe yourself? Do you have curly hair? Do you have dimples when you smile? Are you tall? These are examples of traits. *A* **trait** *is a characteristic that distinguishes one organism from another organism.* An apple tree's traits might include pink flowers and red apples, while a pine tree's traits might include flat needles and cones. Each apple and cone also has a unique set of traits—just as you have unique traits that distinguish you from your classmates.

Determining Traits

Traits are determined by genetic information inside an organism's cells. Inside each cell is a nucleus that contains threadlike structures called chromosomes. Chromosomes contain the genetic information that controls traits. *A* **gene** *(JEEN) is a section of DNA on a chromosome that has genetic information for one trait,* as shown in **Figure 1.**

Genes carry coded instructions for making all parts of an organism. Not all of these instructions are contained in just one gene. Different genes contain different codes. The code of just one gene determines some traits. Other more complex traits are determined by the codes of many genes that work together.

Heredity is the passage of genetic instructions from one generation to the next generation. Genes are inherited. That means the instructions they carry are passed in sex cells from parents to offspring. An organism has genes—and some traits—similar to those of its parents. An offspring inherits two genes for each trait—one from each parent.

Explain

1. How are genes and traits related?

Gene	Trait
Definition:	Definition:

Phenotype and Genotype

You can describe an organism's traits in different ways. **Phenotype** (FEE nuh tipe) *describes an organism's observable set of traits.* The giraffe in **Figure 2** has brown spots, thin legs, and a long neck. These traits are parts of the giraffe's phenotype.

Genotype (JEE nuh tipe) *describes an organism's complete set of genes.* The genotype contains the coded instructions that result in an organism's phenotype. Scientists say that an organism expresses its genotype in its phenotype. Like all organisms, the giraffe has many different traits. Its genotype contains the instructions for all these traits.

Environmental Influence

Genotype does not usually change during an organism's lifetime. The flamingos at the beginning of this lesson are different colors because of the food they eat. They are pink or white depending on the presence of a certain pigment in their diet. Like all organisms, each cell of a flamingo usually contains the same genes throughout the flamingo's life. Its genes do not depend on the food the flamingo eats or what environment it lives in.

Although an organism's genes usually remain the same, an organism's phenotype can change throughout its lifetime. Phenotype can change when factors in an organism's environment change. Factors such as soil quality, water, temperature, or social conditions can change an organism's phenotype without changing its genotype. Some of these factors can cause changes that last a lifetime. Others cause changes that are quickly reversed. For example, the octopus in **Figure 3** can change color quickly as it moves, hunts, and hides in its environment.

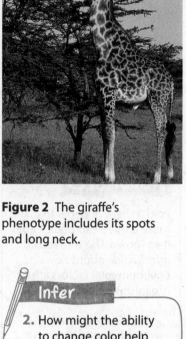
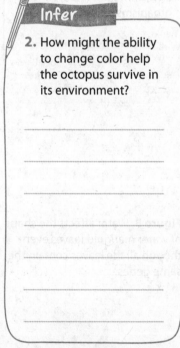

Figure 2 The giraffe's phenotype includes its spots and long neck.

Infer

2. How might the ability to change color help the octopus survive in its environment?

_____

_____

_____

_____

_____

_____

_____

Figure 3 This octopus changes color in a matter of seconds. Despite its color, its genotype remains the same.

Figure 4 Variations in soil acidity determine the color of these hydrangea flowers.

Temperature | Water and Soil | Social Factors

Soil

Just as a flamingo's color can change as its diet changes, the phenotype of many plants can change depending on the nutrients in the soil in which they grow. Low nitrogen in soil might cause a plant to be smaller than usual, or it might cause its leaves to turn yellow.

The acidity of soil can affect phenotype, too. In the case of the hydrangea plants shown in **Figure 4,** soil acidity can determine whether a plant has blue flowers or pink flowers. If it is grown in basic soil, a plant produces pink flowers. If the same plant is grown in acidic soil, it produces blue flowers. However, the plant's genotype remains the same despite the color of its flowers.

Verify

3. Highlight evidence that supports the statement that the genotype of a hydrangea plant is not affected by the acidity of soil.

Figure 5 Water affects the shape of water marigold leaves even though all the leaves contain the same genes.

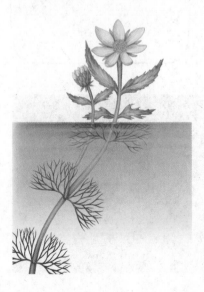

Water

Have you ever forgotten to water a houseplant? What happened to it? The plant might have wilted. A wilted plant looks different than a plant that is well watered. Water can change a plant's phenotype. Lack of water over long periods of time can cause some plants to have smaller leaves than usual, or it can cause leaves to curl. Too much water might cause plants to drop some of their leaves. Water can also affect the leaf shape of some plants, such as the water marigold shown in **Figure 5.** The leaves of the water marigold are thin and branched under the water and broad and wide above the surface.

Temperature

Did you know that the dark areas on a Siamese cat—the nose, ears, and tail—are cooler than the rest of the cat's body? Changes in temperature affect the color of these areas. If the Siamese cat in **Figure 6** lived in a warmer environment for a long period of time, the dark areas would gradually lighten. If the cat moved back to a cool environment, those areas would darken again. However, the cat's genotype in each environment would be the same.

Temperature can affect the phenotype of other organisms. For example, in some reptiles, such as crocodiles and some turtles, temperature determines offspring gender. If the sandy nest in which a crocodile lays her eggs remains about 32°C, the hatchlings are male. In a slightly warmer or cooler nest, the hatchlings are female.

Social Factors

An organism's social environment is the group of like organisms with which it shares a living space. A change in social environment can cause changes in gender, size, or color. For example, the desert locust, shown in **Figure 7,** is brown or green when it lives alone. However, in a crowded social environment, the locust is yellow or orange. Despite the color difference, the locust's genes remain the same.

Figure 6 The dark nose, ears, and tail of this Siamese cat are cooler than the rest of its body.

Identify

4. Underline the traits that can be affected by changes in social factors.

Figure 7 A desert locust's color can change depending on whether the locust lives alone or in a crowded environment.

Organize it!

Complete the cause-and-effect chart to detail how environmental influences affect phenotypes.

Cause	Effect
Type of food a flamingo eats	
Hydrangea growing in acidic soil	
A plant not getting enough water	
A plant getting too much water	
Soil temperature of about 32°C where a crocodile lays its eggs	
A desert locust living in crowded conditions	
The color of an octopus's environment	

Connect it! **Write** a paragraph about how an organism's genotype and phenotype are related. Write your response in your interactive notebook.

Organize it!

Mutations and Phenotype TEKS 7.14(A), (C)

You have read that environmental factors can change an organism's phenotype without changing its genotype. You also read that the environment cannot change genotype. A genotype can be altered only by changes in the gene's DNA code.

What are mutations?

A change in the DNA code of a gene is called a **mutation** (myew TAY shun). Think about the last time you typed something. Did your fingers hit a wrong letter? Mutations are similar. Just as one wrong letter changes a word, a mutation changes a gene.

Sometimes, a mutation in a gene can also change the trait coded by the gene. When it does, the change can appear in the organism's phenotype. The fruit fly with extra wings in **Figure 8** is the result of a mutation in a gene that codes for the number of wings.

Inherited Mutations

Recall that a change to a phenotype that is caused by an environmental factor is not inherited. A pink flamingo's offspring can be pink or white, depending on the offspring's diet. However, changes to genotype can be inherited. If the fly with extra wings in **Figure 8** survives and has offspring, it could pass its wing mutation to future generations. Passing mutations to offspring plays an important role in determining how organisms change over time.

Word Origin

mutation
from Latin *mutare,* means "to change"

Figure 8 The fruit fly with extra wings contains a mutation that appears in its phenotype.

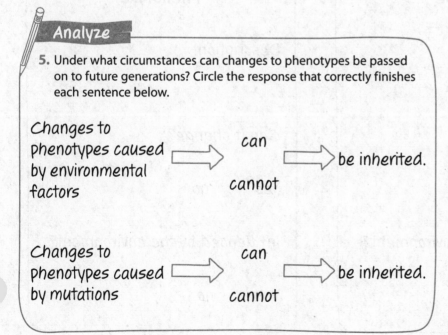

Analyze

5. Under what circumstances can changes to phenotypes be passed on to future generations? Circle the response that correctly finishes each sentence below.

Changes to phenotypes caused by environmental factors → can / cannot → be inherited.

Changes to phenotypes caused by mutations → can / cannot → be inherited.

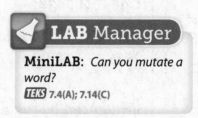

LAB Manager

MiniLAB: *Can you mutate a word?*
TEKS 7.4(A); 7.14(C)

Summarize it!

Describe terms associated with inheritance. **TEKS** 7.14(C)

Term	Description
	a long, tightly coiled molecule that looks like a twisted zipper inside a cell's nucleus
Gene	
Chromosome	

Contrast genotype and phenotype. Describe each term, and then circle *yes* or *no* to answer each question.

Genotype	Phenotype
Description:	Description:
Can it change?	Can it change?
Yes no	Yes no
Influenced by the environment?	Influenced by the environment?
Yes no	Yes no

Use Vocabulary

1. **Distinguish** between phenotype and genotype. **TEKS** 7.14(C) *supporting*

_____

_____

_____

_____

2. **Choose** Which term describes an organism's distinguishing characteristics? **TEKS** 7.14(C) *supporting*

_____

Apply the Essential Questions

3. **Define** the term *heredity*. **TEKS** 7.14(A) *supporting*

_____

_____

_____

4. **Describe** the location of the instructions that code for traits. **TEKS** 7.14(C) *supporting*

_____

_____

_____

_____

_____

H.O.T. Questions (Higher Order Thinking)

5. **Analyze** A rabbit that is raised in northern Maine has different coloring than a rabbit raised in southern Texas. Is it possible for the two rabbits to have the same genes for coloring? Explain your reasoning. **TEKS** 7.14(C) *supporting*

_____

_____

_____

_____

_____

_____

_____

6. **Design an experiment** to test whether a trait in an animal is inherited or the result of an environmental factor. **TEKS** 7.14(A), (C) *supporting*

_____

_____

_____

_____

_____

_____

_____

Sponges for Lunch

The Hawksbill Turtle's Unusual Diet

Meet the Hawksbill

- Weight: 45–90 kg

- Length: 80–100 cm

- Hawksbills inhabit tropical and subtropical regions of the Atlantic, Pacific, and Indian Oceans.

- In the Caribbean, an adult hawksbill eats an average of 544 kg of sponges per year.

- Every 2–3 years, an adult female hawksbill returns to the beach where she hatched to build her nest. She returns 3–5 times per breeding season to build a nest and lays an average of 130 eggs per nest.

AMERICAN MUSEUM Ö NATURAL HISTORY

You might know that a carnivore (KAR nuh vor) is an animal that eats other animals, but have you ever heard of a spongivore (SPUN jih vor)? It is a carnivore that eats sponges. A sponge is a simple animal that has chalky, glasslike spikes that support its body. The hawksbill turtle is a spongivore. Its narrow head has a sharp, curving beak. This enables a hawksbill to remove sponges from small spaces in coral reefs. Hawksbills also have adaptations for digesting and absorbing nutrients from sponges. How did hawksbills evolve as spongivores? Conservation geneticist Eugenia Naro-Maciel of the American Museum of Natural History in New York City is trying to answer this question.

To understand adaptations of sponge-eating turtles, Naro-Maciel analyzed their DNA. She compared the DNA of sea turtle species living today to learn which ones are similar. The more similar the DNA of two species is, the more closely related they are. Her results revealed that hawksbills and other carnivorous sea turtle species are more closely related than hawksbills and plant-eating sea turtle species. Next, Naro-Maciel wants to gather more data about where hawksbills feed and move. Scientists can use this data to find ways to minimize the effects of human actions on hawksbills.

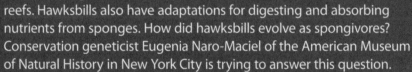

It's Your Turn!

RESEARCH Conduct research about one of the other six sea turtle species. Write a paragraph that describes the turtle's physical characteristics, its feeding and migration habits, and how these traits help it survive.

Time to Split? Unicellular organisms such as these reproduce when one cell divides into two new cells. The two cells are identical to each other. What do you think happened to the contents of the original cell before it divided?

Write your response in your interactive notebook.

LAB Manager

Go to your Lab Manual or visit connectED.mcgraw-hill.com to perform the labs for this lesson.

MiniLAB: *How does mitosis work?*

TEKS 7.1(A); 7.2(E); 7.3(B); 7.14(C)

Explore Activity

Why isn't your cell like mine?

All living things are made of cells. Some are made of only one cell, while others are made of trillions of cells. Where do all those cells come from?

Procedure

1. Read and complete a lab safety form.

2. Ask your team members to face away from you. Draw an animal cell on a sheet of **paper.** Include as many organelles as you can.

3. Use **scissors** to cut the cell drawing into equal halves. Fold each sheet of paper in half so the drawing cannot be seen.

4. Ask your team members to face you. Give each team member half of the cell drawing.

5. Have team members sit facing away from each other. Each person should use a **glue stick** to attach the cell half to one side of a sheet of paper. Then, each person should draw the missing cell half.

6. Compare the two new cells to your original cell.

Think About This

1. How did the new cells compare to the original cell?

_____

_____

_____

_____

2. What are some things that might be done in the early steps to produce two new cells that are more like the original cell?

_____

_____

_____

_____

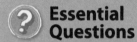

TEKS in this Lesson

7.14(C) Recognize that inherited traits of individuals are governed in the genetic material found in the genes within chromosomes in the nucleus.

Also covers Process Standards: 7.1(A); 7.2(A), (E); 7.3(B)

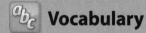 Essential Questions

- What happens during each phase of the cell cycle?
- Why is the result of the cell cycle important?

Vocabulary

cell cycle
interphase
sister chromatid
centromere
mitosis
cytokinesis
daughter cell

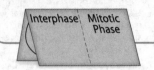

Make a folded book from a sheet of paper. Label the front *The Cell Cycle,* and label the inside of the book as shown. Open the book completely and use the full sheet to illustrate the cell cycle.

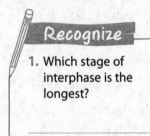

Interphase | Mitotic Phase

The Cell Cycle TEKS 7.14(C)

You have probably noticed that the weather changes in a regular pattern each year. As seasons change, temperature, precipitation, and the number of hours of sunlight vary in a regular cycle. Cells also go through cycles. *Most cells in an organism go through a cycle of growth, development, and division called the* **cell cycle.** Through the cell cycle, organisms grow, develop, replace old or damaged cells, and produce new cells.

Phases of the Cell Cycle

There are two main phases in the cell cycle—interphase and the mitotic (mi TAH tihk) phase. **Interphase** *is the period during the cell cycle of a cell's growth and development.* A cell spends most of its life in interphase, as shown in **Figure 1.** During interphase, most cells go through three stages:

- rapid growth and replication, or copying, of organelles;
- copying of DNA, the genetic information in a cell; and
- preparation for cell division.

Interphase is followed by a shorter period called the mitotic phase. A cell reproduces during this phase. The mitotic phase has two stages, as illustrated in **Figure 1.** The nucleus divides in the first stage, and the cell's fluid, called the cytoplasm, divides in the second stage. The mitotic phase creates two new identical cells. At the end of this phase, the original cell no longer exists.

Figure 1 A cell spends most of its life growing and developing during interphase.

Recognize

1. Which stage of interphase is the longest?

_____

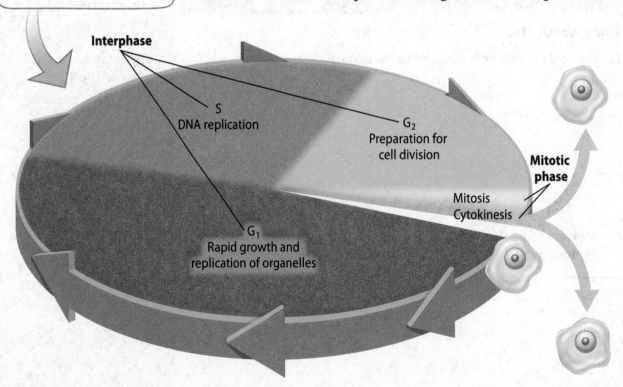

Interphase

S
DNA replication

G₂
Preparation for cell division

Mitotic phase

Mitosis
Cytokinesis

G₁
Rapid growth and replication of organelles

Length of a Cell Cycle

The time it takes a cell to complete the cell cycle depends on the type of cell that is dividing. Recall that a eukaryotic cell has membrane-bound organelles, including a nucleus. For some eukaryotic cells, the cell cycle might last only eight minutes. For other eukaryotic cells, the cycle might take as long as one year. Most dividing human cells normally complete the cell cycle in about 24 hours.

> Describe
>
> **2.** What does the length of a cell cycle depend on?
>
> _____
>
> _____

Interphase TEKS 7.14(C)

As you have read, interphase makes up most of the cell cycle. Newly produced cells begin interphase with a period of rapid growth—the cell gets bigger. This is followed by cellular activities such as making proteins. Next, actively dividing cells make copies of their DNA and prepare for cell division. During interphase, the DNA is called chromatin (KROH muh tun). Chromatin is long, thin strands of DNA, as shown in **Figure 2.** When scientists dye a cell in interphase, the nucleus looks like a plate of spaghetti. This is because the nucleus contains many strands of chromatin tangled together.

Figure 2 During interphase, the nuclei of an animal cell and a plant cell contain long, thin strands of DNA called chromatin.

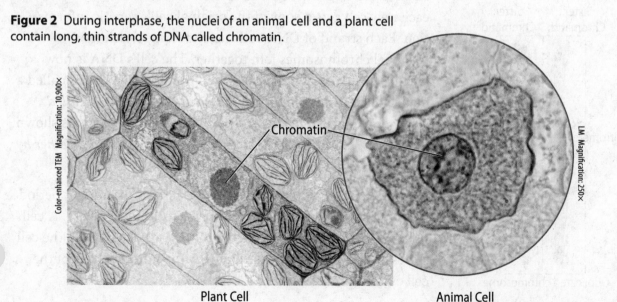

Color-enhanced TEM Magnification: 10,900×

LM Magnification: 250×

Chromatin

Plant Cell

Animal Cell

Table 1 Phases of the Cell Cycle

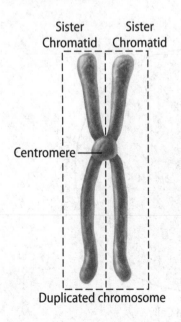

Phase	Stage	Description
Interphase	G_1	growth and cellular functions; organelle replication
	S	growth and chromosome replication; organelle replication
	G_2	growth and cellular functions; organelle replication
Mitotic phase	mitosis	division of nucleus
	cytokinesis	division of cytoplasm

Table 1 The two phases of the cell cycle can each be divided into different stages.

Figure 3 The coiled DNA forms a duplicated chromosome made of two sister chromatids connected at the centromere.

Sister Chromatid   Sister Chromatid

Centromere

Duplicated chromosome

Phases of Interphase

Scientists divide interphase into three stages, as shown in **Table 1.** Interphase begins with a period of rapid growth—the G_1 stage. This stage lasts longer than other stages of the cell cycle. During G_1, a cell grows and carries out its normal cell functions. For example, during G_1, cells that line your stomach make enzymes that help digest your food. Although most cells continue the cell cycle, some cells stop the cell cycle at this point. For example, mature nerve cells in your brain remain in G_1 and do not divide again.

During the second stage of interphase—the S stage—a cell continues to grow and copies its DNA. There are now identical strands of DNA. These identical strands of DNA ensure that each new cell gets a copy of the original cell's genetic information. Each strand of DNA coils up and forms a chromosome. Identical chromosomes join together. The cell's DNA is now arranged as pairs of identical chromosomes. Each pair is called a duplicated chromosome. *Two identical chromosomes, called* **sister chromatids,** *make up a duplicated chromosome,* as shown in **Figure 3.** Notice that the *sister chromatids are held together by a structure called the* **centromere.**

The final stage of interphase—the G_2 stage—is another period of growth and the final preparation for the mitotic phase. A cell uses energy copying DNA during the S stage. During G_2, the cell stores energy that will be used during the mitotic phase of the cell cycle.

Organelle Replication

During cell division, the organelles in a cell are distributed between the two new cells. Before a cell divides, it makes a copy of each organelle. This enables the two new cells to function properly. Some organelles, such as the energy-processing mitochondria and chloroplasts, have their own DNA. These organelles can make copies of themselves on their own, as shown in **Figure 4.** A cell produces other organelles from materials such as proteins and lipids. A cell makes these materials using the information contained in the DNA inside the nucleus. Organelles are copied during all stages of interphase.

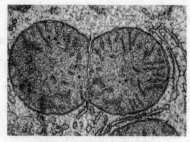

TEM Magnification: Unavailable

Figure 4 This mitochondrion is in the final stage of dividing.

The Mitotic Phase TEKS 7.14(C)

The mitotic phase of the cell cycle follows interphase. It consists of two stages: mitosis (mi TOH sus) and cytokinesis (si toh kuh NEE sus). *In* **mitosis,** *the nucleus and its contents divide. In* **cytokinesis,** *the cytoplasm and its contents divide.* **Daughter cells** *are the two new cells that result from mitosis and cytokinesis.*

During mitosis, the contents of the nucleus divide, forming two identical nuclei. The sister chromatids of the duplicated chromosomes separate from each other. This gives each daughter cell the same genetic information. For example, a cell that has ten duplicated chromosomes actually has 20 chromatids. When the cell divides, each daughter cell will have ten different chromatids. Chromatids are now called chromosomes.

In cytokinesis, the cytoplasm divides and forms the two new daughter cells. Organelles that were made during interphase are divided between the daughter cells.

Organize

3. Complete the diagram at right with information describing the stages in the mitotic phase of the cell cycle.

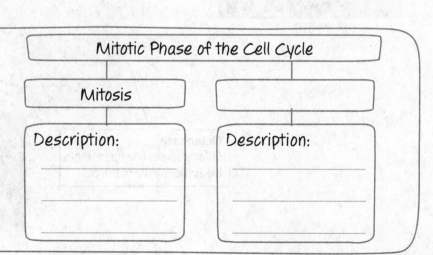

Mitotic Phase of the Cell Cycle

Mitosis

Description:

Description:

Phases of Mitosis

Like interphase, mitosis is a continuous process that scientists divide into different phases, as shown in **Figure 5.**

Prophase During the first phase of mitosis, called prophase, the copied chromatin coils together tightly. The coils form visible duplicated chromosomes. The nucleolus disappears, and the nuclear membrane breaks down. Structures called spindle fibers form in the cytoplasm.

Metaphase During metaphase, the spindle fibers pull and push the duplicated chromosomes to the middle of the cell. Notice in **Figure 5** that the chromosomes line up along the middle of the cell. This arrangement ensures that each new cell will receive one copy of each chromosome. Metaphase is the shortest phase in mitosis, but it must be completed successfully for the new cells to be identical.

Watch

Phases of Mitosis

Go Online!

Figure 5 Mitosis begins when replicated chromatin coils together and ends when two identical nuclei are formed.

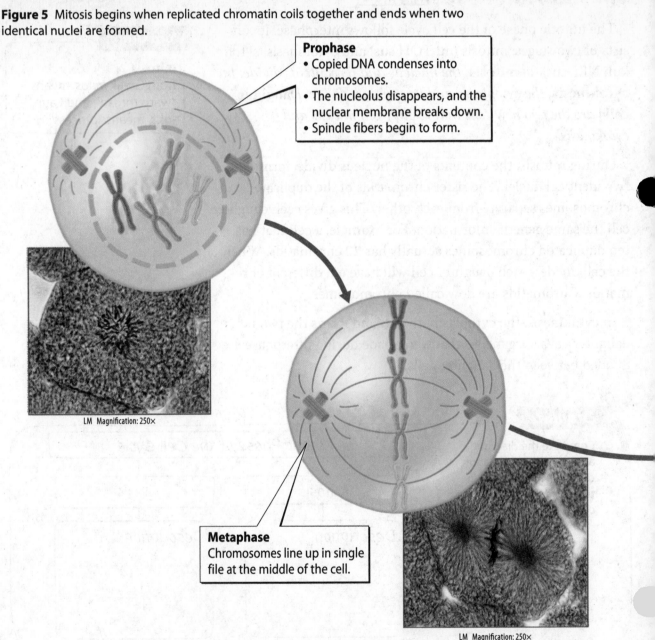

Prophase
- Copied DNA condenses into chromosomes.
- The nucleolus disappears, and the nuclear membrane breaks down.
- Spindle fibers begin to form.

LM Magnification: 250×

Metaphase
Chromosomes line up in single file at the middle of the cell.

LM Magnification: 250×

Anaphase In anaphase, the third stage of mitosis, the two sister chromatids in each chromosome separate from each other. The spindle fibers pull them in opposite directions. Once separated, the chromatids are now two identical single-stranded chromosomes. As they move to opposite sides of a cell, the cell begins to get longer. Anaphase is complete when the two identical sets of chromosomes are at opposite ends of a cell.

Telophase During telophase, the spindle fibers begin to disappear. Also, the chromosomes begin to uncoil. A nuclear membrane forms around each set of chromosomes at either end of the cell. This forms two new identical nuclei. Telophase is the final stage of mitosis. It is often described as the reverse of prophase because many of the processes that occur during prophase are reversed during telophase.

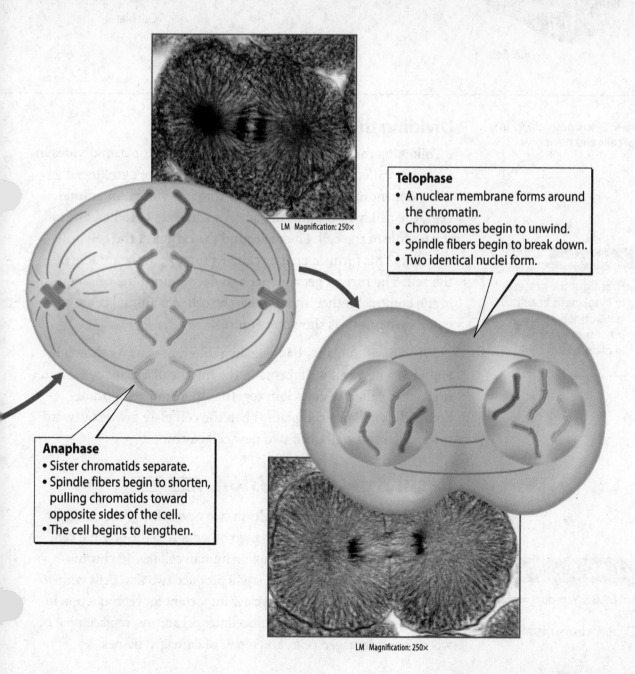

LM Magnification: 250×

Telophase
• A nuclear membrane forms around the chromatin.
• Chromosomes begin to unwind.
• Spindle fibers begin to break down.
• Two identical nuclei form.

Anaphase
• Sister chromatids separate.
• Spindle fibers begin to shorten, pulling chromatids toward opposite sides of the cell.
• The cell begins to lengthen.

LM Magnification: 250×

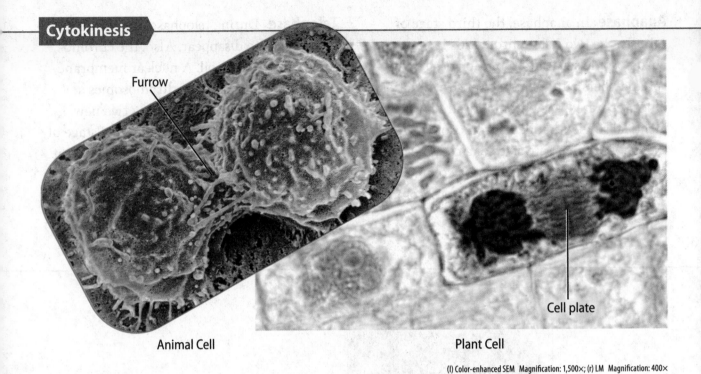

Furrow

Cell plate

Animal Cell

Plant Cell

(l) Color-enhanced SEM Magnification: 1,500×; (r) LM Magnification: 400×

Figure 6 Cytokinesis differs in animal cells and plant cells.

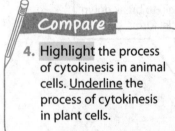

Compare

4. **Highlight** the process of cytokinesis in animal cells. <u>Underline</u> the process of cytokinesis in plant cells.

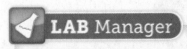

LAB Manager

MiniLAB: *How does mitosis work?*
TEKS 7.1(A); 7.2(E); 7.3(B); 7.14(C)

Dividing the Cell's Components

Following the last phase of mitosis, a cell's cytoplasm divides in a process called cytokinesis. The specific steps of cytokinesis differ depending on the type of cell that is dividing. In animal cells, the cell membrane contracts, or squeezes together, around the middle of the cell. Fibers around the center of the cell pull together. This forms a crease, called a furrow, in the middle of the cell. The furrow gets deeper and deeper until the cell membrane comes together and divides the cell. An animal cell undergoing cytokinesis is shown in **Figure 6.**

Cytokinesis in plants happens in a different way. As shown in **Figure 6,** a new cell wall forms in the middle of a plant cell. First, organelles called vesicles join together to form a membrane-bound disk called a cell plate. Then the cell plate grows outward toward the cell wall until two new cells form.

Results of Cell Division *TEKS* 7.14(C)

Recall that the cell cycle results in two new cells. These daughter cells are genetically identical to each other and to the original cell that no longer exists. For example, a human cell has 46 chromosomes. When that cell divides, it will produce two new cells with 46 chromosomes each. The cell cycle is important for reproduction in some organisms, growth in multicellular organisms, replacement of worn out or damaged cells, and repair of damaged tissues.

Reproduction

In some unicellular organisms, cell division is a form of reproduction. For example, an organism called a paramecium often reproduces by dividing into two new daughter cells or two new paramecia. Cell division is also important in other methods of reproduction in which the offspring are identical to the parent organism.

Growth

Cell division allows multicellular organisms, such as humans, to grow and develop from one cell (a fertilized egg). In humans, cell division begins about 24 hours after fertilization and continues rapidly during the first few years of life. It is likely that during the next few years you will go through another period of rapid growth and development. This happens because cells divide and increase in number as you grow and develop.

Replacement

Even after an organism is fully grown, cell division continues. It replaces cells that wear out or are damaged. The outermost layer of your skin is always rubbing or flaking off. A layer of cells below the skin's surface is constantly dividing. This produces millions of new cells daily to replace the ones that are rubbed off.

Repair

Cell division is also critical for repairing damage. When a bone breaks, cell division produces new bone cells that patch the broken pieces back together.

Not all damage can be repaired, however, because not all cells continue to divide. Recall that mature nerve cells stop the cell cycle in interphase. For this reason, injuries to nerve cells often cause permanent damage.

Use Percentages

A percentage is a ratio that compares a number to 100. If the length of the entire cell cycle is 24 hours, 24 hours equals 100%. If part of the cycle takes 6.0 hours, it can be expressed as 6.0 hours/24 hours. To calculate percentage, divide and multiply by 100. Add a percent sign.

$$\frac{6.0}{24} = 0.25 \times 100 = 25\%$$

Practice

Interphase in human cells takes about 23 hours. If the cell cycle is 24 hours, what percentage is interphase?

Check   Tutor

Go Online! ✓ 💬

Infer

5. Why is the result of the cell cycle important?

_____

_____

_____

_____

_____

_____

Identify each phase of mitosis. *TEKS* 7.14(C)

_____

DNA condenses; spindle fibers begin to form.

_____

Chromosomes line up in single file at the middle of the cell.

_____

Sister chromatids separate and pull to opposite sides.

_____

Nuclear membrane re-forms; chromosomes unwind.

Connect it! **Apply** what you have learned to explain what probably happened when the bean plant grew overnight in the story of *Jack and the Beanstalk*.

_____

_____

_____

_____

_____

_____

Summarize it!

Use Vocabulary

1. **Distinguish** between mitosis and cytokinesis. **TEKS** 7.14(C) *supporting*

_____

_____

_____

_____

Apply the Essential Question

2. **Construct** a table on a separate sheet of paper to show the different phases of mitosis and what happens during each.
TEKS 7.14(C) *supporting*

3. **Give three examples** of why the result of the cell cycle is important.
TEKS 7.14(C) *supporting*

_____

_____

_____

H.O.T. Questions (Higher Order Thinking)

4. **Assess** how the result of mitosis maintains inherited traits from generation to generation. **TEKS** 7.14(C) *supporting*

_____

_____

_____

_____

_____

_____

5. **Evaluate** Why is cell division important for unicellular organisms? For multicellular organisms?
TEKS 7.14(C) *supporting*

_____

_____

_____

_____

_____

_____

_____

Math Skills **Math** **TEKS** 7.1(A); 7.3(A); 7.4(A)

Use Percentages

6. The mitotic phase of the human cell cycle takes approximately 1 hour. What percentage of the 24-hour cell cycle is the mitotic phase?

7. During an interphase lasting 23 hours, the S stage takes an average of 8 hours. What percentage of interphase is taken up by the S stage?

Check   Tutor

Go Online!

DNA Fingerprinting

Solving Crimes One Strand at a Time

▼ **DNA**

Every cell in your body has the same DNA in its nucleus. Unless you are an identical twin, your DNA is entirely unique. Identical twins have identical DNA because they begin as one cell that divides and separates. When your cells begin mitosis, they copy their DNA. Every new cell has the same DNA as the original cells. That is why DNA can be used to identify people. Just as no two people have the same fingerprints, your DNA belongs to you alone.

Using scientific methods to solve crimes is called forensics. DNA fingerprinting is now a basic tool in forensics. Samples collected from a crime scene can be compared to millions of samples previously collected and indexed in a computer.

Every day, everywhere you go, you leave a trail of DNA. It might be in skin cells. It might be in hair or in the saliva you used to lick an envelope. If you commit a crime, you will most likely leave DNA behind. An expert crime scene investigator will know how to collect that DNA.

DNA evidence can prove innocence as well. Investigators have reexamined DNA found at old crime scenes. Imprisoned persons have been proved to be innocent through DNA fingerprinting methods that were not yet available when a crime was committed.

DNA fingerprinting can also be used to identify bodies that had previously been known only as a John or Jane Doe.

▼ **The Federal Bureau of Investigation (FBI) has a nationwide index of DNA samples called CODIS (Combined DNA Index System).**

It's Your Turn!

DISCOVER Your cells contain organelles called mitochondria. They have their own DNA, called mitochondrial DNA. Your mitochondrial DNA is identical to your mother's mitochondrial DNA. Find out how this information is used.

Modern Art? This photo looks like a piece of modern art. It is actually an image of plant cells. The cells are dividing by a process that occurs during the production of sex cells. Why do you think the production of sex cells might differ from the production of body cells?

Write your response in your interactive notebook.

LAB Manager

Go to your Lab Manual or visit connectED.mcgraw-hill.com to perform the labs for this lesson.

MiniLAB: *How does one cell produce four cells?*

TEKS 7.1(A); 7.2(A); 7.3(B); 7.4(A); 7.14(B)

Explore Activity

TEKS 7.1(A); 7.2(A), (C), (E); 7.4(A); 7.14(B)

Why do offspring look different?

Unless you're an identical twin, you probably don't look exactly like any siblings you might have. You might have differences in physical characteristics such as eye color, hair color, ear shape, or height. Why are there differences in the offspring from the same parents?

Procedure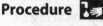

1. Read and complete a lab safety form.

2. Open the **paper bag** labeled *Male Parent* and, without looking, remove three **beads.** Record the bead colors in your Lab Manual or your interactive notebook and replace the beads.

3. Open the **paper bag** labeled *Female Parent* and remove three **beads.** Record the bead colors and replace the beads.

4. Repeat steps 2 and 3 for each member of the group.

5. After each member has recorded his or her bead colors, study the results. Each combination of male and female beads represents an offspring.

Think About This

1. Compare your group's offspring to another group's offspring. What similarities or differences do you observe?

2. What caused any differences you observed? Explain.

3. Why might this type of reproduction be beneficial to an organism?

TEKS in this Lesson

7.14(B) Compare the results of uniform or diverse offspring from sexual reproduction or asexual reproduction

7.14(C) Recognize that inherited traits of individuals are governed in the genetic material found in the genes within chromosomes in the nucleus.

Also covers Process Standards: 7.1(A); 7.2(A), (C), (E); 7.3(B); 7.4(A)

Essential Questions

- What is sexual reproduction, and why is it beneficial?
- What is the order of the phases of meiosis, and what happens during each phase?
- Why is meiosis important?

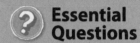 Vocabulary

sexual reproduction
egg
sperm
fertilization
zygote
diploid
homologous chromosomes
haploid
meiosis

547

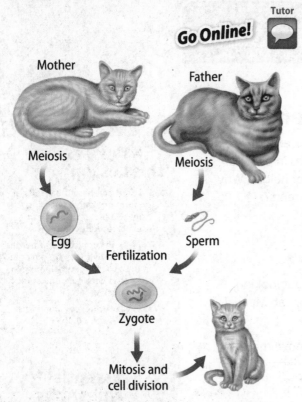

Go Online! Tutor

Mother

Father

Meiosis

Meiosis

Egg

Sperm

Fertilization

Zygote

Mitosis and
cell division

Figure 1 The zygote that forms during fertilization can become a multicellular organism.

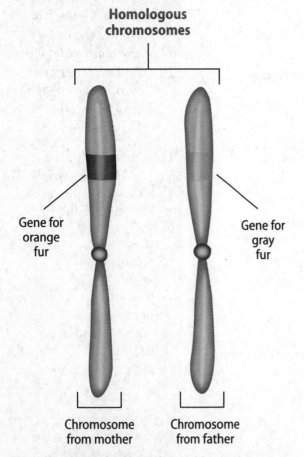

Homologous
chromosomes

Gene for
orange
fur

Gene for
gray
fur

Chromosome
from mother

Chromosome
from father

Figure 2 In this pair of homologous chromosomes, one chromosome carries the gene for orange fur color, and the other chromosome carries the gene for gray fur color.

Sexual Reproduction TEKS 7.14(B), (C)

In a litter of kittens, one kitten might have orange fur like its mother. A second kitten might have gray fur like its father. Another kitten might look like a combination of both parents. How is this possible?

The kittens look different because of sexual reproduction. **Sexual reproduction** *is a type of reproduction in which the genetic materials from two different cells combine, producing an offspring.* The cells that combine are called sex cells. Sex cells form in reproductive organs. *The female sex cell, an* **egg,** *forms in an ovary. The male sex cell, a* **sperm,** *forms in a testis. During a process called* **fertilization** (fur tuh luh ZAY shun), *an egg cell and a sperm cell join together. This produces a new cell. The new cell that forms from fertilization is called a* **zygote.** As shown in **Figure 1,** the zygote develops into a new organism.

Diploid Cells

Following fertilization, a zygote goes through mitosis and cell division. These processes produce nearly all the cells in a multicellular organism. Organisms that reproduce sexually form two kinds of cells—body cells and sex cells. In body cells of most organisms, similar chromosomes occur in pairs. **Diploid** *cells are cells that have pairs of chromosomes.*

Pairs of chromosomes that have genes for the same traits arranged in the same order are called **homologous** (huh MAH luh gus) **chromosomes.** Because one chromosome is inherited from each parent, the chromosomes are not identical. For example, the kittens mentioned earlier inherited a gene for orange fur color from their mother. They also inherited a gene for gray fur color from their father. Both genes for fur color are at the same place on homologous chromosomes, as shown in **Figure 2,** but they code for different colors.

Different organisms have different numbers of chromosomes. Recall that diploid cells have pairs of chromosomes. Notice in **Table 1** that human diploid cells have 23 pairs of chromosomes for a total of 46 chromosomes. A fruit fly diploid cell has 4 pairs of chromosomes, and a rice diploid cell has 12 pairs of chromosomes. Having the correct number of chromosomes is very important. If a zygote has too many or too few chromosomes, it will not develop properly.

Watch
Go Online!

Table 1	Chromosomes of Selected Organisms	
Organism	Number of Chromosomes	Number of Homologous Pairs
Fruit Fly	8	4
Rice	24	12
Yeast	32	16
Cat	38	19
Human	46	23
Dog	78	39
Fern	1,260	630

Haploid Cells

Organisms that reproduce sexually also form egg and sperm cells, or sex cells. Sex cells have only one chromosome from each pair of chromosomes. **Haploid** *cells are cells that have only one chromosome from each pair.* Organisms produce sex cells using a special type of cell division called meiosis. *In* **meiosis,** *one diploid cell divides and makes four haploid sex cells.* Meiosis occurs only during the formation of sex cells.

The Phases of Meiosis

Next, you will read about the phases of meiosis. Many of the phases might seem familiar to you because they also occur during mitosis. Recall that mitosis and cytokinesis involve one division of the nucleus and the cytoplasm. Meiosis involves two divisions of the nucleus and the cytoplasm. These divisions are called meiosis I and meiosis II. They result in four haploid cells—cells with half the number of chromosomes as the original cell. As you read about meiosis, think about how it produces sex cells that have a reduced number of chromosomes.

Infer

1. In **Table 1,** how does the number of chromosomes relate to the number of homologous pairs?

_____

_____

_____

_____

_____

Word Origin

haploid
from Greek *haploeides,*
means "single"

LAB Manager

MiniLAB: *How does one cell produce four cells?*
TEKS 7.1(A); 7.2(A); 7.3(B); 7.4(A); 7.14(B)

Phases of Meiosis I

A reproductive cell goes through interphase before beginning meiosis I, which is shown in **Figure 3.** During interphase, the reproductive cell grows and copies, or duplicates, its chromosomes. Each duplicated chromosome consists of two sister chromatids joined together by a centromere.

❶ **Prophase I** In the first phase of meiosis I, duplicated chromosomes condense and thicken. Homologous chromosomes come together and form pairs. The membrane surrounding the nucleus breaks apart, and the nucleolus disappears.

❷ **Metaphase I** Homologous chromosome pairs line up along the middle of the cell. A spindle fiber attaches to each chromosome.

❸ **Anaphase I** Chromosome pairs separate and are pulled toward the opposite ends of the cell. Notice that the sister chromatids stay together.

❹ **Telophase I** A nuclear membrane forms around each group of duplicated chromosomes. The cytoplasm divides through cytokinesis, and two daughter cells form. Sister chromatids remain together.

Watch
Go Online!

Meiosis

Meiosis I

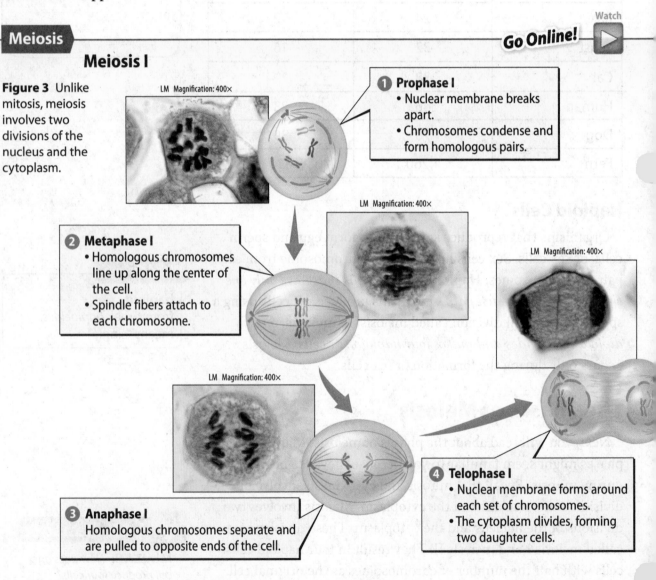

Figure 3 Unlike mitosis, meiosis involves two divisions of the nucleus and the cytoplasm.

LM Magnification: 400×

❶ **Prophase I**
• Nuclear membrane breaks apart.
• Chromosomes condense and form homologous pairs.

LM Magnification: 400×

❷ **Metaphase I**
• Homologous chromosomes line up along the center of the cell.
• Spindle fibers attach to each chromosome.

LM Magnification: 400×

LM Magnification: 400×

❸ **Anaphase I**
Homologous chromosomes separate and are pulled to opposite ends of the cell.

❹ **Telophase I**
• Nuclear membrane forms around each set of chromosomes.
• The cytoplasm divides, forming two daughter cells.

Phases of Meiosis II

After meiosis I, the two cells formed during this stage go through a second division of the nucleus and the cytoplasm. This process, shown in **Figure 3,** is called meiosis II.

5 **Prophase II** Chromosomes are not copied again before prophase II. They remain as condensed, thickened sister chromatids. The nuclear membrane breaks apart, and the nucleolus disappears in each cell.

6 **Metaphase II** The pairs of sister chromatids line up along the middle of the cell in single file.

7 **Anaphase II** The sister chromatids of each duplicated chromosome are pulled away from each other and move toward opposite ends of the cells.

8 **Telophase II** During the final phase of meiosis—telophase II—a nuclear membrane forms around each set of chromatids, which are again called chromosomes. The cytoplasm divides through cytokinesis, and four haploid cells form.

Identify

2. In the text, highlight the end result of telophase I. Underline the end result of telophase II.

Meiosis II

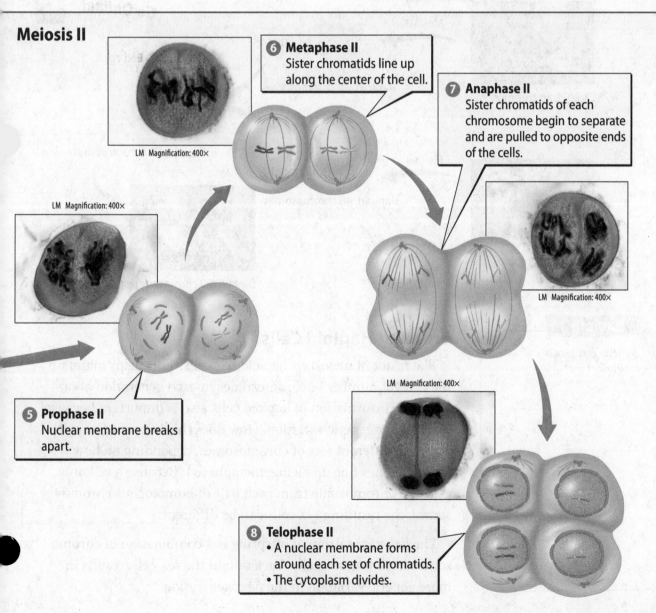

6 **Metaphase II**
Sister chromatids line up along the center of the cell.

LM Magnification: 400×

7 **Anaphase II**
Sister chromatids of each chromosome begin to separate and are pulled to opposite ends of the cells.

LM Magnification: 400×

LM Magnification: 400×

5 **Prophase II**
Nuclear membrane breaks apart.

LM Magnification: 400×

8 **Telophase II**
• A nuclear membrane forms around each set of chromatids.
• The cytoplasm divides.

Why is meiosis important? TEKS 7.14(B), (C)

Meiosis forms sex cells with the correct haploid number of chromosomes. This maintains the correct diploid number of chromosomes in organisms when sex cells join. Meiosis also creates genetic variation by producing haploid cells.

Maintaining Diploid Cells

Recall that diploid cells have pairs of chromosomes. Meiosis helps maintain diploid cells in offspring by making haploid sex cells. When haploid sex cells join together during fertilization, they make a diploid zygote, or fertilized egg. The zygote then divides by mitosis and cell division and creates a diploid organism. **Figure 4** illustrates how the diploid number is maintained in ducks.

Figure 4 Meiosis ensures that the chromosome number of a species stays the same from generation to generation.

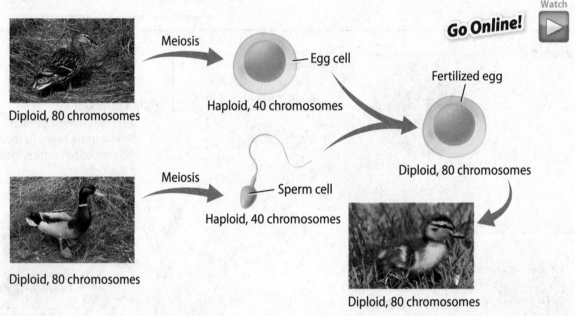

Diploid, 80 chromosomes

Meiosis

Egg cell

Haploid, 40 chromosomes

Go Online!

Watch

Fertilized egg

Diploid, 80 chromosomes

Meiosis

Sperm cell

Haploid, 40 chromosomes

Diploid, 80 chromosomes

Diploid, 80 chromosomes

Explain

3. Why is meiosis important?

Creating Haploid Cells

The result of meiosis is haploid sex cells. This helps maintain the correct number of chromosomes in each generation of offspring. The formation of haploid cells also is important because it allows for genetic variation. How does this happen? Sex cells can have different sets of chromosomes, depending on how chromosomes line up during metaphase I. Because a cell only gets one chromosome from each pair of homologous chromosomes, the resulting sex cells can be different.

The genetic makeup of offspring is a combination of chromosomes from two sex cells. Variation in the sex cells results in more genetic variation in the next generation.

How do mitosis and meiosis differ? TEKS 7.14(B), (C)

Sometimes, it's hard to remember the differences between mitosis and meiosis. Review these processes in **Table 2.**

During mitosis and cell division, a body cell and its nucleus divide once and produce two identical cells. These processes are important for growth and repair or replacement of damaged tissue. Some organisms reproduce by these processes. The two daughter cells produced by mitosis and cell division have the same genetic information.

During meiosis, a reproductive cell and its nucleus divide twice and produce four cells—two pairs of identical haploid cells. Each cell has half the number of chromosomes as the original cell. Meiosis occurs in the reproductive organs of multicellular organisms. Meiosis forms sex cells used for sexual reproduction.

Watch ▶

Table 2	Types of Cell Division	*Go Online!*
Characteristic	**Meiosis**	**Mitosis and Cell Division**
Number of chromosomes in parent cell	diploid	diploid
Type of parent cell	reproductive	body
Number of divisions of nucleus	2	1
Number of daughter cells produced	4	2
Chromosome number in daughter cells	haploid	diploid
Function	forms sperm and egg cells	growth, cell repair, some types of reproduction

---

Math Skills **Math** TEKS 7.1(A); 7.3(A); 7.4(D)

Use Proportions

An equation that shows that two ratios are equivalent is a proportion. The ratios $\frac{1}{2}$ and $\frac{3}{6}$ are equivalent, so they can be written as $\frac{1}{2} = \frac{3}{6}$.

You can use proportions to figure out how many daughter cells will be produced during mitosis. If you know that one cell produces two daughter cells at the end of mitosis, you can use proportions to calculate how many daughter cells will be produced by eight cells undergoing mitosis.

Set up an equation of the two ratios.	$\frac{1}{2} = \frac{8}{y}$
Cross-multiply.	$1 \times y = 8 \times 2$
	$1y = 16$
Divide each side by 1.	$y = 16$

Practice

You know that one cell produces four daughter cells at the end of meiosis. How many daughter cells would be produced if eight sex cells undergo meiosis?

Check Tutor

Go Online! ✓ 💬

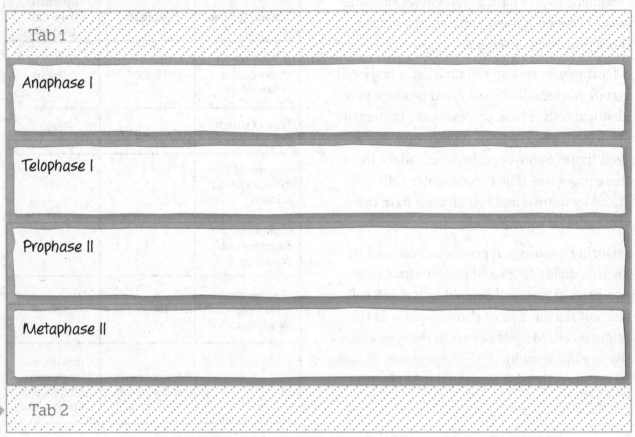

FOLDABLES®

Cut out the Lesson 13.3 Foldable in the back of the book. Use it to describe and illustrate the phases of meiosis.

Tab 1

Anaphase I

Telophase I

Prophase II

Metaphase II

Tab 2

Tape here

Tape here

Connect it! In the space below, **draw** a Venn diagram that compares mitosis and meiosis.

Advantages of Sexual Reproduction TEKS 7.14(B), (C)

Did you ever wonder why a brother and a sister might not look alike? The answer is sexual reproduction. The main advantage of sexual reproduction is that offspring inherit half their DNA from each parent. Offspring are not likely to inherit the same DNA from the same parents. Different DNA means that each offspring has a different set of traits. This results in genetic variation among the offspring.

Genetic Variation

As you just read, genetic variation exists among humans. You can look at your friends to see genetic variation in hair color, eye color, height, and many other physical traits.

Genetic variation occurs in all organisms that reproduce sexually. Consider the plants shown in **Figure 5.** The plants are members of the same species, but they have different traits, such as the ability to resist disease.

Due to genetic variation, individuals within a population have slight differences. These differences might be an advantage if the environment changes. Some individuals might have traits that enable them to survive unusually harsh conditions such as a drought or severe cold. Other individuals might have traits that make them resistant to disease.

Describe

4. How does cassava mosaic disease affect cassava leaves?

_____

_____

_____

_____

_____

_____

Disease-resistant cassava leaves

Cassava leaves with cassava mosaic disease

Figure 5 These plants belong to the same species. However, one is more disease-resistant than the other.

Selective Breeding

Did you know that broccoli, kohlrabi, bok choy, and cabbage descended from one type of mustard plant? It's true. More than 2,000 years ago farmers noticed that some mustard plants had different traits, such as larger leaves or bigger flower buds. The farmers started to choose which traits they wanted by selecting certain plants to reproduce and grow. For example, some farmers chose only the plants with the biggest flowers and stems and planted their seeds. Over time, the offspring of these plants became what we know today as broccoli, shown in **Figure 6.** This process is called selective breeding. Selective breeding has been used to develop many types of plants and animals that have desirable traits. It is another example of the benefits of sexual reproduction.

Selective Breeding

Figure 6 The wild mustard is the common ancestor to all these plants.

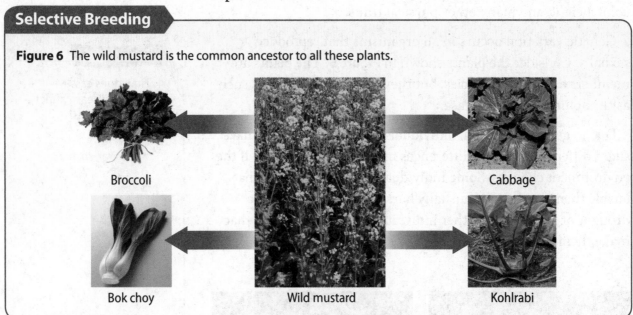

Broccoli

Cabbage

Bok choy

Wild mustard

Kohlrabi

Disadvantages of Sexual Reproduction

Although sexual reproduction produces more genetic variation, it does have some disadvantages. Sexual reproduction takes time and energy. Organisms have to grow and develop until they are mature enough to produce sex cells. Then the organisms have to form sex cells—either eggs or sperm. Before they can reproduce, organisms usually have to find mates. Searching for a mate requires energy and can take a long time. The search for a mate might also expose individuals to predators, diseases, or harsh environmental conditions. In addition, sexual reproduction is limited by certain factors. For example, fertilization cannot take place during pregnancy, which can last as long as two years in some mammals.

Determine

5. Underline the disadvantages of sexual reproduction.

Explain how the process of meiosis relates to the way in which two siblings resemble but are not exact copies of their parents or each other. **TEKS** 7.14(B)

_____

_____

_____

_____

_____

_____

Connect it! **Draw** an example of a family trait that illustrates your explanation. **TEKS** 7.14(B)

Sexual Reproduction and Meiosis

Use Vocabulary

1. **Distinguish** between *haploid* and *diploid*.
   TEKS 7.14(B) *supporting*

Apply the Essential Questions

2. **Define** sexual reproduction.
   TEKS 7.14(B) *supporting*

3. **Explain** how the result of meiosis and cytokinesis affects inherited traits.
   TEKS 7.14(C) *supporting*

4. Which sentence describes an advantage of sexual reproduction? **TEKS** 7.14(B) *supporting*

   A Offspring are identical to the parents.

   B Offspring with genetic variation are produced.

   C Organisms don't have to search for a mate.

   D Reproduction is rapid.

H.O.T. Question (Higher Order Thinking)

5. **Form a hypothesis** about the effect of a mistake in separating homologous chromosomes during meiosis.
   TEKS 7.14(B) *supporting*

Writing in Science

6. **Write** a plot for a short story that describes an environmental change and the importance of genetic variation in helping a species survive that change. Include characters, a setting, a climax, and an ending for your plot.
   TEKS 7.14(B) *supporting*

Math Skills **Math TEKS** 7.1(A); 7.3(A); 7.4(D)

Use Proportions

7. How many daughter cells would be produced if 32 sex cells undergo meiosis?

Check Tutor

Go Online! ✓ 💬

The Spider
Mating Dance

Meet Norman Platnick, a scientist studying spiders.

Norman Platnick is fascinated by all spider species—from the dwarf tarantula-like spiders of Panama to the blind spiders of New Zealand. These are just two of the more than 1,400 species he has discovered worldwide.

How does Platnick identify new species? One way is the pedipalps. Every spider has two pedipalps, but they vary in shape and size among the more than 40,000 species. Pedipalps look like legs but function more like antennae and mouthparts. Male spiders use their pedipalps to aid in reproduction.

Getting Ready When a male spider is ready to mate, he places a drop of sperm onto a sheet of silk he constructs. Then he dips his pedipalps into the drop to draw up the sperm.

Finding a Mate The male finds a female of the same species by touch or by sensing certain chemicals she releases.

Courting and Mating Males of some species court a female with a special dance. For other species, a male might present a female with a gift, such as a fly wrapped in silk. During mating, the male uses his pedipalps to transfer sperm to the female.

What happens to the male after mating? That depends on the species. Some are eaten by the female, and others move on to find new mates.

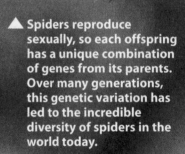

▲ Spiders reproduce sexually, so each offspring has a unique combination of genes from its parents. Over many generations, this genetic variation has led to the incredible diversity of spiders in the world today.

◄ Norman Platnick is an arachnologist (uh rak NAH luh just) at the American Museum of Natural History. Arachnologists are scientists who study spiders.

AMERICAN MUSEUM ᴏꜰ NATURAL HISTORY

It's Your Turn!

RESEARCH Select a species of spider and research its mating rituals. What does a male of the species do to court a female? What is the role of the female? What happens to the spiderlings after they hatch? Use images to illustrate a report on your research.

13.4 Asexual Reproduction

Plants on Plants? Look closely at the edges of this plant's leaves. Tiny plants are growing there. This type of plant can reproduce without meiosis and fertilization. How do you think this happens?

Write your response in your interactive notebook.

LAB Manager

Go to your Lab Manual or visit connectED.mcgraw-hill.com to perform the labs for this lesson.

MiniLAB: *What parts of plants can grow?*

TEKS 7.2(A), (C), (E); 7.4(A); 7.14(B)

LAB: *Mitosis and Meiosis*

TEKS 7.1(A); 7.2(A), (E); 7.3(A), (B); 7.4(A); 7.14(B)

Explore Activity

TEKS 7.1(A); 7.2(A), (C), (E); 7.4(A), (B); 7.14(B)

How do yeast reproduce?

Some organisms can produce offspring without meiosis or fertilization. You can observe this process when you add sugar and warm water to dried yeast.

Procedure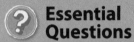

1. Read and complete a lab safety form.

2. Pour 125 mL of **water** into a **beaker.** The water should be at a temperature of 34°C.

3. Add 5 g of **sugar** and 5 g of **yeast** to the water. Stir slightly. Record your observations after 5 minutes in your Lab Manual.

4. Using a **dropper,** put a drop of the yeast solution on a **microscope slide.** Place a **coverslip** over the drop.

5. View the yeast solution under a **microscope.** Draw what you see.

Think About This

1. What evidence did you observe that yeast reproduce?

2. How do you think this process differs from sexual reproduction?

3. How do you think the result of this process might differ from the result of sexual reproduction?

TEKS in this Lesson

7.14(B) Compare the results of uniform or diverse offspring from sexual reproduction or asexual reproduction

Also covers: 7.1(A); 7.2(A), (C), (E); 7.3(A), (B); 7.4(A), (B)

Essential Questions

- What is asexual reproduction, and why is it beneficial?
- How do the types of asexual reproduction differ?

Vocabulary

asexual reproduction
fission
budding
regeneration
vegetative reproduction
cloning

Figure 1 Due to a fast reproduction rate, mold can begin growing on a forgotten sandwich in one or two days.

What is asexual reproduction? **TEKS** 7.14(B)

Lunch is over, and you are in a rush to get to class. You wrap up your half-eaten sandwich and toss it into your locker. A week goes by before you spot the sandwich in the corner of your locker. As shown in **Figure 1,** the surface of the bread is now covered with fuzzy mold—not very appetizing. How did that happen?

The mold on the sandwich is a type of fungus (FUN gus). A fungus releases enzymes that break down organic matter, such as food. It has structures that penetrate and anchor to food, much like roots anchor plants to soil. A fungus can multiply quickly in part because generally a fungus can reproduce sexually or asexually. Recall that sexual reproduction involves two parent organisms and the processes of meiosis and fertilization. Offspring inherit half their DNA from each parent, resulting in genetic variation among the offspring.

In **asexual reproduction,** *one parent organism produces off- spring without meiosis and fertilization.* Because the offspring inherit all their DNA from one parent, they are genetically identical to each other and to their parent.

Identify

1. What are the key points about asexual reproduction? Cross out the terms that do not apply to the process.

single parent organism	~~fertilization~~	genetically identical	~~meiosis~~
~~diploid parent cells~~	offspring produced	~~2 parent organisms~~	haploid daughter cells

Types of Asexual Reproduction TEKS 7.14(B)

There are many different types of organisms that reproduce by asexual reproduction. In addition to fungi, bacteria, protists, plants, and animals can reproduce asexually. In this lesson, you will learn how organisms reproduce asexually.

Fission

Recall that prokaryotes have a simpler cell structure than eukaryotes. A prokaryote's DNA is not contained in a nucleus. For this reason, mitosis does not occur and cell division in a prokaryote is a simpler process than in a eukaryote. *Cell division in prokaryotes that forms two genetically identical cells is known as* **fission.**

Fission begins when a prokaryote's DNA molecule is copied. Each copy attaches to the cell membrane. Then, the cell begins to grow longer, pulling the two copies of DNA apart. At the same time, the cell membrane begins to pinch inward along the middle of the cell. Finally, the cell splits and forms two new identical offspring. The original cell no longer exists.

As shown in **Figure 2,** *E. coli*, a common bacterium, divides through fission. Some bacteria can divide every 20 minutes. At that rate, 512 bacteria can be produced from one original bacterium in about three hours.

Word Origin

fission from Latin *fissionem*, means "a breaking up, cleaving"

Interpret

2. What happens to the original cell's chromosome during fission?

   The chromosomes are copied.

Figure 2 Bacteria can divide very rapidly through fission.

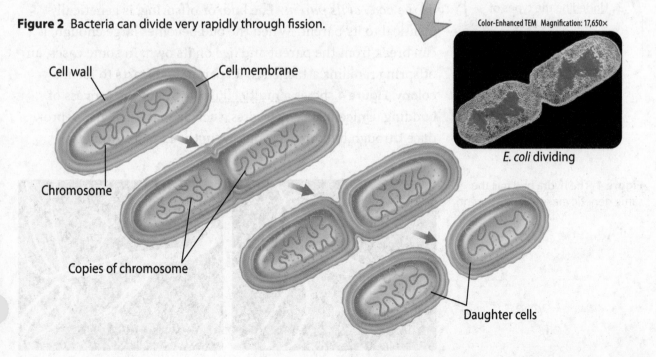

Cell wall

Cell membrane

Chromosome

Copies of chromosome

Color-Enhanced TEM   Magnification: 17,650×

E. coli dividing

Daughter cells

Figure 3 During mitotic cell division, an amoeba divides its chromosomes and cell contents evenly between the daughter cells.

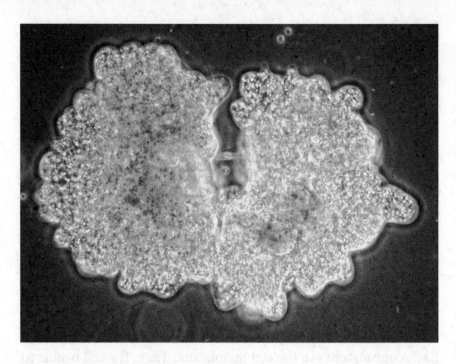

Mitotic Cell Division

Many unicellular eukaryotes reproduce by mitotic cell division. In this type of asexual reproduction, an organism forms two offspring through mitosis and cell division. In **Figure 3,** an amoeba's nucleus has divided by mitosis. Next, the cytoplasm and its contents divide through cytokinesis, and two new amoebas form.

Budding

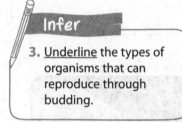

Infer

3. Underline the types of organisms that can reproduce through budding.

In **budding,** *a new organism grows by mitosis and cell division on the body of its parent.* The bud, or offspring, is genetically identical to its parent. When the bud becomes large enough, it can break from the parent and live on its own. In some cases, an offspring remains attached to its parent and starts to form a colony. **Figure 4** shows a multicellular hydra in the process of budding. Unicellular eukaryotes, such as yeast, can also reproduce through budding, as you saw in the Explore Activity.

Figure 4 The hydra bud has the same genetic makeup as its parent.

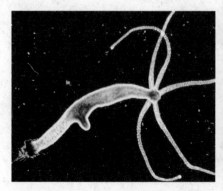
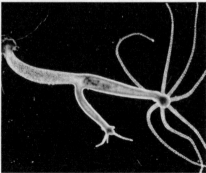

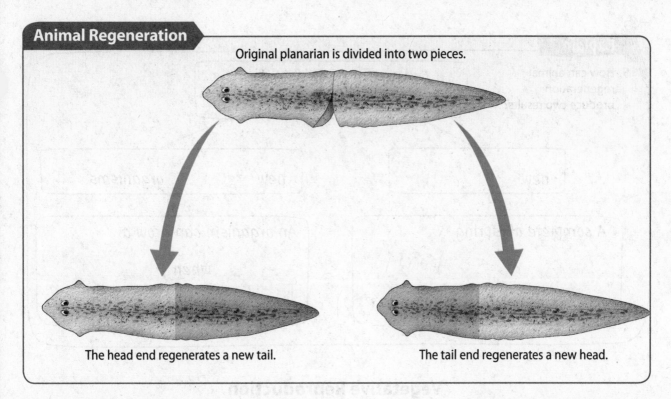

Animal Regeneration

Original planarian is divided into two pieces.

The head end regenerates a new tail.

The tail end regenerates a new head.

Figure 5 A planarian can reproduce through regeneration.

Animal Regeneration

Another type of asexual reproduction, **regeneration,** *occurs when an offspring grows from a piece of its parent.* The ability to regenerate a new organism varies greatly among animals.

Producing New Organisms Some sea stars have five arms. If it is separated from the parent sea star, each arm has the potential to grow into a new organism. To regenerate a new sea star, the arm must contain a part of the central disk of the parent. If conditions are right, one five-armed sea star can produce as many as five new organisms.

Sea urchins, sea cucumbers, sponges, and planarians, such as the one shown in **Figure 5,** can also reproduce through regeneration. Notice that each piece of the original planarian becomes a new organism. As with all types of asexual reproduction, the offspring is genetically identical to the parent.

Producing New Parts When you hear the term *regeneration,* you might think about a salamander regrowing a lost tail or leg. Regeneration of damaged or lost body parts is common in many animals. Newts, tadpoles, crabs, hydras, and zebra fish are able to regenerate body parts. Humans are able to regenerate some damaged body parts, such as the skin and the liver. This type of regeneration, however, is not considered to be asexual reproduction. It only replaces a lost or damaged body part; it does not produce a new organism.

Academic Vocabulary

potential
(noun) possibility

Explain

4. What is true of all cases of asexual reproduction?

The offspring is genetically identical to the parent.

5. How can animal regeneration produce two results?

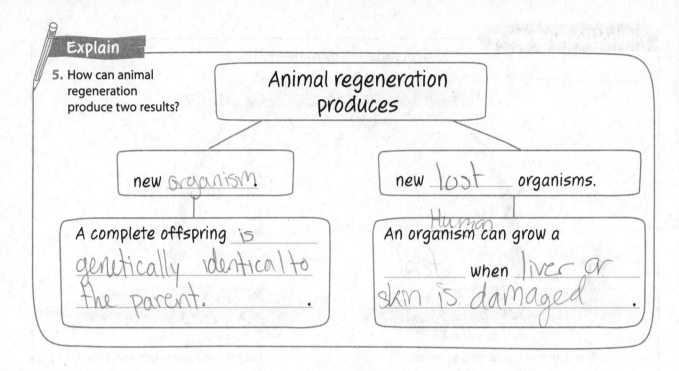

Animal regeneration produces

new ~~organism~~.

A complete offspring is genetically identical to the parent.

new lost organisms.

An organism can grow a Human ____ when liver or skin is damaged.

Vegetative Reproduction

Plants can also reproduce asexually in a process similar to regeneration. **Vegetative reproduction** *is a form of asexual reproduction in which offspring grow from a part of a parent plant.* For example, the strawberry plants shown in **Figure 6** send out long horizontal stems called stolons. Wherever a stolon touches the ground, it can produce roots. When the stolons have grown roots, a new plant can grow—even if the stolons have broken off from the parent plant. Each new plant grown from a stolon is genetically identical to the parent plant.

Vegetative reproduction usually involves structures such as the roots, the stems, and the leaves of plants. In addition to strawberries, many other plants can reproduce by this method, including raspberries, potatoes, and geraniums.

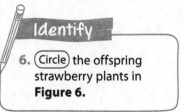

LAB Manager

MiniLAB: *What parts of plants can grow?*
TEKS 7.2(A), (C), (E); 7.4(A); 7.14(B)

Figure 6 The smaller plants were grown from stolons produced by the parent plant.

Identify

6. Circle the offspring strawberry plants in **Figure 6.**

Cloning

Fission, budding, and regeneration are types of asexual reproduction that can produce genetically identical offspring in nature. In the past, the term *cloning* described any process that produced genetically identical offspring. Today, however, the word usually refers to a technique developed by scientists and performed in laboratories. **Cloning** *is a type of asexual reproduction performed in a laboratory that produces identical individuals from a cell or from a cluster of cells taken from a multicellular organism.* Farmers and scientists often use cloning to make copies of organisms or cells that have desirable traits, such as large flowers.

Plant Cloning Some plants can be cloned using a method called tissue culture, as shown in **Figure 7.** Tissue culture enables plant growers and scientists to make many copies of a plant that has desirable traits, such as sweet fruit. Also, a greater number of plants can be produced more quickly by cloning than by vegetative reproduction.

Tissue culture also enables plant growers to reproduce plants that might have become infected with a disease. To clone such a plant, a scientist can use cells from a part of a plant where they are rapidly undergoing mitosis and cell division. This part of a plant is called a meristem. Cells in meristems are disease-free. Therefore, if a plant becomes infected with a disease, it can be cloned using meristem cells.

Figure 7 New carrot plants can be produced from cells of a carrot root using tissue culture techniques.

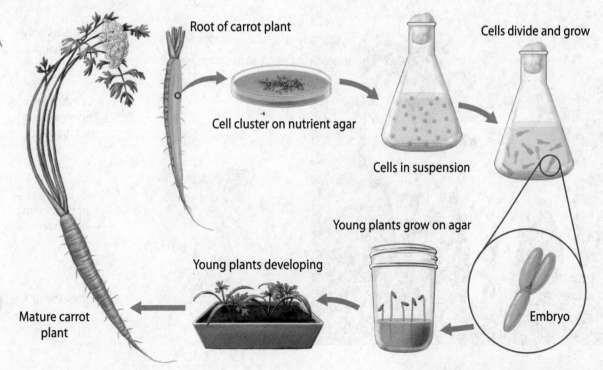

Root of carrot plant

Cell cluster on nutrient agar

Cells divide and grow

Cells in suspension

Young plants grow on agar

Young plants developing

Mature carrot plant

Embryo

Animal Cloning In addition to cloning plants, scientists have been able to clone many animals. Because all of a clone's chromosomes come from one parent (the donor of the nucleus), the clone is a genetic copy of its parent. The first mammal cloned was a sheep named Dolly. **Figure 8** illustrates how this was done.

Scientists are currently working to save some endangered species from extinction by cloning. Although cloning is an exciting advancement in science, some people are concerned about the high cost and the ethics of this technique. Ethical issues include the possibility of human cloning. You might be asked to consider issues like this during your lifetime.

Recall

7. Highlight why an animal clone is a genetic copy of its parent.

Figure 8 Scientists used two different sheep to produce the cloned sheep known as Dolly.

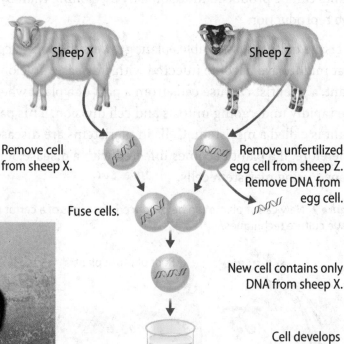

Sheep X

Sheep Z

Remove cell from sheep X.

Remove unfertilized egg cell from sheep Z. Remove DNA from egg cell.

Fuse cells.

New cell contains only DNA from sheep X.

Cell develops into embryo in the laboratory.

Sheep Z

Embryo is implanted in sheep Z.

Dolly

Clone of sheep X

Advantages of Asexual Reproduction

What are the advantages to organisms of reproducing asexually? Asexual reproduction enables organisms to reproduce without a mate. Recall that searching for a mate takes time and energy. Asexual reproduction also enables some organisms to rapidly produce a large number of offspring. For example, the crabgrass shown in **Figure 9** reproduces asexually by underground stems called stolons. This enables one plant to spread and colonize an area in a short period of time.

Disadvantages of Asexual Reproduction

Although asexual reproduction usually enables organisms to reproduce quickly, it does have some disadvantages. Asexual reproduction produces offspring that are genetically identical to their parent. This results in little genetic variation within a population. Why is genetic variation important? Recall that genetic variation can give organisms a better chance of surviving if the environment changes. Think of the crabgrass. Imagine that all the crabgrass plants in a lawn are genetically identical to their parent plant. If a certain weed killer can kill the parent plant, then it can kill all the crabgrass plants in the lawn. This might be good for your lawn, but it is a disadvantage for the crabgrass.

Another disadvantage of asexual reproduction involves genetic changes, called mutations, that can occur. If an organism has a harmful mutation in its cells, the mutation will be passed to asexually reproduced offspring. This could affect the offspring's ability to survive.

Figure 9 Crabgrass can spread quickly because it reproduces asexually.

Classify

8. Which features of asexual reproduction are advantages and which features are disadvantages? Write "A" for advantage and "D" for disadvantage in the center column of the table at right. Explain your reasoning in the right-hand column.

Does not require a mate	A	Searching for a mate takes time and energy.
Can occur rapidly	A	This enables one plant to spread and colonize an area in a short period of time.
Produces little genetic variation	D	Genetic variation gives an organism a better chance of survival in environment changes.

Summarize it!

Identify the 6 types of asexual reproduction. Give an example of each type.

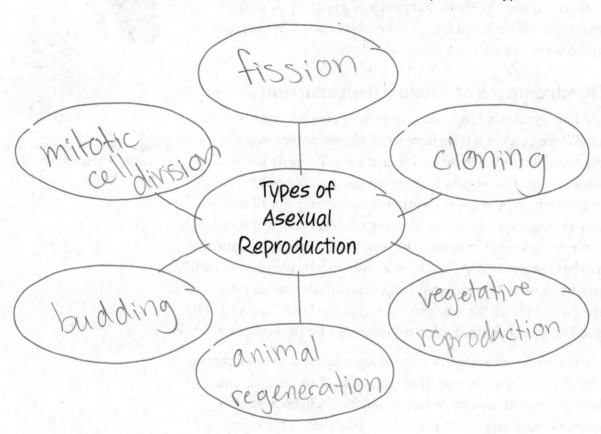

fission

mitotic cell division

cloning

Types of Asexual Reproduction

budding

animal regeneration

vegetative reproduction

Connect it! **Choose** one of the types of asexual reproduction identified above. **Explain** how the results of that type of asexual reproduction differ from the results of sexual reproduction. **TEKS** 7.14(B)

Budding only has one parent. The offspring is genetically identical to its parent. The bud stays attached to its parent and when it is big enough the bud can break away from its parent and live on its own.

Summarize it!

Asexual Reproduction

Use Vocabulary

1. In ___asexual reproduction___, only one parent organism produces offspring. **TEKS** 7.14(B) *supporting*

2. **Define** the term *cloning* in your own words. **TEKS** 7.14(B) *supporting*

   A clone's chromosomes come from only one parent so the offspring is genetically identical.

Apply the Essential Questions

3. **Give** two reasons why asexual reproduction is beneficial.
   TEKS 7.14(B) *supporting*

   Asexual reproduction does not include a mate and can occur rapidly.

4. **Compare and contrast** the results of sexual reproduction and asexual reproduction. **TEKS** 7.14(B) *supporting*

   Asexual reproduction involves the offspring being genetically identical. Sexual reproduction involves the offspring being different than the parents.

 **H.O.T. Questions** (Higher Order Thinking)

5. **Analyze** Explain why the form of reproduction shown in the figure below is an advantage for the organism.
   TEKS 7.14(B) *supporting*

   The plant spreads rapidly to colonize an area in only a short period of time

6. **Critique** the following statement: All organisms have two parents.
   TEKS 7.14(B) *supporting*

   This is false because asexual production does not include a mate and only includes one parent.

Writing in Science

7. Think of all the advantages of sexual and asexual reproduction. Use these ideas to summarize why organisms reproduce. Write your response on a separate sheet of paper. **TEKS** 7.14(B) *supporting*

Test-Taking Strategy

Note Taking Proper study skills will greatly improve your ability to perform well on tests, and a very important study skill to master is note taking. Proper note taking will give you an advantage when reviewing your lessons. Quality notes will help keep you organized, help you analyze the material, and help make the material more meaningful to you. Your stress level will be greatly reduced if you know that you have taken quality notes and used them to prepare for your test.

Note-Taking Strategies

Science Chapter Lesson 2 Notes pg. 1

Reflection Space   Summary Space

1. Take Notes – In your write-in textbook, highlight or underline the most important points or words you cover throughout the lesson.

2. Rewrite – As soon as you can, either after class or at home, summarize your notes in your interactive notebook to make them organized and concise. Make sure to label your notes, including the chapter and lesson number.

3. Reflect – When reviewing your summary, jot down small notes of examples you remember or important points you want to remember beside the paragraph.

4. Review – Take a few minutes each night to review your notes, summary, and important points. Try to recite to yourself why each point is important to the lesson. Repetition helps to engrain the material.

TIP: Do **NOT** cram! Daily review of quality notes is a far more effective and efficient way to learn. This will help you reduce testing anxiety and perform your best!

Multiple Choice

1

> Susana visits with four generations of her family. Her great-grandmother shows her an old family photo of Susana's great-aunts and great-uncles when they were children. Susana is surprised to see that one of the great-uncles looks almost exactly like her younger brother does now. They have the same distinctive hairline and eye shape. Her great-grandmother tells her that it is the result of heredity.

Which best describes the sequence of inheritance that led to Susana having a brother who has the same hairline and eye shape as her great-uncle? **TEKS** 7.14(A)

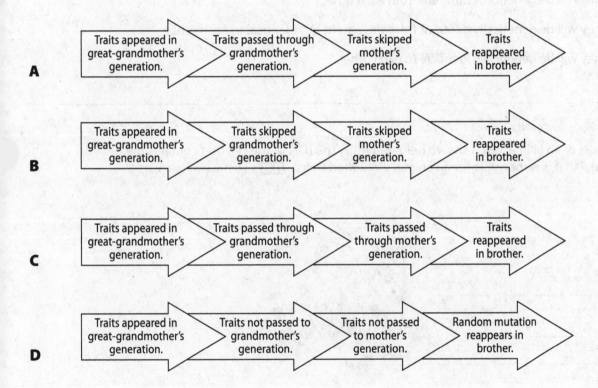

A Traits appeared in great-grandmother's generation. → Traits passed through grandmother's generation. → Traits skipped mother's generation. → Traits reappeared in brother.

B Traits appeared in great-grandmother's generation. → Traits skipped grandmother's generation. → Traits skipped mother's generation. → Traits reappeared in brother.

C Traits appeared in great-grandmother's generation. → Traits passed through grandmother's generation. → Traits passed through mother's generation. → Traits reappeared in brother.

D Traits appeared in great-grandmother's generation. → Traits not passed to grandmother's generation. → Traits not passed to mother's generation. → Random mutation reappears in brother.

2 A planarian, shown below, is a flatworm. It reproduces sexually and also can regenerate from a severed body part. The planarian below has been cut in half. What can you infer about the new individuals produced? **TEKS** 7.14(B) *supporting*

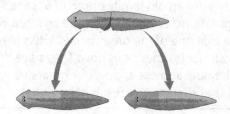

A They will be genetically identical to each other but different from the parent.

B They will be genetically different from each other.

C They will be genetically different from the parent but identical to each other.

D They will be genetically identical to each other.

---

3 A model of an animal cell is shown below. Identify the part of the cell that contains the genetic material that is responsible for an animal's inherited traits. **TEKS** 7.14(C) *supporting;* 7.3(B)

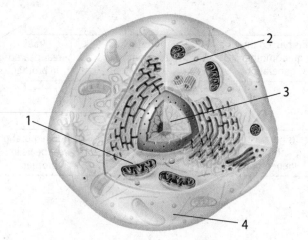

A 1

B 2

C 3

D 4

4   A tree produces seeds in pods when wind-borne pollen from another tree of the same species reaches the flowers. Each seed contains genetic information so the seed can grow into an adult tree. Which statement best describes the result of this process? **TEKS** 7.14(B) *supporting*

   A   The tree produces a large number of genetically diverse offspring.

   B   The tree produces a large number of genetically identical offspring.

   C   The tree produces a small number of offspring that are identical to the female parent.

   D   The tree produces a small number of offspring that are identical to the male parent.

---

5   Hydras are organisms that live in freshwater environments. They have a tubelike body and a mouth at one end. Around the mouth are stinging tentacles that help to capture food. Depending on the conditions, hydras can reproduce sexually or asexually. **TEKS** 7.14(B) *supporting*

Based on your observations, which statement best describes what is happening to the hydra in the figure above?

   A   The hydra is reproducing asexually by budding a new hydra.

   B   The hydra is reproducing asexually by splitting in two.

   C   The hydra is reproducing sexually by grafting to another hydra.

   D   The hydra is reproducing sexually by releasing sex cells into the water.

My Notes

PERIODIC TABLE OF THE ELEMENTS

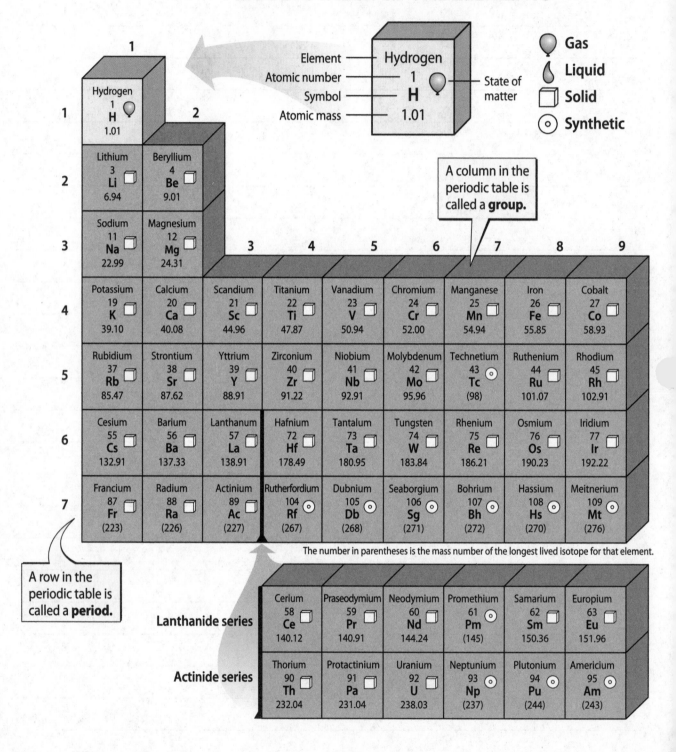

Key

- Metal
- Metalloid
- Nonmetal
- Recently discovered

18					
					Helium 2 He 4.00

13	14	15	16	17	
Boron 5 B 10.81	Carbon 6 C 12.01	Nitrogen 7 N 14.01	Oxygen 8 O 16.00	Fluorine 9 F 19.00	Neon 10 Ne 20.18

			Aluminum 13 Al 26.98	Silicon 14 Si 28.09	Phosphorus 15 P 30.97	Sulfur 16 S 32.07	Chlorine 17 Cl 35.45	Argon 18 Ar 39.95

10	11	12						
Nickel 28 Ni 58.69	Copper 29 Cu 63.55	Zinc 30 Zn 65.38	Gallium 31 Ga 69.72	Germanium 32 Ge 72.64	Arsenic 33 As 74.92	Selenium 34 Se 78.96	Bromine 35 Br 79.90	Krypton 36 Kr 83.80
Palladium 46 Pd 106.42	Silver 47 Ag 107.87	Cadmium 48 Cd 112.41	Indium 49 In 114.82	Tin 50 Sn 118.71	Antimony 51 Sb 121.76	Tellurium 52 Te 127.60	Iodine 53 I 126.90	Xenon 54 Xe 131.29
Platinum 78 Pt 195.08	Gold 79 Au 196.97	Mercury 80 Hg 200.59	Thallium 81 Tl 204.38	Lead 82 Pb 207.20	Bismuth 83 Bi 208.98	Polonium 84 Po (209)	Astatine 85 At (210)	Radon 86 Rn (222)
Darmstadtium 110 Ds (281)	Roentgenium 111 Rg (280)	Copernicium 112 Cn (285)	Ununtrium * 113 Uut (284)	Flerovium 114 Fl (289)	Ununpentium * 115 Uup (288)	Livermorium 116 Lv (293)		Ununoctium * 118 Uuo (294)

* The names and symbols for elements 113, 115, and 118 are temporary. Final names will be selected when the elements' discoveries are verified.

Gadolinium 64 Gd 157.25	Terbium 65 Tb 158.93	Dysprosium 66 Dy 162.50	Holmium 67 Ho 164.93	Erbium 68 Er 167.26	Thulium 69 Tm 168.93	Ytterbium 70 Yb 173.05	Lutetium 71 Lu 174.97
Curium 96 Cm (247)	Berkelium 97 Bk (247)	Californium 98 Cf (251)	Einsteinium 99 Es (252)	Fermium 100 Fm (257)	Mendelevium 101 Md (258)	Nobelium 102 No (259)	Lawrencium 103 Lr (262)

Notebook Foldables

What are they and how do I create them?

Foldables are three-dimensional graphic organizers that help you create study guides for each lesson in your book.

Step 1 Go to the back of your book to find the Notebook Foldable for the lesson you are currently studying. Follow the cutting and assembly instructions at the top of the page.

Step 2 Find the Notebook Foldable page in the lesson. Match up the tabs and attach your Notebook Foldable to this page. Dotted tabs show where to place it on the page. Striped tabs indicate where to tape the Notebook Foldable.

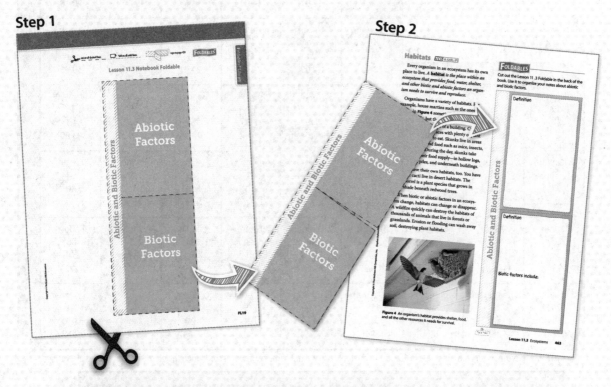

How do I complete my Notebook Foldable?

Each lesson's Notebook Foldable will be different. As you study the lesson, fill out the Notebook Foldable. Use it as a study guide as you learn the lesson material.

Meet Foldables Author Dinah Zike

Dinah Zike is known for designing hands-on manipulatives that are used nationally and internationally by teachers and parents. Dinah is an explosion of energy and ideas. Her excitement and joy for learning inspires everyone she touches.

✂ cut on all dashed lines   ⬜️ fold on all solid lines   ⬛️ tape to page 15   **FOLDABLES**

Lesson 1.1 Notebook Foldable

Results of Scientific Investigations

Technology	New Materials	Possible Explanations

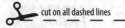 cut on all dashed lines
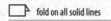 fold on all solid lines
 tape to page 15

FOLDABLES

Lesson 1.1 Notebook Foldable

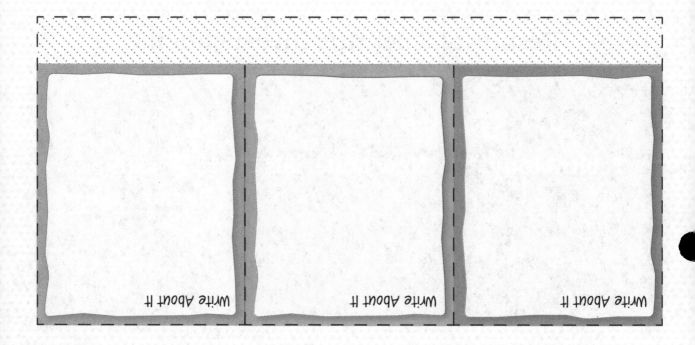

Write About It

Write About It

Write About It

Lesson 2.1 Notebook Foldable

Upper Epidermis

Lower Epidermis

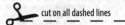 cut on all dashed lines   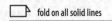 fold on all solid lines   tape to page 42   **FOLDABLES**

Lesson 2.1 Notebook Foldable

Tab 1

Tab 2

Lesson 3.1 Notebook Foldable

Hydrocarbons

| Alkane | Alkene | Alkyne |

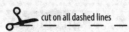 cut on all dashed lines   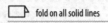 fold on all solid lines   tape to page 86   **FOLDABLES**

Lesson 3.1 Notebook Foldable

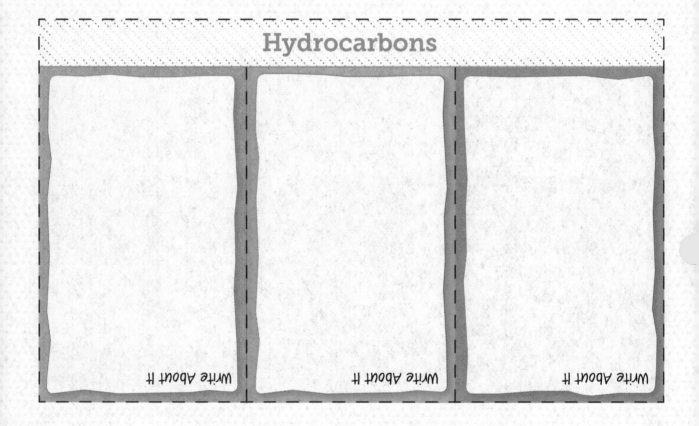

Hydrocarbons

Write About It

Write About It

Write About It

Lesson 4.1 Notebook Foldable

Force is a push or a pull on an object.

Noncontact Forces	Contact Forces

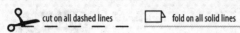 cut on all dashed lines   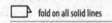 fold on all solid lines   tape to page 132   **FOLDABLES**

Lesson 4.1 Notebook Foldable

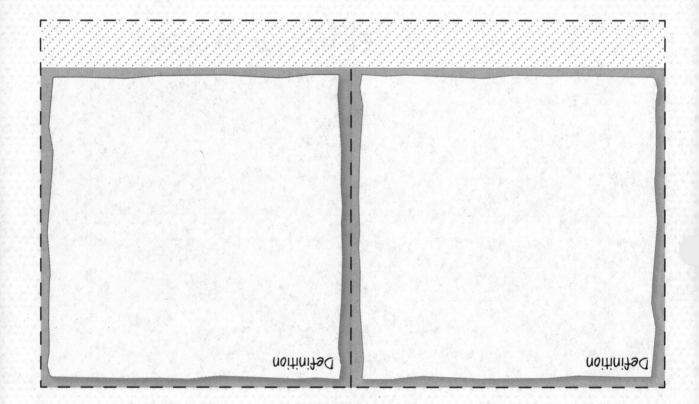

Definition

Definition

Lesson 5.3 Notebook Foldable

Severe Weather

Thunderstorms

Tornadoes

Hurricanes

Winter Storms

Flooding

Extreme Heat/Drought

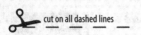 cut on all dashed lines 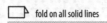 fold on all solid lines tape to page 215   **FOLDABLES**

Lesson 5.3 Notebook Foldable

Write About It

Write About It

Write About It

Write About It

Write About It

Write About It

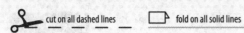
Lesson 6.2 Notebook Foldable

Lakes and Streams

Lakes	Streams

cut on all dashed lines fold on all solid lines tape to page 255

Lesson 6.2 Notebook Foldable

Lakes and Streams

Formation of Streams

Formation of Lakes

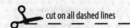 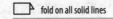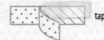
Lesson 7.2 Notebook Foldable

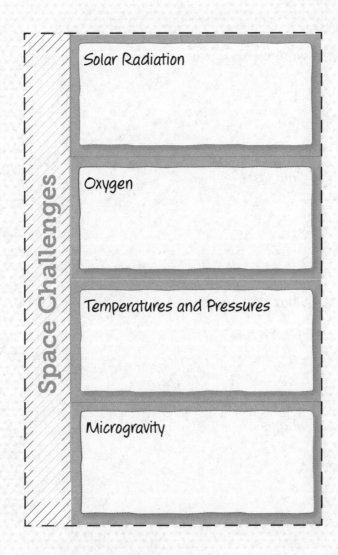

Space Challenges

Solar Radiation

Oxygen

Temperatures and Pressures

Microgravity

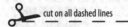 cut on all dashed lines   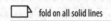 fold on all solid lines   tape to page 293   **FOLDABLES**

Lesson 7.2 Notebook Foldable

What is it?

What is it?

What is it?

What is it?

Lesson 8.1 Notebook Foldable

Two Biomes

| Desert Biome | Temperate Rain Forest Biome |

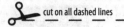 cut on all dashed lines   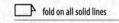 fold on all solid lines   tape to page 311   **FOLDABLES**

Lesson 8.1 Notebook Foldable

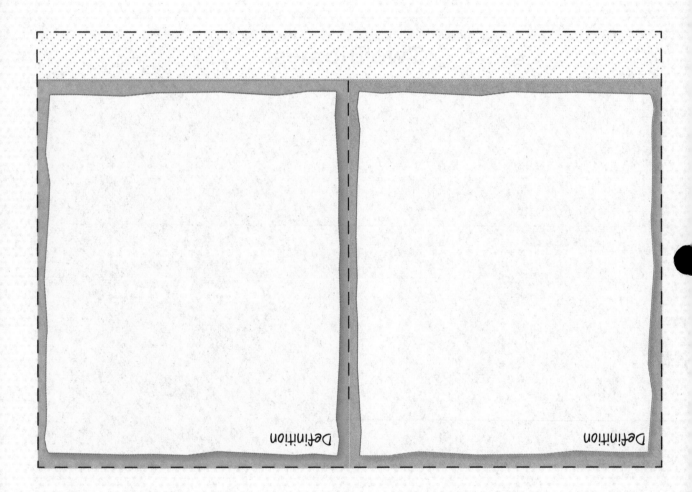

Definition   Definition

Lesson 9.2 Notebook Foldable

Natural Selection	Reproduction	Competition and Predation	Natural Selection
	Variation	Selection	

cut on all dashed lines | fold on all solid lines | tape to page 376 | FOLDABLES

Lesson 9.2 Notebook Foldable

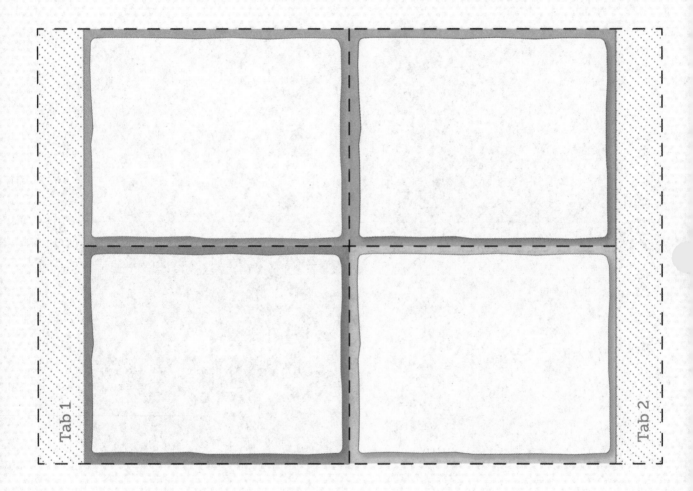

Tab 1

Tab 2

Lesson 10.1 Notebook Foldable

Macromolecules	
Lipids	Nucleic acids
Proteins	Carbohydrates

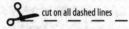 cut on all dashed lines

 fold on all solid lines

tape to page 398

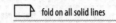 FOLDABLES

Lesson 10.1 Notebook Foldable

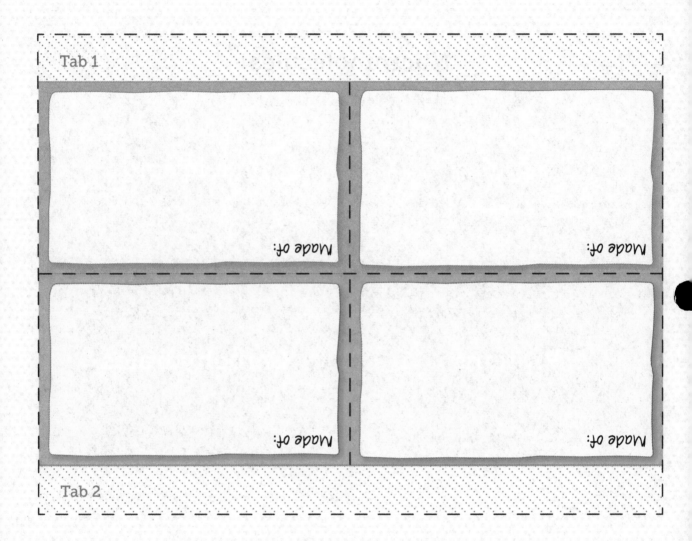

Tab 1

Made of:

Made of:

Made of:

Made of:

Tab 2

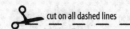 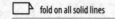
Lesson 11.2 Notebook Foldable

Tab 1   **Human Body Systems**

Skeletal System	**Muscular System**
Nervous System	**Endocrine System**

Tab 2   **Human Body Systems**

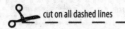 cut on all dashed lines 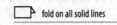 fold on all solid lines 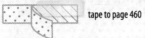 tape to page 460

Lesson 11.2 Notebook Foldable

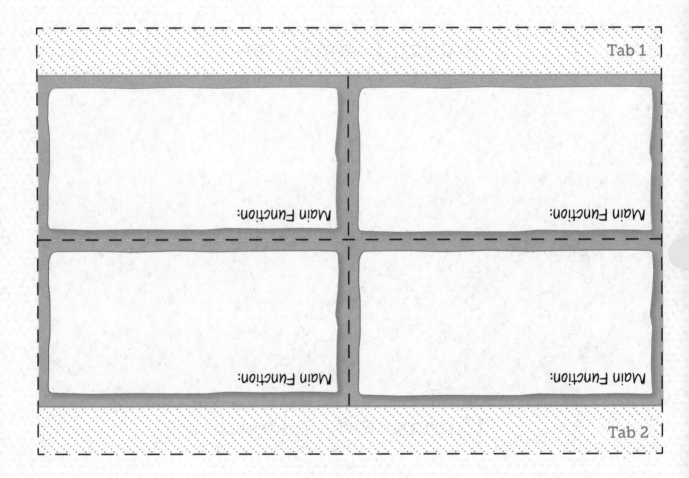

Lesson 12.1 Notebook Foldable

Two Types of Stimuli

Environmental Stimuli	Chemical Stimuli

cut on all dashed lines   fold on all solid lines   tape to page 490   FOLDABLES

Lesson 12.1 Notebook Foldable

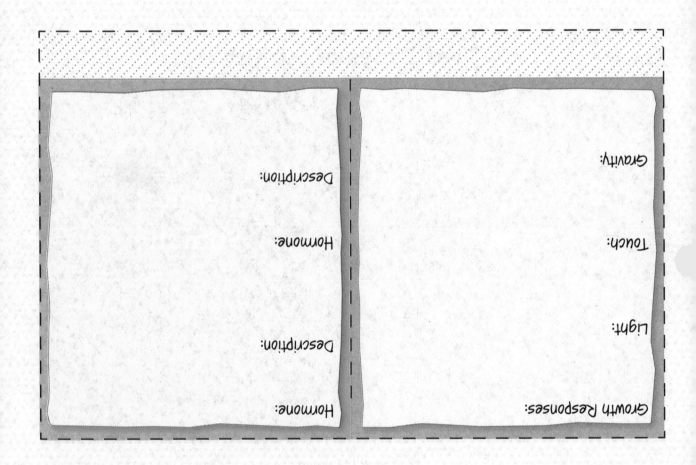

Description:

Hormone:

Description:

Hormone:

Gravity:

Touch:

Light:

Growth Responses:

Lesson 13.3 Notebook Foldable

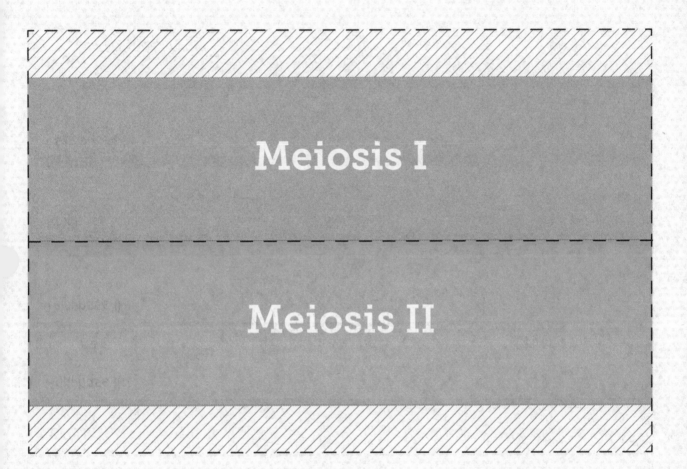

Meiosis I

Meiosis II

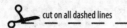 cut on all dashed lines   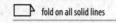 fold on all solid lines   tape to page 554

Lesson 13.3 Notebook Foldable

Tab 1

Metaphase I

Prophase I

Telophase II

Anaphase II

Tab 2

Pronunciation Key

Use the following key to help you sound out words in the glossary.

a	back (BAK)		**ew**	food (FEWD)
ay	day (DAY)		**yoo**	pure (PYOOR)
ah	father (FAH thur)		**yew**	few (FYEW)
ow	flower (FLOW ur)		**uh**	comma (CAH muh)
ar	car (CAR)		**u (+ con)**	rub (RUB)
e	less (LES)		**sh**	shelf (SHELF)
ee	leaf (LEEF)		**ch**	nature (NAY chur)
ih	trip (TRIHP)		**g**	gift (GIHFT)
i (i + com + e)	idea (i DEE uh)		**j**	gem (JEM)
oh	go (GOH)		**ing**	sing (SING)
aw	soft (SAWFT)		**zh**	vision (VIH zhun)
or	orbit (OR buht)		**k**	cake (KAYK)
oy	coin (COYN)		**s**	seed, cent (SEED)
oo	foot (FOOT)		**z**	zone, raise (ZOHN)

English Español

adaptation/amino | **adaptación/aminoácido**

adaptation (a dap TAY shun): an inherited trait that increases an organism's chance of surviving and reproducing in a particular environment (p. 376)

air mass: a large area of air that has uniform temperature, humidity, and pressure (p. 201)

air pressure: the pressure that a column of air exerts on the air, or a surface, below it. (p. 189)

alpine glacier: a glacier that forms in the mountains. (p. 241)

amino (uh MEE noh) **acid:** a carbon compound that contains the two functional groups, amino and carboxyl. (p. 110)

amino (uh MEE noh) **group:** a group consisting of a nitrogen atom covalently bonded to two hydrogen atoms (—NH2). (p. 103)

adaptación: rasgo heredado que aumenta la oportunidad de un organismo de sobrevivir y reproducirse en un medioambiente. (pág. 376)

masa de aire: gran área de aire que tiene temperatura, humedad y presión uniformes. (pág. 201)

presión del aire: presión que una columna de aire ejerce sobre el aire o sobre la superficie debajo de ella. (pág. 189)

glacial alpino: glacial que se forma en las montañas. (pág. 241)

aminoácido: compuesto de carbono que contiene los dos grupos funcionales amino y carboxilo (pág. 110)

aminoácido: compuesto de carbono que contiene los dos grupos funcionales amino y carboxilo (pág. 103)

aquifer: an area of permeable sediment or rock that holds significant amounts of water. (p. 265)

artificial satellite: any human-made object placed in orbit around a body in space (p. 290)

asexual reproduction: a type of reproduction in which one parent organism produces offspring without meiosis and fertilization. (p. 562)

astrobiology: the study of the origin, development, distribution, and future of life on Earth and in the universe (p. 280)

acuífero: área de sedimento permeable o roca que conserva cantidades significativas de agua. (pág. 265)

satélite artificial: cualquier objeto hecho por el ser humano y puesto en órbita alrededor de un cuerpo en el espacio. (pág. 290)

reproducción asexual: tipo de reproducción en la cual un organismo parental produce crías sin mitosis ni fertilización. (pág. 562)

astrobiología: estudio del origen, desarrollo, distribución y futuro de la vida en la Tierra y el universo. (pág. 280)

B

balanced forces: forces acting on an object that combine and form a net force of zero (p. 134)

behavior: the way an organism reacts to other organisms or to its environment (p. 502)

binomial nomenclature (bi NOH mee ul • NOH mun klay chur): a naming system that gives each organism a two-word scientific name. (p. 364)

biological molecule: a large organic molecule in any living organism. (p. 110)

biome: a geographic area on Earth that contains ecosystems with similar biotic and abiotic features. (p. 310)

budding: the process during which a new organism grows by mitosis and cell division on the body of its parent. (p. 564)

fuerzas en equilibrio: fuerzas que actúan sobre un objeto, se combinan y forman una fuerza neta de cero. (pág. 134)

comportamiento: forma en la que un organismo reacciona hacia otros organismos o hacia su medioambiente. (pág. 502)

nomenclatura binomial: sistema de nombrar que le da a cada organismo un nombre científico de dos palabras. (pág. 364)

molécula biológica: molécula orgánica grande de cualquier organismo vivo. (pág. 110)

bioma: área geográfica en la Tierra que contiene ecosistemas con características bióticas y abióticas similares. (pág. 310)

germinación: proceso durante el cual un organismo nuevo crece por medio de mitosis y división celular en el cuerpo de su progenitor. (pág. 564)

C

calorie: the amount of energy it takes to raise the temperature of 1 kg of water by 1°C (p. 441)

carbohydrate (kar boh HI drayt): a group of organic molecules that includes sugars, starches and cellulose. (pp. 112, 400)

carboxyl (kar BAHK sul) group: a group consisting of a carbon atom with a single bond to a hydroxyl group and a double bond to an oxygen atom (—COOH). (p 102)

cell cycle: a cycle of growth, development, and division that most cells in an organism go through. (p. 534)

cell differentiation (dihf uh ren shee AY shun): the process by which cells become different types of cells. (p. 421)

caloría: cantidad de energía necesaria para aumentar la temperatura de 1 kg de agua en 1°C. (pág. 441)

carbohidrato: grupo de moléculas orgánicas que incluye azúcares, almidones y celulosa. (pág. 112, 400)

grupo carboxilo: grupo que consiste en un átomo de carbono unido a un grupo hidroxilo mediante un enlace sencillo y a un átomo de oxígeno mediante un enlace doble (–COOH). (pág. 102)

ciclo celular: ciclo de crecimiento, desarrollo y división por el que pasan la mayoría de células de un organismo. (pág. 534)

diferenciación celular: proceso por el cual las células se convierten en diferentes tipos de células. (pág. 421)

Glossary

cell membrane: a flexible covering that protects the inside of a cell from the environment outside the cell. (p. 407)

cell theory: the theory that states that all living things are made of one or more cells, the cell is the smallest unit of life, and all new cells come from preexisting cells. (p. 395)

cell wall: a stiff structure outside the cell membrane that protects a cell from attack by viruses and other harmful organisms. (p. 407)

cellular respiration: a series of chemical reactions that convert the energy in food molecules into a usable form of energy called ATP. (p. 46)

centromere: a structure that holds sister chromatids together. (p. 536)

chemical energy: energy that is stored in and released from the bonds between atoms (p. 143)

chemosynthesis (kee moh sihn THUH sus): the process during which producers use chemical energy in matter rather than light energy to make food. (p. 69)

chloroplast (KLOR uh plast): a membrane-bound organelle that uses light energy and makes food—a sugar called glucose— from water and carbon dioxide in a process known as photosynthesis. (p. 412)

cladogram: a branched diagram that shows the relationships among organisms, including common ancestors. (p. 366)

climate: the long-term average weather conditions that occur in a particular region (p. 223)

climax community: a stable community that no longer goes through major ecological changes. (p. 344)

cloning: a type of asexual reproduction performed in a laboratory that produces identical individuals from a cell or a cluster of cells taken from a multicellular organism. (p. 567)

compact bone: the hard outer layer of bone (p. 461)

complex machine: two or more simple machines working together (p. 169)

condensation (kahn den SAY shun): the process during which water vapor changes into liquid water. (pp. 55, 191)

membrana celular: cubierta flexible que protege el interior de una célula del ambiente externo de la célula. (pág. 407)

teoría celular: teoría que establece que todos los seres vivos están constituidos de una o más células (la célula es la unidad más pequeña de vida) y que las células nuevas provienen de células preexistentes. (pág. 395)

pared celular: estructura rígida en el exterior de la membrana celular que protege la célula del ataque de virus y otros organismos dañinos. (pág. 407)

respiración celular: serie de reacciones químicas que convierten la energía de las moléculas de alimento en una forma de energía utilizable llamada ATP. (pág. 46)

centrómero: estructura que mantiene unidas las cromátidas hermanas. (pág. 536)

energía química: energía almacenada en y liberada por los enlaces entre los átomos. (pág. 143)

quimiosíntesis: proceso durante el cual los productores usan la energía química en la materia en vez de la energía lumínica, para elaborar alimento. (pág. 69)

cloroplasto: organelo limitado por una membrana que usa la energía lumínica para producir alimento –un azúcar llamado glucosa– del agua y del dióxido de carbono en un proceso llamado fotosíntesis. (pág. 412)

cladograma: diagrama de brazos que muestra las relaciones entre los organismos, incluidos los ancestros comunes. (pág. 366)

clima: promedio a largo plazo de las condiciones del tiempo atmosférico que ocurre en una región particular. (pág. 223)

comunidad clímax: comunidad estable que ya no sufrirá mayores cambios ecológicos. (pág. 344)

clonación: tipo de reproducción asexual realizada en un laboratorio que produce individuos idénticos a partir de una célula o grupo de células tomadas de un organismo pluricelular. (pág. 567)

hueso compacto: capa externa y dura del hueso. (pág. 461)

máquina compleja: dos o más máquinas simples que trabajan juntas. (pág. 169)

condensación: proceso mediante el cual un gas cambia a líquido. (pág. 55, 191)

conditioning: a way of learning new behaviors where a behavior is modified so that a response to one stimulus becomes associated with a different stimulus (p. 509)

constants: the factors in an experiment that remain the same (p. 22)

contact force: a push or a pull on one object by another object that is touching it (p. 131)

convection: the circulation of particles within a material caused by differences in thermal energy and density (p. 190)

coral reef: an underwater structure made from outside skeletons of tiny, soft-bodied animals called coral. (p. 337)

critical thinking: comparing what you already know with the information you are given in order to decide whether you agree with it. (p. 14)

cumulonimbus cloud: the cloud type that can form thunderstorms (p. 208)

cytokinesis (si toh kuh NEE sus): a process during which the cytoplasm and its contents divide. (p. 537)

cytoplasm the liquid part of a cell inside the cell membrane; contains salts and other molecules (p. 408)

cytoskeleton: a network of threadlike proteins joined together that gives a cell its shape and helps it move. (p. 408)

condicionamiento: forma de aprender comportamientos en la cual se modifica una conducta, de tal manera que la respuesta a un estímulo se asocia con un estímulo diferente. (pág. 509)

constantes: factores en un experimento que permanecen iguales. (pág. 22)

fuerza de contacto: empuje o arrastre ejercido sobre un objeto por otro que lo está tocando. (pág. 131)

convección: circulación de partículas en el interior de un material causada por diferencias en la energía térmica y la densidad. (pág. 190)

arrecife de coral: estructura bajo el agua formada por exoesqueletos de animales diminutos y de cuerpo blando. (pág. 337)

pensamiento crítico: comparación que se hace cuando se sabe algo acerca de información nueva, y se decide si se está o no de acuerdo con ella. (pág. 14)

nube cumulonimbus: tipo de nube que forma tormentas. (pág. 208)

citocinesis: proceso durante el cual el citoplasma y sus contenidos se dividen. (pág. 537)

citoplasma: fluido en el interior de una célula que contiene sales y otras moléculas. (pág. 408)

citoesqueleto: red de proteínas en forma de filamentos unidos que le da forma a la célula y le ayuda a moverse. (pág. 408)

D

daughter cell: the two new cells that result from mitosis and cytokinesis. (p. 537)

dependent variable: the factor a scientist observes or measures during an experiment. (p. 22)

deposition: the laying down or settling of eroded material (p. 227)

desert: a biome that receives very little rain. (p. 312)

dichotomous key: a series of descriptions arranged in pairs that lead the user to the identification of an unknown organism. (p. 365)

diploid: a cell that has pairs of chromosomes. (p. 548)

drought: a period of below-average precipitation (p. 216)

células hija: las dos células nuevas que resultan de la mitosis y la citocinesis. (pág. 537)

variable dependiente: factor que el científico observa o mide durante un experimento. (pág. 22)

deposición: establecimiento o asentamiento de material erosionado. (pág. 227)

desierto: bioma que recibe muy poca lluvia. (pág. 312)

clave dicotómica: serie de descripciones organizadas en pares que dan al usuario la identificación de un organismo desconocido. (pág. 365)

diploide: célula que tiene pares de cromosomas. (pág. 548)

sequía: período con bajo promedio de precipitación. (pág. 216)

E

ecological succession: the process of one ecological community gradually changing into another. (p. 344)

ecoregion: a large area of land that has a distinct group of plants, animals, and other species (p. 222)

efficiency: the ratio of output work to input work (p. 171)

egg: the female reproductive, or sex, cell; forms in an ovary (p. 548)

electric energy: energy carried by an electric current (p. 141)

energy: the ability to cause change (p. 140)

energy pyramid: a model that shows the amount of energy available in each link of a food chain (p. 73)

energy transformation: the conversion of one form of energy to another (p. 154)

erosion: the moving of weathered material, or sediment, from one location to another (p. 227)

estuary (ES chuh wer ee): a coastal area where freshwater from rivers and streams mixes with salt water from seas or oceans (pp. 254, 333)

eutrophication (yoo troh fuh KAY shun): the process of a body of water becoming nutrient-rich. (p. 348)

evaporation (ih va puh RAY shun): the process of a liquid changing to a gas at the surface of the liquid (pp. 55. 191)

sucesión ecológica: proceso en el que una comunidad ecológica cambia gradualmente en otra. (pág. 344)

ecorégión: gran área de tierra que tiene un grupo de plantas, animales y otras especies. (pág. 222)

eficiencia: relación entre energía invertida y energía útil. (pág. 171)

óvulo: célula reproductiva femenina o sexual; forma en un ovario. (pág. 548)

energía eléctrica: energía transportada por una corriente eléctrica. (pág. 141)

energía: capacidad de ocasionar cambio. (pág. 140)

pirámide energética: modelo que explica la cantidad de energía disponible en cada vínculo de una cadena alimentaria. (pág. 73)

transformación de energía: conversión de una forma de energía a otra. (pág. 154)

erosión: transporte de material meteorizado, o de sedimento, de un lugar a otro. (pág. 227)

estuario: área costera donde el agua dulce de ríos y arroyos se mezcla con el agua salada de los mares u océanos. (pág. 254, 333)

eutrofización: proceso por el cual un cuerpo de agua se vuelve rico en nutrientes. (pág. 348)

evaporación: proceso de cambio de un líquido a un gas en la superficie del líquido. (pág. 55, 191)

F

fertilization (fur tuh luh ZAY shun): a reproductive process in which a sperm joins with an egg (pp. 474, 548)

fission: cell division that forms two genetically identical cells. (p. 563)

food chain: a model that shows how energy flows in an ecosystem through feeding relationships (p. 71)

food web: a model of energy transfer that can show how the food chains in a community are interconnected (p. 72)

force: a push or a pull on an object (p. 130)

freshwater: water that has less than 0.2 percent salt dissolved in it. (p. 240)

fertilización: proceso reproductivo en el cual un espermatozoide se une con un óvulo. (pág. 474, 548)

fisión: división celular que forma dos células genéticamente idénticas. (pág. 563)

cadena alimentaria: modelo que explica cómo la energía fluye en un ecosistema a través de relaciones alimentarias. (pág. 71)

red alimentaria: modelo de transferencia de energía que explica cómo las cadenas alimentarias están interconectadas en una comunidad. (pág. 72)

fuerza: empuje o arrastre ejercido sobre un objeto. (pág. 130)

agua dulce: agua que tiene menos de 0,2 porciento de sal disuelta en ella. (pág. 240)

friction: a contact force that resists the sliding motion of two surfaces that are touching (p. 132)

front: a boundary between two air masses (p. 202)

functional group: an atom or group of atoms that determine the function or properties of the compound. (p. 101)

fricción: fuerza de contacto que resiste el movimiento de dos superficies que están en contacto. (pág. 132)

frente: límite entre dos masas de aire. (pág. 202)

grupo funcional: átomo o grupo de átomos que determina la función o las propiedades de un compuesto. (pág. 101)

G

gamete(GA meet): human reproductive cell (p. 474)

gene (JEEN): a section of DNA on a chromosome that has genetic information for one trait (p. 522)

genotype (JEE nuh tipe): the alleles of all the genes on an organism's chromosomes; controls an organism's phenotype (p. 523)

genus (JEE nus): a group of similar species. (p. 364)

geyser: a warm spring that sometimes ejects a jet of liquid water or water vapor into the air (p. 284)

grassland: a biome where grasses are the dominant plants. (p. 313)

gravity: an attractive force that exists between all objects that have mass (p. 132)

groundwater: water that is stored in cracks and pores beneath Earth's surface (pp. 224, 262)

gameto: célula reproductora humana. (pág. 474)

gen: parte del ADN en un cromosoma que contiene información genética para un rasgo. (pág. 522)

genotipo: juego completo de genes de un organismo. (pág. 523)

género: grupo de especies similares. (pág. 364)

géiser: manantial caliente que algunas veces expulsa un chorro de agua líquida o vapor de agua al aire. (pág. 284)

pradera: bioma donde los pastos son las plantas dominantes. (pág. 313)

gravedad: fuerza de atracción que existe entre todos los objetos que tienen masa. (pág. 132)

agua subterránea: agua almacenada en grietas y poros debajo de la superficie de la Tierra. (pág. 224, 262)

H

halide group: a functional group which contains group 17 halogens – fluorine, chlorine, bromine, and iodine. (p. 102)

haploid: a cell that has only one chromosome from each pair. (p. 549)

hibernation: a response in which an animal's body temperature, activity, heart rate, and breathing rate decrease during periods of cold weather (p. 506)

homeostasis (hoh mee oh STAY sus): an organism's ability to maintain steady internal conditions when outside conditions change (p. 438)

homologous (huh MAH luh gus) chromosomes: pairs of chromosomes that have genes for the same traits arranged in the same order. (p. 548)

hormone: a chemical signal that is produced by an endocrine gland in one part of an organism and carried in the bloodstream to another part of the organism (p. 467)

grupo halide: grupo funcional que contiene 17 halógenos–flúor, cloro, bromo y yodo. (pág. 102)

haploide: célula que tiene solamente un cromosoma de cada par. (pág. 549)

hibernación: respuesta en la cual la temperatura corporal, el ritmo cardíaco y la tasa de respiración de un animal disminuyen durante los periodos fríos. (pág. 506)

homeostasis: capacidad de un organismo de mantener las condiciones internas estables cuando las condiciones externas cambian. (pág. 438)

cromosomas homólogos: pares de cromosomas que tienen genes de iguales rasgos dispuestos en el mismo orden. (pág. 548)

hormona: señal química producido por una glándula endocrina en una parte de un organismo y llevado en la corriente sanguínea a otra parte del organismo. (pág. 467)

humidity (hyew MIH duh tee): the amount of water vapor in the air (p. 199)

hurricane: an intense tropical storm with winds exceeding 119 km/h (p. 212)

hydrocarbon: a compound that contains only carbon and hydrogen atoms. (p. 90)

hydroxyl (hi DRAHK sul) **group:** the chemical group consisting of one atom of hydrogen and one atom of oxygen (—OH). (p. 101)

hypothesis: a possible explanation for an observation that can be tested by scientific investigations. (p. 10)

humedad: cantidad de vapor de agua en el aire. (pág. 199)

huracán: tormenta tropical intensa con vientos que exceden los 119 km/h. (pág. 212)

hidrocarburo: compuesto que contiene solamente átomos de carbono e hidrógeno. (pág. 90)

grupo hidroxilo: grupo químico que consiste en un átomo de hidrógeno y un átomo de oxígeno (–OH). (pág. 101)

hipótesis: explicación posible de una observación que se puede probar por medio de investigaciones científicas. (pág. 10)

I

ice core: a long column of ice taken from a glacier. (p. 245)

ice sheet: a glacier that spreads over land in all directions. (p. 242)

immunity: the resistance to specific pathogens (p. 449)

imprinting: behavior that occurs when an animal forms an attachment to an organism or place within a specific time period after birth or hatching (p. 508)

inclined plane: a simple machine that consists of a ramp, or a flat, sloped surface (p. 166)

independent variable: the factor that you want to test. It is changed by the investigator to observe how it affects a dependent variable. (p. 22)

inference: a logical explanation of an observation that is drawn from prior knowledge or experience. (p. 10)

innate behavior: a behavior that is inherited rather than learned (p. 504)

instinct (IHN stingt): a complex pattern of innate behaviors (p. 505)

interphase: the period during the cell cycle of a cell's growth and development. (p. 534)

intertidal zone: the ocean shore between the lowest low tide and the highest high tide. (p. 336)

isomer (I suh mur): one of two or more compounds that have the same molecular formula but different structural arrangements. (p. 90)

núcleo de hielo: columna larga de hielo tomado de un glacial. (pág. 245)

capa de hielo: glacial que se extiende sobre la tierra en todas las direcciones. (pág. 242)

inmunidad: resistencia a patógenos específicos o a agentes causantes de enfermedades. (pág. 449)

impronta: comportamiento que ocurre cuando un animal forma un apego a otro organismo o lugar dentro de un período específico de tiempo, después de nacer o eclosionar. (pág. 508)

plano inclinado: máquina simple que consiste en una rampa, o superficie plana inclinada. (pág. 166)

variable independiente: factor que el investigador cambia para observar cómo afecta la variable dependiente. (pág. 22)

inferencia: explicación lógica de una observación que se extrae de un conocimiento previo o experiencia. (pág. 10)

comportamiento innato: comportamiento heredado más que aprendido. (pág. 504)

instinto: patrón complejo de comportamientos innatos. (pág. 505)

interfase: período durante el ciclo celular del crecimiento y desarrollo de una célula. (pág. 534)

zona intermareal: playa en medio de la marea baja más baja y la marea alta más alta. (pág. 336)

isómero: uno de dos o más compuestos que tienen la misma fórmula molecular, pero diferentes arreglos estructurales. (pág. 90)

K

kinetic (kuh NEH tik) **energy:** energy due to motion (p. 141)

energía cinética: energía debida al movimiento. (pág. 141)

L

lake: a large body of water that forms in a basin surrounded by land. (255)

law of conservation of energy: law that states that energy can be transformed from one form to another, but it cannot be created or destroyed (p. 154)

lever: a simple machine that consists of a bar that pivots, or rotates, around a fixed point (p. 167)

lightning: an electric discharge within a cloud, between clouds, or between a cloud and the ground (p. 209)

lipid: a type of biological molecule that includes fats, oils, hormones, waxes, and components of cellular membranes. (p. 114)

lipid: a large macromolecule that does not dissolve in water. (p. 398)

lymphocyte(LIHM fuh site): a type of white blood cell that is made in the thymus, the spleen, and bone marrow (p. 448)

lago: cuerpo extenso de agua que se forma en una cuenca rodeada de tierra. (pág. 255)

ley de la conservación de la energía: ley que plantea que la energía puede transformarse de una forma a otra, pero no puede crearse ni destruirse. (pág. 154)

palanca: máquina simple que consiste en una barra que gira, o rota, alrededor de un punto fijo. (pág. 167)

rayo: descarga eléctrica en el interior de una nube, entre nubes o entre una nube y el suelo. (pág. 209)

lípido: tipo de molécula biológica que incluye grasas, aceites, hormonas, ceras y componentes de las membranas celulares. (pág. 114)

lípido: macromolécula extensa que no se disuelve en agua. (pág. 398)

linfocito: tipo de glóbulos blancos que se producen en el timo, el bazo y la médula del hueso. (pág. 448)

M

macromolecule: substance that forms from joining many small molecules together (p. 397)

mechanical energy: sum of the potential energy and the kinetic energy in a system (p. 144)

meiosis: a process in which one diploid cell divides to make four haploid sex cells. (p. 549)

migration: the instinctive, seasonal movement of a population of organisms from one place to another (p. 506)

mitosis (mi TOH sus): a process during which the nucleus and its contents divide. (p. 537)

monomer (MAH nuh mur): one of the small organic molecules that make up the long chain of a polymer. (p. 104)

mutation (myew TAY shun): a permanent change in the sequence of DNA, or the nucleotides, in a gene or a chromosome (p. 527)

macromolécula: sustancia que se forma al unir muchas moléculas pequeñas. (pág. 397)

energía mecánica: suma de la energía potencial y de la energía cinética en un sistema. (pág. 144)

meiosis: proceso en el cual una célula diploide se divide para constituir cuatro células sexuales haploides. (pág. 549)

migración: movimiento instintivo de temporada de una población de organismos de un lugar a otro. (pág. 506)

mitosis: proceso durante el cual el núcleo y sus contenidos se divide. (pág. 537)

monómero: una de las moléculas orgánicas pequeñas que forman la larga cadena de un polímero. (pág. 104)

mutación: cambio permanente en la secuencia de AND, o de nucleótidos, en un gen o en un cromosoma. (pág. 527)

Glossary

N

natural selection: the process by which organisms with variations that help them survive in their environment live longer, compete better, and reproduce more than those that do not have the variation (p. 374)

neuron (NOO rahn): the basic functioning unit of the nervous system; a nerve cell (p. 464)

nitrogen fixation (NI truh jun • fihk SAY shun): the process that changes atmospheric nitrogen into nitrogen compounds that are usable by living things. (p. 57)

noncontact force: a force that one object applies to another object without touching it (p. 131)

nuclear energy: energy stored in and released from the nucleus of an atom (p. 143)

nucleic acid (new KLEE ihk • A sud): a biological polymer that stores and transmits genetic information. (pp. 113, 399)

nucleus: part of a eukaryotic cell that directs cell activity and contains genetic information stored in DNA. (p. 410)

nutrient: a part of food used by the body to grow and survive (p. 441)

selección natural: proceso por el cual los organismos con variaciones que les ayudan a sobrevivir en sus medioambientes viven más, compiten mejor y se reproducen más que aquellos que no tienen esas variaciones. (pág. 374)

neurona: unidad básica de funcionamiento del sistema nervioso; célula nerviosa. (pág. 464)

fijación del nitrógeno: proceso que cambia el nitrógeno atmosférico en componentes de nitrógeno útiles para los seres vivos. (pág. 57)

fuerza de no contacto: fuerza que un objeto puede aplicar sobre otro sin tocarlo. (pág. 131)

energía nuclear: energía almacenada en y liberada por el núcleo de un átomo. (pág. 143)

ácido nucleico: polímero biológico que almacena y transmite información genética. (pág. 113, 399)

núcleo: parte de la célula eucariótica que gobierna la actividad celular y contiene la información genética almacenada en el ADN. (pág. 410)

nutriente: parte del alimento que el cuerpo usa para crecer y vivir. (pág. 441)

O

observation: the act of using one or more of your senses to gather information and taking note of what occurs. (p. 10)

organ: a group of different tissues working together to perform a particular job. (p. 424)

organ system: a group of organs that work together and perform a specific task (pp. 425, 438)

organelle: membrane-surrounded component of a eukaryotic cell with a specialized function. (p. 409)

organic: a class of chemical compounds in living organisms that are based on carbon (p. 282)

organic compound: chemical compound that contains carbon atoms usually bonded to at least one hydrogen atom. (p. 87)

ovum(OH vum): female reproductive cell, or gamete (p. 474)

observación: acción de usar uno o más sentidos para reunir información y tomar notar de lo que ocurre. (pág. 10)

órgano: grupo de diferentes tejidos que trabajan juntos para realizar una función específica. (pág. 424)

sistema de órganos: grupo de órganos que trabajan juntos y realizar una función específica. (pág. 425, 438)

organelo: componente de una célula eucariótica rodeado de una membrana con una función especializada. (pág. 409)

orgánico: clase de compuestos químicos en los organismos vivos con base en carbono. (pág. 282)

compuesto orgánico: compuesto químico que contienen átomos de carbono generalmente unidos a, al menos, un átomo de hidrógeno. (pág. 87)

óvulo: célula reproductora femenina, o gameto. (pág. 474)

permeability: the measure of the ability of water to flow through rock and sediment. (p. 264)

phenotype (FEE nuh tipe): how a trait appears, or is expressed (p. 523)

photoperiodism: a plant's response to the number of hours of darkness in its environment (p. 494)

photosynthesis (foh toh SIHN thuh sus): a series of chemical reactions that convert light energy, water, and carbon dioxide into the food-energy molecule glucose and give off oxygen (p. 43)

pioneer species: the first species that colonizess new or undisturbed land. (p. 345)

plant hormone: a substance that acts as a chemical messenger within a plant (p. 495)

polymer (PAH luh mur): a molecule made up of many of the same small organic molecules covalently bonded together, forming a long chain. (p. 104)

polymerization (pah luh muh ruh ZAY shun): the chemical process in which small organic molecules, or monomers, bond together to form a chain. (p. 104)

porosity: the measure of a rock's ability to hold water. (p. 264)

potential (puh TEN chul) energy: stored energy due to the interactions between objects or particles (p. 142)

precipitation (prih sih puh TAY shun): water, in liquid or solid form, that falls from the atmosphere. (pp. 55, 200)

prediction: a statement of what will happen next in a sequence of events. (p. 11)

pressure system: a moving air mass with a particular pressure (p. 201)

protein (PROH teen): a long chain of amino acid molecules; contains carbon, hydrogen, oxygen, nitrogen, and sometimes sulfur (p. 400)

protein (PROH teen): a biological polymer made of amino acid monomers. (p. 110)

pulley: a simple machine that consists of a grooved wheel with a rope or cable wrapped around it (p. 167)

permeabilidad: medida de la capacidad del agua para fluir a través de la roca y el sedimento. (pág. 264)

fenotipo: forma como aparecen o se expresan los rasgos. (pág. 523)

fotoperiodismo: respuesta de una planta al número de horas de oscuridad en su medioambiente. (pág. 494)

fotosíntesis: serie de reacciones químicas que convierte la energía lumínica, el agua y el dióxido de carbono en glucosa, una molécula de energía alimentaria, y libera oxígeno. (pág. 43)

especie pionera: primera especie que coloniza tierra nueva o tierra virgen. (pág. 345)

fitohormona: sustancia que actúa como mensajero químico dentro de una planta. (pág. 495)

polímero: molécula hecha de muchas de las mismas moléculas orgánicas pequeñas unidas por enlaces covalentes, y que forman una cadena larga. (pág. 104)

polimerización: proceso químico en el que moléculas orgánicas pequeñas, o monómeros, se unen para formar una cadena. (pág. 104)

porosidad: medida de la capacidad de una roca para almacenar agua. (pág. 264)

energía potencial: energía almacenada debido a las interacciones entre objetos o partículas. (pág. 142)

precipitación: agua, en forma líquida o sólida, que cae de la atmósfera. (pág. 55, 200)

predicción: afirmación de lo que ocurrirá después en una secuencia de eventos. (pág. 11)

sistema de presión: masa de aire en movimiento con una presión determinada. (pág. 201)

proteína: larga cadena de aminoácidos; contiene carbono, hidrógeno, oxígeno, nitrógeno y, algunas veces, sulfuro. (pág. 400)

proteína: polímero biológico hecho de monómeros de aminoácidos. (pág. 110)

polea: máquina simple que consiste en una rueda acanalada rodeada por una cuerda o cable. (pág. 167)

Glossary

R

radiant energy: energy carried by an electromagnetic wave (p. 147)

reflex: an automatic movement in response to a stimulus (p. 465)

regeneration: a type of asexual reproduction that occurs when an offspring grows from a piece of its parent. (p. 565)

reproduction: the process by which new organisms are produced (p. 474)

rocket: a vehicle propelled by the exhaust made from burning fuel (p. 290)

runoff: water that flows over Earth's surface. (p. 252)

energía radiante: energía que transporta una onda electromagnética. (pág. 147)

reflejo: movimiento automático en respuesta a un estímulo. (pág. 465)

regeneración: tipo de reproducción asexual que ocurre cuando un organismo se origina de una parte de su progenitor. (pág. 565)

reproducción: proceso por el cual se producen nuevos organismos. (pág. 474)

cohete: vehículo propulsado por gases de escape producidos por la ignición de combustible. (pág. 290)

escorrentía: agua que fluye sobre la superficie de la Tierra. (pág. 252)

S

salinity (say LIH nuh tee): a measure of the mass of dissolved salts in a mass of water (p. 328)

saturated hydrocarbon: hydrocarbon that contains only single bonds. (p. 91)

science: the investigation and exploration of natural events and of the new information that results from those investigations. (p. 8)

scientific law: a rule that describes a pattern in nature. (p. 13)

scientific theory: an explanation of observations or events that is based on knowledge gained from many observations and investigations. (p. 13)

screw: a simple machine that consists of an inclined plane wrapped around a cylinder (p. 167)

sea ice: ice that forms when sea water freezes. (p. 244)

seismic energy: the energy transferred by waves moving through the ground (p. 146)

selective breeding: the selection and breeding of organisms for desired traits (p. 380)

sexual reproduction: type of reproduction where the genetic material from two different cells—a sperm and an egg—combine, producing an offspring (p. 548)

simple machine: a machine that does work using one movement (p. 166)

sister chromatids: two identical chromosomes that make up a duplicated chromosome. (p. 536)

sound energy: energy carried by sound waves (p. 146)

salinidad: medida de la masa de sales disueltas en una masa de agua. (pág. 328)

hidrocarburos saturados: hidrocarburo que solamente contiene enlaces sencillos. (pág. 91)

ciencia: la investigación y exploración de los eventos naturales y de la información nueva que es el resultado de estas investigaciones. (pág. 8)

ley científica: regla que describe un patrón dado en la naturaleza. (pág. 13)

teoría científica: explicación de observaciones o eventos con base en conocimiento obtenido de muchas observaciones e investigaciones. (pág. 13)

tornillo: máquina simple que consiste en un plano inclinado incrustado alrededor de un cilindro. (pág. 167)

hielo marino: hielo que se forma cuando el agua del mar se congela. (pág. 244)

energía sísmica: energía transferida por ondas que se mueven a través del suelo. (pág. 146)

cría selectiva: selección y cría de organismos para características deseadas. (pág. 380)

reproducción sexual: tipo de reproducción en la cual el material genético de dos células diferentes de un espermatozoide y un óvulo se combinan, produciendo una cría. (pág. 548)

máquina simple: máquina que hace trabajo con un movimiento. (pág. 166)

cromátidas hermanas: dos cromosomas idénticos que constituyen un cromosoma duplicado. (pág. 536)

energía sonora: energía que transportan las ondas sonoras. (pág. 146)

space probe: an uncrewed spacecraft sent from Earth to explore objects in space (p. 291)

species (SPEE sheez): a group of organisms that have similar traits and are able to produce fertile offspring. (p. 364)

sperm: a male reproductive, or sex, cell; forms in a testis (pp. 474, 548)

spongy bone: the interior region of bone that contains many tiny holes (p. 461)

stem cell: an unspecialized cell that is able to develop into many different cell types. (p. 422)

stimulus (STIHM yuh lus): a change in an organism's environment that causes a response (p. 490)

storm surge: rising ocean water along the coast, caused by hurricane winds pushing the ocean water higher as the hurricane approaches land (p. 212)

stream: a body of water that flows within a channel. (p. 253)

substituted hydrocarbon: an organic compound in which a carbon atom is bonded to an atom, or group of atoms, other than hydrogen. (p. 100)

surface water: the water that fills lakes and rivers (p. 224)

sonda espacial: nave espacial sin tripulación enviada desde la Tierra para explorar objetos en el espacio. (pág. 291)

especie: grupo de organismos que tienen rasgos similares y que están en capacidad de producir crías fértiles. (pág. 364)

espermatozoide: célula reproductora masculina o sexual; forma en un testículo. (pág. 474, 548)

hueso esponjoso: región interior de un hueso que contiene muchos huecos diminutos. (pág. 461)

célula madre: célula no especializada que tiene la capacidad de desarrollarse en diferentes tipos de células. (pág. 422)

estímulo: un cambio en el medioambiente de un organismo que causa una respuesta. (pág. 490)

marejada ciclónica: ascenso del agua del océano en la costa, causado por vientos huracanados que empujan el agua del océano más alto a medida que el huracán se acerca a tierra. (pág. 212)

corriente: cuerpo de agua que fluye por un canal. (pág. 253)

hidrocarburo de sustitución: compuesto orgánico en el cual un átomo de carbono está unido a un átomo, o grupo de átomos, diferente del hidrógeno. (pág. 100)

agua superficial: agua que llena los lagos y ríos. (pág. 224)

taiga (TI guh): a forest biome consisting mostly of cone-bearing evergreen trees. (p. 319)

technology: the practical use of scientific knowledge, especially for industrial or commercial use. (p. 12)

temperate: the term describing any region of Earth between the tropics and the polar circles. (p. 316)

thermal energy: the sum of the kinetic energy and the potential energy of the particles that make up an object (p. 144)

thunderstorm: a weather event that includes rain, strong winds, thunder, and lightning (p. 208)

tissue: a group of similar types of cells that work together to carry out specific tasks. (p. 423)

tornado: a violent, whirling column of air in contact with the ground (p.210)

trait: a distinguishing characteristic of an organism (p. 522)

taiga: bioma de bosque constituido en su mayoría por coníferas perennes. (pág. 319)

tecnología: uso práctico del conocimiento científico, especialmente para uso industrial o comercial. (pág. 12)

temperatura: término que describe cualquier región de la Tierra entre los trópicos y los círculos polares. (pág. 316)

energía térmica: suma de la energía cinética y potencial de las partículas que componen un objeto. (pág. 144)

tormenta: evento del tiempo atmosférico que incluye lluvia, vientos fuertes, truenos y rayos. (pág. 208)

tejido: grupo de tipos similares de células que trabajan juntas para llevar a cabo diferentes funciones. (pág. 423)

tornado: columna de aire violenta y rotativa en contacto con el suelo. (pág. 210)

rasgo: característica distintiva de un organismo. (pág. 522)

Glossary

Glossary

tropism (TROH pih zum): plant growth toward or away from an external stimulus (p. 491)

troposphere (TRO puh sfihr): the atmospheric layer closest to Earth's surface (p. 189)

tundra (TUN druh): a biome that is cold, dry, and treeless. (p. 320)

tropismo: crecimiento de las plantas hacia o lejos de un estímulo externo. (pág. 491)

troposfera: capa atmosférica más cercana a la Tierra. (pág. 189)

tundra: bioma frío, seco y sin árboles. (pág. 320)

U

unbalanced forces: forces acting on an object that combine and form a net force that is not zero (p. 134)

unsaturated hydrocarbon: a hydrocarbon that contains one or more double or triple bonds. (p .91)

fuerzas no balanceadas: fuerzas que actúan sobre un objeto, se combinan y forman una fuerza neta diferente de cero. (pág. 134)

hidrocarburos insaturados: hidrocarburo que contiene uno o más enlaces dobles o triples. (pág. 91)

V

variable: any factor that can have more than one value. (p. 22)

variation (ver ee AY shun): a slight difference in an inherited trait among individual members of a species (p. 374)

vegetative reproduction: a form of asexual reproduction in which offspring grow from a part of a parent plant. (p. 566)

variable: cualquier factor que tenga más de un valor. (pág. 22)

variación: ligera diferencia en un rasgo hereditario entre los miembros individuales de una especie. (pág. 374)

reproducción vegetativa: forma de reproducción asexual en la cual el organismo se origina a partir de una planta parental. (pág. 566)

W

water table: the upper limit of the underground region in which the cracks and pores within rocks and sediment are completely filled with water. (p. 264)

watershed: an area of land that drains runoff into a particular stream, lake, ocean, or other body of water (pp. 224, 254)

wedge: a simple machine that consists of an inclined plane with one or two sloping sides; it is used to split or separate an object (p. 166)

wetland: an area of land that is saturated with water for part or all of the year. (p. 266)

wetland: an aquatic ecosystem that has a thin layer of water covering soil that is wet most of the time. (p. 332)

wheel and axle: a simple machine that consists of an axle attached to the center of a larger wheel, so that the shaft and wheel rotate together (p. 167)

work: the amount of energy used as a force moves an object over a distance (p. 157)

nivel freático: límite superior de la región subterránea en la cual las grietas y los poros dentro de las rocas y el sedimento están completamente llenos de agua. (pág. 264)

cuenca hidrográfica: área de tierra que drena escorrentía hacia un arroyo, lago, océano u otro cuerpo de agua específico. (pág. 224, 254)

cuña: máquina simple que consiste en un plano inclinado con uno o dos lados inclinados; se usa para partir o separar un objeto. (pág. 166)

lago: área de tierra saturada con agua durante parte del año o todo el año. (pág. 266)

humedal: ecosistema acuático que tiene una capa delgada de suelo cubierto de agua que permanece húmedo la mayor parte del tiempo. (pág. 332)

rueda y eje: máquina simple que consiste en un eje insertado en el centro de una rueda grande, de manera que el eje y la rueda rotan juntos. (pág. 167)

trabajo: cantidad de energía usada como fuerza que mueve un objeto a cierta distancia. (pág. 157)

Z

zygote (ZI goht): the new cell that forms when a sperm cell fertilizes an egg cell (pp. 474, 548)

zigoto: célula nueva que se forma cuando un espermatozoide fertiliza un óvulo. (pág. 474, 548)

Index

Abiotic factors

Italic numbers = illustration/photo   **Bold numbers** = vocabulary term
lab = indicates entry is used in a lab on this page

Brain

Index

Index

Index